Big Data Analytics for Improved Accuracy, Efficiency, and Decision Making in Digital Marketing

Amandeep Singh
Chitkara Business School, Chitkara University, Punjab, India

A volume in the Advances in Marketing, Customer Relationship Management, and E-Services (AMCRMES) Book Series

IGI Global
PUBLISHER of TIMELY KNOWLEDGE

Published in the United States of America by
IGI Global
Business Science Reference (an imprint of IGI Global)
701 E. Chocolate Avenue
Hershey PA, USA 17033
Tel: 717-533-8845
Fax: 717-533-8661
E-mail: cust@igi-global.com
Web site: http://www.igi-global.com

Library of Congress Cataloging-in-Publication Data

Names: Singh, Amandeep, 1982- editor.
Title: Big data analytics for improved accuracy, efficiency, and decision making in digital marketing / Amandeep Singh, editor.
Description: Hershey, PA : Business Science Reference, 2021. | Includes bibliographical references and index. | Summary: "This book will help the digital marketers to understand the Big Data in a better way and to get a meaning full information, which, will help the marketers to better market their products to the consumers"-- Provided by publisher.
Identifiers: LCCN 2020058387 (print) | LCCN 2020058388 (ebook) | ISBN 9781799872313 (hardcover) | ISBN 9781799872320 (paperback) | ISBN 9781799872337 (ebook)
Subjects: LCSH: Internet marketing--Statistical methods. | Decision making--Statistical methods. | Big data.
Classification: LCC HF5415.1265 .B54 2021 (print) | LCC HF5415.1265 (ebook) | DDC 658.8/72--dc23
LC record available at https://lccn.loc.gov/2020058387
LC ebook record available at https://lccn.loc.gov/2020058388

This book is published in the IGI Global book series Advances in Marketing, Customer Relationship Management, and E-Services (AMCRMES) (ISSN: 2327-5502; eISSN: 2327-5529)

British Cataloguing in Publication Data
A Cataloguing in Publication record for this book is available from the British Library.

For electronic access to this publication, please contact: eresources@igi-global.com.

Advances in Marketing, Customer Relationship Management, and E-Services (AMCRMES) Book Series

ISSN:2327-5502
EISSN:2327-5529

Editor-in-Chief: Eldon Y. Li, National Chengchi University, Taiwan & California Polytechnic State University, USA

MISSION

Business processes, services, and communications are important factors in the management of good customer relationship, which is the foundation of any well organized business. Technology continues to play a vital role in the organization and automation of business processes for marketing, sales, and customer service. These features aid in the attraction of new clients and maintaining existing relationships.

The Advances in Marketing, Customer Relationship Management, and E-Services (AMCRMES) Book Series

addresses success factors for customer relationship management, marketing, and electronic services and its performance outcomes. This collection of reference source covers aspects of consumer behavior and marketing business strategies aiming towards researchers, scholars, and practitioners in the fields of marketing management.

COVERAGE

- Data mining and marketing
- E-Service Innovation
- Relationship Marketing
- Database marketing
- CRM and customer trust
- Legal Considerations in E-Marketing
- Ethical Considerations in E-Marketing
- Customer Retention
- B2B marketing
- Web Mining and Marketing

IGI Global is currently accepting manuscripts for publication within this series. To submit a proposal for a volume in this series, please contact our Acquisition Editors at Acquisitions@igi-global.com or visit: http://www.igi-global.com/publish/.

The Advances in Marketing, Customer Relationship Management, and E-Services (AMCRMES) Book Series (ISSN 2327-5502) is published by IGI Global, 701 E. Chocolate Avenue, Hershey, PA 17033-1240, USA, www.igi-global.com. This series is composed of titles available for purchase individually; each title is edited to be contextually exclusive from any other title within the series. For pricing and ordering information please visit http://www.igi-global.com/book-series/advances-marketing-customer-relationship-management/37150. Postmaster: Send all address changes to above address.

Titles in this Series

For a list of additional titles in this series, please visit:
http://www.igi-global.com/book-series/advances-marketing-customer-relationship-management/37150

Developing Successful Global Strategies for Marketing Luxury Brands
Fabrizio Mosca (University of Turin, Italy) Cecilia Casalegno (University of Turin, Italy) and Rosalia Gallo (Universitat Autònoma de Barcelona, Spain)
Business Science Reference • ©2021 • 351pp • H/C (ISBN: 9781799858829) • US $225.00

Insights, Innovation, and Analytics for Optimal Customer Engagement
Samala Nagaraj (Woxsen University, India)
Business Science Reference • ©2021 • 334pp • H/C (ISBN: 9781799839194) • US $195.00

New Techniques for Brand Management in the Healthcare Sector
Ana Pinto Borges (European Business School and Research Group, ISAG (NIDISAG), Portugal) and Paula Rodrigues (Lusíada University of Porto, Portugal)
Business Science Reference • ©2021 • 244pp • H/C (ISBN: 9781799830344) • US $225.00

Impact of ICTs on Event Management and Marketing
Kemal Birdir (Mersin University, Turkey) Sevda Birdir (Mersin University, Turkey) Ali Dalgic (Isparta University of Applied Sciences, Turkey) and Derya Toksoz (Mersin University, Turkey)
Business Science Reference • ©2021 • 357pp • H/C (ISBN: 9781799849544) • US $195.00

Building Consumer-Brand Relationship in Luxury Brand Management
Paula Rodrigues (Lusíada University of Porto, Portugal) and Ana Pinto Borges (Instituto Superior de Administração e Gestão, Portugal)
Business Science Reference • ©2021 • 318pp • H/C (ISBN: 9781799843696) • US $225.00

Innovations in Digital Branding and Content Marketing
Subhankar Das (Duy Tan University, Vietnam) and Subhra Rani Mondal (Duy Tan University, Vietnam)
Business Science Reference • ©2021 • 311pp • H/C (ISBN: 9781799844204) • US $195.00

For an entire list of titles in this series, please visit:
http://www.igi-global.com/book-series/advances-marketing-customer-relationship-management/37150

IGI Global
PUBLISHER of TIMELY KNOWLEDGE

701 East Chocolate Avenue, Hershey, PA 17033, USA
Tel: 717-533-8845 x100 • Fax: 717-533-8661
E-Mail: cust@igi-global.com • www.igi-global.com

Editorial Advisory Board

Table of Contents

Detailed Table of Contents

In every field, during a particular era, there is someone who stands up to a cause. There is a "North Star" in the sky to guide the "navigator" who might erringly go astray to reach the destination. The star gives direction through sheer stability. Consumer analytics as such is widely accepted throughout the world. It especially has a firm footing in enriching user experience thanks to the gigantic data collection exercise. The popularity seems to have stemmed from the fact that analytics is the real "navigator" based on data facts and the panacea for the business problems and leads the way forward whenever required. Customer journey analytics is a key instrument in the profitability framework. It also aims to provide a view of customers that is essentially dynamic in nature and other key data points observed during the life cycle of a customer. It further covers ahead of the prevailing product ownership and user data for inculcating the information such as digital channel interactions, social media, voice-of-the-consumer interactions, sentiment analysis, and more.

Multi-document summarization extracts and summarizes the information without affecting its original context from the different sources of documents. It has been carried out using extractive text summarization and abstractive text summarization. Extractive summarization extracts summaries from verbatim lines, and abstractive summarization extracts new lines of summary from the source documents. Abstractive summarization is an advanced technology compared to extractive summarization. This research studies extractive summarization of multi documents from internet resources using word frequency counting and with maximum coverage using K-means clustering. In an internet search, the search algorithm shows the results from different websites using crawling and indexing. However, the search and text summary take place from hundreds, thousands, maybe millions of documents. To handle and manipulate these huge amounts of information, big data and its techniques are applied widely. This research also addresses big data techniques and tools that are available for multi-document summarization.

Intense competition and price wars in the retail sector provide the impetus to examine consumer behavior in the retail industry. It has become increasingly important to scrutinize what drives consumer choice of retail stores. This chapter addresses this need and aims to establish the factors that drive consumer retail choice behavior. The empirical setting for the study was five organized Indian retail stores: Easy Day, Big Bazaar, More, Reliance Fresh, and Freshmart. Data were collected with the help of a questionnaire (n=700) in a store-intercept survey. Data were analyzed using multivariate data analysis techniques. A model identifying the variables that predicts retail store choice probabilities was developed and tested. Results establish that atmospherics, merchandise assortment, and customer satisfaction have a significant positive impact on retail store choice. On the other hand, price has a significant negative impact on retail store choice. Implications are discussed.

Digital marketing managers are feeling the ever-increasing pressure to show the contribution of marketing activities and it's their primary concern towards their organization. The absence of responsibility has harmed the expected outcomes from

COVID-19 has affected our educational sector adversely, which resulted in the closure of all academic institutions. This global health crisis demands social distancing as the way to keep the virus away and forced the academic institutions to adapt to this physical distancing from the students as well as colleagues. The faculty needs to be motivated in order to be innovative, interactive, and accessible. The pandemic has not only led to the disappearance of old teaching methods but also the adoption of the modular concept of e-learning. Through a review-based study, the authors discuss the diverse response by the academic institutions and assesses their resilience towards education and transition to online learning during challenging times. Through this study, the authors opined that significant opportunities are there which will help in learning from pedagogical developments of other academic institutions. This will help in strengthening the collective response to COVID 19.

The digital economy has brought in its wake numerous issues of a technological kind. It has affected every element within the organization (e.g., structure, informal work relationships, culture, and most importantly, managerial leadership). Because of new technologies emerging every day, the process of change has become persistent, and a paradigm shift has been witnessed in the management of workplace behaviour. The chapter has three sections. Concepts underlying organizational behaviour and the meaning of digitalization are discussed in the first section; the second section is an analysis of the changing leadership framework and its role in digital business transformation, and the third section highlights the positive and negative effects of a digital workplace on employee behaviour. The discussion concludes with comments on the significance of a digital workplace in COVID-19 era. The primary objective of this chapter is to identify and organize the accumulated knowledge on the implications of digital transformation for organizational behaviour and provide critical insights.

Our lifestyle cravings are voracious. The hospitality sector ensures guests are pleased with every new application and connected system that continues to become a business success. For guests, digital technology means a simple life where customer service is all about it. The transition of hospitality is at its tilt stage where everything is possible due to digital technology, where the ability to be improved by the correct technique from the movement of the reservation to check-out and from the ease of connecting to the hotel guest network to the temperature of the guest room when entering for the first time. Therefore, advancement in emerging technologies provides an opportunity for the hospitality business. Hotels strive for their growth to have more guest satisfaction with better experience, provisions, and management.

The buying behaviors of the consumers are changing very rapidly in the today's consumer-oriented market. New technologies are evolving in the market to attract the customers. Smart phones have become necessities to cope with the changing dynamics of the market and society as a whole. Due to competitive price offer by the various cellular operators, it has become easy for all to reach the internet. Due to ease of use, the young generations are using the application of internet for various uses especially for purchasing goods and services. Today, every company is applying the digital marketing tool to attract customers, especially the young generation. As per a report published in Economics, the internet users in India are expected to reach 627 million by the end 2020. Due to the digital marketing, a new concept of shopping has evolved in the market, which the authors call off-the-shop retailing.

i-Branding is one of the fastest-growing aspects of internet marketing. Internet marketing is still an experimental area that continues to grow, evolve, and adapt. The use of the internet as a branding tool is an important area of study since the literature on internet branding is currently in the formative stage. This study investigated the relationship of various factors with respect to customer satisfaction of youths towards purchasing through the internet. The sample size is comprised of 520 respondents from various regions of Punjab. For this purpose, CFA has been applied to analyze the customer satisfaction of internet marketing among youngsters. Finally, this chapter would help academicians as well as industry experts to analyze the potential of i-branding in the future.

From a humble beginning in 2013, OYO is today the world's second-largest hospitality chain of franchised and leased hotels, living spaces, and homes. OYO has a global presence with large-scale operations in many countries. This case outlines OYO's complicated growth journey from a rapidly growing startup to an ethically maligned business venture. It also underscores OYO's business and revenue model, work culture, and growth strategies. It also provides a sneak peek about the major problems faced by OYO and how OYO should cope with these challenges.

Businesses are growing rapidly. They are using different strategies to connect customers. In this process, marketing is the most important thing. Most people use social media, and it has become one of the best platforms for marketing products. On social media, people can share their views and opinions and also get knowledge about the product and its updates. One of the fundamental reasons for utilizing social media in marketing is as a specialized apparatus that makes the organizations open to those interested in their products and makes them visible to the individuals

Preface

The availability of Big Data, low-cost commodity hardware, and new information management and analytic software have produced a unique moment in the history of data analysis. The convergence of these trends means that we have the capabilities required to analyse astonishing data sets quickly and cost-effectively for the first time in history. These capabilities are neither theoretical nor trivial. They represent a genuine leap forward and a clear opportunity to realize enormous gains in terms of efficiency, productivity, revenue, and profitability. Every business organization, small or big, needs valuable data and insights. When it comes to understanding your target audience and customer's preferences, big data plays a very important role. It even helps you anticipate their needs. The right data needs to be effectively presented and properly analyzed. It can help a business organization achieve various goals. This book will strengthen the research in the following fields:

- Role of Big Data Analytics in attaining competitive advantage.
- How Big Data is shaping the future of the business
- Improving Business Marketing Efficiency using Big Data
- Drawing Meaning Out of Big Data- In-Depth Insights
- Big Data a Big Profit-Making and productive way of business
- Big Data a Big Way Forward
- Faster, Better Decision Making Using Big Data
- Big Data for Society as a Whole.

Data plays a huge role in understanding valuable insights about target demographics and customer preferences. From every interaction with technology, regardless of whether it's active or passive, we are creating new data that can describe us. With data being captured through products, video cameras, credit cards, cell phones, and other touchpoints, our data profile is growing exponentially. If analyzed correctly, these data points can explain a lot about our behavior, personalities, and life events. Companies can leverage these insights for product improvements, business strategy, and marketing campaigns to cater to the target customers. With this focus in mind, this book is written that will help the digital marketers to understand the Big Data in a better way and to get a meaning full information out of that.

Chapter 1: Enriching User Experience by Transforming Consumer Data Into Deeper Insights

In every field, during a particular era, there is someone, who stands up to a cause. There is a "North Star" in the sky, to guide the "navigator", who might erringly go astray to reach destination. The star gives direction, through sheer stability. Consumer analytics as such is widely accepted throughout the world. It specially has a very firm footing in enriching user experience, thanks to the gigantic data collection exercise. The popularity seems to have stemmed from the fact that, Analytics is the real "navigator", based on data facts, has the panacea for the business problems and leads the way forward, whenever required. Customer journey analytics as a key instrument in the profitability framework. It also aims to provide a view of customers which is essentially dynamic in nature and other key data points observed during the life cycle of a customer. It further covers ahead of the prevailing product ownership and user data for inculcating the information such as digital channel interactions, social media, voice-of-the-consumer interactions, sentiment analysis, and more.

Chapter 2: A Study on Text Summarization From Multi Documents for Big Data Analytics – Text Summarization With Big Data Analytics

Multi-document summarization extracts and summarizes the information without affecting its original context from the different sources of documents. It has been carried out using extractive text summarization and abstractive text summarization. Extractive text summarization extracts summaries from verbatim lines and abstractive text summarization extracts and generates new lines of summary from the source documents. Abstractive summarization is an advanced technology compared to extractive summarization. In most internet searches, the search algorithm shows the results from different websites. However, the search takes place from hundreds, thousands, maybe millions of documents. To handle and manipulate these huge amounts of data big data and its techniques are applied widely. This research addresses big data techniques and tools available for multi-document summarization. It also studies extractive summarization of multi documents from internet resources with maximum coverage and word frequency counting using K-means clustering.

Chapter 3: Determinant Attributes of Store Choice in Organized Retail

Intense competition and price wars in the retail sector provide impetus to examine consumer behavior in the retail industry. It has become increasingly important to scrutinize what drives consumers' choice of retail stores. This paper addresses this need and aims to establish the factors that drive consumers' retail choice behavior. The empirical setting for the study was five organized Indian retail stores: Easy Day, Big Bazaar, More, Reliance Fresh and Freshmart. Data were collected with the help of a questionnaire (n=700) in a store-intercept survey. Data were analyzed using multivariate data analysis techniques. A model identifying the variables that predict retail store choice probabilities was developed and tested. Results establish that atmospherics, merchandise assortment and customer satisfaction have a significant positive impact on retail store choice. On the other hand, price has a significant negative impact on retail store choice. Implications are discussed.

Chapter 4: Digitalization and Work Behaviour

The digital economy has brought in its wake numerous issues of a technological kind. It has affected every element within the organization viz. structure, informal work relationships, culture and most importantly managerial leadership. Because of new technologies emerging every day, the process of change has become persistent and a paradigm shift has been witnessed in the management of workplace behaviour. The article comprises of 3 sections: Concepts underlying organizational behaviour and the meaning of digitalization are discussed in the first section; the second section is an analysis of the changing leadership framework and its role in digital business transformation; and the third section highlights the positive and negative effects of a digital workplace on employee behaviour. The discussion concludes with comments on the significance of a digital workplace in Covid-19 era. The primary objective of this chapter is to identify and organize the accumulated knowledge on the implications of digital transformation for organizational behaviour and provide critical insights thereof.

Chapter 5: Social Media, Crowdsourcing, and Marketing

Social media has emerged as a new playing ground for digital marketing. Supporting the resource view of the organization, crowdsourcing is a strong platform for social media marketing. Crowdsourcing on social media for marketing is strengthening companies in terms of saving marketing expenditure, promoting at speed of light and enhancing the organizational learning, collaboration and performance. The chapter tries to focus on the relevance of social media, crowdsourcing and marketing which help the company to improve, innovate and cultivate on the crowdsourced wisdom. The future of social media, crowdsourcing and marketing depends on how companies change the way they perceive about the stakeholders, business and processes.

Chapter 6: Big Data Impacts in Tourism Research

Big data is one of the most in-demand and generally uses the term to illustrate the mounting increase and availability of data in the modern age which is believed to be maintained or either it is also expected to grow in the nearby future. Talking about tourism research even at an early-stage big data has shown very wondrous improvement in tourism research. This might be the first attempt to present a capacious literature review on different types of big data tourism research. By data informant the big data related to tourism comes into web search data, online booking data, web page visiting data, etc. Which carries different information, different data types address and different tourism-related issues? As mentioned above each type a structural analysis is conducted from the perspective of research focuses on the characteristics of data the techniques which are used in the analysis, major challenges, and further directions. This chapter simplifies a meticulous understanding of this sunrise research and offers a valuable vision into its future possibilities.

Chapter 7: Resilience by Academic Institutions During COVID-19 – A Review-Based Study

COVID 19 has affected our educational sector adversely which resulted in the closure of all academic institutions. This global health crisis demanding social distancing as the way to keep the virus away, also forced the academic institutions to adapt this physical distancing from the students as well as colleagues. The faculty at this time of the hour needs to be motivated in order to be innovative, interactive and accessible. The Pandemic event has not only led to the disappearance of old teaching methods but also the adoption of the modular concept of E-Learning solving the problem of teaching the students at home. Through a review-based study, we will discuss the diverse response by the academic institutions and assess their resilience towards education and transition to online learning during challenging times. Through this study, we opined that significant opportunities are there which will help in learning from pedagogical developments of other academic institutions. This will help in strengthening the collective response to COVID 19.

Chapter 8: Digitalization and Work Behaviour – A Paradigm Shift

Digital marketing managers are feeling the ever-increasing pressure to show the contribution of marketing activities and it's their primary concern towards their organization. The absence of responsibility has harmed the expected outcomes from the marketing campaigns. The best way to recover its impact is to show the results of advertising in financial terms to top administration. Previous research shows that the capacity to quantify marketing performance significantly affects firm execution, benefit, stock returns, top administration fulfilment with advertising, and advertisers' standing inside an association. This research paper discusses about the various challenges faced by the organizations in measuring the digital marketing performance and significance of measuring the online marketing performance through better online execution. The findings of this study reveal that data produced through digital analytics can be utilized for estimating and optimizing performance of digital marketing campaigns.

Chapter 9: Online Advertising Strategies in Indian and Australian E-Commerce Companies – A Comparative Study

Online advertising and marketing in which promote the different types of products through various kinds of advertising modes to customers. Online advertising is promotional messages that show up on the monitors of online laptops, desktops, tablets, televisions, and smart phones. The main objective of the study is to analyze the online advertising and impact comparison of online advertising strategy which is adopted by Indian and Australian e-commerce companies. To achieve the objectives of this study, take the sample of 5 Indian and 5 Australian e-commerce companies. This study also found that the Indian and Australian e-commerce companies have inter-connected. Online advertising in India has been flouring and also increasing because of launched 4G connections which is good for the future of online marketing. This chapter explains comparisons of Indian and Australian e-commerce companies and also focuses on the top ten platforms to increase sales and customer attraction through advertising. The future of online advertising is brilliant and unlimited.

Chapter 10: An Empirical Study on Pharmaceutical and Personal Care Stocks Using Sharpe's Single Index Model

As the various avenues for better returns in India are slowly dwindling due to various global scenarios as well as due to domestic government policies, more and more people are turning towards stock market for better returns. This poses a challenge to the fund managers during when they have to construct a portfolio, which maximizes return and minimizes risk. This has become more and more challenging in the recent years as the investors are also becoming more knowledgeable. Timely and correct investment decision on part of the investor requires an in-depth knowledge of the stock that he intends to procure and the theories behind portfolio management. This research paper mainly focuses on construction of an optimal portfolio comprising of top Pharmaceutical companies and FMCG companies in India. Sharpe ratio return analysis is the tool that is used to construct the optimal portfolio. Monthly returns data of last 10 years of the said companies are regressed against monthly return data of Nifty for better comparison.

Chapter 11: An influence of Digitalization and Recent Innovations on the Hospitality and Tourism Sector

Our lifestyle cravings are voracious. The hospitality sector ensures guests are pleased with every new application & connected system that continues to become a business success. For guests, digital technology means a simple life where customer service is all about it. The transition of hospitality is at its tilt stage where everything is possible due to digital technology, where the ability to be improved by the correct technique from the movement of the reservation to check-out and from the ease of connecting to the hotel guest network to the temperature of the guest room when entering for the first time. Therefore, advancement in emerging technologies provides an opportunity for the hospitality business. As hotels strive for their growth to have more guest satisfaction with better experience, provisions, and management, hotels are forging and forging.

Chapter 12: Impact of Digital Marketing on the Buying Behaviour of Youth With Special Reference to Uttarakhand State

The buying behaviours of consumers are changing very rapidly in today's consumer-oriented market. New technologies are evolving in the market to attract customers. Today smartphone becomes our necessity to cope with the changing dynamics of the market and society as a whole. Due to the competitive price offer by the various cellular operators, the reach of the Internet become easy for all. Due to ease of use the young generations are using the application of the internet for various uses especially for purchasing goods and services. Today every company is applying digital marketing tool to attract customers, especially the young generation. As per the report published in Economics time the internet user in India is expected to reach 627 million by the end of 2020. Due to digital marketing, the new concept of shopping evolved in the market which we call off shop retailing.

Chapter 13: i-Branding as a tool of Integrated marketing – An Empirical Study of Youngster Satisfaction

I-branding is one of the fastest-growing aspects of internet marketing. Internet marketing is still an experimental area that continues to grow, evolve and adapt. The use of the Internet as a branding tool is an important area of study since the literature on Internet branding is currently in the formative stage. This study investigated the relationship of various factors with respect to customer satisfaction of youths towards purchasing through the internet. The sample size is comprised of 520 respondents from various regions of Punjab. For this purpose, CFA has been applied to analyze the customer satisfaction of internet marketing among youngsters. Finally, this paper would help academicians as well as an industry expert to analyze the potential of I-branding in the coming future.

Chapter 14: OYO (The Journey) – The Deeper Insights

From a humble beginning in 2013, OYO is today the world's second largest hospitality chain of franchised and leased hotels, living spaces and homes. OYO has a global presence with large-scale operations in many countries. This case outlines OYO's complicated growth journey from a rapidly growing start-up to an ethically maligned business venture. It also underscores OYO's business and revenue model, work culture and growth strategies. It also provides a sneak peek about the major problems faced by OYO and how should OYO cope up with these challenges now.

Chapter 15: Social Media Marketing – Social Media Marketing as New Marketing Tool

Nowadays, businesses are growing very rapidly. To connect with every customer or a person they are using different strategies. In this process, marketing becomes the most important thing. As now most of the people are using social media, it has become one of the best platforms for marketing the product. On social media, people can share their views and opinions and also get knowledge about the product and its updates. One of the fundamental reasons for utilizing social media in marketing is as a specialized apparatus that makes the organizations open to those interested in their product and makes them visible to the individuals who have no information of their products. These companies utilize social media to make a buzz, and learn from and target customers. Therefore, companies need to look at various social media platforms where their customers exist in this chapter, the concept of social media marketing is discussed with some brief with practical examples of companies applying social media marketing tool.

Chapter 16: Developing a Framework to Study the Impact of Contingent Factors on Business Performance Using Strategic Cost Management – A Meta-Analysis Study

In the present scenario, cost and management accounting techniques have proved effectiveness in decision making as it provides value creation. Therefore, the need for transforming of traditional cost and management accounting to strategic cost management has been recognized. Manufacturing or service industries continuously seek to achieve business performance with the help of strategic cost management using contingency theory. This paper provides a semi-systematic review of the articles and research papers examining major themes found in the literature focusing on impact of various factors that are contingent in nature on the business performance through usage of strategic cost management. Systematic analysis of literature identified numerous relevant articles and research papers in eminent journals. The results indicated that there exists an interrelationship among variables and the finding supports central proposition of contingency theory where business performance increases with the usage of strategic cost management and contingent factors.

Amandeep Singh
Chitkara Business School, Chitkara University, India

Chapter 1
Enriching User Experience by Transforming Consumer Data Into Deeper Insights

Devesh Bathla
Chitkara Business School, Chitkara University, India

Shraddha Awasthi
Chitkara Business School, Chitkara University, India

Kuber Singh
University of Waterloo, Canada

ABSTRACT

In every field, during a particular era, there is someone who stands up to a cause. There is a "North Star" in the sky to guide the "navigator" who might erringly go astray to reach the destination. The star gives direction through sheer stability. Consumer analytics as such is widely accepted throughout the world. It especially has a firm footing in enriching user experience thanks to the gigantic data collection exercise. The popularity seems to have stemmed from the fact that analytics is the real "navigator" based on data facts and the panacea for the business problems and leads the way forward whenever required. Customer journey analytics is a key instrument in the profitability framework. It also aims to provide a view of customers that is essentially dynamic in nature and other key data points observed during the life cycle of a customer. It further covers ahead of the prevailing product ownership and user data for inculcating the information such as digital channel interactions, social media, voice-of-the-consumer interactions, sentiment analysis, and more.

DOI: 10.4018/978-1-7998-7231-3.ch001

INTRODUCTION

Huge set of information are these days gathered and stored by organisations, with the desire for being valuable later on. This represents the test of overseeing such heaps of information and separating from it fitting information for supporting choices. Huge Data is right now internationally spread and broadly acknowledged, speaking to likewise an equivalent word of vanguard as far as data the executives, in spite of the fact that this doesn't come without contention (Fan and Bifet, 2013). Actually, as Chen, Chiang, and Story (2012) contended, specialists need to step forward "from Big Data to Big Impact" for adequately profiting by the focal points gave by Big Data. The help of dynamic is a key issue for advertisers, by giving bits of knowledge to help with responding to basic inquiries, for example, the best fit item pertaining to a specific market; ways to publicize such item in corresponding showcase; via which correspondence channels; with given focuses in time and for the decided cost; and bolstered by which sort of limited time and promotional activity. Given these premises, it is with nothing unexpected that Marketing has proven from the beginning an area for tries of different things with Big Data draws near (Bendle and Wang, 2016). Ongoing wellsprings of heaps of information incorporate internet based life and portable applications: both have demonstrated to majorly affect clients' choices, straightforwardly influencing brand building (Moro, Rita, and Vala, 2016).

This paper draws a research review of literature analysing the Big Data in Marketing confined in second decade of this ongoing century. Considering Big Data itself possibly holds esteem on the off chance that it is bridled targeting removing adroit information, examination has developed as a vital pattern to answer the difficulties of Big Data in Marketing. Actually, promoting examination arrangements are presently being spread all through associations trying to profit by Big Data arrangements (Laurent, 2013), albeit most executions are not yet accomplished to adequately exploit from such coordinated Marketing-Big Data arrangements (Chen et al., 2012). As the analytics likewise apply to miniscule volumes, developing difficulties in regards to huge volumes have as of late risen, for example, coordinating a wide number of unmistakable sources, managing both organized and unstructured information, and execution issues. Along these lines, examination have additionally been incorporated inside this investigation. All things considered, it ought to be featured that the primary focal point of study is to see how Big Data is being overseen and handled to use Marketing difficulties. Along these lines, by dissecting research led in this area, the current investigation gives a general image of the momentum best in class, adding to a superior comprehension of this subject. With the point of covering a huge range of the writing, a semi-robotized content mining approach utilizing theme displaying was embraced. The points found give the required research bits of knowledge on Big Data in Marketing that helps to enrich the user experience by leveraging the available insights.

Marketing analysts have noticed that advertising science and practice are experiencing an investigation interruption, thinking about the blast of information, the development of computerized showcasing, online life, and showcasing examination (Moorman 2016). A junction is additionally subjected in estimation of the effect, enormous information, and on the online or otherwise reconciliation, as researchers have highlighted testing in incorporating of all shapes and sizes information and showcasing examination into advertising choice and tasks (Hanssens and Pauwels 2016). Analysts predict significantly progressively broad advancement of huge information, because of shrewd innovation gadgets, for example, watches, cameras, and for the most part, the IOT (Baesens et al. 2016). Researchers have suggested further research with respect to utilization of client investigation specific to numerous zones of advertising, that includes retail (Griffith and Hoppner 2015), firm execution (Germann 2014), processing innovations, expository techniques in promoting (Li and Kannan 2017), predictive investigation (Koppius and Shmueli 2011), and large information examination (Wamba et al. 2017). Industry specialists stress upon the significance of inter-departement activity to cater a significant true issue that is past the limit of a solitary control. This would include the use of large information and examination (Ketter et al. 2016).

Analysts likewise observe benefits of enormous information for research for having a clearer interpretation of shopping designs utilizing trucks with RFIDs, cell phone applications, or camcorders. Such advances are of utmost use in overseeing store network and business forms (Davenport 2006; Venkatesan 2017), just as in the territories of website improvement, and web based life investigation (Kumar et al. 2017). With regards to online networking, analysts have contended that advertisers should concentrate not just on utilizing it as a correspondence channel with customers yet in addition as a wellspring of showcasing bits of knowledge (Moe and Schweidel 2017).

While huge information, showcasing investigation, and information mining appear to be setting down deep roots in promoting (Jobs et al. 2016), organizations consider information examination an especially basic test (Verhoef et al. 2016). Showcasing investigation assume a focal job under these conditions, considering the requirements for sufficient measurements and systematic strategies to improve information driven advertising activities and dynamic (Kannan and Wedel 2016). Ever since the closure of studies, organizations can accomplish positive and feasible execution results through optimum utilization of promoting examination (Germann 2013).

Concurrent reason for this research aims at examining the ebb and flow condition of research in showcasing investigation and evaluate the focal examination subjects,

subjects of premium, discoveries, just as strategies for examination utilized. We additionally have as target to assess the utilization of advertising investigation in showcasing research practice and contrast this present reality premiums and those of scholastics in distributed examinations, just as in college courses. This article adds to the promoting writing with an efficient audit of studies and discoveries on advertising investigation, which take into consideration further suggestions. We start by portraying the authentic setting, and afterward we present the aftereffects of a complete writing survey of promoting diaries, looking at co-events of words as seen as scholarly research that comprehends of advertising firms dealing in research to speak to the specialist perspective, likewise to business schools for mirroring the flow standards of instruction and training during MBA. Then, at that point it is intended to close with suggestions for academicians as researchers or teachers and as trainers, and for working professionals.

OVERVIEW OF MARKETING ANALYTICS

Many years prior, promoting information was typically accessible at a gross measure, on a month to month basis or annually. In the year 1923, A C Nielsen made one of the most notable research among organizations to quantify item deals in stores. Subsequently, till 1950, Nielsen started estimating TV crowds and radio listeners (Kannan et al. 2016). Then, almost three decades back, advertisers were becoming acclimated to the adaptability of the scanner information, UPCs, and every other month review information from Nielsen (Bijmolt et al. 2010).

1990s was the time, when in the field of conventional examination developed, Internet showcasing started being sent, and Blemish Keters understood this chance of gauging details of site guests with the help of log records. Likewise, around then, CRM programming opened up, from organizations like Salesforce, Oracle and others (Kannan et al. 2016). The foremost web investigation merchant in the commercial space, I/PRO Corp, was propelled in 1994, followed by WebTrends in the year 1995, which was then taken ahead by Omniture in 2002, and then largely by Google Analytics in 2005 (Patron and Chaffey 2012). The twentieth century spoke to a chance to grow new information and channels and to make different correlative marketing studies. These progressed with the advancement of the Internet and the sensational increment in information handling pace and information stockpiling abilities, as per Law of Moore, expressing that digital capacity limit per unit volume copies at regular intervals (Huang and Rust 2015).

The latest research works have influenced showcasing research, giving specialists a chance to utilize electronic intelligent study instruments, online subjective investigation, mining, and breaking down huge databases (Hauser 2007). On account of the computerized stage, organizations began approaching huge client databases, with data on buy conduct, advertising contacts, and other client qualities were put away. The Internet and online life brought a blast of ongoing information, combined with improved information age and assortment, decrease in processing expenses, and developments in measurements (Verhoef et al. 2017). In the given scenario, organizations are utilizing investigation as a huge upper hand since they can, yet in addition since they should (Davenport 2006). By and large, advertisers can utilize investigation in deciding the allotment of promoting assets, client lifetime esteem, in recognizing and holding gainful clients and getting maximum from every given transaction. The next section showcases the practising of marketing analytics techniques.

Figure 1. Marketing analytics definition analysis

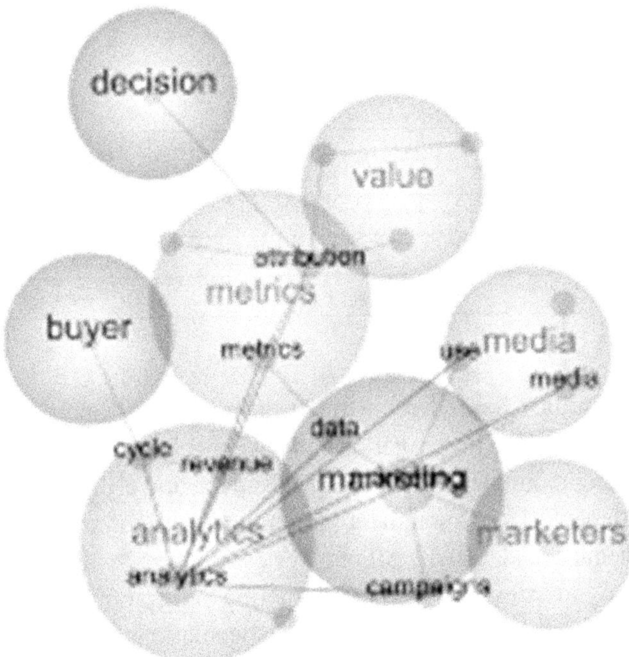

PRACTISING THE MARKETING ANALYTICS

To evaluate distinctions as well as similitudes of the process of marketing analytics as is seen in advertising exploration, practice, and the scholarly world, this research was carried out, while comparing the research articles' abstracts, the portrayal of showcasing examination administrations from information about organizations, just as the depictions of the course from business schools. Table 1 displays the essential headings associated with marketing analytics and their level of significance for showcasing specialists, professionals, and scholastics.

Customers are seen as focal point of this training related piece of the model in Table 1, which suggest and highlights their basic job in drawing in with respect to organizations and as a beneficiary of administrations (Pauwels and Hanssens 2016). On account of current innovation, the Internet, and web based life, organizations can offer customized types of assistance and utilize the CRM or Customer Relationship Management to provide better experiences for clients (Maklan et al. 2015). The current state of marketing has revolutionised the manner in which advertisers impart and draw in with shoppers, just as the techniques for picking up bits of knowledge in customers' conduct, because of showcasing investigation (Kerr and Kelly 2017; Huang and Rust 2017).

Table 1. Theme importance

	Analytics (%)	Customer (%)	Data (%)	Management (%)	Marketing (%)
Courses	21.9	5.9	26.7	6.1	39.4
Practice	13.9	23.8	12.5	6.5	43.3
Research	20.2	12.5	20.8	9.3	37.1

Marketing studies have demonstrated an across the board increment in the utilization of showcasing investigation and wise specialist advancements, even from organizations, for example, Amazon, IBM, Netflix, and eBay, for collective sifting, suggestion frameworks, personalization, and value examination motors (Verhoef et al. 2016; Kumar et al. 2016). All out worldwide uses in advertising dashboards, expository programming, and other promoting programming frameworks reach about $24 billion every year, and generous speculations have been made in large information new businesses in previous years (Krush et al. 2016). For some experts, enormous information has become the standard and an approach to keep up intensity in the commercial centre (Chaffey and Patron 2012; Petrescu and Krishen 2017; Krishen and Petrescu 2017). Researchers have highlighted that Business2Business experts see huge potential in utilizing Business2Business client research to take care of organisational issues, despite the fact that they don't yet appear to profit by the devices not the direction to accomplish the same (Lilien 2016). Studies reveal that organizations utilize prescient examination suppliers based on cloud, (for example,

Mintigo and Lattice) to interpret on both inside information reference points and sources of information available outside to distinguish new prospects (Lilien 2016). Moreover, directors appear to experience issues with respect to the determination of the correct measurements, the translation of the outcomes and their reconciliation, which prompts dissatisfaction and disillusionment, which needs further research and appearance in research and scholarly articles (Pauwels 2015; Verhoef et al. 2016; Wedel and Kannan 2016).

The focal point of marketing research organizations with respect to advertising examination is increasingly focused on couple of primary factors: the business, and the customers. Fundamentally high significance granted to purchasers is likewise clear in Table 1. The premium is identified with utilizing promoting investigation to define advertising methodologies and settle on choices on evaluating and item. Simultaneously, lifetime customer value, a crucial ROI viewpoint, likewise being highlighted by advertisers. Connection among training and research is for the most part dependent on execution and procedures, focuses that have been recognized as requiring improvement for promoting examination. With respect to and showcasing the scholarly world, the model shows the noticeable quality granted to business choices by the two classifications, which will be additionally examined in the following segment. Additionally, in this specific situation, professionals are significantly more inclined towards specialized side of showcasing examination and optimum utilization of particular software.

ACADEMIC APPLICATION OF MARKETING ANALYTICS

Diverse scholarly advancements gave been stressed by research that influence promoting work on, including organizations being established by the researchers or on their work of research (Wedel and Kannan 2016). An imperative critical supporters of this dissemination and development towards showcasing research, practically speaking and research is explained by the researchers, by means of the training and teaching offered by business colleges often called as business schools. Pertaining to the said reason, research on websites of the best 20 best worldwide colleges for business and economics, as recognized by U.S. News (2019), and separated data with respect to the contributions towards course and specializations on advertising investigation, just as their course depictions. Majority top colleges offer a set of courses identified with advertising investigation, numerous at the alumni level, and some additionally at the undergrad level. A few schools additionally have degrees in promoting examination, for example, University of Chicago offers a Master's Program in the field of Marketing Analytics and while the New York University offers a B.S. in this very field of Marketing Analytics. The Wharton Customer Analytics

Initiative has been built up by The University of Pennsylvania, a scholarly research place concentrating on the turn of events and use of client examination strategies and offer this Marketing Analytics - where the free MOOC stage EdX platform offers the seminar on Data Tools and Techniques. Different colleges, for example, Columbia University and the University of California at Berkeley likewise possess on EdX, free advertising examination courses, other than there are house courses. Additionally, it was imperative to assess their level of enthusiasm for promoting examination in business colleges saw to be less present day. For this reason, a research on half of the business colleges from this league, which is ten of them, that of later certified by the AACSB in the previous year. Just one of them included notices of a promoting examination seminar on its site.

As to reasonable concentration in the promoting examination courses, Table 1 shows that information investigation is focal, including plans of action, business choices, showcasing measurements, and information. While relapse shows up as the most com-mon technique even in the theoretical guide, there are different programming bundles utilized, including Excel, SPSS, R, just as various apparatuses, for example, serious investigation, quantitative key arranging network (QSPM) choice model, Monte Carlo investigation choice model, conjoint examination, advancement examination, and spending plans for conventional and internet based life. As in Table 1, the attention is on showing understudies the essentials of information examination, to settle on choices and think of models from the information gathered.

ROLE AS AN EDUCATOR OF ACADEMIA

Marketing division in academic system ought to incorporate advertising examination into their general educational program to furnish understudies with a convincing profession advantage, thinking about the exploration and particularly expert (and job market) enthusiasm for this territory. This coursework probably begins while uncurtaining strong insights class, in addendum to promoting examination, and afterward may length out to cater various modelling techniques for various types of information, in any event for MBAs and perhaps at the same time for cutting edge students.

Marketing division in academic system ought to likewise furnish their understudies with true chances to work on showcasing investigation, information assortment, examination, translation, and dynamic. This can remember coordinated effort with neighbourhood organizations for reasonable activities, entry level positions, and understudy business hatcheries. Doing so would assist understudies with understanding our standard alerts in summing up results, managing populaces (rather than tests) and one-sided tests as the reason for getting clients, in settling on choices and creating hypothesis. Much like deciphering subjective research, the consequences of non-arbitrary examples can't be summed up. Presentation to at least one major information datasets will assist understudies with understanding that with huge examples and populaces, each impact turns out to be measurably critical in spite of being of no significance at all. There are likewise numerous exclusive exhibition estimation models accessible that are emotional and have no hypothetical premise.

Lastly, a component of training that can be actualized moderately rapidly is official projects. Customarily, variation or enhancement in regular programs need an extra degree of administration and confirming, though official projects can be created, promoted, manned, and executed with moderately less postponement. There is probably as of now neglected interest for such retooling and can be said as retraining in the sphere of showcasing experts, who have not been presented to similar content and study material as part of the MBA or undergrad study however those who could value should be effortless with ideas and systematic instruments as a piece of the present advertising exchange.

PRACTICING MARKETING ANALYTICS IN THE MANAGERIAL ROLES

The information and imperative innovation are significant, yet it isn't just about information and innovation. Our models demonstrated a chose specialist centre around business choices and prescriptive data, yet we as a whole know the information and the innovation are helpful just to the degree to which they are effectively and thoroughly utilized to make bits of knowledge and inferences from the information. The translation and the hypothesis behind it are basic.

As the huge number of marketing analytics and strategies for study as available in the various research articles, it was observed that a set of papers could not provide all inclusive information or pedagogy or settled guidelines. The assorted variety is acknowledged and ought to be empowered, while at any rate till certain sorts of information make evident achievements. Advertising examination requires a comprehensive methodology, a mix of strategies, in a perfect world with various sorts of information, fitting the profile of the organization, and deciphered related. The same number of statistical surveying organizations were established by scholastics (Wedel and Kannan 2016), it is a perhaps natural to try to work together with scientists and educators on various market investigation points, particularly at universities where this zone is created.

CONCLUSION

A proficient review of the marketing research regarding the subject of marketing analytics has been presented. In an analytics of cluster and semantic procedures, the central subjects and thoughts concerned with marketing analytics in the field of marketing research, inclusive of, metrics of marketing, marketing analytics value, and the big data. This furthermore gave an assessment structure to segments of marketing analytics as observed by publicizing practitioners, educators and researchers.

Deriving from the outcomes of the analytics, researchers will be able to draw recommendations, as for future research needs concerned with marketing analytics. The main fixation in this point of view should be on building the theory and progression, similarly as the arrangement of integrative models. As far as the practitioners are concerned, they could in leverage the research and get benefitted by a dynamically proficient, theory based strategy and the use of a holistic framework. Educational instructors can add to the improvement of both these fields and the readiness of prepared managers.

This paper adds to the literature of marketing by consolidating fundamental studies in marketing analytics and giving a gross information of the research state. Specialists get proposals and an abstract of the review, for a continuously trademark way to deal with applied findings of the relevant theory. Academicians can in like manner use these results in the lecture-hall to present and show the application and focal points of marketing analytics.

RECOMMENDATION

This review on the state of marketing analytics in higher education, research, and practice has given revelations as for the necessities and priorities for all of the three categories, the variations, and shared attributes amongst them, similarly as information with respect to the central research answers regarding this matter. There are so far various inquiries and questions that ought to be answered and gives that should be disclosed regarding marketing analytics, especially keeping in mind about their vast use and accelerating advancements.

REFERENCES

Aggarwal, P., Vaidyanathan, R., & Venkatesh, A. (2009). Using lexical semantic analysis to derive online brand positions: An application to retail marketing research. *Journal of Retailing*, *85*(2), 145–158. doi:10.1016/j.jretai.2009.03.001

Alcaraz, R. (2014). The business case for better analytics: A retrospective and the future of theory and practice of marketing science. *Journal of Brand Strategy*, *3*(3), 295–303.

Alves, Fernandes, & Raposo. (2016). Value co-creation: Concept and contexts of application and study. *Journal of Business Research, 69*(5), 1626–1633. es.2015.10.029 doi:10.1016/j.jbusr

AMA. (2017). *2017 AMA gold global top 25 market research companies*. Retrieved from https://www.ama.org/publications/MarketingNews/Pages/2017-ama-gold-global-report.aspx

Atwong, C. T. (2015). A social media practicum: An action-learning approach to social media marketing and analytics. *Marketing Education Review*, *25*(1), 27–31. doi:10.1080/10528008.2015.999578

Ayanso, A., & Lertwachara, K. (2014). *Harnessing the power of social media and web analytics*. IGI Global. doi:10.4018/978-1-4666-5194-4

Baesens, B., Bapna, R., Marsden, J. R., Vanthienen, J., & Zhao, J. L. (2016). Transformational issues of big data and analytics in net- worked business. *Management Information Systems Quarterly*, *40*(4), 807–818. doi:10.25300/MISQ/2016/40:4.03

Barczak, G. (2017). Writing a review article. *Journal of Product Innovation Management, 34*(2), 120–121. doi:10.1111/jpim.12365

Bendle, N. T., Farris, P. W., Pfeifer, P. E., & Reibstein, D. J. (2015). *Marketing metrics: The manager's guide to measuring marketing performance* (3rd ed.). Pearson Education.

Bijmolt, T. H. A., Leeflang, P. S. H., Block, F., Eisenbeiss, M., Hardie, B. G. S., Lemmens, A., & Saffert, P. (2010). Analytics for customer engagement. *Journal of Service Research, 13*(3), 341–356. doi:10.1177/1094670510375603

Bradlow, E. T., Gangwar, M., Kopalle, P., & Voleti, S. (2017). The role of big data and predictive analytics in retailing. *Journal of Retailing*, *93*(1), 79–95. doi:10.1016/j.jretai.2016.12.004

Chaffey, D., & Patron, M. (2012). From web analytics to digital marketing optimization: Increasing the commercial value of digital analytics. *Journal of Direct, Data and Digital Marketing Practice*, *14*(1), 30–45. doi:10.1057/dddmp.2012.20

Chandrasekaran, D., Srinivasan, R., & Sihi, D. (2017). Effects of offline ad content on online brand search: Insights from super bowl advertising. *Journal of the Academy of Marketing Science*, *46*(3), 403–430. doi:10.100711747-017-0551-8

Chung, T. S., Wedel, M., & Rust, R. T. (2016). Adaptive personalization using social networks. *Journal of the Academy of Marketing Science, 44*(1), 66–87. doi:10.100711747-015-0441-x

Corrigan, H. B., Craciun, G., & Powell, A. M. (2014). How does Target know so much about its customers? Utilizing customer analytics to make marketing decisions. *Marketing Education Review, 24*(2), 159–165. doi:10.2753/MER1052-8008240206

Côrte-Real, N., Oliveira, T., & Ruivo, P. (2017). Assessing business value of Big Data Analytics in European firms. *Journal of Business Research, 70*, 379–390. doi:10.1016/j.jbusres.2016.08.011

Coursaris, C. K., van Osch, W., & Balogh, B. A. (2016). Informing brand messaging strategies via social media analytics. *Online Information Review, 40*(1), 6–24. doi:10.1108/OIR-02-2015-0062

Culotta, A., & Cutler, J. (2016). Mining brand perceptions from Twitter social networks. *Marketing Science, 35*(3), 343–362. doi:10.1287/mksc.2015.0968

Dann, S. (2010). Redefining social marketing with contemporary commercial marketing definitions. *Journal of Business Research, 63*(2), 147–153. doi:10.1016/j.jbusres.2009.02.013

Davenport, T. H. (2006). Competing on analytics. *Harvard Business Review, 84*(1), 99–107. PMID:16447373

Davenport, T. H., & Harris, J. G. (2007). *Competing on analytics: The new science of winning*. Harvard Business School Press.

Erevelles, S., Fukawa, N., & Swayne, L. (2016). Big Data consumer analytics and the transformation of marketing. *Journal of Business Research, 69*(2), 897–904. doi:10.1016/j.jbusres.2015.07.001

Fluss, D. (2010). Why marketing needs speech analytics. *Journal of Direct, Data and Digital Marketing Practice, 11*(4), 324–331. doi:10.1057/dddmp.2010.12

Furness, P. (2011). Applications of Monte Carlo Simulation in marketing analytics. *Journal of Direct, Data and Digital Marketing Practice, 13*(2), 132–147. doi:10.1057/dddmp.2011.25

Germann, F., Lilien, G. L., Fiedler, L., & Kraus, M. (2014). Do retailers benefit from deploying customer analytics? *Journal of Retailing, 90*(4), 587–593. doi:10.1016/j.jretai.2014.08.002

Germann, F., Lilien, G. L., & Rangaswamy, A. (2013). Performance implications of deploying marketing analytics. *International Journal of Research in Marketing*, *30*(2), 114–128. doi:10.1016/j.ijresmar.2012.10.001

Goh, T. T., & Sun, P.-C. (2015). Teaching social media analytics: An assessment based on natural disaster postings. *Journal of Information Systems Education*, *26*(1), 27–38.

Gunasekaran, A., Papadopoulos, T., Dubey, R., Wamba, S. F., Childe, S. J., Hazen, B., & Akter, S. (2017). Big data and predictive analytics for supply chain and organizational performance. *Journal of Business Research*, *70*, 308–317. doi:10.1016/j.jbusres.2016.08.004

Hair, J. F. Jr. (2007). Knowledge creation in marketing: The role of predictive analytics. *European Business Review*, *19*(4), 303–315. doi:10.1108/09555340710760134

Hanssens, D. M., & Pauwels, K. H. (2016). Demonstrating the value of marketing. *Journal of Marketing*, *80*(6), 173–190. doi:10.1509/jm.15.0417

Hanssens, D. M., Pauwels, K. H., Srinivasan, S., Vanhuele, M., & Yildirim, G. (2014). Consumer attitude metrics for guiding marketing mix decisions. *Marketing Science*, *33*(4), 534–550. doi:10.1287/mksc.2013.0841

Hauser, W.J. 2007. Marketing analytics: The evolution of marketing research in the twenty-first century. *Direct Marketing: An Inter- national Journal, 1*(1), 38–54.

Ho, Y., Chung, Y., & Lau, K. (2010). Unfolding large-scale marketing data. *International Journal of Research in Marketing*, *27*(2), 119–132. doi:10.1016/j.ijresmar.2009.12.009

Hofacker, C. F., Malthouse, E. C., & Sultan, F. (2016). Big Data and consumer behaviour: Imminent opportunities. *Journal of Consumer Marketing*, *33*(2), 89–97. doi:10.1108/JCM-04-2015-1399

Hoppner, J. J., & Griffith, D. A. (2015). Looking back to move forward: A review of the evolution of research in international marketing channels. *Journal of Retailing*, *91*(4), 610–626. doi:10.1016/j.jretai.2015.04.005

Huang, M.-H., & Rust, R. T. (2017). Technology-driven service strategy. *Journal of the Academy of Marketing Science*, *45*(6), 906–924. doi:10.100711747-017-0545-6

Järvinen, J., & Karjaluoto, H. (2015). The use of Web analytics for digital marketing performance measurement. *Industrial Marketing Management*, *50*, 117–127. doi:10.1016/j.indmarman.2015.04.009

Jobs, C. G., Aukers, S. M., & Gilfoil, D. M. (2015). The impact of big data on your firms marketing communications: A framework for understanding the emerging marketing analytics industry. *Inter- national. Academy of Marketing Studies Journal, 19*(2), 81–94.

Jobs, C. G., Gilfoil, D. M., & Aukers, S. M. (2016). How marketing organizations can benefit from big data advertising analytics. *Academy of Marketing Studies Journal, 20*(1), 18–36.

Kannan, P. K., & Li, H. A. (2017). Digital marketing: A framework, review and research agenda. *International Journal of Research in Marketing, 34*(1), 22–45. doi:10.1016/j.ijresmar.2016.11.006

Kerr, G., & Kelly, L. (2017). IMC education and digital disruption. *European Journal of Marketing, 51*(3), 406–420. doi:10.1108/EJM-08-2015-0603

Ketter, W., Peters, M., Collins, J., & Gupta, A. (2016). Competitive benchmarking: An IS research approach to address wicked problems with big data and analytics. *Management Information Systems Quarterly, 40*(4), 1057–1080. doi:10.25300/MISQ/2016/40.4.12

Krishen, A. S., & Petrescu, M. (2017). The world of analytics: Interdisciplinary, inclusive, insightful, and influential. *Journal of Marketing Analytics, 5*(1), 1–4. doi:10.105741270-017-0016-4

Krush, M. T., Agnihotri, R., & Trainor, K. J. (2016). A contingency model of marketing dashboards and their influence on marketing strategy implementation speed and market information management capability. *European Journal of Marketing, 50*(12), 2077–2102. doi:10.1108/EJM-06-2015-0317

Kumar, A., Bezawada, R., Rishika, R., Janakiraman, R., & Kannan, P. K. (2016b). From social to sale: The effects of firm-generated content in social media on customer behavior. *Journal of Marketing, 80*(1), 7–25. doi:10.1509/jm.14.0249

Kumar, V., Dixit, A., Javalgi, R. G., & Dass, M. (2016a). Research frame- work, strategies, and applications of intelligent agent technologies (IATs) in marketing. *Journal of the Academy of Marketing Science, 44*(1), 24–45. doi:10.100711747-015-0426-9

Kumar, V., Sharma, A., & Gupta, S. (2017). Accessing the influence of strategic marketing research on generating impact: Moderating roles of models, journals, and estimation approaches. *Journal of the Academy of Marketing Science, 45*(2), 164–185. doi:10.100711747-017-0518-9

LaPointe, P. (2012). The dog ate my analysis: The hitchhiker's guide to marketing analytics. *Journal of Advertising Research*, *52*(4), 395–396. doi:10.2501/JAR-52-4-395-396

Lau, R. Y. K., Li, C., & Liao, S. S. Y. (2014). Social analytics: Learning fuzzy product ontologies for aspect-oriented sentiment analysis. *Decision Support Systems*, *65*, 80–94. doi:10.1016/j.dss.2014.05.005

Leventhal, B. (2010). An introduction to data mining and other techniques for advanced analytics. *Journal of Direct, Data and Digital Marketing Practice*, *12*(2), 137–153. doi:10.1057/dddmp.2010.35

Lilien, G. L. (2011). Bridging the academic–practitioner divide in marketing decision models. *Journal of Marketing*, *75*(4), 196–210. doi:10.1509/jmkg.75.4.196

Lilien, G. L. (2016). The B2B knowledge gap. *International Journal of Research in Marketing*, *33*(3), 543–556. doi:10.1016/j.ijresmar.2016.01.003

Littell, J., Corcoran, J., & Pillai, V. (2008). *Systematic reviews and meta-analysis*. Oxford University Press. doi:10.1093/acprof:oso/9780195326543.001.0001

Liu, X., Singh, P. V., & Srinivasan, K. (2016). A structured analysis of unstructured big data by leveraging cloud computing. *Marketing Science*, *35*(3), 363–388. doi:10.1287/mksc.2015.0972

Maklan, S., Peppard, J., & Klaus, P. (2015). Show me the money: Improving our understanding of how organizations generate return from technology-led marketing change. *European Journal of Marketing*, *49*(3/4), 561–595. doi:10.1108/EJM-08-2013-0411

Martens, D., Provost, F., Clark, J., & de Fortuny, E. J. (2016). Mining massive fine-grained behavior data to improve predictive analytics. *Management Information Systems Quarterly*, *40*(4), 869–888. doi:10.25300/MISQ/2016/40.4.04

Martin, K. D., & Murphy, P. E. (2017). The role of data privacy in marketing. *Journal of the Academy of Marketing Science*, *45*(2), 135–155. doi:10.100711747-016-0495-4

Miles, D. A. (2014). Measuring customer behavior and profitability: Using marketing analytics to examine customer and marketing behavioral patterns in business ventures. *Academy of Marketing Studies Journal*, *18*(1), 141–170.

Moe, W. W., & Schweidel, D. A. (2017). Opportunities for innovation in social media analytics. *Journal of Product Innovation Management*, *34*(5), 697–702. doi:10.1111/jpim.12405

Moorman, C. (2016). Celebrating marketing's dirty word. *Journal of the Academy of Marketing Science, 44*(5), 562–564. doi:10.100711747-016-0483-8

Motamarri, S., Akter, S., & Yanamandram, V. (2017). Does big data analytics influence frontline employees in services marketing? *Business Process Management Journal, 23*(3), 623–644. doi:10.1108/BPMJ-12-2015-0182

Nair, H. S., Misra, S., Hornbuckle, W. J. IV, Mishra, R., & Acharya, A. (2017). Big data and marketing analytics in gaming: Combining empirical models and field experimentation. *Marketing Science, 36*(5), 699–725. doi:10.1287/mksc.2017.1039

Netzer, O., Feldman, R., Goldenberg, J., & Moshe, F. (2012). Mine your own business: Market structure surveillance through text mining. *Marketing Science, 31*(3), 521–543. doi:10.1287/mksc.1120.0713

Ozimek, J. F. (2010). Issues with statistical forecasting: The problems with climate science—And lessons to be drawn for marketing analytics. *Journal of Database Marketing & Customer Strategy Management, 17*(2), 138–150.

Pauwels, Aksehirli, & Lackman. (2016). Like the ad or the brand? Marketing stimulates different electronic word-of-mouth content to drive online and offline performance. *International Journal of Research in Marketing, 33*(3), 639–655.

Pauwels, K. (2015). Truly accountable marketing: The right metrics for the right results. *GfK Marketing Intelligence Review, 7*(1), 8–15.

Persson & Ryals. (2014). Making customer relationship decisions: Analytics v rules of thumb. *Journal of Business Research, 67*(8), 1725–1732.

Petersen, McAlister, Reibstein, Winer, Kumar, & Atkinson. (2009). Choosing the right metrics to maximize profit-ability and shareholder value. *Journal of Retailing, 85*(1), 95–111.

Petrescu & Krishen. (2017). Marketing analytics: From prac-tice to academia. *Journal of Marketing Analytics, 5*(2), 45–46.

Quinn, Dibb, & Simkin, Canhoto, & Analogbei. (2016). Troubled waters: The transformation of marketing in a digital world. *European Journal of Marketing, 50*(12), 2103–2133.

Raich, Müller, & Abfalter. (2014). Hybrid analysis of textual data: Grounding managerial decisions on intertwined qualitative and quantitative analysis. *Management Decision, 52*(4), 737–754.

Ringel & Skiera. (2016). *Visualizing asymmetric competition among more than 1,000 products using big search data*. Marketing.

Rust & Huang. (2014). The service revolution and the transformation of marketing science. *Marketing Science, 33*(2), 206–221.

Saboo, Kumar, & Park. (2016). Using big data to model time-varying effects for marketing resource (re)allocation. *Management Information Systems Quarterly, 40*(4), 911–939.

Salehan & Kim. (2016). Predicting the performance of online consumer reviews: A sentiment mining approach to big data analytics. *Decision Support Systems, 81*, 30–40.

Shmueli & Koppius. (2011). Predictive analytics in information systems research. *Management Information Systems Quarterly, 35*(3), 553–572.

Skiera, B. (2016). Data, data and even more data: Harvesting insights from the data jungle. *GfK Marketing Intelligence Review, 8*(2), 10–17.

Smith & Humphreys. (2006). Evaluation of unsupervised semantic mapping of natural language with Leximancer concept mapping. *Behavior Research Methods, 38*(2), 262–279.

Sridhar, Naik, & Kelkar. (2017). Metrics unreliability and marketing overspending. *International Journal of Research in Marketing, 34*(4), 761–779.

Trusov, Ma, & Jamal. (2016). Crumbs of the cookie: User profiling in customer-base analysis and behavioral targeting. *Marketing Science, 35*(3), 405–426.

U.S. News. (2018). *Best global universities for economics and business*. Accessed January 15, 2018, from https://www.usnews.com/educaion/best-global-universities/economics-business?page=3

Venkatesan, R. (2017). Executing on a customer engagement strategy. *Journal of the Academy of Marketing Science, 45*(3), 289–293.

Verhoef, Kooge, & Walk. (2016). *Creating Value with Big Data Analytics: Making Smarter Marketing Decisions*. London: Routledge.

Vorvoreanu, Boisvenue, Wojtalewicz, & Dietz. (2013). Social media marketing analytics: A case study of the public's perception of Indianapolis as Super Bowl XLVI host city. *Journal of Direct. Data and Digital Marketing Practice, 14*(4), 321–328.

Wedel & Kannan. (2016). Marketing analytics for data-rich environments. *Journal of Marketing, 80*(6), 97–121.

Wilson, R. D. (2010). Using clickstream data to enhance business-to- business web site performance. *Journal of Business and Industrial Marketing*, *25*(3), 177–187.

Xu, Frankwick, & Ramirez. (2016). Effects of big data analytics and traditional marketing analytics on new product success: A knowledge fusion perspective. *Journal of Business Research*, *69*(5), 1562–1566.

Chapter 2
A Study on Tools and Techniques of Big Data Analytics for Text Summarization From Multi-Documents

Martin Aruldoss
Central University of Tamil Nadu, India

Miranda Lakshmi Travis
St.Joseph's College of Arts and Science (Autonomous), India

ABSTRACT

Multi-document summarization extracts and summarizes the information without affecting its original context from the different sources of documents. It has been carried out using extractive text summarization and abstractive text summarization. Extractive summarization extracts summaries from verbatim lines, and abstractive summarization extracts new lines of summary from the source documents. Abstractive summarization is an advanced technology compared to extractive summarization. This research studies extractive summarization of multi documents from internet resources using word frequency counting and with maximum coverage using K-means clustering. In an internet search, the search algorithm shows the results from different websites using crawling and indexing. However, the search and text summary take place from hundreds, thousands, maybe millions of documents. To handle and manipulate these huge amounts of information, big data and its techniques are applied widely. This research also addresses big data techniques and tools that are available for multi-document summarization.

DOI: 10.4018/978-1-7998-7231-3.ch002

INTRODUCTION

As the information online is increasing day by day, it is important to process that information in multiple ways. The literature of online content is nevertheless, mostly in recent times such as news articles, web blogs, research journals, social media posts, etc. The information is vast; it is as vast as the human doesn't put the required time to analyze those for effective or optimal use. Hence, researchers are working on better ways in information engineering since mid 20th century, nowadays it is known as Natural Language Processing (Chen et al., 2002). Natural Language Processing (NLP) is a subset of Artificial Intelligence, using NLP one can understand or generate text & speech similar to how the human does these. NLP uses Machine Learning algorithms to achieve these. Now, we are going to see one of the Text Processing techniques of NLP, i.e Text Summarization, Summarizing large bodies of text into few sentences. Few sentences can be extracted in many ways; many ways were implemented so far by researchers (Kiani & Akbarzadeh, 2006).

Different kinds of research are going on Text Summarization since last 50 years; Researchers understood that it is not that easy to build a framework that does the task of summarizing a text. The results with extractive Summarization is considered better in some cases when it is compared with Abstractive Summarization, even though the idea of Abstractive Summarization is powerful but the ways to implement this is not deterministic. Several stages in text Summarization must be designed in a more efficient way(Jaruskulchai & Kruengkrai, 2003).

So, while text or document is fed into the Algorithm, the text has to be cleaned so that the Algorithm can exploit it to get a better results and another stage of Summarization Algorithm is feature extraction, the features should be selected in such a way that the most relevant and context-based text has to be maintained, finally the conversion of text features into vectors, it is important because the computer program can apply math operations on mathematical symbols or digits only and finally the algorithm generates summary (Radev et al., 2000).

LITERATURE REVIEW

Big Data Support for Text Summarization

Big data is a technology used to handle a very large volume of data. It is a technology to store, distribute and process a huge amount of data. Due to technological advancements and with HTML 2.0 the possibility of transmitting data without any specified tag is simplified. Specifically, social media techniques like WhatsApp, Facebook, Instagram, Google, and other techniques are very useful to transmit a huge volume of structured and unstructured data. When you watch a video on YouTube specific advertisements that matches your interest are shown infrequent intervals. This advertisement is selected based on your browsing history and preference. Based on the trends in twitter one can find the recent developments in a particular topic. Moreover, today searches are simplified with help of Google text search and voice-based search. Today most people are using mobile phones to do all kinds of transactions, as well as these mobile phones, are used to track user locations. Today there are many mobile applications are available and depend on the user preference and user requirement these applications are installed. These mobile applications are very much useful to understand the user interest and how much time they are spending can be known. These different scenarios indicate voluminous generation of data and data is being generated in a large volume at every moment. Hence a special kind of text summarization technique is required to better understand the hidden knowledge or information behind this information.

Big Data Formats

Generally, big data is available in both structured and unstructured formats. Employee data and student data are the best examples of structured data. A predefined format is followed to frame data. For example, the employee name which is in alphanumeric format. The next type is unstructured data which is a combination of different fields. For example, in social media text, multilingual text, video clippings, audio clippings, images (different formats), documents (Pdf, word doc, text, and other formats) satellite images, scientific data, photographs, and video, radar, or sonar data are shared.

All these shared things are available in different formats (unstructured format). The important characteristics of big data are volume, velocity, variety, veracity, and value. All these characteristics are equally important and the important character required for multi-document summarization is value. Volume indicates the handling of a large volume of data and velocity indicates the speed at which the data is manipulated. In big data, manipulation consists of ingesting, persisting, computing and analyzing, and finally visualizing the data. Another important character is variety which is a very important multi-document summarization. When a user searches anything on the net which involves different kinds of documents and the summary should provide a result based on all these documents. Another important character is veracity which talks about inconsistency present in the data. By applying all these characters to text summarization it should produce a value for decision making. By analyzing the huge amount of data one must get valuable insight from these data and in-text summarization the output should be a meaningful value obtained from the different variety of data.

Big Data Tools for Summarization

Big data offers different kinds of tools for text summarization and the backbone for big data is cluster computing. It combines different resources from various nodes. The nodes which are available in different places are combined together to summarize the results. The different benefits of cluster computing are high availability, resource pooling, and easy scalability. High availability indicates that failure of a node or cluster will not stop processing as well as high fault tolerance. It is also providing the guarantee that software or hardware failure will not affect the processing of data for summarization.

Resource pooling shares the resources with multiple clients according to the demand. The special feature of resource pooling is the assignment and reassignment of resources according to the demand with the limited number of required resources. Multitenancy technology is widely applied to implement resource pooling in big data. The last and important advantage of cluster computing is easy scalability which adds resources horizontally. The special feature is one need not add resources to a physical machine instead according to the demand the resources can be added or removed virtually.

Activities Involved With Big Data Processing for Text Summarization

There are four important steps are followed in big data to carry out the data summarization which are listed as follows.

Step 1: Ingesting data into the Hadoop Distributed File System (HDFS)

Step 2: Persisting the data in storage (NoSQL)

Step 3: Computing and Analyzing data

Step 4: Visualizing the results

The different tools and its functionalities of each step are described as follows.

Step 1: Ingesting data into the Hadoop Distributed File System (HDFS)

Data ingestion is a process of taking data from the different nodes into a centralized system. In this case Hadoop Distributed File System (HDFS) is applied for data storage. Intern HDFS stores and manipulates the data in different nodes. In this process, both structured and unstructured data are ingested into HDFS (Prudhvi et al., 2021). To carry out the ingestion process big data tools such as Apache Flume, Apache Chukwa, and Apache Sqoop are used widely. Apache Flume and Apache Chukwa are used to ingest the unstructured tools whereas Apache Sqoop is applied to ingest the structure data (Zhang & Liu, 2021).

Step 2: Persisting the data in storage (NoSQL)

The important step of big data processing is persisting of the data into the NoSQL. It stands for "non-sql" or "non-relational" and used to store unstructured data (Ranjan & Foropon, 2021). When compared to the traditional models like SQL, No SQL stores the data with less constrained consistency. It has four types which are listed as follows.

1. Key-value pair
2. Document-based storage
3. Column based storage
4. Graph-based storage

In key-value pair, each collection of data is stored through keys and the single key will have more values. For example, in an online book catalog system, each book has an item code. A particular data item (book code) would have values such as customer id, order items, product id, quantity, cost, and order data, and so on (Sun & Stranieri, 2021). In key-value pair, a single key for example the book id "3756824" may have values such as customer-id (45789IND), order items (product id=2010, quantity=5, cost=245) and order data (22/02/2021). This method is very efficient to store unstructured textual data.

Document Store Languages

It is a very peculiar method to store unstructured data using document store languages. In this kind of storage XML and JSON are applied and data is retrieved using their id (Essakimuthu et al., 2021). The following example helps to better understand the document store language using JSON.

```
'_id': 1,
'artistName': { ' Ilaiyaraaja ' },
'albums': [
{
'albumname': 'How to name it',
'datereleased': 1986,
'songs': '3'
}, {
'albumname': 'Nothing but Wind',
'datereleased': 1988,
'songs': '3'
}, {
'albumname': 'Time',
```

First name	Last name	DOB	Job Category	Salary	Data of Hire	Employer	Insurance ID	Emergency contact	Hospital Name

"personal data" "professional data" "Medical data"

```
'datereleased': 1996,
'songs': '3'
}
]
}
```

Column Store Database

This is another efficient method that is widely applied to store unstructured data. It stores the data in a column-oriented model. A single row may have many numbers of columns and each group of columns may have different kinds of data (Hajjaji et al., 2021). For example, in a particular row the first three columns contains data about "personal data", a group of columns may have "professional data" and another set of columns may have "medical data" which is represented in the following table.

In this particular method in a given row, the first three columns contain "personal data" and next four-column contains "professional data" and the last three columns contain "medical data". The next method is graph-based storage.

Graph-Based Storage

In this method, graph-based storage is used to model and store the data. It is a very efficient method to model the relationship among the data items using graphs (Rehman et al., 2021). In an ecommerce system, the relationship between the different data items and different customers is represented as graphs that simplify the maintenance of data (Kaffash et al., 2021).

Processing and Analyzing of Multisource Documents

In big data to process the data batch processing and stream processing are applied. In batch processing, data are processed in batches and in-stream processing data is processed in real times. To perform real data analytics, stream processing is applied whereas when you have a huge volume of data and analytics is not required immediately then batch processing is applied (Yu et al., 2021). To process the data using batch processing Hadoop is applied and for real-time processing, Spark is applied (Roul, 2021).

These techniques are applied to process the big data and as well as to process the document from multiple sources. There is continuous research is going on Natural Language Processing in which document summarization is a part. From the literature, it has been found that better algorithms are applied to improve the performance of summarization. In many research papers and blogs, many solutions were addressed regarding the Summarization problem. Still much is needed to achieve expected results (Osborne, 2002).

From the literature, it has been found that text summarization using probabilistic methods has shown limited results. Hence supervised and unsupervised machine learning algorithms are applied to improve the text summarization results. K-Means Algorithm is an unsupervised clustering algorithm that shows better results for text summarization. It is also found that very limited research is carried out to apply a hybrid of algorithms for text summarization (Neto et al., 2002).

Making a framework for any problems will be useful for future use. Hence for text summarization, a framework should be developed to find better results. The next section describes big data support for text summarization.

When you consider, few papers addressed this issue regarding the framework for summarizing the text, but it is in the initial phase which lacks the comprehensive capability and contextual sentence formation. Hence extractive summary is used because the sentences are not modified or generated (Edmundson, 2008). In the future Abstractive Summarization, techniques could be used to identify the better results and make an efficient framework for this text summarization from multiple documents. Hence this research proposes to summarize information from multiple documents by dividing all the sentences in the information into different Clusters using the K-Means clustering algorithm. By identifying or selecting a sentence from each cluster will give a summary from multiple documents.

APPLYING OF K-MEANS CLUSTERING ALGORITHM FOR TEXT SUMMARIZATION FROM MULTI DOCUMENTS

The program may collect the data from Google Search regarding the topic (Searched Keyword). The collection of documents is made into a collection of Sentences by splitting them to the end of each sentence. By using K means clustering algorithm make all the sentences into separate groups so that all the sentences that give similar meaning may be clustered into one single cluster.

Then from all the available clusters pick up one sentence from each cluster and join them to form the summary. In the second step, documents need to be split into sentences. Calculate numerical values to sentences based on their frequency and compare to word frequency (ratio of occurrence of the word to a number of words), TF-IDF (**Term Frequency * Inverse Document Frequency**) (product of word frequency and Inverse document frequency [ratio of number of documents to a number of documents the word contained in]).

Number of Clusters – According to the number of sentences the number of clusters is designed for the summary. Moreover, as the sentences are clustered to their closest sentences, one sentence from each cluster might give a sentence that gives a meaning different from other cluster sentences.

EXPERIMENTATION

To implement the K means clustering algorithm Python is applied. Moreover, Python is easy to code, and lots of pre-written libraries are available to simplify the product development phases. SciKit Learn is very useful to develop text summarization for machine learning programs.

The pre-built libraries always give perfect results, because they are made to enhance that particular programming language, like SKlearn in python. SKlearn feature extraction library such as TFTDFVectorizer, Vectorizing the textual data using TFTDF. K-Means Algorithm mostly depends on a math equation, the Euclidean distance between two data points. Here, the TFTDF matrix is high dimensional, nearly hundreds or thousands, so the program that is written from scratch may not be efficient for better results. So, we used SKlearn clustering, KMeans. While visualizing the results, plotting the graph, the scatterplot takes two-dimensional data as input, so SKlearn Principal Component Analysis will be helpful in reducing the multiple dimensional data.

Libraries Used for Experimentation

· from sklearn.cluster import KMeans
· from sklearn.feature_extraction.text import TFTDFVectorizer
· from sklearn.decomposition import KMeans

RESULTS AND DISCUSSIONS

Google search is conducted for the keyword 'Protection from CoronaVirus' and results obtained for this search is considered as data set for this experimentation. The **TFIDF Vector obtained for the experimentation is described in Figure 1.**

Figure 1. TFIDF MATRIX

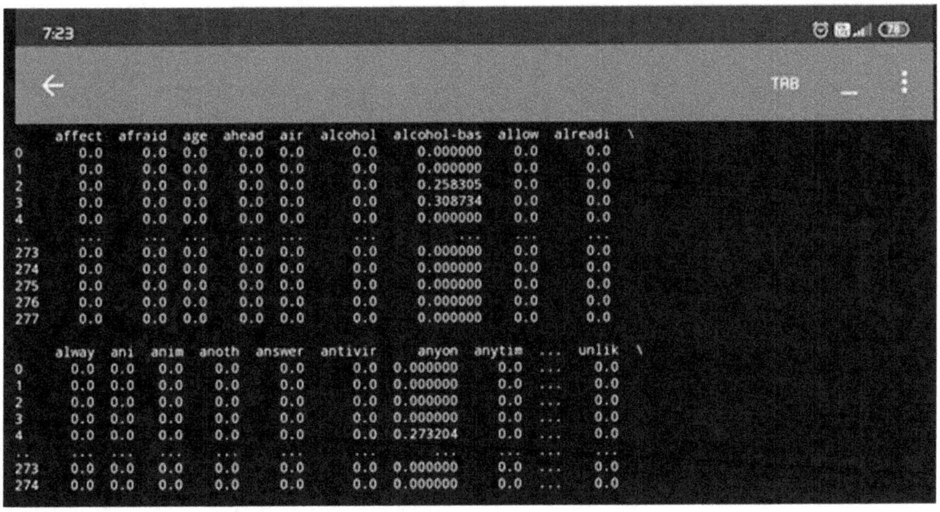

```
     affect  afraid  age  ahead  air  alcohol  alcohol-bas  allow  alreadi  \
0       0.0     0.0  0.0    0.0  0.0      0.0     0.000000    0.0      0.0
1       0.0     0.0  0.0    0.0  0.0      0.0     0.000000    0.0      0.0
2       0.0     0.0  0.0    0.0  0.0      0.0     0.258305    0.0      0.0
3       0.0     0.0  0.0    0.0  0.0      0.0     0.308734    0.0      0.0
4       0.0     0.0  0.0    0.0  0.0      0.0     0.000000    0.0      0.0
..      ...     ...  ...    ...  ...      ...          ...    ...      ...
273     0.0     0.0  0.0    0.0  0.0      0.0     0.000000    0.0      0.0
274     0.0     0.0  0.0    0.0  0.0      0.0     0.000000    0.0      0.0
275     0.0     0.0  0.0    0.0  0.0      0.0     0.000000    0.0      0.0
276     0.0     0.0  0.0    0.0  0.0      0.0     0.000000    0.0      0.0
277     0.0     0.0  0.0    0.0  0.0      0.0     0.000000    0.0      0.0

     alway  ani  anim  anoth  answer  antivir     anyon  anytim  ...  unlik  \
0      0.0  0.0   0.0    0.0     0.0      0.0  0.000000     0.0  ...    0.0
1      0.0  0.0   0.0    0.0     0.0      0.0  0.000000     0.0  ...    0.0
2      0.0  0.0   0.0    0.0     0.0      0.0  0.000000     0.0  ...    0.0
3      0.0  0.0   0.0    0.0     0.0      0.0  0.000000     0.0  ...    0.0
4      0.0  0.0   0.0    0.0     0.0      0.0  0.273204     0.0  ...    0.0
..     ...  ...   ...    ...     ...      ...       ...     ...  ...    ...
273    0.0  0.0   0.0    0.0     0.0      0.0  0.000000     0.0  ...    0.0
274    0.0  0.0   0.0    0.0     0.0      0.0  0.000000     0.0  ...    0.0
```

Figure 2. Summary from K Means

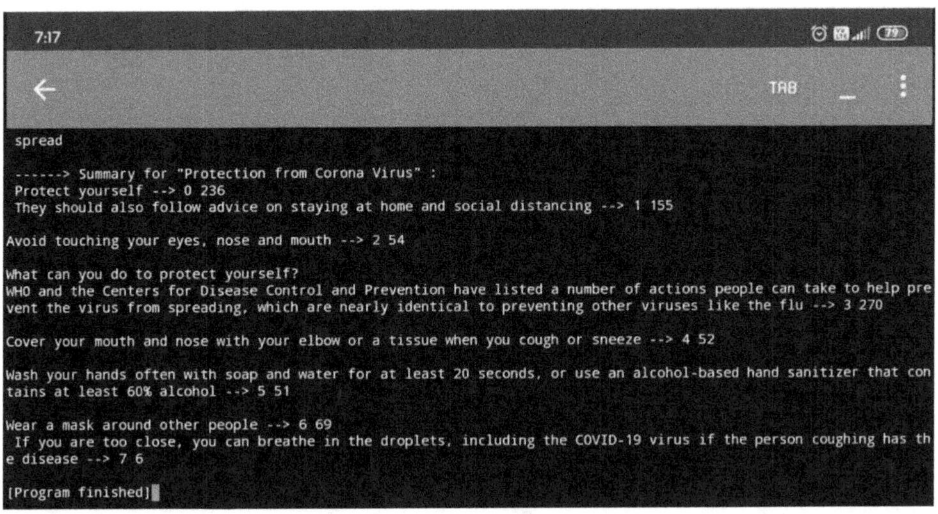

```
spread

------> Summary for "Protection from Corona Virus" :
Protect yourself --> 0 236
They should also follow advice on staying at home and social distancing --> 1 155

Avoid touching your eyes, nose and mouth --> 2 54

What can you do to protect yourself?
WHO and the Centers for Disease Control and Prevention have listed a number of actions people can take to help pre
vent the virus from spreading, which are nearly identical to preventing other viruses like the flu --> 3 270

Cover your mouth and nose with your elbow or a tissue when you cough or sneeze --> 4 52

Wash your hands often with soap and water for at least 20 seconds, or use an alcohol-based hand sanitizer that con
tains at least 60% alcohol --> 5 51

Wear a mask around other people --> 6 69
 If you are too close, you can breathe in the droplets, including the COVID-19 virus if the person coughing has th
e disease --> 7 6

[Program finished]
```

The summary obtained for the resultant documents obtained in the Google search is represented in Figure 2.

Figure 3. TFIDF Summary

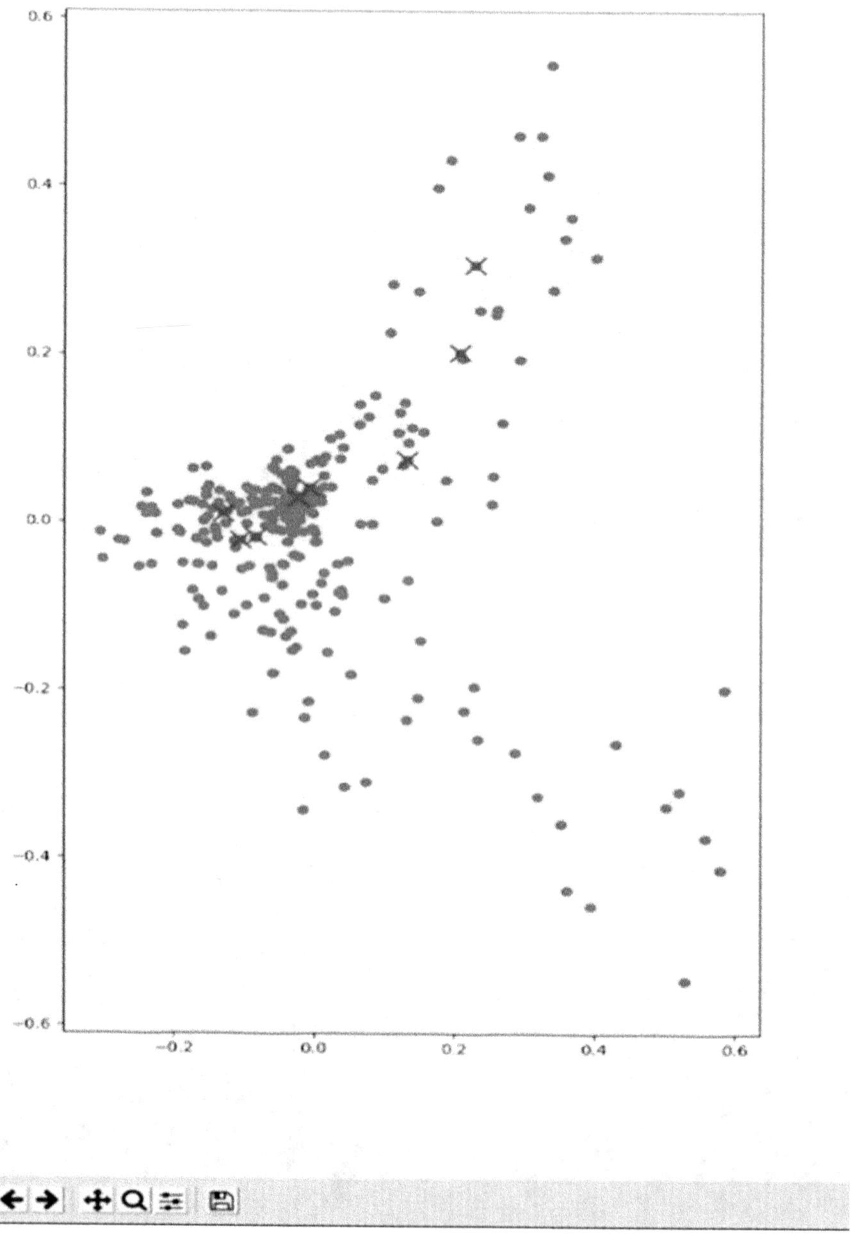

The comparative analysis on clusters obtained using TFIDF and K-Means is described in the Figure 3 and Figure 4.

Figure 4. K-Means Summary

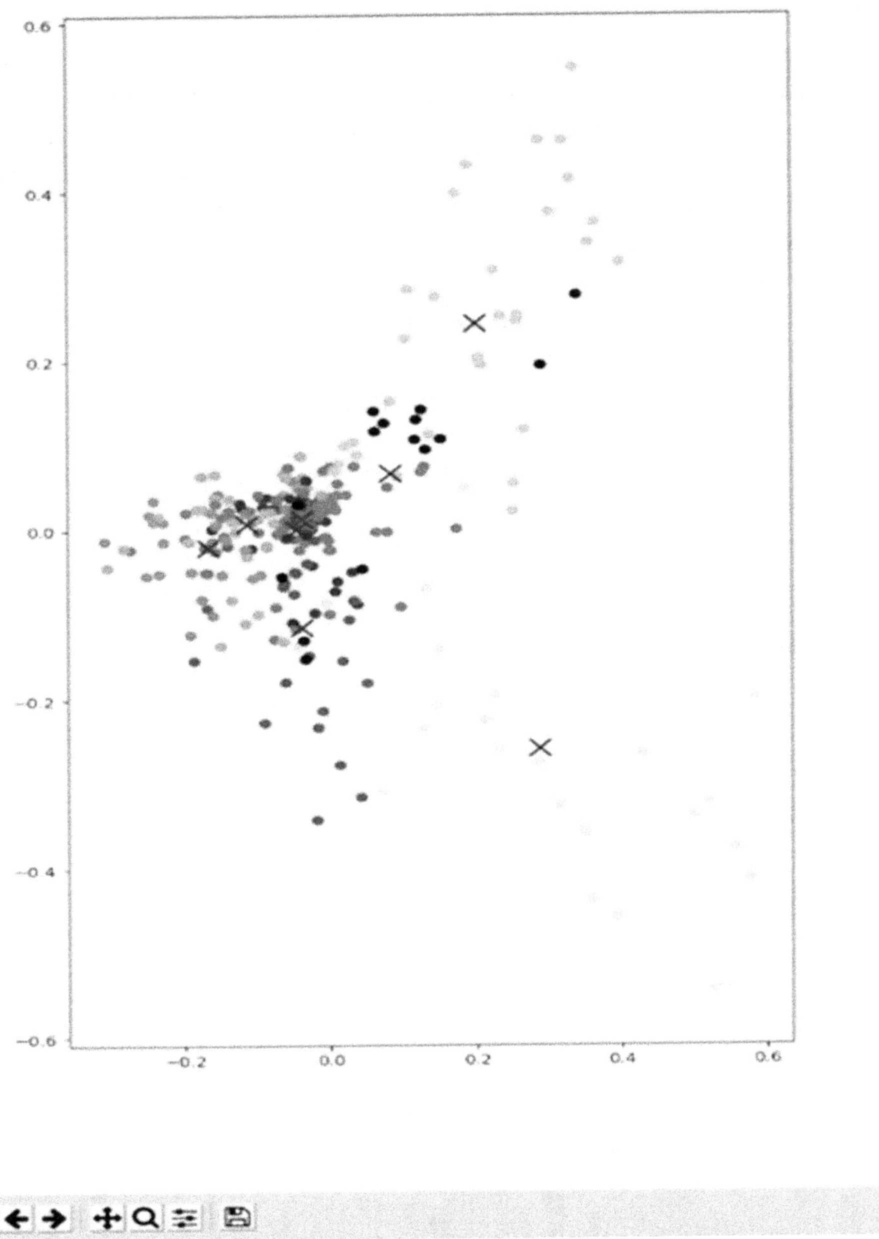

In the above two cases, the TFIDF graph left few sentences (at the bottom right part). In K-Means graph most of the sentences are covered and split into clusters. Hence K Means gives a better result for text summarization from multiple documents.

CONCLUSION

The results with K Means clustering the algorithm is better compared to probabilistic methods because in some way the relationship between words in the document is identified and based in that few groups are divided such that each group is different from the other. So picking one sentence from one group, finally, all these sentences from different groups will give broader information, may spread all over the information in the documents. So, by reading the summary we can understand the whole information approximately. The implemented results are proofs for the conclusion. The obtained results with K-means clustering on document Summarization are better compared to Summarizing with word frequency counting. However, K-Means each sentence in the summary is selected from different clusters.

In this process, neural networks can be applied to improve the results in extractive text Summarization. Improving Algorithms of Abstractive text Summarization will give better results because a meaningful and efficient summary generation could be expected. And data cleaning, feature selection is also important to research areas which help in forming meaningful summary.

REFERENCES

Chen, F., Han, K., & Chen, G. (2002). An Approach to sentence selection based text summarization. *Proceedings of the IEEE, TENCON02*, 489–493.

Edmundson, H. P. (2008, April). New methods in automatic extracting. *Journal of the Association for Computing Machinery, 16*(2), 264–285. doi:10.1145/321510.321519

Essakimuthu, A., Ganesh, R. K., Krishnan, R. S., & Robinson, Y. H. (2021). Enhanced Hadoop Distribution File System for Providing Solution to Big Data Challenges. *Further Advances in Internet of Things in Biomedical and Cyber Physical Systems, 193*, 71–83. doi:10.1007/978-3-030-57835-0_7

Hajjaji, Y., Boulila, W., Farah, I. R., Romdhani, I., & Hussain, A. (2021). Big data and IoT-based applications in smart environments: A systematic review. *Computer Science Review, 39*, 100318. doi:10.1016/j.cosrev.2020.100318

Jaruskulchai, C., & Kruengkrai, C. (2003). Text Summarization Using Local and Global Properties. *Proceedings of the IEEE/WIC International Conference on web Intelligence*, 201-206.

Kaffash, S., Nguyen, A. T., & Zhu, J. (2021). Big data algorithms and applications in intelligent transportation system: A review and bibliometric analysis. *International Journal of Production Economics*, *231*, 107868. doi:10.1016/j.ijpe.2020.107868

Kiani, & Akbarzadeh. (2006). AutomaticText Summarization Using: Hybrid Fuzzy GA-GP. *IEEE International Conference on Fuzzy Systems*, 977-983.

Neto, Freitas, & Kaestner. (2002). Automatic Text Summarization using a Machine Learning Approach. In *Advances in Artificial Intelligence: Lecture Notes in Computer Science*. Springer.

Osborne, M. (2002). Using Maximum Entropy for Sentence Extraction. *ACL Workshop on Text Summarization*. 10.3115/1118162.1118163

Prudhvi, K., Chowdary, A. B., Reddy, P. S. R., & Prasanna, P. L. (2021). Text Summarization Using Natural Language Processing. In *Intelligent System Design* (pp. 535–547). Springer. doi:10.1007/978-981-15-5400-1_54

Radev, D. R., Jing, H., & Budzikowska, M. (2000). *Centroid-based summarization of multiple documents: Sentence extraction, utility based evaluation, and user studies*. In ANLP/NAACL Workshop on Summarization, Seattle, WA.

Ranjan, J., & Foropon, C. (2021). Big data analytics in building the competitive intelligence of organizations. *International Journal of Information Management*, *56*, 102231. doi:10.1016/j.ijinfomgt.2020.102231

Rehman, A., Naz, S., & Razzak, I. (2021). Leveraging big data analytics in healthcare enhancement: Trends, challenges and opportunities. *Multimedia Systems*, 1–33.

Roul, R. K. (2021). Topic modeling combined with classification technique for extractive multi-document text summarization. *Soft Computing*, *25*(2), 1113–1127. doi:10.100700500-020-05207-w

Sun, Z., & Stranieri, A. (2021). The Nature of Intelligent Analytics. In *Intelligent Analytics With Advanced Multi-Industry Applications* (pp. 1–21). IGI Global. doi:10.4018/978-1-7998-4963-6.ch001

Yu, W., Zhao, G., Liu, Q., & Song, Y. (2021). Role of big data analytics capability in developing integrated hospital supply chains and operational flexibility: An organizational information processing theory perspective. *Technological Forecasting and Social Change*, *163*, 120417. doi:10.1016/j.techfore.2020.120417

Zhang, X., & Liu, S. (2021, January). Automatic Text Summarization for Marine Natural Products Literature. *Journal of Physics: Conference Series*, *1732*(1), 012047. doi:10.1088/1742-6596/1732/1/012047

Chapter 3
Determinant Attributes of Store Choice in Organized Retail

Dilpreet Singh
Chitkara Business School, Chitkara University, India

Namrata Sandhu
https://orcid.org/0000-0003-4428-5821
Chitkara Business School, Chitkara University, India

ABSTRACT

Intense competition and price wars in the retail sector provide the impetus to examine consumer behavior in the retail industry. It has become increasingly important to scrutinize what drives consumer choice of retail stores. This chapter addresses this need and aims to establish the factors that drive consumer retail choice behavior. The empirical setting for the study was five organized Indian retail stores: Easy Day, Big Bazaar, More, Reliance Fresh, and Freshmart. Data were collected with the help of a questionnaire (n=700) in a store-intercept survey. Data were analyzed using multivariate data analysis techniques. A model identifying the variables that predicts retail store choice probabilities was developed and tested. Results establish that atmospherics, merchandise assortment, and customer satisfaction have a significant positive impact on retail store choice. On the other hand, price has a significant negative impact on retail store choice. Implications are discussed.

DOI: 10.4018/978-1-7998-7231-3.ch003

INTRODUCTION

Of late, retail has been one of the fastest growing global industries. Retail has witnessed exponential growth in the advanced economies and is all set to replicate the same growth pattern in emerging economies (Tripathi & Sinha, 2008). But, while growth is a significant feature of this industry, so is competition. The ever-increasing competition has made price wars, overlapping merchandise, special schemes and offers to attract customers etc. a regular feature of this industry.

If we categorically talk about organized retail in India, it has had a bumpy ride in the last decade. A number of companies opened stores, experimented with different formats and struggled to understand customer preferences. While some retail giants bet on the traditional brick and mortar format, others banked on online retail (Ganesha et al., 2020). The latter include big names such as Future Group, Reliance Industries, Aditya Birla, Spencer's to name a few. Despite stringent efforts over the years, only a few retailers succeeded to swim through the turbulent competitive waters (Business Standard, 2012). Some argue that it is the understanding of customers and the right operating model that helped the retailers (Khare et al., 2012); others contend that deep pockets of promoters such as Reliance helped the retailers stay afloat (Business Today, 2012).

The share of organized retail is around nine percent today and is expected to touch 10 percent in another two years (IBEF, 2018). Given this background, it is imperative for the retail companies to make the most of this boom and understand customer preferences to further groom their business.

From a research perspective, the intense competition in the retail industry has captured the attention of many researchers (Popkowski et al., 2000). Many studies addressing different facets of this industry have been conducted both inside and outside India. In particular, past researchers have emphasized the need to scrutinize how consumers choose retail stores. Therefore, literature is replete with calls to examine store choice decision criteria of consumers (Tripathi & Sinha, 2008). The present study addresses this call for further research and empirically examines the drivers of consumers' store choice in organized retail.

In the next section of this study, a survey of the relevant literature is presented. Subsequent sections focus on methodology, analysis and implications. The study ends with a discussion on the limitations of the study and the scope for future research.

LITERATURE REVIEW: CONSUMER STORE CHOICE DECISION CRITERIA

This section presents a survey of the extant relevant literature. The purpose of this section is twofold. First, this section attempts to provide an orientation to the dependent variable of the study – store choice. Second, this section helps shortlist the variables that form the basis of the research instrument.

Over five decades of research is available on the drivers of store choice. Existing research on the factors that influence store choice indicates that distance and travelling cost (Huff, 1964; Craig et al., 1984; Brown, 1989), merchandise display (Levy & Weitz, 1998), store image and ambience (Martineau, 1958; Woodside & Trappey, 1992; Medina & Ward, 1999) service output (Gale & Klavans, 1985) and price (Freymann, 2002) significantly impact store choice.

Substantial literature is available that examines the link between distance and choice of store. Generally speaking, these studies establish a negative relation between the two variables (Loudon & Bitta, 1993). These studies establish that farther the distance of the store from the customer's home, higher the probability of selection of alternatives and lower the store patronage (Loudon & Bitta, 1993). Some researchers content that this relation may not hold true in all cases. These researchers examine the impact of age and background of customers on store choice decision. They establish that the elderly customers are less sensitive to price and travelling cost than the young and consider shopping a recreational activity. Hence, in the case of the elderly, the proximity of the store to their homes is not an effective determinant of store choice (Dodge & Summer, 1969; Lumpkin et al., 1985). Therefore, it can be said that store choice is determined by both shopper characteristics and distance (Bellenger et al., 1977; Kim & Park, 1997; Leszczyc et al., 2000).

Engel and colleagues (1995) propose that the width and depth of the merchandise significantly influences the store choice decision. Levy and Weitz (1998) and Sinha and Banerjee (2004) endorse this and add another dimension of merchandise display: visual merchandising, to the variables impacting the customer behavior of the shoppers.

Kotler (1973), and Baker and colleagues (1992) establish that store ambience and environment also influence store choice. Bloch and colleagues (1994) highlight the importance of atmospherics in retail customer decision-making. Goodwin and McElwee (1999) points out that staff attitude forms an important part of atmospherics and cannot be ignored. Good staff-customer relationships mean increased loyalty, resistance to switching and higher conversion (Reynolds & Arnold, 2000). Similarly, music played in a store contributes to store atmospherics. Herrington and Capella (1994) discuss the impact of music on customer preferences. Slow tempo music causes the shoppers to move slowly and results in higher sales (Berman & Evans,

2007). Further, space in the store also positively improves the atmospherics and impacts store choice (Berman & Evans, 2007). Shoppers prefer and spend more time in stores with ample space to roam freely (Berman & Evans, 2007).

Past researchers believe that service also has a significant impact on the choice of a retail store (Sinha et al., 2002). This finding has been confirmed by studies conducted by many authors (Stern & El-Ansary, 1988; Bucklin et al., 1996; Baker et al., 2002). These researchers closely examine the link between a store's service output and store choice. As long back as 1966, Bucklin defined a store's service output as the sum total of what a consumer obtains/receives from a store. A strong positive correlation between a store's service output and customers' perceived value exists (Gale & Klavans, 1985). Customers' perceived value in turn impacts customer satisfaction. If the perceived value is less than the expectations, the customer is dissatisfied (Oliver, 1980). This negatively impacts store choice (Gale & Klavans, 1985).

Hildebrandt (1988) undertook extensive work on retail store choice criteria. The author contends that quality, atmosphere and price impact the choice of a retail store. Hildebrandt (1988) also proposed a scale to examine the drivers of store choice decision.

Past scholars also establish a significant link between price and store choice (Bell et al., 2001; Freymann, 2002). Price negatively impacts store choice (Arnold et al., 1978; Walters & Heikki, 1986). Previous authors point out two price formats – Everyday Low Prices (EDLP) and High Low (HILO) and establish that perceived utilities impact the choice of store. Any change in the price format significantly impacts customers' choice and in turn the choice and profitability of the retail store (Bell & Lattin, 1998).

To sum up, the work of Ghosh and colleagues (2010) and, Sandhu and colleagues (2012) can be cited. Ghosh et al. (2010) argue that convenience and merchandise mix, store atmospherics and service are the three primary factors that impact choice of retail outlets. Sandhu et al. (2012) establish product and store attributes, merchandise assortment, schemes, exterior atmospherics, and interior atmospherics as the drivers of store choice (Sandhu et al., 2012). Vashishtha and Sharma (2016) replicated these results in a recent study. It may be pertinent to point out here that there is a high degree of concurrence in the findings of the studies conducted in India (Ghosh et al., 2010; Sandhu et al., 2012; Vashishtha & Sharma, 2016) and the studies conducted abroad (Kotler, 1973; Baker et al., 1992; Bloch et al., 1994). Both Indian and foreign studies have displayed similar findings. The studies conducted to understand the determinants are not very recent and it becomes important to understand if the factors hold true in the current scenario. Given this gap, the current study attempts to assess the determinants of store choice.

METHODOLOGY

Instrument Design and Data Collection

For the purpose of data collection, a questionnaire was designed. The questionnaire contained 20 statements representative of the probable variables that influence retail store choice. This inventory of statements was developed based on a review of the extant relevant literature. In particular, suggestions put forth by Hildebrandt (1988) and Hansen and colleagues (2004) were referred to. Importance of each statement was captured using a five-point Likert scale. The questionnaire also contained questions on the demographic profile of the respondents.

Some of the statements used in the questionnaire were negatively worded to reduce bias due to the tendency of the respondents to provide affirmative responses (Streiner & Norman, 1995). At the time of data entry, responses to these statements were reverse-coded.

A store-intercept survey was conducted to collect data. The empirical setting for the study was five organized retail stores in Tricity (Chandigarh, Mohali and Panchkula): Easy Day, Big Bazaar, More, Reliance Fresh and Freshmart. These stores were chosen on the basis of convenience. A priori sample size estimation was done and although 150 questionnaires were administered at each of the five retail stores (n = 750), the number of usable questionnaires obtained was 700. Table 1 exhibits the details of data collection.

Table 1. Details of data collection

Name of store	Number of filled questionnaires obtained	Number of usable questionnaires obtained
Easy Day	150	144
Big Bazaar	150	134
More	150	132
Reliance Fresh	150	144
Freshmart	150	146

Source: Authors' study

Profile of Respondents

An attempt was made to have representation from different demographic groups. Table 2 displays the profile of the respondents. The maximum number of respondents

(296) was from the age group of 18-30 years. 36 senior citizens were also part of the sample. The number of female respondents was 406 (sample size=700). The number of female shoppers in these stores was comparatively higher than the males (n=294). 47.86 percent of the respondents were graduates while 42.57 percent were postgraduates. Finally, the majority of the respondents fell in 6,00,000-12,00,000 annual income (in INR) category. This number was 309 as against 52 and 126 who earned less than 3,00,000 INR and between 3,00,000 INR and 6,00,000 INR respectively.

Table 2. Respondent profile (n = 700)

Variable	Categories of variable	Frequency	Percentage
Age (in years)	< 18	106	15.14
	18-30	296	42.29
	30-45	160	22.86
	45-60	102	14.57
	> 60	36	05.14
Gender	Female	406	58.00
	Male	294	42.00
Qualification	Graduate	335	47.86
	Postgraduate	298	42.57
	Any other	67	09.57
Annual income (in INR)	< 3 00 000	52	07.43
	3 00 000-6 00 000	126	18.00
	6 00 000-12 00 000	309	44.14
	> 12 00 000	213	30.43

Source: Authors' study

Data Analysis Techniques

The collected data were analyzed using multivariate data analysis techniques: factor analysis and regression analysis (for details refer to next section).

ANALYSIS

Factor Analysis

To start with, the collected data were reduced with the help of factor analysis. Appropriateness of the use of factor analysis was verified before subjecting the data to analysis (refer to table 3 and 4). Kaiser-Meyer-Oklin value worked out to .707 and the results of Bartlett's test of sphericity were also significant (p = .000) (refer to table 3). Table 4 exhibits the correlation matrix. As can be seen from this matrix, there are sufficient correlations among different pairs to variables to proceed with factor analysis. As such, the data were subjected to factor analysis.

The results of factor analysis are exhibited in table 5. As can be seen, six factors accounting for 66.89 percent of the total variance were extracted. Only the factors with Eigen values exceeding 1.0 and variables which clearly loaded on a factor with a loading of over 0.5 (17 out of the 20 variables included in the questionnaire) were retained (Malhotra, 2008). The extracted factors, in decreasing order of importance are atmospherics, distance, merchandise assortment, quality, price, and customer satisfaction. The reliability of the factors was established with the help of Cronbach's coefficient α (α = .814).

Table 3. KMO and Bartlett's test

Kaiser Meyer Oklin measure of sampling adequacy	**.707**	
Bartlett's test of sphericity	Approx. χ^2	1420.524
	df	21
	Sig.	.000

Source: Authors' study

The most important factor that has emerged after the analysis is 'atmospherics'. With an Eigen value of 6.814, this factor accounts for 23.13 percent of the total variance. Store characteristics such as background music, staff, cleanliness and hygiene, in-store atmosphere and ambience constitute atmospherics. The next factor is 'distance'. This factor has an Eigen value of 2.092. Four variables are loaded on this factor. These variables are indicative of the distance between the customer's home and the store, total travel time, travel expense and availability of parking facility at the store. The third factor is merchandise assortment. The three variables loaded on this factor represent three different aspects of merchandise assortment: product variety, product choice/range and product availability. The fourth factor

Table 4. Correlation matrix

	V1	V2	V3	V4	V5	V6	V7	V8	V9	V10	V11	V12	V13	V14	V15	V16	V17	V18	V19	V20	V21
V1	1																				
V2	.765**	1																			
V3	.176**	.204**	1																		
V4	.158**	.193**	.497**	1																	
V5	.093*	.120**	.305**	.322**	1																
V6	.105**	.135**	.415**	.470**	.352**	1															
V7	.447**	.470**	.149**	.279**	.121**	.075*	1														
V8	.272**	.299**	.204**	.172**	.181**	.349**	.192**	1													
V9	.419**	.395**	.397**	.303**	.291**	.301**	.413**	.368**	1												
V10	.505**	.436**	.201**	.326**	.202**	.238**	.515**	.358**	.473**	1											
V11	.414**	.394**	.366**	.436**	.296**	.439**	.415**	.450**	.501**	.658**	1										
V12	.514**	.493**	.221**	.318**	.178**	.271**	.475**	.343**	.480**	.572**	.587**	1									
V13	.467**	.446**	.222**	.306**	.209**	.318**	.460**	.424**	.493**	.597**	.619**	.767**	1								
V14	.444**	.428**	.194**	.279**	.194**	.292**	.451**	.455**	.502**	.549**	.587**	.745**	.844**	1							
V15	.287**	.275**	.372**	.360**	.263**	.388**	.531**	.374**	.569**	.567**	.571**	.538**	.633**	.625**	1						
V16	.354**	.373**	.280**	.217**	.162**	.127**	.377**	.355**	.578**	.459**	.475**	.493**	.628**	.653**	.625**	1					
V17	.169**	.168**	.200**	.126**	.124**	.151**	.142**	.326**	.355**	.262**	.351**	.318**	.504**	.605**	.377**	.620**	1				
V18	.159**	.255**	.234**	.190**	.085*	.164**	.339**	.290**	.267**	.262**	.239**	.161**	.323**	.371**	.475**	.549**	.343**	1			
V19	.204**	.280**	.292**	.204**	.125**	.173**	.180**	.164**	.232**	.184**	.295**	.099**	.141**	.073	.217**	.241**	.141**	.346**	1		
V20	.487**	.407**	.278**	.202**	.106**	.107**	.405**	.213**	.391**	.502**	.430**	.365**	.289**	.265**	.371**	.329**	.094*	.206**	.337**	1	
V21	.242**	.312**	.468**	.354**	.318**	.431**	.313**	.348**	.478**	.347**	.565**	.408**	.513**	.499**	.559**	.494**	.463**	.322**	.436**	.299**	1

** Correlation is significant at the 0.01 level (2-tailed)
* Correlation is significant at the 0.05 level (2-tailed).

Table 5. Factors impacting store choice in organized retail

Factor	Eigen value	Cumulative variance (%)	Variables	Loadings
Factor 1 – Atmospherics	6.814	23.13	The background music in the store is soothing.	.922
			This store has good staff.	.763
			Cleanliness and hygiene of the store is appreciable.	.641
			This store has a good in-store atmosphere.	.606
			I like the ambience of the store.	.598
Factor 2 – Distance	2.092	35.07	This store is far away from my house.	.833
			I don't visit this store often because travel time to reach the store is a lot.	.713
			It is expensive to travel to the store from my house.	.589
			This store does not have adequate parking.	.502
Factor 3 – Merchandise assortment	1.888	45.10	This store offers a wide variety of products.	.789
			I always get what I am looking for at this store.	.745
			Unique products are available at this store.	.543
Factor 4 – Quality	1.631	53.78	This store stocks latest and fresh products.	.687
			This store offers products of good quality.	.663
Factor 5 – Price	1.218	60.20	This store does not offer value for money.	.718
			This store offers low prices.	.555
Factor 6 – Customer satisfaction	1.117	66.89	I would recommend this store to others.	.628

Source: Authors' study

has an Eigen value of 1.631 and has been named 'quality'. The variables loaded on this factor are suggestive of the freshness and quality of products. The fifth factor impacting store choice is 'price'. This factor has two variables loaded on it. The last and the sixth factor has been named 'customer satisfaction'. This factor has one variable indicative of customer satisfaction: recommendation to other prospective customers, loaded on it.

Model Development

To examine the impact of the six extracted factors on retail store choice, the model depicted in table 6 was developed. The six factors were presumed to be the independent variables and store choice was presumed to be the dependent variable. The hypotheses exhibited in table 7 were proposed.

Figure 1. Model to be tested
Source: Authors' study

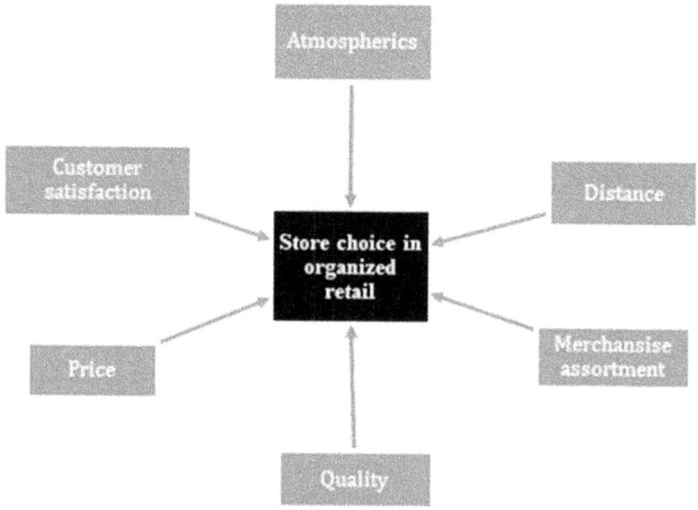

Table 6. Model development

Independent variables	Dependent variable
Atmospherics	Store choice
Distance	
Merchandise assortment	
Quality	
Price	
Customer satisfaction	

$Y = a + b_1x_1 + b_2x_2 + b_3x_3 + b_4x_4 + b_5x_5 + b_6x_6$.. ....Equation 1,
where Y = store choice, a = constant, x_1 = atmospherics, x_2 = distance, x_3 = merchandise assortment, x_4 = quality, x_5 = price, x_6 = customer satisfaction, and b_1 to b_6 = slope coefficients

Source: Authors' study

Table 7. Hypotheses

Null hypotheses	Alternate hypotheses
H_{01}: There is no significant impact of atmospherics on store choice.	H_1: There is a significant impact of atmospherics on store choice.
H_{02}: There is no significant impact of distance on store choice.	H_2: There is a significant impact of distance on store choice.
H_{03}: There is no significant impact of merchandise assortment on store choice.	H_3: There is a significant impact of merchandise assortment on store choice.
H_{04}: There is no significant impact of quality on store choice.	H_4: There is a significant impact of quality on store choice.
H_{05}: There is no significant impact of price on store choice.	H_5: There is a significant impact of price on store choice.
H_{06}: There is no significant impact of customer satisfaction on store choice.	H_6: There is a significant impact of customer satisfaction on store choice.

Source: Authors' study

Model Testing

The model developed in the preceding sub-section was tested with the help of regression analysis. Before proceeding, it was ensured that multicollinearity was not a concern in the present study. The pair –wise correlation between all pairs of regressors was under 0.8 (refer to table 8) and the VIF of all variables was under 10 (refer to table 9) (Gujarati, 2008). This ensures that the data are free from the problem of multicollinearity.

Table 8. Correlation matrix

	F1	F2	F3	F4	F5	F6	Y
F1	1						
F2	.176**	1					
F3	.158**	.497**	1				
F4	.093*	.305**	.322**	1			
F5	.105**	.415**	.470**	.352**	1		
F6	.765**	.204**	.193**	.120**	.135**	1	
Y	.447**	.149**	.297**	.121**	.075*	.470**	1
**Significant at 5 per cent level of significance *Significant at 1 per cent level of significance							

Source: Authors' study

The results of regression analysis are displayed in tables 9 to11. The overall regression model is significant (p = .000). Individually, four factors: atmospherics, merchandise assortment, price and customer satisfaction significantly impact the dependent variable. As such, H_1, H_3, H_5 and H_6 are supported. Distance and quality do not significantly impact the dependent variable. Hence, H_2 and H_4 are rejected. Further, atmospherics, merchandise assortment and customer satisfaction positively impact the dependent variable and price negatively impacts the dependent variable. The final model thus takes the shape of equation (2).

$$Y = a + b_1x_1 + b_3x_3 + b_5x_5 + b_6x_6 \quad (2)$$

Table 9. Regression analysis

Factors	Unstandardized coefficients		Standardized coefficients	t	Significance (*p* value)	VIF
	B	SE	Beta			
Atmospherics	.315	.076	.208	4.154	.000*	2.412
Distance	-.082	.087	-.036	-.934	.351	1.450
Merchandise assortment	.510	.083	.245	6.151	.000*	1.532
Quality	.054	.054	.035	-990	.323	1.205
Price	-.161	.063	.097	-2.540	.011*	1.422
Customer satisfaction	.480	.086	.208	5.564	.000*	2.454
*Significant at 5 per cent level of significance; intercept (constant) = .565; R^2=.284; adjusted R^2=.278						

Source: Authors' study

Table 10. Model summary

Model	R^2	Adjusted R^2	SE of the estimate
1	.284	.278	1.41593

Source: Authors' study

Table 11. ANOVA for regression

Sources of variation	Sum of squares	df	Mean square	F	Significance
Regression	550.551	6	91.759	45.768	.000
Residual	1385.353	691	2.2005		
Total	1935.904	697			

Source: Authors' study

where Y = store choice, a = constant, x_1 = atmospherics, x_3 = merchandise assortment, x_5 = price, and x_6 = customer satisfaction

Previous researchers have examined the impact of atmospherics on store choice and have found a significant correlation between the two variables (Hildebrandt, 1988; Baker et al., 1992; Sandhu et al., 2012). The results of the current study reinforce this relationship. The study also supports the work of previous scholars who suggest that merchandise assortment is a significant store choice decision criterion (Baker et al., 2002). Extant literature also documents the significant impact of price (Arnold et al., 1983; Bell et al., 2001) and customer satisfaction on store choice (Hildebrandt, 1988). Once again, the findings of the current study support literature in this context.

Many scholars content that distance has a significant negative impact on store choice (Hansen et al., 2004). However, in the current study, distance and store choice were not significantly correlated. The present study also refutes the work of Hildebrandt (1988), who contends that quality is a significant driver of store choice.

CONCLUSION AND IMPLICATIONS

To conclude it can be said that the results of the current study establish that atmospherics, merchandise assortment and customer satisfaction have a significant positive impact on retail store choice. This is in conjunction with the previous studies

Figure 2. Proposed model: Store choice criteria in organized retail

(Baker et al., 2002; Gale & Klavans, 1985) On the other hand, price has a significant negative impact on retail store choice. Figure 2 exhibits the conclusion of the study.

The present study has cogent implications for retail managers. To attract customers and gain a competitive edge in the marketplace, retail managers must focus on improving store atmospherics and merchandise assortment. They must also aim to augment customer satisfaction and offer competitive prices.

LIMITATIONS AND SCOPE FOR FUTURE RESEARCH

The present study suffers from some limitations. First, regional bias may prevent generalization of results. Second, the model could not explain the total variance, and third, the study did not assess the impact of customer demographics on store choice. The study only concentrated on the impact of store attributes on store choice.

Future researchers may replicate this study devoid of its limitations. They may also integrate store formats into the model. Future researchers can also use structural equation modeling to assess the linkages between the drivers of retail store choice decision. For example: the current study establishes that both price and customer satisfaction impact store choice. Pervious literature indicates that reduction in price can significantly enhance customer satisfaction (Gale & Klavans, 1985). Future investigators can empirically verify this correlation in the Indian context. They can also uncover correlations between other factors that impact store choice decision.

REFERENCES

Arnold, S. J., Ma, S., & Tigert, D. J. (1978). A comparative analysis of determinant attributes in retail store selection. *Advances in Consumer Research. Association for Consumer Research (U. S.)*, *5*(1), 663–667.

Arnold, S. J., Oum, T. H., & Tigert, D. J. (1983). Determinant attributes in retail patronage: Seasonal, temporal, regional, and international comparisons. *JMR, Journal of Marketing Research*, *20*(2), 149–157. doi:10.1177/002224378302000205

Baker, J., Grewal, D., & Levy, M. (1992). An experimental approach to making retail store environmental decisions. *Journal of Retailing*, *68*(4), 445–460.

Baker, J., Parasuraman, A., Grewal, D., & Voss, G. B. (2002). The influence of multiple store environment cues on perceived merchandise value and patronage intentions. *Journal of Marketing*, *65*(1), 120–141. doi:10.1509/jmkg.66.2.120.18470

Bell, D. R., Ho, T., & Tang, C. S. (2001). Store choice and shopping behavior: How price format works. *California Management Review*, *43*(2), 352–369.

Bell, D. R., & Lattin, J. M. (1998). Shopping behavior and consumer preference for retail price format: Why 'large basket' shoppers prefer EDLP. *Marketing Science*, *17*(1), 66–88. doi:10.1287/mksc.17.1.66

Bellenger, D. N., Robertson, D. H., & Greenberg, B. A. (1977). Shopping centre patronage motives. *Journal of Retailing*, *53*(2), 29–38.

Berman, B., & Evans, J. R. (2007). *Retailing management: A strategic approach* (8th ed.). Pearson Education.

Bloch, P. H., Dawson, S., & Ridgway, N. M. (1994). The shopping mall as consumer habitat. *Journal of Retailing*, *70*(1), 132–145. doi:10.1016/0022-4359(94)90026-4

Brown, S. (1989). Retail location theory: The legacy of Harold hoteling. *Journal of Retailing*, *65*(4), 450–470.

Bucklin, L. P. (1966). *A theory of distribution channel structure*. Institute of Business and Economic Research.

Bucklin, L. P., Ramaswamy, V., & Majumdar, S. K. (1996). Analyzing channel structures of business markets via the structure-output paradigm. *International Journal of Research in Marketing*, *13*(1), 73–87. doi:10.1016/0167-8116(95)00035-6

Business Standard. (2012). *Madras HC orders shutdown of Subhiksha*. Available at: https://www.business-standard.com/article/companies/madras-hc-orders-shutdown-of-subhiksha-112030100064_1.html

Business Today. (2012). *The devil is in retail*. Available at: https://www.businesstoday.in/magazine/cover-story/organised-retail-india-problems/story/184980.html

Craig, S. C., Ghosh, A., & McLafferty, S. (1984). Department store cross-shoppers. *JMR, Journal of Marketing Research*, *14*(2), 187–192.

Dodge, R. H., & Summer, H. (1969). Choosing between retail stores. *Journal of Retailing*, *45*(3), 11–21.

Engel, J. F., Blackwell, R. D., & Miniard, P. W. (1995). *Consumer behaviour*. Dryden Press.

Freymann, J. V. (2002). Grocery store pricing and its effect on initial and ongoing store choice. *Marketing Management Journal*, *12*(1), 107–119.

Gale, B. T., & Klavans, R. (1985). Formulating a quality improvement strategy. *The Journal of Business Strategy*, *5*(3), 21–31. doi:10.1108/eb039072

Ganesha, H. R., Aithal, P. S., & Kirubadevi, P. (2020). Changes in Consumer Perspective towards Discount at Brick-and-Mortar Stores owing to Emergence of Online Store Format in India. I*nternational Journal of Management. Technology, and Social Sciences*, *5*(1), 43–83.

Ghosh, P., Tripathi, V., & Kumar, A. (2010). Customer expectations of store attributes: A Study of organized retail outlets in India. *Journal of Retail & Leisure Property*, *9*(1), 75–87. doi:10.1057/rlp.2009.27

Goodwin, D., & McElwee, R. (1999). Grocery shopping and an ageing population: Research note. *International Journal of Retail, Distribution and Consumer Research*, *9*(4), 403-409.

Gujarati, D. N. (2008). *Basic econometrics*. McGraw Hill.

Hansen, T., Cumberland, F., & Sologaard, H. S. (2004). *How the measurement of store choice behavior moderates the relationship between distance and store choice behavior*. Available at: www.marketing-trends-congress.com/archives/2013/pages/PDF/665.pdf

Herrington, J. D., & Capella, L. M. (1994). Practical applications of music in retail and service settings. *Journal of Services Marketing*, *8*(4), 50–65. doi:10.1108/08876049410065615

Hildebrandt, L. (1988). Store image and the prediction of performance in retailing. *Journal of Business Research*, *17*(1), 91–100. doi:10.1016/0148-2963(88)90026-4

Huff, D. (1964). Declining and estimating a trading area. *Journal of Marketing*, *28*(3), 34–38. doi:10.1177/002224296402800307

IBEF. (2018). *Retail industry in India*. Available at: https://www.ibef.org/industry/retail-india.aspx

Khare, A., Khare, A., & Singh, S. (2012). Attracting Shoppers to Shop Online—Challenges and Opportunities for the Indian Retail Sector. *Journal of Internet Commerce*, *11*(2), 161–185. doi:10.1080/15332861.2012.689570

Kim, B., & Park, K. (1997). Studying patterns of grocery shopping trips. *Journal of Retailing*, *73*(4), 501–517. doi:10.1016/S0022-4359(97)90032-4

Kotler, P. (1973). Atmospherics as a marketing tool. *Journal of Retailing*, *49*(4), 48–64.

Leszczyc, P. T. L. P., Sinha, A., & Timmermans, H. J. P. (2000). Consumer store choice dynamics: An analysis of the competitive market structure for grocery stores. *Journal of Retailing*, *76*(3), 323–345. doi:10.1016/S0022-4359(00)00033-6

Levy, M., & Weitz, B. (1998). *Retailing management* (3rd ed.). McGraw Hill.

Loudon, D. L., & Bitta, A. J. (1993). *Consumer behavior: Concepts and applications*. McGraw-Hill.

Lumpkin, J. R., Greenberg, B. A., & Goldstucker, J. L. (1985). Marketplace needs of the elderly: Determinant attributes and store choice. *Journal of Retailing*, *61*(2), 75–105.

Malhotra, N. K. (2008). *Marketing research: An applied orientation*. Prentice-Hall. doi:10.1108/S1548-6435(2008)4

Martineau, P. (1958). The personality of the retail store. *Harvard Business Review*, *36*(1), 47–56.

Medina, S., & Ward, R. W. (1999). A model of retail outlet selection for beef. *The International Food and Agribusiness Management Review*, *2*(2), 195–219. doi:10.1016/S1096-7508(00)00021-5

Oliver, R. L. (1980). A cognitive model of the antecedents and consequences of satisfaction decisions. *JMR, Journal of Marketing Research*, *17*(4), 46–49. doi:10.1177/002224378001700405

Popkowski, L., Sinha, A., & Timmermans, H. J. P. (2000). Consumer store choice dynamics: An analysis of the competitive market structure for grocery stores. *Journal of Retailing*, *76*(3), 323–345. doi:10.1016/S0022-4359(00)00033-6

Reynolds, K. E., & Arnold, M. J. (2000). Customer loyalty to the salesperson and the store: Examining relationship customers in an upscale retail context. *Journal of Personal Selling & Sales Management*, *20*(2), 89–98.

Sandhu, N., Singh, D., & Dhall, R. (2012, March). *Determinants of retail store choice: An empirical analysis*. Paper presented at 2nd National Conference on Retailing in India: Opportunities and Challenges, BFCMT, Bathinda, India.

Sinha, P. K., & Banerjee, A. (2004). Store choice behavior in an evolving market. *International Journal of Retail & Distribution Management*, *32*(10), 482–494. doi:10.1108/09590550410558626

Sinha, P. K., Banerjee, A., & Uniyal, D. P. (2002). Deciding where to buy: Store choice behaviour of Indian shoppers. *Vikalpa*, *27*(2), 13–28. doi:10.1177/0256090920020203

Stern, L. W., & El-Ansary, A. I. (1988). *Marketing channels*. Prentice-Hall Inc.

Streiner, D., & Norman, G. (1995). *Health measurement scales: A practical guide to their development and use*. Oxford University Press.

Tripathi, S., & Sinha, P. K. (2008). *Choice of a retail store and retail store format: A hierarchical logit model*. Available at: www.iimahd.ernet.in/publications/data/2008-04-03Tripathi.pdf

Vashishtha, S., & Sharma, S. (2016). Store choice behaviour in a developing economy: An empirical evidence on household consumer durables. *IOSR Journal of Business and Management, 18*(8), 30–35. doi:10.9790/487X-1808013035

Walters, R. G., & Heikki, J. R. (1986). An empirical investigation into the imapct of price promotions on reatil store performance. *Journal of Retailing, 62*(3), 237–266.

Woodside, A. G., & Trappey, R. J. (1992). Finding out why customers shop your store and buy your brand. *Journal of Advertising Research, 32*(6), 59–78.

Chapter 4
Digital Marketing Performance:
Understanding the Challenges and Measuring the Outcomes

Tejinder Pal Singh Brar
Chandigarh Group of Colleges, India

ABSTRACT

Digital marketing managers are feeling the ever-increasing pressure to show the contribution of marketing activities and it's their primary concern towards their organization. The absence of responsibility has harmed the expected outcomes from the marketing campaigns. The best way to recover its impact is to show the results of advertising in financial terms to top administration. Previous research shows that the capacity to quantify marketing performance significantly affects firm execution, benefit, stock returns, top administration fulfillment with advertising, and advertisers' standing inside an association. This chapter discusses the various challenges faced by the organizations in measuring the digital marketing performance and significance of measuring the online marketing performance through better online execution. The findings of this study reveal that data produced through digital analytics can be utilized for estimating and optimizing performance of digital marketing campaigns.

INTRODUCTION

Digital marketing as defined by The Digital Marketing Institute as "the utilization of advanced technologies to make an incorporated, directed and quantifiable communication which assists with not only gaining and retaining customers but also building relationships with them" (Wilson, 2010). Digital technologies are

DOI: 10.4018/978-1-7998-7231-3.ch004

most certainly not just utilized as stages or channels for conveying digital marketing activities, but at the same time they are applied for creating, focusing on, and estimating those activities. Direct advertising was progressively supplanted by the term interactive marketing in the scholarly writing during the 1990s. This reflects that marketing was getting more conversational (Li, 2011). It is important to note that direct marketing was based on one-directional communications, on the other hand interactive marketing was based on two directional communications and cross-channel conversations (Zahay, 2014).

The essential utilization of databases remained a significant component of interactive advertising, yet new channels arisen for directing intelligent communications. This prompted the thought of multi-channel marketing; and as the significance of Internet grew, the core interest of interactive marketing extended to include marketing in digital media (Malthouse and Hofacker, 2010). These changes in terminologies also reflected through titles of academic journal like Journal of Direct Marketing became the Journal of Interactive Marketing in 1998. Later on, Direct Marketing: An International Journal also changed its name to Journal of Research in Interactive Marketing. Finally the term interactive marketing is replaced with the more relevant term i.e. Digital Marketing. There are number of areas where digital marketing is related and the direct marketing is one such area where it can be related. Direct marketing is based on the concept of competent use of databases that facilitate marketers to target customers based on their individual characters and behaviors as well as to measure their responses (Wymbs, 2011) and because the databases were largely digitized therefore direct marketing can be considered an early form of digital marketing.

Different ideas identified with digital marketing include Internet/web based marketing, electronic marketing. While recognizing that these ideas are frequently utilized equivalently with digital marketing, a few differentiations can be made. To begin with, the term Internet/web based marketing alludes just to one innovation (i.e., Internet), while digital marketing incorporates a variety of other innovations, including SMSs, MMSs, mobile applications, and databases that can be utilized without an Internet connection (Chaffey and Smith, 2013). According to Zahay (2014) components of direct marketing and interactive marketing like databases etc. are integral part of digital marketing but in its advanced form digital marketing as in this the customer upto some extent taken control of online communication through various online platforms like social media and also taken control of the purchase decision by conducting online research. Overall, digital marketing supports many-to-many communications, which are increasingly commenced not by the companies but by the customers. The researchers has been witnessed the growth of digital

Figure 1. Increase in the search results for the word "Digital Marketing"
Source: Takala (2016)

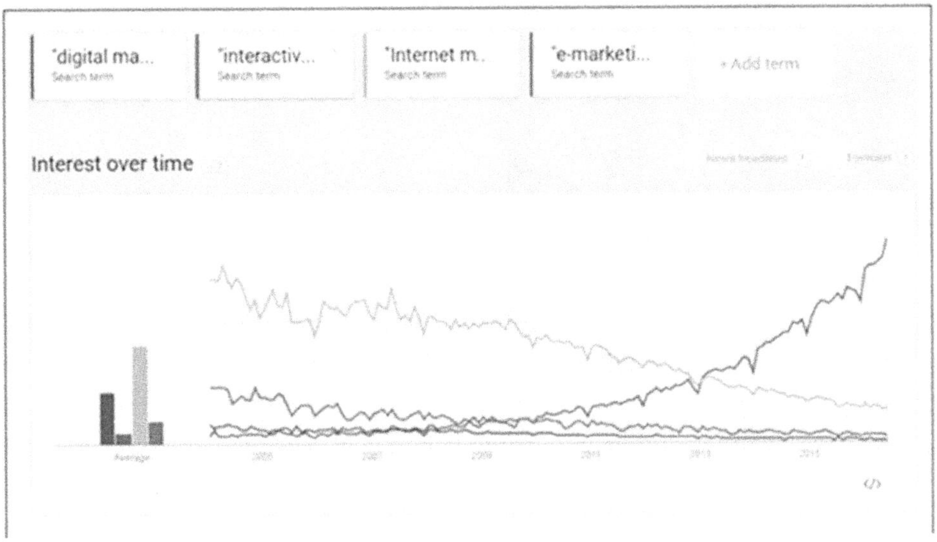

marketing over the past 10 years. Takala (2016) illustrates the volume of Google search terms "digital marketing," "interactive marketing," "Internet marketing," and "e-marketing" with the help of following figure which reveals the volume of searches on digital marketing. This verification provides support for the terminological shift toward digital marketing.

The Effects of Digitalization on Customer Behavior

Advances in data innovation and with new developments in online technologies have changed customer behavior and marketing practices. The absolute and the most extremist advancements empowered by IT include the Internet and cell phones. These developments have expanded the volume and openness of computerized data by making it universal (i.e., data can be used anyplace), and have encouraged the quick and smooth trade of data among individuals and associations through computerized correspondence channels (Kozinets et al. 2010). Accordingly, conduct of customers' has fundamentally changed regarding media utilization propensities, correspondences examples, and buying patterns. Following figure shows usage of various online platforms for searching for online products and usage of social media.

Figure 2. Usage of various online platforms
Source: HubSpot Research (2020)

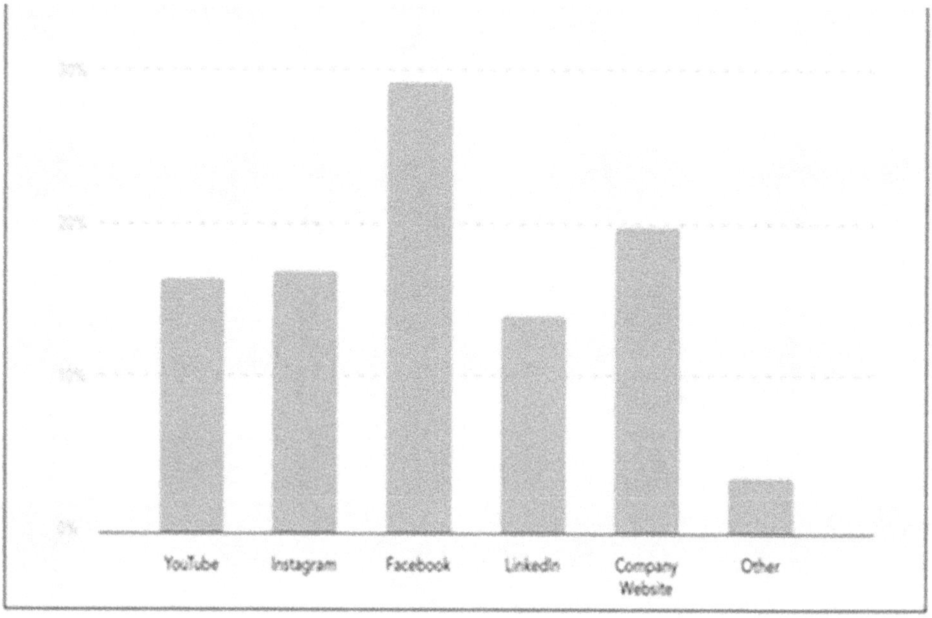

Digital Marketing Goals and Strategic Trends

Computerized advertising techniques, strategies, and execution measurements ought to be based on marketing objectives (Krishnamurthy, 2006; Miller and Cioffi, 2004). An organization may have strategic destinations explicitly custom fitted to digital marketing, for example, traffic development and an expansion in deals sourced from computerized channels; be that as it may, the essential objectives of advertising normally meet across channels. The objective is to produce positive income and net benefit (Ambler and Roberts, 2008; Clark et al. 2006).

Content marketing: Clients have more power over the marketing messages they are willing to devour in light of the fact that they have better approaches for evading marketing messages like online adblocks (Malthouse et al. 2013). Hence, organizations should shift their communication approaches from promoting the products to offering some benefit for clients through appropriate content.

Personalization of marketing communications: Personalization of marketing communications is identified with content advertising that convey significant content to the right customer at the right time requires personalized actions. The idea behind personalization is to regard every individual as a one of a kind individual with particular necessities and to furnish them with personalized arrangements (Ho and

Bodoff, 2014). By and large, personalization alludes to fitting the components of the promoting blend for similarity at an individual level (Montgomery and Smith, 2009).

Data-driven marketing: Digital media propels the accessibility of client related information, which has in turn made an essential development toward information driven promoting (Mulhern, 2009). Data driven marketing alludes to the utilization of information to advise and enhance the execution of marketing activities (Kirk, 2018). Different authors have inferred that the period of marketers making decisions based on various choices dependent on instinct and senses [Kshetri and Voas (2019); Marr (2018).; Mraznica (2017); Peacock (2014), Brar and Basra (2018)].

DIGITAL MARKETING TACTICS

With the increase usage of online platforms, the overall environment has been changed. Organizations spend a normal of 10.2% of their yearly income on marketing activities, and around one-fourth of their all out promoting consumption is spent on digital advertising activities (Gartner, 2014). Since the arranging and execution of marketing activities require HR, it is in all actuality frequently hard to assess marketing use precisely. This is apparent in the field of online advertising, where numerous activities don't require direct money related ventures so consumption is rather dictated when spent on the activities, for example, composing a blog entry or having a discussion by means of online media.

CHALLENGES OF MARKETING PERFORMANCE MEASUREMENT

Two important terms were used in 1950's to check the marketing effectiveness, there are marketing productivity analysis and marketing audit. Marketing productivity analysis associated with costs and revenue, Zahay (2014), whereas marketing audits review marketing performance through the overall condition of marketing activities within a firm (Peacock, 2014). Many authors emphasized the need of MPM conceptual frameworks that link marketing activities and operations with profitability and firm performance. With this keeping in mind, Spiegel (2014) constructed an all encompassing MPM structure by coordinating both efficiency investigation and advertising review approaches under a similar system.

Universal challenges: Despite progress in measuring the analysis, marketing productivity analysis suffers from limited knowledge of causal relationships and time lags between marketing input and resultant changes in output (Siry, 2019). Following are two universal MPM unsolved challenges

Figure 3. Digital Marketing Strategies
Source: Takala (2016)

Tactic	Description
Websites	A company website is usually the home base for a firm's digital presence. It is used for multiple purposes, such as providing firm-related information to customers, building brand image, and fostering direct and indirect sales (Hwang, Mcmillan, & Lee, 2003). Along with the main company website, firms may also use campaign websites, which are focused on specific themes or events (e.g., a new product launch) (Krishnamurthy, 2006).
Display/ banner advertising	Hyperlinked pixel displays on websites, which are used for gaining visibility, generating traffic for the corporate website, and building brands (Briggs & Hollis, 1997).
Search engine advertising	A form of advertising where firms pay fees to search engines (e.g., Google, Bing, Yahoo!) to be displayed in search results with specified keywords. The goal is to drive the targeted audience to the company website or other firm-related media space (e.g., a firm's LinkedIn page) (Ghose & Yang, 2009).
Search engine optimization	A process of identifying and fine-tuning the elements and content of a website to achieve a high ranking to relevant queries in search result listings, and subsequently attract the targeted audience (Zhang & Dimitroff, 2005).
Email marketing/ newsletters	Electronic mail for reaching potential and existing customers with targeted marketing messages (Phelps, Lewis, Mobilio, Perry, & Raman, 2004).
Affiliate marketing	The contractual placement of hyperlinks on third-party websites (i.e., affiliate sites), which are aimed at drawing visitors to the company website as a result of clicking on the hyperlinks (Papatla & Bhatnagar, 2002). Examples of affiliate marketing are the inclusion of company products on price comparison sites or special rebate sites and banner ads on affiliate websites.
Blogging	A company blog (i.e., a Web log) is a website or a section on a company website where company representatives or invited writers provide perspectives on topical issues related to the company or industry. A blog consists of blog posts presented in reverse chronological order that may include text, graphics, videos, and/or links to other web pages (Berthon, Pitt, Plangger, & Shapiro, 2012).
Microblogging	A tool for sharing topical firm- or industry-related information with a confined length (e.g., Twitter) (Jansen et al., 2009). It is used for branding purposes, connecting with potential customers, and attracting them to other online channels.

(1) linking marketing activities with long-term impacts
(2) isolating the impact of specific marketing activities from other influences

Linking marketing activities with long-term impacts: financial metrics to a great extent disregard the drawn out impacts of marketing activities and may accordingly prompt to inconsistent solutions. As per Ambler and Roberts (2008), this limitation is showed by top administration's longing for monetary measurements that are easy to catch and straightforward. The explanation behind administration's craving to assess marketing with financial measurements is that researchers have been not able to give significant evaluation approaches. In the CMO Council review Kantrowitz, A. (2014), the head marketing officials were disappointed with the performance metrics evaluating long term impacts.

Isolating marketing impacts from other influences: Another MPM challenge is identified with troubles isolating the effect of an individual advertising action from different impacts. For instance, if the sale of a company related with consumer goods increased after an marketing campaign, then it is difficult to assess which segment of the total sales increased because of that specific campaign and what amount can be clarified by different elements, for example, recently presented items, reports distributed about the organization during the campaign, value advancements, the circumstance of the mission, enhancements in the monetary circumstance of the objective market, or the insolvency of at least one significant contenders.

In general, there is a lack of academic research on how organizations use MPM systems in practice (Verhoef et al. 2014). A number of studies have investigated the marketing metrics used by firms, but knowledge is limited in terms of how organizations can design and implement effective MPM systems that will drive better marketing decisions. In the following section, the

organizational challenges of designing and implementing MPM systems are reviewed in the light of existing research, with a particular emphasis on the use of digital analytics as part of the system. There is an absence of scholastic exploration on how organizations use MPM frameworks (Verhoef et al. 2014). Various investigations have explored the marketing measurements utilized by firms, yet information is restricted regarding how organizations can plan and execute viable MPM frameworks that will drive better marketing choices.

Metrics Selection

One if the most difficult task in MPM is selecting metrics as there is no clear standards for making set of metrics as per the requirements of the organization. Metrics are very significant in aligning digital analytics with a digital marketing strategy. As per defined (Ambler, 2000), the metrics must be clearly as properly defined performance metrics help organizations to investigate the performance and avoid common misunderstandings.

MEASURING THE PERFORMANCE

According to (Li, 2011; Brar and Basra 2018), digital analytics is based on the idea of web investigation. Web analytics is characterized as the "estimation, assortment, investigation and detailing of data for the motivations behind arrangement and optimizing Web usage". In accordance with this definition, perhaps the most persuasive Web examination specialists, (Sharma et al. 2020) characterized the idea as "the scrutiny of qualitative and quantitative information from your site". Web analytics is an umbrella term used for estimating, investigating and improving digital data for business purposes. Now the term has been progressively reprimanded because of its solid affiliation with "website analytics" (Kirk, 2018). Following table shows various tools that can be utilized for analyzing the performance of marketing campaigns.

Figure 4. Digital Analytics tools
Source: Takala (2016)

Tool	Description
Web analytics	Web analytics collects clickstream data regarding the source of website traffic (e.g., email, search engines, display ads, social links), navigation paths, and the behavior of visitors during their website visits (Nakatani & Chuang, 2011). The data can be used for understanding customer behavior on the website, measuring the outcomes of website visits, and optimizing website structure and content to maximize results.
Social media monitoring	Social media monitoring tracks and classifies eWOM information regarding specific keywords (Sponder, 2012). It enables firms to monitor and measure the volume and valence of online discussions related to the company, competitors, industry, or particular marketing campaigns.
Marketing automation	Marketing automation refers to the automatic personalization of marketing mix activities (Heimbach, Gottschlich, & Hinz, 2015). It capitalizes on behavioral tracking techniques similar to Web analytics, but employs more advanced features for identifying individual customers and following their behaviors over extended periods of time. It can be used for targeting potential buyers through the use of personalized content.

Measurement Process

Choosing proper metrics to evaluate marketing performance will bring limited benefits if the firm has not planned the process for refining the metrics. As per Underwood (2016), organizations are frequently anxious to receive computerized analytics measurements but come up short on a key plan for how to utilize them to improve performance, which therefore delivers them nothing productive. Following phases (in a particular manner) needs to be carefully considered for effective measurements:

Figure 5. Phases for effective measurement
Source: Developed by the researcher

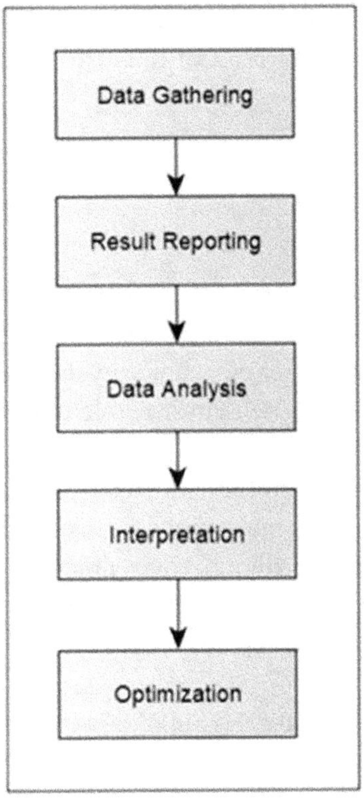

The Development of Appropriate Measures

The output of a campaign test might be viewed as remotely substantial if the whole campaign has been effectively estimated and if different factors, which may impact these "checked" results, have been taken into account in estimating the general impact of the campaign; for instance, the presence and impact of the TV media plan on account of a TV in addition to online campaign.

Validity and Reliability of Measurement

Validity and reliability are the two vital conditions for guaranteeing the nature of the instruments utilized and along these lines the outcomes obtained. Validity alludes to the limit of the measure to effectively evaluate or address the idea or build being estimated. All in all, if the estimation of adequacy looks for, for instance, to confirm the effect on brand picture, a valid measure should have the option to accurately gauge the expected effect of the online campaign on the brand image. The reliability of an estimation instrument alludes to its ability to replicate a similar outcome when a similar event is estimated a few times with a similar instrument. Thus, affectability alludes to the limit of the instrument to record generally little varieties in the event estimated.

CONCLUSION

The outcomes of this investigation are predictable with prior recommendations that marketing estimation challenges are especially clear in organizations because of their having less clients and longer buy choice cycles (Webster et al. 2005). In fact, modern organizations appear to be almost feeble to exhibit how much marketing communication activities impact a specific purchase decision, and to decide their drawn out long term effect. Albeit these difficulties were likewise recognizable in the financial organization, it was much more idealistic about overcoming marketing measurement challenges in the digital environment. Therefore the investigation offered help to the possibility that the operational environment may affect marketing measurement challenges and the apparent chance of overcoming them in an online environment.

Despite its contributions to the existing knowledge, this study has limitations that must be acknowledged. The first important limitation stems from the fact that the study investigated only three industrial companies and the results were compared to just one financial services corporation. Consequently the results are not transferable and more research is needed to confirm these preliminary findings. Nevertheless, there were no major differences between the results found for the industrial companies, suggesting that the results of this study may be applicable as the basis of a broader quantitative investigation. Regardless of its contributions to the current information, this article has restrictions that should be recognized and the primary limitation is the outcomes are not adaptable and more examination is expected to affirm the findings.

REFERENCES

Ambler, T., & Roberts, J. H. (2008). Assessing marketing performance: Don't settle for a silver metric. *Journal of Marketing Management*, *24*(7-8), 733–750. doi:10.1362/026725708X345498

Brar, T. P. S., & Basra, R. (2018). Business Intelligence Technology: A Study Of Bi Implementation And Challenges. Advances in Wireless Communication and Mathematics.

Chaffey, D., & Smith, P. R. (2013). *Emarketing excellence: Planning and optimizing your digital marketing* (4th ed.). Taylor & Francis. doi:10.4324/9780203082812

Clark, B. H., Abela, A. V., & Ambler, T. (2006). Behind the wheel: Align marketing goals and corporate strategies through dashboards. *Marketing Management, 15*(3), 19–23.

Gartner. (2014, November). *Gartner Survey Reveals Digital Marketing Budgets Will Increase by 8 Percent in 2015.* Available at: https://www.gartner.com/newsroom/id/2895817

Ho, S. Y., & Bodoff, D. (2014). The effects of Web personalization on user attitude and behavior: An integration of the Elaboration Likelihood Model and consumer search theory. *Management Information Systems Quarterly, 38*(2), 497–520. doi:10.25300/MISQ/2014/38.2.08

Kantrowitz, A. (2014). The CMO's guide to marketing automation. *Advertising Age, 85*(17), 24.

Kirk, N. (2018). Compliance and Personal Data Protection: The EU is getting serious about data protection via the GDPR. *Journal of Property Management, 83*(3), 40–41.

Kozinets, R. V., de Valck, K., Wojnicki, A. C., & Wilner, S. J. S. (2010). Networked narratives: Understanding word-of-mouth marketing in online communities. *Journal of Marketing, 74*(March), 71–89. doi:10.1509/jm.74.2.71

Krishnamurthy, S. (2006). Introducing e-markplan: A practical methodology to plan e-marketing activities. *Business Horizons, 49*(1), 51–60. doi:10.1016/j.bushor.2005.05.008

Kshetri, N., & Voas, J. (2019). Online Advertising Fraud. *Computer, 52*(1), 58–61. doi:10.1109/MC.2018.2887322

Leeflang, P. S. H., Verhoef, P. C., Dahlström, P., & Freundt, T. (2014). Challenges and solutions for marketing in a digital era. *European Management Journal, 32*(1), 1–12. doi:10.1016/j.emj.2013.12.001

Li, L. (2011). Marketing metrics' usage: Its predictors and implications for customer relationship management. *Industrial Marketing Management, 40*(1), 139–148. doi:10.1016/j.indmarman.2010.09.002

Malthouse, E., & Hofacker, C. (2010). Looking back and looking forward with interactive marketing. *Journal of Interactive Marketing*, *24*(3), 181–184. doi:10.1016/j.intmar.2010.04.005

Malthouse, E. C., Haenlein, M., Skiera, B., Wege, E., & Zhang, M. (2013). Managing customer relationships in the social media era: Introducing the social CRM house. *Journal of Interactive Marketing*, *27*(4), 270–280. doi:10.1016/j.intmar.2013.09.008

Marr, B. (2018). A Very Brief History Of Blockchain Technology Everyone Should Read. *Forbes*. Available via: https://www.forbes.com/sites/bernardmarr/2018/02/16/a-very-brief-history-of-blockchain-technology-everyone-should-read/#68257227bc47

Miller, A., & Cioffi, J. (2004). Measuring marketing effectiveness and value: The Unisys marketing dashboard. *Journal of Advertising Research*, *44*(3), 237–243. doi:10.1017/S0021849904040334

Montgomery, A. L., & Smith, M. D. (2009). Prospects for personalization on the Internet. *Journal of Interactive Marketing*, *23*(2), 130–137. doi:10.1016/j.intmar.2009.02.001

Mraznica, E. (2017). GDPR: A new challenge for personal data protection. *Bankarstvo*, *46*(4), 166–177. doi:10.5937/bankarstvo1704166M

Mulhern, F. (2009). Integrated marketing communications: From media channels to digital connectivity. *Journal of Marketing Communications*, *15*(2-3), 85–101. doi:10.1080/13527260902757506

Peacock, S. E. (2014). How web tracking changes user agency in the age of Big Data: The used user. *Big Data & Society*, *1*(2), 1–11. doi:10.1177/2053951714564228

Sharma, R., Brar, T. P. S., & Gandhi, P. (2020). Defense and Isolation in the Internet of Things. *Internet of Things in Business Transformation: Developing an Engineering and Business Strategy for Industry*, *5*(0), 141–168.

Siry, L. (2019). Cloudy days ahead: Cross-border evidence collection and its impact on the rights of EU citizens. *New Journal of European Criminal Law*, *10*(3), 227–250. doi:10.1177/2032284419865608

Spiegel, E. (2014). *Six challenges of Big Data*. https://blogs.wsj.com/experts/2014/03/26/six-challenges-of-big-data/

Takala, T. (2016). *The Use of Digital Analytics for Measuring and Optimizing Digital Marketing Performance. Jyväskylä University Printing House.*

Underwood, S. (2016). Blockchain Beyond Bitcoin: Blockchain technology has the potential to revolutionize applications and redefine the digital economy. *Communications of the ACM*, *59*(11), 15–17. doi:10.1145/2994581

Webster, F. E., Malter, A. J., & Ganesan, S. (2005). The decline and dispersion of marketing competence. *MIT Sloan Management Review*, *46*(4), 35–43.

Wilson, R. (2010). Using clickstream data to enhance business-to-business web site performance. *Journal of Business and Industrial Marketing*, *25*(3), 177–187. doi:10.1108/08858621011027768

Wymbs, C. (2011). Digital marketing: The time for a new "academic major" has arrived. *Journal of Marketing Education*, *33*(1), 93–106. doi:10.1177/0273475310392544

Zahay, D. (2014). Beyond interactive marketing. *Journal of Research in Interactive Marketing*, *8*(4). Advance online publication. doi:10.1108/JRIM-08-2014-0047

Chapter 5
Social Media, Crowdsourcing, and Marketing

Shivani Inder
https://orcid.org/0000-0002-4805-4118
Chitkara Business School, Chitkara University, India

ABSTRACT

Social media has emerged as a new playing ground for digital marketing. Supporting the resource view of the organization, crowdsourcing is a strong platform for social media marketing. Crowdsourcing on social media for marketing is strengthening companies in terms of saving marketing expenditure; promoting at speed of light; and enhancing the organizational learning, collaboration, and performance. The chapter tries to focus on the relevance of social media, crowdsourcing, and marketing, which help the company to improve, innovate, and cultivate on the crowdsourced wisdom. The future of social media, crowdsourcing, and marketing depends on how companies change the way they perceive stakeholders, business, and processes.

INTRODUCTION

Social media is an expanding and growing platform for communicating expectations among the stakeholders. According to a survey conducted by Misco International Limited, in association with the Ornate Group, it has been found that two out of three business feel that social media is important for sending a message (Times, 2021). According to Kaplan and Haenlein (2010), Social media is "a group of internet based applications that build on the ideological and technological foundations of Web 2.0, and that allow the creation and exchange of user-generated content." Adding to this, Kietzmann, Hermkens, McCarthy and Silverstre (2010) defined

DOI: 10.4018/978-1-7998-7231-3.ch005

social media as media that "employ mobile and web based technologies to create highly interactive platforms via which individuals and communities share, co-create, discuss and modify user-generated content."

Social media made pervasive, substantial alterations in the communications and businesses have been pointed at the centre of a new communication landscape (Kietzmann et al., 2010). Social media is considered as a subset of internet marketing. Businesses mostly prefer to use social media like Facebook (90%), followed by LinkedIn (71%), Instagram (62%) & YouTube (36%) (Times, 2021). 'The honeycomb of social media' offers seven functional blocks like sharing, presence, relationships, identity, conversations, groups and reputation (Kietzmann et al, 2010) at the disposal of companies for the purpose of marketing. For companies to fully leverage social media and reap the benefits of marketing, companies must learn and acquire new skills and strategies (Scott, 2015). Outsourcing the non core activities and diverting such activities to experts helps companies to explore benefits cost effective expert generated solutions. Combining outsourcing with social media, crowdsourcing offers a much desirable strategic way to reach solutions to an array of problems. Businesses can develop capabilities and enhance performance by effectively employing social media resources (Paniagua and Sapena, 2014).

CROWDSOURCING

Management literature has broadly analyzed the outsourcing concept (Parmigiani, 2007). Focusing on the resource based view of the organization, companies attempt to be competitive by channelizing its resources towards the core activities and outsourcing the non-core activities to outside parties and reduce the cost substantially. Therefore, "companies should commit most of their resources to their core competence, while outsourcing the rest of their functions to specialized entities." (Li and Petrick, 2008,p. 237). With internet, technology and globalization on the one edge of organizational environment, information travels at the speed of light. Additionally, companies also try to develop and nurture the mechanisms to attract experts to focus and provide solutions to the problems or work that suits them the most. This brings the attention of the companies to ensure that the experts must come under the ambit or in close proximity of the companies, so that the expertise can be accessed at ease and earliest. In other words, companies are shifting their attention to "folk capital", or "community capital" or "global capital" or "masscapital".

Building on the merge of concepts of 'community' and 'outsourcing', crowdsourcing has emerged as concept of twenty first century. Jeff Howe and Mark Robinson coined the term "crowdsourcing" in 2005. Surwiecki (2005) suggests "many hands make light work" to the concept. Crowdsourcing is "the act of taking a task traditionally performed by a designated agent (such as an employee or a contractor) and outsourcing it by making an open call to an undefined but large group of people" (Howe, 2008). Brabham (2008) defined crowdsourcing as "an online, distributed problem solving and production model." Whitla (2009) elaborated the concept as a process of arranging work for organisations and offering returns to whosoever in the group completes the work. Crowdsourcing is an emerging trend which pools in the wisdom of crowd on internet and helps firms in solving problems or handling tasks that require huge human capital (Li, Hsieh, Lin and Wei, 2020).

SOCIAL MEDIA AND CROWDSOURCING

Crowdsourcing is emerging as a strong platform for social media marketing. Social media contributes in marketing generally by two main forms, i.e. one is to employ crowdsourcers for completing tasks and carrying out marketing of products, and the second is to employ the crowdsourcers as experts for contributing in promoting and advertising campaigns.

Ford et al (2015) point that crowdsourcing offers a unique outsourcing approach as the willing and capable individuals join the task sourced. Saxton et al (2013) points three basic element to crowdsourcing: the crowd, outsourcing and the social network or web. Crowdsourcing is a sort of online movement in which a party i.e. crowdsourcer (may be organization, non profit organization, or individual) makes a call for the achievement of task to a group of people. Individuals participating in the achievement of task get rewards either in the form of monetary rewards, social acknowledgment, skill advancement etc whereas the crowdsourcer achieves the task.

Crowdsourcing plays a crucial role in social media marketing. As whenever the time to make a purchase decision arrives, the probability of trusting a fellow customer is comparatively much higher than a brand. A number of social media platforms have been used crowdsourcing to market brands than just selling products. Social media marketing enables marketers to market a lifestyle, idea or culture rather than just a brand. With crowdsourcing and social media, marketers bring in the brand story to life by embedding audience preferences rather than visual content marketing.

Considering one end of the scale, companies may consider crowdsourcing to carry out activities to spread the word or message regarding the product/service on the network of communities or social circles via social media. For example, a small scale company may crowdsource its promotional material for marketing on social media and distribute it across different communities and locations at a specified period of time. Moreover, social media crowdsourcing enables the companies to modify the message as a response to stakeholder's expectations. Additionally, companies may have crowdsourcers to navigate and analyse the reviews and posts on social media and increase the product visibility.

Over the recent years, marketing practices have started focusing on reading the conversations between different stakeholders and interpreting expectations rather marketing focused on transactions. Considering social network and exchange theories (Morgan & Hunt, 1994) the value of relationships stem out from trust, faith, understanding, commitment, customs etc. Literature has not given the role of social media marketing and crowdsourcing much deserved attention, especially the exploration of ways social media contribute in innovation processes and learning processes of organisations.

Crowdsourcing and online social network complement and contribute in the organizational learning and helps in improving the organization performance (Palacios-Marques, Gallego-Nicholls and Guijarro-Gracia, 2021). Zupic (2013) suggests that social media acts crowdsourcing enabler via two mechanisms i.e. peer-to-peer learning and motivation. Palacios et al (2016) points five emerging trends in relation to crowdsourcing such as problem solving, learning paradigms, open innovation, new product development and collaborative initiative. Pacauskas, Rajala, Westerlund and Mantymaki (2018) investigated user innovation for crowdsourcing based marketing initiatives. They emphasized on the importance of activities and technical features that enable socializing with other participants, support active participation and create a participatory experience. They suggest that crowdsourcing can be leverage for marketing purposes and user innovation as a building block for engagement mechanism in crowdsourcing initiative.

Piller, Vossen and Ihl (2012) highlight the use of crowdsourcing to establish social collaboration between producer and customer for the process of new product

Figure 1. Block of social media, medium and business performance
(Source: Adapted from Paniagua and Sapena, 2014)

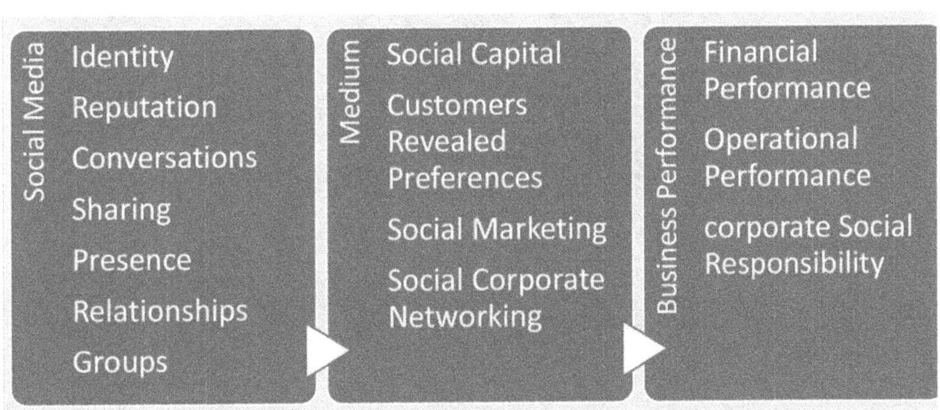

development. Businesses generally choose four main channels of social media to increase performance i.e. social capital, customer's revealed preferences, social marketing and social corporate networking (Paniagua and Sapena, 2014).

Alongwith, crowdsourcing equip brands with much user generated content which is much more engaging. Crowdsourcing leads to collective, thoughtful engagement. It offers a multiplayer experience. Marketing on social media via crowdsourcing helps the brands to convert the users into brand advocates and engage users to brands.

Companies deploy a number of methods to crowdsource social media marketing campaigns like asking for feedback, conducting contests and giveaways, polls, sruveys etc. Nike's Nike idea, Starbuck's MyStarbucks Idea, Threadless.com T-shirt idea project Crowdflower, Lego's Lego factory are the few examples for the companies that have successfully employed the combination of social media and crowdsourcing to promote the business. Toyota crowdsourced its marketing campaign with '#FeelingTheStreet campaign' for a period of six weeks in 2015. Toyota was able to crowdsource best content from social media platforms Instagram and Facebook. The company received more than 1.2 million likes, comments and shares on social media. Additionally, there was a 440% increase year-on-year in ad engagement without any extra expenditure.

Figure 2. Glimpse of Toyota's '#FeelingTheStreet' campaign

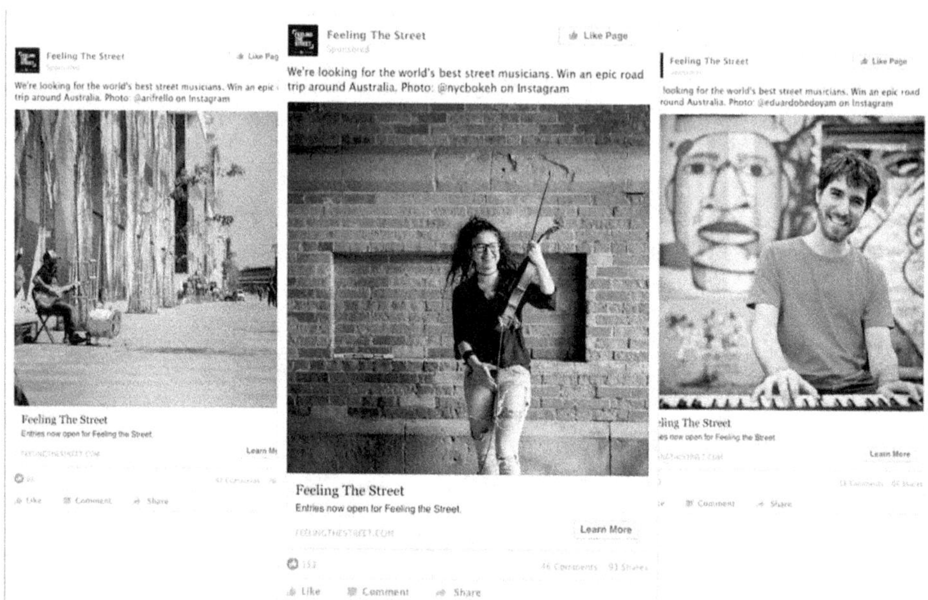

Another excellent example for crowdsourcing and social media marketing is of 'Porche' They crowdsourced a campaign on social media with statement "the best expert panel in the world: our fans" to choose an exterior color for the car. This led to huge response of 16,000 likes, 1200 comments for the color Aquablue Metallic to top the list. Considering crowdsourced wisdom, the company released the car on August 2, 2013 and posted its photos on their Facebook page.

Figure 3. Porsche Facebook post on August 2013

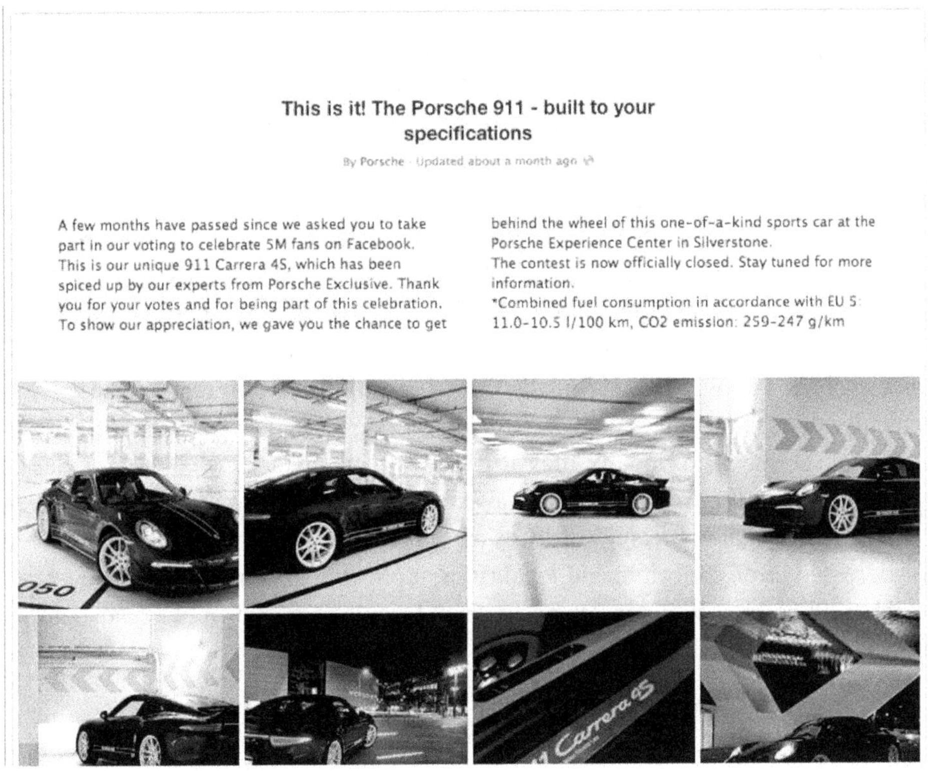

Similarly, Mountain Dew and Lays have resorted to crowdsourcing marketing and products on social media.

HOW CROWDSOURCE MARKETING WORKS

Challenges

Though social media provides a platform for crowdsourcing, still crowdsourcing faces a number of challenges like ill-prepared proposals and solutions (Whitla, 2009). Social media, crowdsourcing and marketing has few challenges. The medium offers a lack of credibility as no minimum standard has been established to ensure quality level of local crowdsourcing platforms. As it has been rightly put forward by Jeff Howe "sometimes crowds can be wise, but sometimes they can also be stupid." Establishing the ground for assigning the responsibility and putting procedures to effectively filtering ideas for future consideration is a challenge in case of assigning a marketing campaign through social media crowdsourcing (Hempel, 2006)

Belsky (2010) points that a large number of participants in the crowd sourced projects are novices that ultimately affect the quality of the work provided. Another challenge is lack of skilled and experienced talents to support growth of local platforms. Out of motivations, Acar (2019) comments that intrinsic and extrinsic motivations have association with quality of solutions, whereas motivations pinned in prosocial and learning have negative relation with solution quality. Ren, Han, Genc, Yeoh & Popovic (2021) find that crowd contributes more creatively in solving generalist tasks than professionals, whereas professionals tend to have more creativity in specialist tasks. Additionally, they also establish understanding on the boundaries on the creativity for crowdsourcing and how to break these boundaries.

Assigning legal ownership of ideas and part work done by an individual need to addressed through formal and legal rules applicable uniformly across countries (Stibbe, 2006). Few other challenges for social media marketing and crowdsourcing are weak payment systems and global levels of competition.

CONCLUSION

In the today's digital and age of social media, the discovery of the capabilities for the firms to stay competitive is not inside the company but stays outside the firm. The chapter tries to postulate the relevance of social media, crowdsourcing and marketing which help the company to improve, innovate and cultivate on the crowdsourced wisdom. The future of social media, crowdsourcing and marketing depends on how companies change the way they perceive about the stakeholders, business and processes.

REFERENCES

Acar, O. A. (2019). Why Crowdsourcing Often Leads to Bad Ideas. *Harvard Business Review*.

Belsky, S. (2010). *Crowdsourcing is broken: How to fix it*. Bloomberg Businessweek.

Brabham, D. C. (2008). Crowdsourcing as a model for problem solving: An introduction and cases. *Convergence*, *14*(1), 75–90. doi:10.1177/1354856507084420

Ebner, W., Leimeister, J. M., & Krcmar, H. (2009). Community engineering for innovations: The ideas competition as a method to nurture a virtual community for innovations. *R & D Management*, *39*(4), 342–356. doi:10.1111/j.1467-9310.2009.00564.x

eYeka. (2015). *The state of crowdsourcing in 2015*. Analyst report #CSReport 2015.

Ford, R. C., Richard, B., & Ciuchta, M. P. (2015). Crowdsourcing: A new way of employing non-employees? *Business Horizons*, *58*(4), 377–388.

HBS Digital Initiative. (2017). *The biggest challenge to the future of crowdsourcing in business*. Retrieved from: https://digital.hbs.edu/platforms-crowds/biggest-challenge-future-crowdsourcing-business/

Hempel, J. (2006). Crowdsourcing: Milk the masses for inspiration. *Business Week*, *25*, 38–39.

Howe, J. (2008). *Crowdsourcing: How the power of the crowd is driving the future of business*. Random House.

Ikediego, H. O., Ilkan, M., Abubakar, A. M., & Victor Bekun, F. (2018). Crowdsourcing (who, why and what). *International Journal of Crowd Science*, *2*(1), 27–41. doi:10.1108/ijcs-07-2017-0005

Kaplan, A. M., & Haenlein, M. (2010). Users of the world, unite! The challenges and opportunities of Social Media. *Business Horizons*, *53*(1), 59–68.

Kietzmann, J. H., Hermkens, K., McCarthy, I. P., & Silvestre, B. S. (2011). Social media? Get serious! Understanding the functional building blocks of social media. *Business Horizons*, *54*(3), 241–251.

Li, X., & Petrick, J. F. (2008). Examining the antecedents of brand loyalty from an investment model perspective. *Journal of Travel Research*, *47*(1), 25–34.

Li, Y.-M., Hsieh, C.-Y., Lin, L.-F., & Wei, C.-H. (2020). A social mechanism for task-oriented crowdsourcing recommendations. *Decision Support Systems*, 113449.

Majchrzak, A., & Malhotra, A. (2013). Towards an information systems perspective and research agenda on crowdsourcing for innovation. *The Journal of Strategic Information Systems*, *22*(4), 257–268.

Majchrzak, A., & Malhotra, A. (2013). Towards an information systems perspective and research agenda on crowdsourcing for innovation. *The Journal of Strategic Information Systems*, *22*(4), 257–268.

Miner, T. (2005). The wisdom of crowds: Why the many are smarter than the few, and how collective wisdom shapes business, economies, societies, and nations. *Journal of Experiential Education*, *27*(3), 351.

Morgan, R. M., & Hunt, S. D. (1994). The commitment-trust theory of relationship marketing. *Journal of Marketing*, *58*(3), 20–38.

Pacauskas, D., Rajala, R., Westerlund, M., & Mäntymäki, M. (2018). Harnessing user innovation for social media marketing: Case study of a crowdsourced hamburger. *International Journal of Information Management*, *43*, 319–327.

Palacios, M., Martinez-Corral, A., Nisar, A., & Grijalvo, M. (2016). Crowdsourcing and organizational forms: Emerging trends and research implications. *Journal of Business Research*, *69*(5), 1834–1839.

Palacios-Marqués, D., Gallego-Nicholls, J. F., & Guijarro-García, M. (2021). A recipe for success: Crowdsourcing, online social networks, and their impact on organizational performance. *Technological Forecasting and Social Change*, *165*, 120566.

Paniagua, J., & Sapena, J. (2014). Business performance and social media: Love or hate? *Business Horizons*, *57*(6), 719–728.

Parmigiani, A. (2007). Why do firms both make and buy? An investigation of concurrent sourcing. *Strategic Management Journal*, *28*(3), 285–311.

Paul, W. (2009). Crowdsourcing and its application in marketing activities. *Contemporary Management Research*, *5*(1).

Piller, F., Vossen, A., & Ihl, C. (2012). From social media to social product development: The impact of social media on co-creation of innovation. *Die Unternehmung*, *66*, 7–27.

Ren, J., Han, Y., Genc, Y., Yeoh, W., & Popovič, A. (2021). The boundary of crowdsourcing in the domain of creativity. *Technological Forecasting and Social Change*, *165*, 120530.

Saxton, G. D., Oh, O., & Kishore, R. (2013). Rules of crowdsourcing: Models, issues, and systems of control. *Information Systems Management, 30*(1), 2–20.

Scott, D. M. (2015). *The new rules of marketing and PR: how to use social media, blogs, news releases, online video, and viral marketing to reach buyers directly.* John Wiley & Sons.

Stibbe, M. (2006). All contributions welcome. *Director, 60*(4), 76–81.

Surwiecki, J. (2005). *The Wisdom of Crowds: Why the Many Are Smarter than the Few and How Collective Wisdom Shapes Business, Economies, Societies, and Nations*. Doubleday.

Times Malta. (2021). *Two out of the three believe social media 'very important' for their business*. Retrieved from: https://timesofmalta.com/articles/view/two-out-of-three-believe-social-media-very-important.850025

Whitla, P. (2009). Crowdsourcing and its application in marketing activities. *Contemporary Management Research, 5*(1).

Župič, I. (2013). Social media as enabler of crowdsourcing. In *Social Media in Human Resources Management.* Emerald Group Publishing Limited.

Chapter 6
Big Data Impacts in Tourism Research

Arjun Singh
Manipal University Jaipur, India

Surbhi Chauhan
Jaipur Institute of Engineering and Management, India

Nitin Sharma
Manipal University Jaipur, India

Vijay Kumar Sharma
Manipal University Jaipur, India

Raguru Jaya Krishna
Manipal University Jaipur, India

ABSTRACT

Big data has shown improvement in tourism research. This might be the first attempt to present a capacious literature review on different types of big data tourism research. By data informant, the big data related to tourism comes into web search data, online booking data, web page visiting data, etc. Each type of structural analysis is conducted from the perspective of research focused on the characteristics of data techniques that are used in the analysis, major challenges, and further directions. This chapter simplifies a meticulous understanding of this research and offers a valuable vision into its future possibilities.

DOI: 10.4018/978-1-7998-7231-3.ch006

INTRODUCTION

Social media sites have become a very important part of our lives nowadays and somewhere it affects our ability to decide. Big data generated on the social media sites has fabricated countless opportunities for bringing more sagacity to decision makers. Few studies on big data analytics have demonstrated its support for tactical decision making. A formal method for analysing the big data generated on social media for decision support is yet to be developed, especially in tourism sector. The aim of this study is to design and valuate a 'big data analytics' method to support strategic decision making tourism destination management by using design science research approach. Everyday many types of data are constantly growing within social media (Such as Twitter, Facebook, Instagram, Line & WeChat etc.) because of their large user base, and frequent uploads of digital photos and videos.

Big data has allowed companies to track study shopping patterns, recommendations, and the purchasing behaviour that are known to influence sales and it has provided an exceptional insight into customers decision making process. Big data has given more power to the agencies and the merchants involved in tourism that they can find ingenious ways to use a variety of data resources to connect with a particular visitor or the potential visitor at every stage of a trip and they can use these big data sources to enhance an timely understand the fastest growing visitors demographics.

It is fact that both consumers and tourism product providers will be benefited by using big data. It is clear that big data can provide better, targeted, and profitable products to consumers (Pries & Dunnigan, 2015). Personalized marketing and targeted product designs are very powerful opportunities for both consumers and tourism product providers. For instance, Big data gets the information about the interest of the consumer from photos posted on social networks by the consumer or what he searches for. This provide a very useful information to the product providers about the type of product the user is looking for. It is up to the researchers how efficiently they are going to examine the digital footprint left by activities on internet and make the use of these data or whether these data will create a new research epitome that tangles new methodologies and will develop our theoretical understanding of tourism. Till date the online data source is mainly used in applied research, and by means of that advantage was taken of the large and often free-of-charge volumes of data that brings the understanding of the activities of the tourism /travel industry and its patrons.

Background

Business Intelligence and Big data are just about to unfold their full potential for the tourism domain. Big data can be a very useful source of information for the tourism sector seems to be still ignored by the researchers. Same situation seems to happen with Business intelligence also. Big data is to be considered an incredible opportunity it can provide answers about people's behaviours and views (Rodolfo Baggio 2016). In the last years, everyone need to recognised customer-focused approach in order to increase the tourism. Big data have also started to be a source for Business Intelligence Activities. The tourism scholars have well understood the capability of BD to provide insights that are useful or should be used for enriching the BI practices for destinations and operators. This note presents the results of an analysis of the recent literature on BD and BI and the application of the related technique to the fields of travel and tourism.

Smart tourism is become more and more important for the local government to raise the economy. Nowadays, many researchers draw much attention to the smart tourism. By the use of new technologies we can extract useful information from social media contents and then it help people to make more efficient and economic travel decisions. Author uses urban tourism check algorithm in which can find out the visitors who come from other country using social media check-in-data. Author chooses the Shanghai as a research target to analyse the data and the tourism place are Renmin Square, Yu Garden, The Bund and Chenhuang Temple in 2016 from Sino Weibo .We divide the tourists in two parts, one is local tourists and the other is outside tourists (Kai Yang, Wanggen Wan 2016).In order to make sure the accuracy of algorithm, Author uses the PLSA algorithm to analyze the Web text content. Through this analysis of outsider tourists it is possible to provide a reference to the government which can use the tourism to rise in urban economy.

Social websites, smart phones and other equipments of customers including PCs and laptops have allowed billions of people across the world to participate in data production and nowadays, data has been increased rapidly. Analysis of large sets of data that is referred to as big data. Big data helps in analyzing the traveler trends by collecting information from different consumer centers and developing a specific marketing strategy for the target audience or customers. Definitely companies such as eBay, Google, Facebook, and Linkedln have been established on big data since the beginning. Because users produce high amount of data in different formats and they have to adopt new methodologies and technologies (Sanaz Shafiee 2016). Big data can be regarded as an innovation source for tourism organizations and tourism industry. Aditya patel, Lalit Nagla 2014, purposes a model for doing customer analytics on social media using big data for improving target advertising and improved business decision making. Using social media networking, they influence others and reveal their buying interests in products and services. Various research papers, case studies and industry white papers recently published, demonstrate the use of big data related technologies and models to harness the large amount of data for strategic business advantage. Organizations capture as much as information as they can about customers and analyze it effectively to discover patterns, trends and other vital clues. Social media marketing is very powerful medium for customer engagement, collaboration and active communication.

A paper presents a knowledge infrastructure which has recently been implemented as a genuine novelty at the leading Swedish mountain tourism destination. They proposed a Destination Management Information System are derives knowledge creation and application as a precondition for organizational learning at tourism destination (Matthias Fuchs 2016).They addressed both the generation of customer-based knowledge within a tourism destination as well as the BI based supplier-oriented knowledge application to support supplier's decision making. The knowledge generation layer, though methods of information gathering, extraction and storage, makes knowledge accessible to stakeholders. The knowledge application layer offers e-services that inform about supply elements and tourist's activities. The knowledge level of tourism stakeholders can be significantly increased. The agenda considers, for instance, the application of real- time Business Intelligence to gain real-time knowledge on tourists' on-site behaviour at tourism destination.

Jingjing Li present a comprehensive literature review on the application of big data to tourism research. In such a big data era, a variety of data is used in various fields. Big data have been generated from three primary sources-users, devices and operations. Among them, UGC data were dominant with 47% after that the device data have 36% and in contrast the transaction (operations) data was 17%. Web search data have improved tourism demand prediction and online marketing. Based on this big data sources, tourist behaviour and tourism market can be better explored and understood by both academia and industries. This paper attempts to fill such a literature gap to present a comprehensive literature review on different types of big data in tourism research and provide a systematically analysis.

Xiaolu Zhou, effectively detected and ranked popular tourism destinations in multiple cities and also leveraged cloud computing to expedite Flickr tag processing and similarity graph preparation. This study provides a method for extracting tourist spots using Flickr images and a big data approach. The number of geo-tagged digital photos has grown exponentially. Increasing numbers on digital photos with geo-tags are available on many photo-sharing websites such as Flickr and Instagram. Flickr, the most popular, hosts over 5 billion photos. We have great opportunities to study people's travel experiences. The temporal and geographic features of the photos are very useful in separating the tourist-related photos from event-related photos. This study also demonstrates the application of using R Hadoop cloud computing infrastructure to crunch big geospatial data.

Slava Kisilevich, Daniel Keim, present a GIS based decision support system that can both, estimate objective hotel room rates using hotel locational characteristics and predict temporal room rates. This paper makes three major contributions. First, we present a GIS based decision support system like for hotel brokers. Second the DSS can be applied virtually any part which makes it attractive business tool. Third, it integrates data mining framework and it offers the possibility of adding new algorithms. The system has been designed and evaluated in close cooperation with a company that develops travel technology solutions. Company has also provided real large datasets to evaluate the system.

BIG DATA SOURCES

Online Textual Data

In today's scenario, the thrive in technology and social media has fiercely changed the way the travelling industry was by providing a vast platform to share user generated data. And these data has been used to promote tourism research, including two types: one is the online textual data like the reviews given by the users of a particular product and by means of blogs on social media sites and another is through the online shared photos on photo sharing sites. Due to the unexpected growth of the internet in the last few decades' social media offers a copious platform for tourists to spread a variety of information related to tourism, such as travelling reviews and experiences. The user can generate a big mine of online reviews data by expressing their likes and dislikes toward tourism products. They can also share their few point and experiences in blogs or websites such as Facebook, Twitter and Instagram. Which provide valuable information to the required user. And this online reviews data, blogs data in the textual style compose special type of big data in tourism research online textual data.

The very first process is to collect the online textual data (including reviews related to tourism, blogs and online shared photos) from the social media sites by using web crawling technology. For instance, Xiang pt al.(2017) transmitting emotions and opinion of tourists used the web crawlers, by the programming languages like python and java, to acquire hotel related reviews. Guo et al.(2017) developed a web crawler to assemble review data from trip advisor periodically.

In the second step the online textual data which is collected will be evaluated to excerpt the useful knowledge for tourism research, by means of two sub-stages: first is the data pre-processing and another is interpretation evaluation.

Data Cleaning

Below are the steps for data cleaning-

a) Fill the missing values (attribute or column value)
b) Ignore the tuple: normally done when class label is missing.
c) To fill the missing values use the attribute mean.

Figure 1. Model for processing textual data

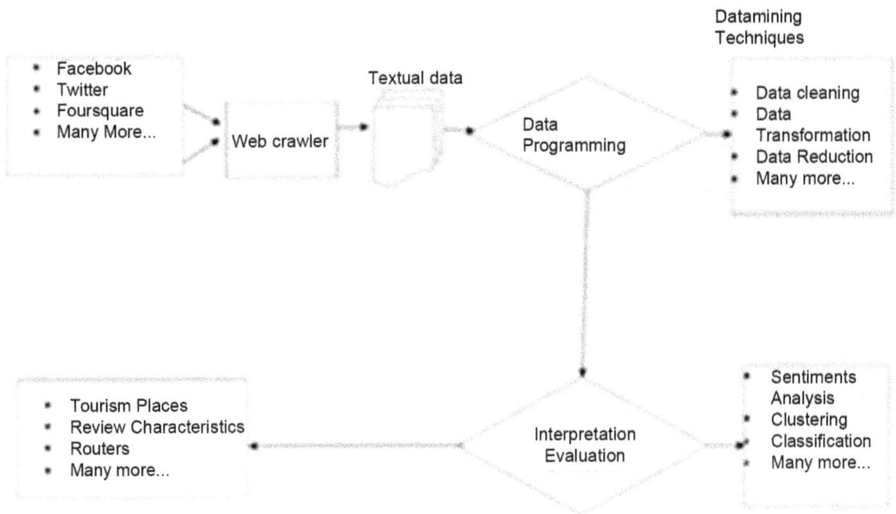

d) For filling all the samples that belong to the same class use the attribute mean (or majority nominal value).
e) Remain missing values can be predicted by using a learning algorithm: consider the attribute with the missing value as a dependent (class) variable and run a learning algorithm (Bayes or decision tree) to predict the missing values.
f) Identify Outliers and smooth out noisy data
g) Binning: Sort the attribute value and split them into bins then smooth by bin median, bin means, bin boundaries.
h) Clustering: Group the values in cluster and then identify and eliminate outliers.
i) Regression: smooth the data by fitting the data into the regression function.
j) Correct inconsistent data: use domain knowledge or expert decision.

Data Transformation

a) **Normalization:** Scaling attribute values to fall within a specified range.
b) **Aggregation:** Moving up in the concept hierarchy on numeric attributes.

c) **Generalization:** Moving up in the concept hierarchy on nominal attributes.
d) **Attribute construction:** Replacing or adding new attributes inferred by existing attributes.

Data Reduction

a) Reducing the number of attributes
b) Data cube aggregation: applying roll-up, slice or dice operation.
c) Removing irrelevant attributes: attributes selection (filtering and wrapper methods), searching the attribute space.
d) Principle component analysis (numeric attributes only): searching for a lower dimensional space that can be best represent the data.
e) Reducing the number of attribute values & tuples
f) Binning: Reducing the number of attributes by grouping them into intervals.
g) Clustering: grouping values in clusters.
h) Aggregation or Generalization Sampling

Online Photo Data

Various data are posted and spread on social media sites that come in the category of user generated data. Like textual data and especially photos uploaded by the tourists. The user generated data contains very much information in relation to the users, location and time, providing a new aspect to study the behavior of the tourist, tourism recommendation, and tourism marketing. Therefore this online data mainly the photos uploaded by the users (tourists) has aroused an increasingly large attention in tourism research. Online photo data have also been used in promoting tourism marketing. Online photo data have become a very efficient medium to form tourism destination for potential visitor (Deng & Li, 2018). For example Deng & Li, (2018) intended a machine learning based model to select the photo elements from the viewer's perspective and assist destination for photo selection. The Big data related to the photo in the tourism research mainly comes from various social media sites and photo sharing websites or platform: Flickr, Instagram, pinterest etc.

Among these platforms, Flickr is the most dominant source of photo data used in tourism research. Various useful APIs are provided by this platform, for the easy access of photo data and the embedded metadata. An online photo contains a very useful message in terms of metadata. Because of the heterogeneous information embedded in photos. There are three primary categories for metadata in tourism research.

User Related Information

Photo ID: ID of the photo downloaded from websites.

User ID: ID of the tourist uploading the photo.

Temporal Information

Taken Date: The date and time to take the photo.

Uploaded Date: The date and time to upload the photo.

Textual Information

Textual metadata: Tourist defined textual information like title, description and tags of the photo.

MAJOR CHALLENGES & SOLUTIONS

In tourism research varieties of big data generated by the users have been applied, making ominous employments and innovations. These big data originated from user end. Which carries different information, different data type addresses, different tourism issues? The user generated data remain dominant in tourism research which gives the information about tourist sentiment analysis, behavior of the tourist analysis, marketing and recommendation related to tourism.

Online textual data enforced in tourism research is of two types, i.e., Reviews by the user which can be called as reviews data and another one is blogs data. Reviews data and blogs data that carries peculiar information have their own respective research focuses. Tourist's attitude towards the tourism products can be known by reviews data and it can also be applied for measuring tourist satisfaction. This topic includes exploring the attributes of tourist satisfaction in the connection between tourist satisfaction and other related points such as guest experience and its position in the competition.

Tourism research adopting online photo data can be enhanced by flourishing research areas and perfecting analytic approach. As far as research areas are concerned, discovering tourism spots (i.e., where to travel) from the endemic dimension of online photos has been studied very abundantly. On the subject of analytic techniques to investigate about tourism related data in the present tourism research clustering and sequencing analysis have been used popularly. For estimation, classification, prediction, homogeneity grouping and association rule new big data mining technique can also be introduced into a fresh research. Apart from metadata the photo data themselves contain a plenty of information, and powerful mining techniques that will work directly on the images are needed.

The increase in the users of the social media in the last few years has created a positive effect on tourism research, as it has made the researchers to pay more attention on applying online textual big data reviews and blogs to tourism research. But there are still many things left in this field to work on and develop new research. Therefore, for future researches big sample size is despicable. Lot of work has done on the user generated data i.e., in the field of knowing tourists sentiments (or opinions) towards tourism product or destination. But, still how to use this to tourism product design and tourism marketing in practice is somewhat lacking.

But some issues are still there like data reliability. For example, sometimes the user give fake reviews about the destination or product for avoiding unnecessary troubles or for gaining bonus (Schuckert et at.,2015 B). This type of reviews needs to be studied very deeply in the nearby future. Due to the amorphous composite feature of tourism related online reviews and blog data, the processing analytic techniques were fooled with some tricky challenges.

Lots of thing can be done to collect the information about the interest of the tourist at a particular place and what attracts the most and the real time number of the tourist can be known through the checking particular place by getting the data from different sources like Facebook, Foursquare, Flicker etc. So that the tourist can get the idea about the gather of that particular place. And it will help in finding the foot-falls of the tourism places.

For helping the tourist to know about the following tourism plan or getting plan information about them. A Decision Support System (DSS) can be built. And the data can be collected through API provided by different sources like Facebook, Foursquare etc. (On the other hand the researches on the different types of big data is very much data characteristics dependent. For example, for analyzing tourist satisfaction, about tourism product or destination. Online textual data (conveying tourist sentiments) is very much helpful. On the other side web search data shows the public attention towards tourism markets, parallel to inherent demands have improved tourism demands prediction and online marketing. It is important to see that even some type of big data has been used in the same issue; each of them has its own peculiar analysis prospective.

CONCLUSION

Instead of prodigious improvement and innovation, there are still abundant places left to develop the tourism research using big data, mainly from the viewpoint of exploring research area and developing analytic techniques. To embellish the tourism research using big data, some more valuable big data and captivating tourism issues should be considered. Big data relatively makes very small contribution to tourism research, due to some tricky issues like high cost and privacy concerns. Therefore, the application of these big data to tourism research can be predominantly improved by intensifying the corporation and tourism industries. However, the data contains very useful information about the things that can be utilized to provide a new context of understanding tourist behavior, tourism management and tourism market. For instance, with the progress in smart tourism, most of the tourism places are equipped with monitoring system, which generates a large volume of video data. And this data is analyzed for understanding the behaviour of the tourist that will support the tourism management. Beside this tangential data or cross-domain data such as health, insurance and education data are also very important for tourism research, because they can influence the tourist preference greatly.

Till now, most of the studies are focused on single type of big data; it may be insufficient to capture characteristics of complex tourism system. Therefore, study on multi-data type is vigorously recommended for development of tourism research. There are some common issues like tourism demand prediction, tourist sentiments analysis, tourist behavior analysis and tourism recommendation that are using big data. But there are some issues left to work on like tourism precaution, tourism online marketing, scene spots programming, tourism product design and tourism capacity estimation. Moreover, various analytic methods such as machine learning and deep learning are really promising for tourism research.

REFERENCES

Artola, C., Pinto, F., & García, D. P. (2015). Can internet searches forecast tourism inflows? *International Journal of Manpower*, *36*(1), 103–116. doi:10.1108/IJM-12-2014-0259

Berezina, K., Bilgihan, A., Cobanoglu, C., & Okumus, F. (2016). Understanding satisfied and dissatisfied hotel customers: Text mining of online hotel reviews. *Journal of Hospitality Marketing & Management*, *25*(1), 1–24. doi:10.1080/1936 8623.2015.983631

Deng & Li. (2018). Feeling a destination through the 'right' photos: A machine learning model for DMOs' photo selection. *Tourism Management*, 267-278.

Fang, Kucukusta, & Law. (2016). Analysis of the perceived value of online tourism reviews: Influence of readability and reviewer characteristics. *Tourism Management*, 498–506.

Gandomi & Haider. (2017). Beyond the hype: Big data concepts, methods, and analytics. *International Journal of Information Management*, 137–144.

Pries & Dunnigan. (2015). *Big Data Analytics: A practical guide for managers.* CRC Press.

Schuckert, Liu, & Law. (2015). Hospitality and tourism online reviews: Recent trends and future directions. *Journal of Travel & Tourism Marketing*, 608-621.

Silva & Schegg. (2015). The interactive effects of online reviews on the determinants of Swiss hotel performance: A neural network analysis. *Tourism Management*, 130–141.

Chapter 7
Resilience by Academic Institutions During COVID-19:
A Review-Based Study

Rashmi Aggarwal
Chitkara Business School, Chitkara University, India

Tanvi Verma
Chitkara Business School, Chitkara University, India

Rishu Chhabra
Chitkara University Institute of Engineering and Technology, Chitkara University, India

ABSTRACT

COVID-19 has affected our educational sector adversely, which resulted in the closure of all academic institutions. This global health crisis demands social distancing as the way to keep the virus away and forced the academic institutions to adapt to this physical distancing from the students as well as colleagues. The faculty needs to be motivated in order to be innovative, interactive, and accessible. The pandemic has not only led to the disappearance of old teaching methods but also the adoption of the modular concept of e-learning. Through a review-based study, the authors discuss the diverse response by the academic institutions and assesses their resilience towards education and transition to online learning during challenging times. Through this study, the authors opined that significant opportunities are there which will help in learning from pedagogical developments of other academic institutions. This will help in strengthening the collective response to COVID 19.

DOI: 10.4018/978-1-7998-7231-3.ch007

INTRODUCTION

Pandemics have influenced and may continue to influence, the potential of the educational institutions to enhance the learning of the students. Sloan Consortium (2008) has analysed that the capacity of the colleges & universities to continue with enhancing the learning of the students despite any catastrophe is called as academic continuity. The catastrophe situation could be caused by natural disaster, human induced disaster or any unexpected factor like pandemic. Many educational institutions are affected by these disasters and hereby affecting the academic performance of the students also. Recent occurrences of H1N1 and H5N1 influenza (Monto, 2009) and the severe acute respiratory syndrome (SARS) (Goh et al., 2006) led to the need by educational institutions to embrace measure like closure of the institutions and quarantine in order to control the spread of infection. Sifferlin (2014) mentioned that during the outbreak of Ebola, nearly 5 million children faced the closure of schools in Africa. Paye-Layleh (2015) highlighted that the schools were shut down for 9 months in Sierra Leone while the schools were closed in Guinea and Liberia for 6 months. The schools remained suspended until October whereas they were supposed to open in August (BBC News, 2014).

COVID 19 emerged in Wuhan city of China during Dec, 2019, was declared as epidemic globally with major concern for health of the public (Lai, Shih, Ko, Tang & Hsueh, 2020). Later on Jan 30, 2020 WHO (World Health Organisation) declared it as Global Public Health Emergency which can pose threat to countries across world (Lupia et al.,2020; Sohrabi et al., 2020).This pandemic had substantial impact on the education sector globally. An emergency policy initiative was started by the Chinese government called "Suspending Classes without Stopping Learning" (Zhang, Wang, Yang, & Wang, 2020). As such no decision was taken nationwide for the shutting down of the educational institutions (Mansoor, 2020), most of the governments in their regions have decided to shut down educational institutions (The Economist, 2020). Delhi schools also got closed from 13th March (Press Trust of India, 2020). The University Grants Commission advised the universities on 19th March, 2020 to defer the assessments till March end (The Economic Times, 2020).

By April 06, 2020, almost in 170 countries academic institutions were closed and more than 13% of the students globally had to either face disruptions or they had to end up with their studies during this COVID 19. There is a global impact in almost every region What we are seeing globally is impact on every region and noticeable impact was seen on upper and lower middle income countries (Bassett, 2020). It has been proclaimed that more than 1.5 billion learners from all age groups around the universe are afflicted by educational institutions closure amid COVID 19(UNESCO, 2020a; UNICEF, 2020). But keeping in mind the maxim that "Learning never stops", steps were taken instantly to continue system of education (UNESCO, 2020a; 2020c; 2020d; 2020e).

Educational institutions have always been at the forefront in responding to the pandemic or disaster event but this is very challenging for them and many are still in the crawling stage. The question here arises that would these educational institutions be able to adapt immediately to the virtual or e-learning environment in place of traditional face to face lecture delivery presently being followed? Would these educational institutions be able to continue with the lectures in spite of the fact that majority of their faculty, staff and students are unable to be physically present on the campus. During the Pandemic event it is well accepted practice to close the educational institutions and credit to the students on the basis of whatever covered in the class.

Keeping the pandemic situations in mind, it was dexterity on the part of the educational institutions to transforming the content to an online environment (Wu, 2020). It was also manifestation of impact of educational institutions with limited resources along with socially disadvantaged learners who have limited access to technology. Not to be forgotten is the impact of internet on the ability of the students to engage in the online learning environment (Zhing, 2020). It was a cause of concern for many authors whether the educational institutions were ready to take the upcoming challenge of digitalized learning (Houlden & Veletsianos, 2020).

There is no doubt about this that spread of COVID-19 has posed the challenges for higher education at an enormity which we have never witnessed since the advent of technology and online learning. Main focus of the study is to review and discuss whether the academic institutions are resilient to this hurricane and their quick transition to E- Learning methodology which can be most effective in the field of education during this lockdown. The Systematic analysis of selected countries and their response to higher education highlighted steps taken across the world during this challenge.

Resilience is ability of an individual to withstand despite the unfavorable circumstances (Rutter, 2008) & also considered as process where recovery is from specific events (Zautra, Hall, & Murray, 2010). Few researchers are of the opinion that it is like attributes of the personality (Fredrickson, Tugade, & Waugh, 2003; Campbell-Sills, Cohan, & stein, 2006), while few consider that it is procedure (Egeland, Carlson, & Sroufe, 1993; Luthar 2006). Resilience is salient skill for successful leaders who can easily realize the differentiation in 'being strong' in distressed situations and being resilient. 'Being strong' is experiencing difficult circumstances while being resilient uses experience & intuition to deal with the distress (Hudgins, 2016).

McManus et al (2008) mentioned that organizational resilience is a function for organizational situation awareness, managing the keystone vulnerabilities and capacity to be adaptive in the complex & interrelated surroundings. It will include constituents like contingent rectitude, strategic capacity & action which will ultimately lead to organizational expansion (Kantur & Iseri-Say, 2012). Being resilient is a pragmatic aspect of organizational factor which ultimately results in increased productivity, raising the welfare and reduction in absenteeism & staff turnover (Andolo, 2013).

REVIEW OF LITERATURE

COVID 19 is an infectious disease which is induced by a virus called "coronavirus." This disease is contagious in nature (World Health Organization, 2020) later called as (2019-nCoV). To decelerate its spread, strict protocols were observed by many countries like complete lockdowns or pronouncements of having social distancing while other countries still chose flock immunity. The steps taken for the purpose included work from homes, flexible working hours, closing many institutions where there are chances of people infecting each other. Our biggest treasure is 34 crore students in the country which is more than America's population. It is of utmost importance to the government to look after the safety of the teaching fraternity and the students- Ramesh Pokhriyal, Union HRD Minister (Barman & Das, 2020).

As opined by Dutta (2020), pronouncements to shut down buildings had impact on universities and many other academic institutions. This forced the academic institutions at all the levels to follow the emergency remote teaching. The shutdown led to lot of apprehensions among the students and teaching fraternity. But the innovative methods to deliver the content to the students were adopted by the teaching fraternity with focus on the curriculum (Bozkurt & Sharma, 2020).

In a matter of just few weeks or months, this virus has reformed that how the learners across the world are educated. These changes give us a sign that how the teaching learning process can be changed for better and the worse in the long term period. The educational institutions which were closed worldwide have provoked the professionals to reconsider the conventional method of teaching learning (Crawford, Butler-Henderson, Rudolph, & Glowatz, 2020)

In order to assure that the study was conducted across the globe. An attempt was made to attain the equality amongst countries across the World Health Organisations' (2020) six regions. The countries that are selected are more affected by COVID-19 spread. The focus of the study was to explore a country from each region and review the different strategies adopted by them during COVID 19.

The regions selected to review the resilience by universities across the world are distributed by World Health Organisations. One country from each region is chosen on the basis of the number of cases infected by virus. The countries are then further distributed on the basis of high income and middle income.

Table 1. Summary of countries reviewed by region

Region	Countries
Africa	South Africa, Nigeria
America	United States of America, Canada
Eastern Mediterranean	Iran, Saudi Arabia
Europe	Spain, United Kingdom
South East Asia	India, Bangladesh
Western Pacific	China, Singapore

High Income Countries

United States of America

Located at the epicenter of the Pandemic with 18, 42,101 confirmed cases including 107029 deaths as on 4th June, 2020, and the educational system at US- largest in the world has taken the huge hit (CDC, 2020). With first suspected on-campus case which was reported on 17th February, 2020, the response by higher educational institutions across the US was to brace the staff and well-being of the students. When most of the authorities were busy with reducing the effect of COVID 19, and spring break left the universities vacant, the academic institutions didn't took initiative to start online education till March, with many prestigious institutions made a statement in the beginning of March and others joined by mid- March.(Crawford. Butler-Henderson, Rudolph, & Glowatz, 2020).

The University of Washington also closed the university on March 07, 2020 and started with the online classes for approximately 50,000 students, and there were others who responded by cancelling activities like conferences, workshops, fitness and also re-location to online platforms from in person platform. (Duong, Pham, Yang, Wang, & Luo, 2020). Harvard University (Herpich, 2020) pronounced moving to complete e-delivery by 23rd March(as did Massachusetts Institute of Technology). Yale, Princeton, Stanford and the University of California announced on 19th March that the online delivery of the instructions will start from that date only. The academic institutions also moved spring break by 1 week for allowing the transformation to remote teaching. The study of higher education in Texas (Bawab, 2020) depicted that while most will come back to remote way of teaching, but few institutions have yet to take call on the same as on 22nd March. Clark (2020) mentioned that at the same time only 5 percent of higher educational institutions decided that they will adopt the virtual instruction with very less presence on the campus.

Saudi Arabia

The second largest country in Arab world, Saudi Arabia, has a population of more than 34 million. Majority population is in t middle age group 15-64 while those in age group of 0-14 and more than 65 are nearly 32.4% and 2.8% respectively. Online education was also initiated in Saudi Arabia when the activities at educational institutions were suspended because of coronavirus issues, although problems were faced by students and transition to digital education environment was problematic. The main concerns by the students were weak connectivity in certainareas,difficulty logging into the network and taking classes, including lack of resources (Obaid, 2020). There were few awkward moments during the time when the lectures were delivered- students went to sleep, loudly eating lunch, arguing with peer when researchers failed to mute the headsets on the computers. While Saudi Arabia's higher education worked a lot by starting campaigns to promote distant learning classes but it was incomparable to the student's problems. Artificial intelligence can never be trusted to an extent no matter how powerful and intellectual that is, since most places do not have fibre optics to make the internet connectivity easier. Many respondents complained that the course work was very hard and difficult to be self - studied. The assignments were also pending as the study material was not readily available. (Tanveer, Bhaumik, & Hassan, 2020).

United Kingdom

There were 2,74,766 confirmed cases with 1936 fresh cases as on June 01,2020 (World Health Organisation, 2020a). The risk level throughout England is quite on a higher side. In the beginning of February, the first case which was detected in the country was a student from China from University of York (BBC News, 2020a). The universities from UK were also having tough times in regard to unknown factors related to Brexit and influence of leaving European nation, and they were also handling the query of majority of students regarding their place in University due to restrictions in their travel and there was almost nil solution (Gov. UK, 2020). Flurry of actions were declared by the British Govt. from March 20 which required change in methods of teaching and learning of higher education. They are seeing the measures like shifting to remote teaching to the extent possible, motivating them for work from home, extending the time for conducting graduation ceremonies, and also changing the pattern of exam. The same measures were adopted by Scotland's Universities (BBC News, 2020c). University of Hull & University of Exeter already waved traditional method of teaching since March. It was also required to help the international students who are separated from friends and family (Morgan, 2020). The tension was also growing amongst those seeking entry to next academic cycle to the University. Bothwell (2020) opined that educational institutions should go in for flexible process to admission; start dates to be delayed and also relax the entry requirements. Advance HE (2020) have started giving remote services to have a service as flexible as possible. There were also controversies regarding the student making a choice of the course which may not be in the best interest (BBC News, 2020g). The students also joined together voluntarily in order to support the fellow students & members from their group during social distancing and isolation actions (BBC News, 2020h, 2020i).

Middle Income Countries

South Africa

South Africa had 32,683 cases with 1,716 fresh cases on 4th June, 2020. The first confirmed case of COVID in South Africa was recorded on March 05, 2020. The national state of disaster was declared on 15th March, 2020 by President from South Africa. President Cyril Ramaphosa in the beginning contained partial ban on travel, travel advisories, public transport discouraged, schools were closed, and prohibited the gathering of more than 100 people (South African News Agency, 2020). Later on 23rd March, President Ramaphosa issued national lockdown for 21 days from 26th March, 2020 (Government of South Africa, 2020). The lockdown had led to the closure of schools & the institutions of higher learning. To curtail the extent of disruptions in academic, several learning institutions reacted by transferring few courses to online platforms. The initiative which was led through ministers and the announcement was made that the departments of communications and digital technologies and basic education have joined forces, to ensure virtual learning (Itweb, 2020). In the initiative, the South African Broadcasting Corporation (SABC) and DSTV channel availed channels entirely dedicated to education (Government of South Africa, 2020). Some higher academic institutions undertook precautionary actions followed by concerns for absence of urgency raised by students from South African Union (Kyama et al., 2020). University of Johannesburg, Wits, Fort Hare and Cape Town also had suspension of traditional way of teaching. Other Universities like Atellenbosch, Witwatersrand and Rhodes also suspended ceremony of graduation (Sobuwa, 2020). It was also advised to all those with recent international travel to self-isolate themselves. Seminars and conferences should be conducted with alternative formats. The mitigation plans were also developed for the students residing on the Universities. The advice was also given to 12,000 students from South Africa who were studying abroad to maintain contact with in-country contacts so as to get the needed help and evacuation (South African Government, 2020)

India

Having neighbouring border with China, the no. of cases were 1.90,535 as on June 01, 2020 (WHO,2020a) left many concerned that being the large population size, the no. of community infected cases was more than what was disclosed(Mansoor,2020). Due to the Novel Corona virus lockdown of 40 days(first and second phase), in all the institutions a total of about 10 million academic hours will be compromised, which will be rather difficult to compensate. Dutta further mentioned that the University Grants Commission advised the institutes to continue with their classes in online mode and engage ICT resources which are available for use in the academic discourse. The faculty members of the University and colleges are also requested by its advisory to make use of the various online tools in order to reach out to the students.

Mahalakshmi and Radha (2020) reviewed that the way of teaching mode has been changed drastically with the emergence of online learning, in which teaching is done through digital platform. Several application tools are made available to conduct the teaching and learning process. Applications such as Zoom, Google classroom, You Tube, Google Meet are common among students' community. Harsha and Bai (2020) found that different apps for teaching the students for live streaming/ conferences/ lecture series, zoom was being used and for assigning the student assignments Easy class app and Google classrooms were used. For the students who can't join the online because of internet connectivity, PPTs were uploaded on slide share keeping in mind that the students can get access to the same as they get the internet and the doubts can be clarified by their faculty through calls.

Many online courses are available (free and paid) whereby students can enrich their knowledge in a better way. The most important and attractive aspects of online learning are its convenience, affordability and effectiveness.

Lall and Singh (2020) analysed that many government and private institutions like IITs and IIMs, have taken a leap from conventional classroom teaching to digital teaching. The campuses were shut down but professors were busy working from home, preparing effective study material for the students so that there isn't any halt in the teaching learning process.

To enable the practical knowledge of labs, many universities and organizations have also come forward and provide virtual labs for the students.

China

China's higher education system had little time to prepare as it was the country to have first case of Coronavirus. The students up to doctoral were told to be at home and can carry on with online learning. The pandemic had affected 30 million tertiary level learners in approximately 3000 learning foundations. According to (Bao,2020;

UNESCO,2020), most of these institutions have rushed to create online classes to fill the gaps that are likely to remain for rest of the academic years in affected areas. Approximately half a million international students' returned to their own countries and had to log in from their homes to continue studying and also access necessary learning materials (Bao, 2020). To ensure that content and services are accessible to majority students including those in remote areas, the government has sought to share teaching knowledge in different ways using satellite Television in areas without internet access (Ministry of Education of the People's Republic of China 2020e). To help students prepare for home based learning, the teaching pedagogies and time schedules were continuously changed. The goal was to build independent thinking skills for the students. The standardized tests were cancelled on January 28, including Graduate Management Admission Test, Graduate record Examination and the test of English a foreign language (TOEFL; ICEF, 2020).

There were conflicting reports for the resilience of the higher education sector. Few universities announced rapid transformation by February 2 (Leung & Sharma, 2020), and for others the same was not there starting from mid to end of February (Mckenzie, 2020; Qu, 2020).

Hardly any higher educational institution was doing online delivery until this pandemic and majority were unequipped also. As virtual teaching had not been major form of education in Chinese academic institutions, most of the faculty had no prior online teaching experience. Even though teachers were provided with diverse training during virus outbreak, the short term effect of this training is likely to remain minimal. Additionally the teachers' differing attitude and the ability to learn IT also impacted on the overall effectiveness of online education (Zhang et al., 2015).

DISCUSSION AND CONCLUSION

The systematic literature review of studies conducted in six countries across six WHO (2020c) regions shows distinct similarities and differences towards the resilience by academic institutions during COVID 19. The below table summarises the countries into High income and Middle income on the basis of Gross National income per capita taken from World bank data. The countries are further categorized according to the no. of confirmed COVID 19 cases by WHO region. The analysis highlights the resilience of academic institutions across the world by adopting the different strategies.

As summarized above most of the academic institutions irrespective of their income status are resilient during COVID 19 and closed their campuses followed by online learning for the students. However moving from traditional learning to complete remote & online strategy is not going to occur overnight and is also associated with

Table 2. Systematic analysis of resilience of Academic Institutions

World Bank data	Countries	COVID 19 cases as on 1st June,2020	Resilience by Academic Institutions	Adopting online education and closure of the campuses
High Income Countries	United States of America	1 734 040	Some what	Yes
	Saudi Arabia	85 261	Yes	Yes
	United Kingdom	274766	Yes	Yes
Middle Income Countries	South Africa	32683	Yes	Yes
	India	190 535	Some what	Yes
	China	84 588	Yes	Yes

many challenges like lack of infrastructure, internet facilities at students' place, skill set required by the faculty to deliver the content online.

But above all, the students welcomed this online learning open hearted. They are very pleased that the institutions are making efforts to keep the curriculum going in midst of the lockdown, on top of all the difficulties and against the backdrop of these challenges. Initially the focus of the academic institutions was on transitioning to the virtual environment but now they are more focused on improvising online pedagogy. The academic institutions across the world are undergoing rapid change & they need to be aware of their capacity to monitor the quality of learning design on a continuous basis.

It has been observed that majority of the academic institutions are resilient to this hurricane and they quickly made transition to E- Learning methodology which is most effective in the field of education during this lockdown.

FUTURE SCOPE

By having more accurate data and inclusion of more countries as per WHO regions, it would be possible to keep a check on the rate of technological adoption among the countries' universities. There are few academic institutions which are partially prepared to move to digitalized education as they were following the pattern before this challenge also. Other institutions had a lot more ground to cover.

Significant opportunities are there to learn from other universities' pedagogical innovations. This will help in strengthening the collective response to COVID 19. We are doubtful that the status reports from each of University's position will change significantly in the next few days as academic institutions are now improving their online pedagogy on a daily basis by updating their curriculum accordingly. The educational institutions have a important role to play in transition to support society leading to valuable addition to productive home environments.

REFERENCES

Advance, H. E. (2020). *Coronavirus (COVID-19) updates*. https://www.advance-he.ac.uk/coronavirus-COVID-19-updates

Andolo, D. (2013). From time to talk about workplace stress. In Personal Resilience for Healthcare Staff. When the Going Gets Tough. Radcliffe Publishing.

Bao, W. (2020). COVID -19 and online teaching in higher education: A case study of Peking University. *Human Behavior and Emerging Technologies*, *2*(2), 113–115. doi:10.1002/hbe2.191 PMID:32510042

Barman, A., & Das, K. (2020). *E-Learning and E-education during COVID-19 Pandemic -A study on the e-learning initiatives with special reference to North-East India*. Academic Press.

Bassett, R. M. (2020, May). *Sustaining the Values of Tertiary Education during the COVID-19 Crisis.* Retrieved from https://www.internationalhighereducation.net/api-v1/article/!/action/getPdfOfArticle/articleID/2922/productID/29/filename/article-id-2922.pdf

Bawab, N. (2020, March 19). *Here's what Texas universities and colleges are doing in response to COVID-19*. WFAA8 ABC. https://www.wfaa.com/article/news/health/coronavirus/ list-texas-universities-that-have-suspended-study-abroad-or-travel-programs/287-4242e7fe-f39b-4322-a8d1-3de59cff46f3

BBC News. (2020a, February 1). *Health: Coronavirus: UK patient is University of York student*. BBC. https://www.bbc. com/news/health-51337400

BBC News. (2020c, March 15). *Coronavirus: Scottish universities and colleges announce new measures.* BBC. https://www.bbc.com/news/uk-scotland-51880666

BBC News. (2020g, March 23). *Universities must stop unconditional offers in virus confusion*. BBC. https://www.bbc.com/news/education-52010858

BBC News. (2020h, March 18). *Coronavirus: Oxford University students set up help group*. BBC. https://www.bbc.com/news/uk-england-oxfordshire-51946854

BBC News. (2020i, March 18). *Coronavirus: Oxford University students set up help group*. BBC. https://www.bbc.com/news/uk-england-oxfordshire-51946854

BBC News. *(2014, August 27). Ebola Outbreak: Nigeria Closes All Schools until October*. BBC News.

Bothwell, E. (2020, March 18). Flexible admissions could mitigate COVID-19 impact. *Times Higher Education*. https:// www.timeshighereducation.com/news/flexible-admissions-could-mitigate-COVID-19-impact

Bozkurt, A., & Sharma, R. C. (2020). Emergency remote teaching in a time of global crisis due to CoronaVirus pandemic. *Asian Journal of Distance Education, 15*(1).

Campbell-Sills, L., Cohan, S. L., & Stein, M. B. (2006). Relationship of resilience to personality, coping, and psychiatric symptoms in young adults. *Behaviour Research and Therapy, 44*(4), 585–599. doi:10.1016/j.brat.2005.05.001 PMID:15998508

Clark, E. (2020, March 13). Hundreds of universities closing across the US in response to coronavirus threat. *Chemistry World*. https://www.chemistryworld.com/news/hundredsof- universities-closing-across-the-us-in-response-to coronavirus-threat/4011337.article

Coronavirus disease 2019 (COVID-19) in the U.S. (2020, May 21). Retrieved from https://www.cdc.gov/coronavirus/2019-ncov/cases-updates/cases-in-us.html

Crawford, J., Butler-Henderson, K., Rudolph, J., & Glowatz, M. (2020). COVID-19: 20 Countries' Higher Education Intra-Period Digital Pedagogy Responses. *Journal of Applied Teaching and Learning, 3*(1).

Definition of regional groupings. (n.d.). Retrieved from https://www.who.int/healthinfo/global_burden_disease/definition_regions/en/

Duong, V., Pham, P., Yang, T., Wang, Y., & Luo, J. (2020). *The ivory tower lost: How college students respond differently than the general public to the covid-19 pandemic*. arXiv preprint arXiv:2004.09968.

Dutta, A., & Goswami, A. L. (2020, May 4). *Corona Pandemic and Higher Education*. Academic Press.

Egeland, B., Carlson, E., & Sroufe, L. A. (1993). Resilience as process. *Development and Psychopathology, 5*(4), 517–528. doi:10.1017/S0954579400006131

Fredrickson, B. L., Tugade, M. M., Waugh, C. E., & Larkin, G. R. (2003). What good are positive emotions in crises? A prospective study of resilience and emotions following the terrorist attacks on the United States on September 11th, 2001. *Journal of Personality and Social Psychology, 84*(2), 365–376. doi:10.1037/0022-3514.84.2.365 PMID:12585810

Goh, K. T., Cutter, J., Heng, B. H., Ma, S., Koh, B. K., Kwok, C., ... Chew, S. K. (2006). Epidemiology and control of SARS in Singapore. *Annals of the Academy of Medicine, Singapore*, *35*(5), 301. PMID:16829997

Government of South Africa. (2020). *Minister Angie Motshekga on Basic Education Sector Plans to support learners during Coronavirus COVID-19 lockdown*. Accessed 08/04/2020, available from https://www.gov.za/speeches/minister-angie-motshekga-basic-educationsector-plans-support-learners-during-covid-19

Gov.UK. (2020). *Travel advice: Coronavirus (COVID-19)*. https://www.gov.uk/guidance/travel-advice-novel-coronavirus

Herpich, N. (2020, March 10). Q&A on Harvard's move to online learning. *Harvard Gazette*. https://news.harvard.edu/ gazette/story/2020/03/officials-detail-university's-move-to online- learning-to-combat-coronavirus/

Houlden, S., & Veletsianos, G. (2020). Coronavirus pushes universities to switch to online classes – but are they ready? *The Conversation*. https://theconversation.com/coronaviruspushes-universities-to-switch-to-online-classes-but-arethey-ready-132728

Hudgins, T. A. (2016). Resilience, job satisfaction and anticipated turnover in nurse leaders. *Journal of Nursing Management*, *24*(1), E62–E69. doi:10.1111/jonm.12289 PMID:25782613

ICEF. (2020). Coronavirus triggers travel restrictions and other countermeasures. *ICEF Monitor*. https://monitor.icef.com/2020/01/coronavirus-triggers-travel-restrictions-andother-countermeasures/

Itweb. (2020). *Government makes provision for virtual learning during lockdown*. Accessed 08/04/2020, available from https://www.itweb.co.za/content/Gb3BwMW8LQKq2k6V

Kantur, D., & İşeri-Say, A. (2012). Organizational resilience: A conceptual integrative framework. *Journal of Management & Organization*, *18*(6), 762–773. doi:10.5172/jmo.2012.18.6.762

Kyama, R., Kokutse, F., & Dell, S. (2020, February 21). COVID-19 – Kenya, Ghana, and South Africa students stay put. *University World News*. https://www.universityworldnews.com/post. php?story=20200221140301259

Lai, C., Shih, T., Ko, W., Tang, H., & Hsueh, P. (2020). Severe acute respiratory syndrome coronavirus 2 (SARS-Cov-2) and coronavirus disease-2019 (COVID-19): The epidemic and the challenges. *International Journal of Antimicrobial Agents, 55*(3), 105924. doi:10.1016/j.ijantimicag.2020.105924 PMID:32081636

Lall, S., & Singh, N. (2020). CoVid-19: Unmasking the new face of Education. *International Journal of Research in Pharmaceutical Sciences, 11*(SPL1), 48-53.

Leung, M., & Sharma, Y. (2020, February 21). *Online classes try to fill education gap during epidemic.* University World News. https://www.universityworldnews.com/post.php?story=20200221083603 25

Lupia, T., Scabini, S., Mornese Pinna, S., Di Perri, G., De Rosa, F. G., & Corcione, S. (2020). 2019 novel coronavirus (2019-nCoV) outbreak: A new challenge. *Journal of Global Antimicrobial Resistance, 21*, 22–27. doi:10.1016/j.jgar.2020.02.021 PMID:32156648

Luthar, S. (2006). Resilience in development: a synthesis of research across five decades. In D. Cicchetti & D. Cohen (Eds.), *Risk, Disorder, and Adaptation* (pp. 740–795). Wiley.

Mahalakshmi & Radha. (2020). COVID 19: A massive exposure towards web based learning. *Journal of Xidian University, 14*(4). . doi:10.37896/jxu14.4/266

Mansoor, S. (2020, March 12). India is the world's second most populous country. Can it handle the coronavirus outbreak? *Time*. https://time.com/5801507/coronavirusindia/

McKenzie, L. (2020, February 25). Coronavirus forces universities online. *Inside Higher Education.* https://www. insidehighered.com/news/2020/02/25/coronavirus-forcesus-universities-online-china

McManus, S., Seville, E., Vargo, J., & Brunsdon, D. (2008). Facilitated process for improving organizational resilience. *Natural Hazards Review, 9*(2), 81–90. doi:10.1061/(ASCE)1527-6988(2008)9:2(81)

Ministry of Education of the People's Republic of China. (2020e). *Relevant Person in Charge of the Ministry of Education Answered Reporters' Questions on the Postponement of the "Suspending Classes without Stopping Learning" in Primary and Secondary Schools.* Available online: http://www.moe.gov.cn/jyb_xwfb/s271/202002/t20200211_420109.html

Monto, A. (2009). The risk of seasonal and pandemic influenza: Prospects for control. *Clinical Infectious Diseases, 48*(S1), S20–S25. doi:10.1086/591853 PMID:19067611

Morgan, J. (2020, March 19). Schools shutdown creates UK university admissions uncertainty. *Times Higher Education*. https://www.timeshighereducation.com/news/schoolsshutdown-creates-uk-university-admissions-uncertainty

Niranjan, P. S. (2020). Corona virus Pandemic impact on Global Education: A Blessing in disguise. *Sustainable Humanosphere, 16*(2), 68–72.

Obaid, R. (2020). *Saudi students, educators take on virtual education challenge amid coronavirus suspension*. Retrieved from https://www.arabnews.pk/node/1640211/saudi-arabia

Paye-Layleh, J. (2015, February 17). Liberia Schools Reopen after 6-month Ebola Closure. *The Boston Globe*.

Press Trust of India. (2020, March 13). Several states in shutdown mode, total number of coronavirus cases 81. *Press Trust of India*. https://www.indiatoday.in/india/story/states-shutdown-coronavirus-case-1655258-2020-03-13

Rutter, M. (2008). Developing concepts in developmental psychopathology. *Developmental psychopathology and wellness: Genetic and environmental influences*, 3-22.

Sifferlin, A. (2014, Dec. 17). Million Kids Aren't in School Because of Ebola. *Time*.

Sloan Consortium. (2008). *About academic continuity*. Retrieved from http://www.academiccontinuity.org/node/272

Sobuwa, Y. (2020). Universities cancelling in-person classes due to coronavirus. *Sowetan Live*. https://www.sowetanlive. co.za/news/south-africa/2020-03-16-universitiescancelling-in-person-classes-due-to-coronavirus/

Sohrabi, C., Alsafi, Z., O'Neill, N., Khan, M., Kerwan, A., Al-Jabir, A., Iosifidis, C., & Agha, R. (2020). World Health Organization declares global emergency: A review of the 2019 novel coronavirus (COVID-19). *International Journal of Surgery, 76*, 71–76. doi:10.1016/j.ijsu.2020.02.034 PMID:32112977

South African Government. (2020). *Minister Blade Nzimande: Measures to deal with the Coronavirus COVID-19 in the post-school education and training sector*. https://www. gov.za/speeches/minister-higher-education-science-andinnovation-statement-measures-deal-COVID-19-threat

South African News Agency. (2020). *Coronavirus 101*. https:// www.sanews.gov.za/south-africa/coronavirus-101

Tanveer, M., Bhaumik, A., & Hassan, S. (2020). Covid-19 Pandemic, Outbreak Educational Sector and Students Online Learning in Saudi Arabia. *Journal of Entrepreneurship Education, 23*(3).

The Economic Times. (2020, March 19). *UGC tells universities to postpone exams, suspend evaluation work due to COVID-19*. https://economictimes.indiatimes.com/industry/ services/education/ugc-tells-universities-to-postpone exams- suspend-evaluation-work-due-to-COVID-19-spread/articleshow/74707411.cms?from=mdr

The Economist. (2020, March 21). The billion-person question if covid-19 takes hold in India the toll will be grim. *The Economist*. https://www.economist.com/asia/2020/03/21/if-covid-19-takes-hold-in-india-the-toll-will-be-grim

The total population. (2020, January 1). Retrieved from https://www.stats.gov.sa/en/indicators/1

UNESCO. (2020, March 13). *COVID-19 educational disruption and response*. Retrieved from https://en.unesco.org/covid19/educationresponse

UNESCO. (2020a). *COVID-19 education response*. Retrieved from https://en.unesco.org/covid19/educationresponse/globalcoalition

UNESCO. (2020b). *COVID-19 Educational disruption and response*. Retrieved from https://en.unesco.org/covid19/educationresponse

UNESCO. (2020c). *Global education coalition*. Retrieved from https://en.unesco.org/covid19/educationresponse/globalcoalition

UNESCO. (2020d). *National learning platforms and tools*. Retrieved from https://en.unesco.org/covid19/educationresponse/nationalresponses#WESTERN%20EUROPE%20&%20NORTH%20AMERICA

UNESCO. (2020e). *Distance learning solutions*. Retrieved from https://en.unesco.org/covid19/educationresponse/solutions

UNICEF. (2020). *UNICEF and Microsoft launch global learning platform to help address COVID-19 education crisis*. Retrieved from https://www.unicef.org/press-releases/unicef-and-microsoft-launch-global-learning-platform-help-address-covid-19-education

World Health Organization. (2020a). *Coronavirus disease (COVID-2019) situation reports*. Situation report – 64 (29 March 2020). https://www.who.int/emergencies/diseases/ novel-coronavirus-2019/situation-reports

Wu, Z. (2020). *How a top Chinese university is responding to coronavirus.* https://www.weforum.org/agenda/2020/03/coronavirus-china-the-challenges-of-online-learning-foruniversities/

Zautra, A., Hall, J., & Murray, K. (2010). Resilience: a new definition of health for people and communities. In J. Reich, A. Zautra, & J. Hall (Eds.), Handbook of Adult Resilience (pp. 3–34). Academic Press.

Zhang, W., Wang, Y., Yang, L., & Wang, C. (2020). Suspending classes without stopping learning: China's education emergency management policy in the COVID-19 outbreak. *Journal of Risk and Financial Management, 13*(3), 55. doi:10.3390/jrfm13030055

Zhang, Y., Liu, X., Fan, F., Zhou, P., & Bai, Q. (2015). Factors Influencing on Teachers' ICT Application Level of Primary and Secondary Schools: An Empirical Analysis Based on the 14 cities of X Province. *Modern Educational Technology, 25*, 44–50.

Zhong, R. (2020, March 17). The coronavirus exposes education's digital divide. *The New York Times.* https://www.nytimes.com/2020/03/17/technology/china-schoolscoronavirus.html

Chapter 8
Digitalization and Work Behaviour:
A Paradigm Shift

Navreet Kaur
Chitkara Business School, Chitkara University, India

ABSTRACT

The digital economy has brought in its wake numerous issues of a technological kind. It has affected every element within the organization (e.g., structure, informal work relationships, culture, and most importantly, managerial leadership). Because of new technologies emerging every day, the process of change has become persistent, and a paradigm shift has been witnessed in the management of workplace behaviour. The chapter has three sections. Concepts underlying organizational behaviour and the meaning of digitalization are discussed in the first section; the second section is an analysis of the changing leadership framework and its role in digital business transformation, and the third section highlights the positive and negative effects of a digital workplace on employee behaviour. The discussion concludes with comments on the significance of a digital workplace in COVID-19 era. The primary objective of this chapter is to identify and organize the accumulated knowledge on the implications of digital transformation for organizational behaviour and provide critical insights.

INTRODUCTION

Information and communication technology has had a massive impact on business and work life as a whole. With the onset of organizational digitalization, spread of the internet and a change in the economic superstructure, a paradigm shift has been

DOI: 10.4018/978-1-7998-7231-3.ch008

witnessed in workplace behaviour and its management. The primary objective of this review article is to identify and organize the accumulated knowledge on the implications of digital transformation for organizational behaviour and provide critical insights thereof. The chapter comprises of 3 sections: Concepts underlying organizational behaviour and the meaning of digitalization are discussed in the first section; the second section is an analysis of the changing leadership framework and its role in digital business transformation; and the third section highlights the positive and negative effects of a digital workplace on employee behaviour. The discussion concludes with comments on the significance of a digital workplace in Covid-19 era.

THE MODEL OF ORGANIZATIONAL BEHAVIOUR IN THE CONTEXT OF A DIGITAL TRANSFORMATION

The effects of digitalization on all aspects of business have been quite widespread. However, a study of the impact of such a change on organizational work life remained neglected for quite some time (Foerster-Metz et al., 2018). The two salient features of the third wave economy are a boom in the service sector and a complex, ever changing IT mainframe. A change in the nature of work, the workplace and the worker is witnessed with the evolution of the industrial economy into a knowledge-based one. Hojeghan & Esfangareh (2011, p. 309) state that this digital economy "is based on electronic goods and services produced by an electronic business and traded through electronic commerce."

Of the various macro and micro variables that affect behaviour within organizations, an individual himself is the most significant entity. As per the OB model (Newstrom & Davis, 1997), there are three basic elements that define an organization and are in a reciprocal relationship with each other viz. structure, technology, and informal social groups. The organization is not located in a vacuum; there is a socio-economic-political-cultural environment around it which acts and interacts with it (Richards, 2018). The change in the economic structure and order very conspicuously depicts the interdependences between the three determinants mentioned. The external factors have influenced the internal environment of the enterprise: its goals, vision and mission. The technological revolution apart from changing the reporting lines and the direction of businesses has impacted work environments and workflows and also individual and group behaviour. The induction of tech-savvy and digitally sound Gen Y has brought with it a distinct value system and new attitudes (DuBrin, 2002). In sum, technology has affected both the composition of the work force and its psyche.

The onslaught of technologies like advanced algorithms, robotics, and analytics is a megatrend that demands companies to be proactive in their approach. It is important here to understand the minute differences in terms associated with a software-controlled economy. The 2 stages preceding digital transformation are:

a. Digitization

According to Ernst & Young (2011), "Digitization means the conversion of analogue information to digital (computer-readable) information." The analogue information is encoded into zeroes and ones so that computers can store, process, and transmit such information (Bloomberg, 2018).The manufacturing of a transistor and microprocessor in the 20th century paved the way for the conversion of traditional media such as video, sound or picture into the binary language of bits and bytes. Converting handwritten or typewritten text into digital form is also an example of digitization. With an increase in the amount and complexity of digital information, the global storage capacity has also increased manifolds.

b. Digitalization

The application of IT or digital technologies by enterprises to attain efficiency in business processes (Li et al., 2016) such as communication (Ramaswamy & Ozcan, 2016; Van Doorn et al., 2010), distribution (Leviäkangas, 2016), or business relationship management (Baraldi & Nadin, 2006), achieve data transparency and thus, enhance customer experiences is referred to as digitalization (Pagani & Pardo, 2017). For instance, creating mobile communication channels for better customer relationship management (Ramaswamy & Ozcan, 2016). Automation and the use of computer-controlled equipment results in a change in job descriptions. The global consulting firm, Simon-Kucher & Partners reports that a company on operating an online platform may already be 80 percent digitalized thus requiring only 20% to create customer value. However, implementing the technology behind such an online platform is not digitalization; it is shifting the business process to such a platform.

'Digital transformation' is not possible without digitization and digitalization. It is an organization-wide response to ever evolving digital technologies involving a transformational change in the management of front line areas such as information technology, operations, marketing, supply chain, and strategy formulation, leading to development of new business models (Iansiti & Lakhani, 2014; Kane et al., 2015; Pagani & Pardo, 2017). Digital transformation is inherently linked to innovative changes in the business model as a result of implementation of digital technologies (Sebastian et al., 2017) which is beset with challenges since it shakes the status quo by making the core business model obsolete (Teece, 2010). However, as the new business logic gets internalized in the company's culture, it leads to value creation (e.g., Pagani & Pardo, 2017; Zott & Amit, 2008).

The drivers of digital transformation viz. digital technology, digital competition, and digital customer behaviour reflect the influence of the external environment on the organization. Web 2.0, big data, cloud computing, crypto currencies, artificial intelligence, and block chain have resulted in virtual businesses (Chen et al., 2012; Iansiti & Lakhani, 2014; Ng & Wakenshaw, 2017) and in firms becoming increasingly capital intensive. The coming in of new technologies has had far reaching effects on the retail sector in particular. Digital information rich firms such as Apple, Microsoft, Amazon, Facebook and Chinese companies like Alibaba have an edge over others in terms of valuation. Furthermore, the digital revolution has brought about a change in the consumer mindset and behaviour. Consumer focus has shifted to the online market place affecting both online and offline sales (Kannan & Li, 2017).This is an era of the 'knowledge customer' who is more connected and aware of what the market offers (e.g., Lamberton & Stephen, 2016; Verhoef et al., 2017) by virtue of new social media tools and new AI-based technologies. Firms need to appropriately adapt to these changes.

Research shows that there are four interlinked 'strategic imperatives of digital transformation' (Verhoef et al., 2019) viz. required digital resources, required organizational structure, digital growth strategies, and required metrics. Some of these prerequisites for a successful technological transformation are in the purview of this paper. The utilization of digital resources, both tangible and intangible, lies in the hands of the employees. Barney's (1991) resource-based view about factors that make the workforce a source of competitive advantage is particularly relevant here. The intellectual capital of a firm and knowledge management through maintaining of extensive databases, are of prime importance today. Delivering value to the customer is at the heart of a digital transformation and efficient storage of data helps identify trends in consumer behaviour.

Digital resources include digital assets, digital agility, digital networking capacity, and big data analytics capability. Digital assets (both hardware and software) are the basis for transforming a business digitally. For instance, big data containing customer metrics can be analyzed by employees possessing analytical skills and digital capabilities resulting in customization of services (e.g., Verhoef et al., 2016). 'Digital agility' defined as the ability of cashing upon market opportunities well in time, a flexibility in terms of modifying existing digital assets and discarding skills that have become obsolete (Eggers & Park, 2018; Lavie, 2006) is a crucial digital capability in the 21st century workplace. A quick response to market changes in a dynamic and unpredictable environment (Lee et al., 2015; Lu & Ramamurthy, 2011; Tallon & Pinsonneault, 2011) might involve interchanging of organizational roles and responding to customer needs amidst intensified competition due to the advent of new technology (Chakravarty et al., 2013). Social capital building through digital networking capability is another much needed skill. Competitive advantage depends upon the strength of partners and ecosystems that companies choose to collaborate with (Accenture, 2017).A network comprising of heterogeneous stakeholders like customers and suppliers results in value creation and growth of platforms (McIntyre & Srinivasan, 2017; Thomas et al., 2014).

Gathering of digital data and possessing of digital technologies by organizations has no utility in the absence of big data analytics capability which includes data management, data visualization and business skills (Verhoef et al., 2016). Formulation of strategies depends on quick decision making which further relies on reliable data (Accenture, 2018). To create value from big data, it is imperative to have a workforce that has strong digital and analytical skills and is continuously trained for skill updation (e.g., Kübler et al., 2017). Digital transformation is unlikely without restructuring marked by separate business units, agile organizational forms and digital functional areas (Eggers & Park, 2018). The disconnection of headquarters from autonomous business units allows room for experimentation and idea generation; agile organizational forms marked by flexibility, decentralization, effective communication and an atmosphere of innovation and creativity are the result of de-layering of the tall bureaucratic structure. The IT function apart from facilitating data flows must also play a supportive role in digital value creation via fast and explorative responses (Leonhardt et al., 2017) and by the data analyst assuming the role of a marketing researcher.

Undertaking digitalization projects like automating processes or up-skilling workers in using digital devices do not amount to digital transformation. Bloomberg (2018, para. 22) calls it a "customer-driven strategic business transformation' that requires cross-cutting organizational change as well as the implementation of digital technologies". To sum up, digitization and digitalization are essentially about technology, but digital transformation is about the customer and requires the organization to make a change in its core competency.

E-LEADERSHIP

The decisive influence of the leader in the evolution of a digitally run enterprise cannot be negated. In today's turbulent business environment marked by volatility, complexity and discontinuous, often disruptive changes, the traditional model of leadership has become obsolete in many ways (Horner-Long & Schoenberg, 2002). The cardinal personality characteristics of a leader today are agile thinking, tolerance for ambiguity, and digital skills which translate into his capacity to lead employees through fast paced changes – mainly technological in nature – and to make them change ready. Larjovuori et al. (2016) defined digital leadership as "the leaders' ability to create a clear and meaningful vision for the digitalization process and the capability to execute strategies to actualize it." (p. 1144). VOPA plus model for digital leadership designed by Buhse (2014) delineates four aspects that are central to the leader gaining trust of the employees viz. Networking, Openness, Agility, and Participation.

New digital tools have made the dissemination and access of information faster and easier thus bestowing employees with both expert and informational power (French & Raven, 1959) which has made them efficient and professionally independent. This autonomy has in turn enhanced their sense of responsibility and their ability to actively participate in strategic decision making. (Barley, 2015; Schwarzmüller et al., 2018).There is a change in power relationships and organizations have become 'starfish like' (Brafman & Beckstrom, 2007) with a wider span of control. The leader in such a situation is mainly a facilitator and is expected to manifest an inclusive style of leading and not a control-seeking one (e.g., Schwarzmüller et al., 2018). An interesting paradox here is that autonomy sometimes leads to isolation, worker alienation, poor accountability and weak social bonding (Lynn Pulley & Sessa, 2001; Van Wart et al. 2017; Roman et al. 2018) particularly in employees who find empowerment difficult to handle. Hence, leaders need to be mentors who enable followers to face the challenges that accompany increased autonomy (Schwarzmüller et al., 2018).

A learning environment must be created wherein the leader without losing sight of the vision and mission of the organization instils in the workforce a collective ambition (Lynn Pulley & Sessa, 2001). E-leadership as opposed to traditional face-to-face leadership is marked by the ability to communicate via ICTs viz. Information and Communication Technologies which involves choosing the right digital tool and sending unambiguous messages in both synchronous and asynchronous modes (Roman et al. 2018, p. 5). Studies by Horner-Long & Schoenberg (2002) and Schwarzmüller et al. (2018) show that virtual communication is the key to effective leadership and emotional intelligence needs to be supplemented by entrepreneurial and risk-taking competencies along with decisiveness, a tolerance for ambiguity, and problem-solving abilities. 'High speed decision making' and the accompanying innovative solutions can only be possible if leaders have the capability to process Big Data. This points at the need to collaborate with IT managers, for data analysis and for deriving meaningful conclusions (Harris & Mehrotra, 2014; Vidgen et al., 2017). In this digital age, an exchange of ideas between different stakeholders results in tangible benefits in the form of innovation and e-leaders need to make optimal use of networking opportunities (Avolio et al., 2014). Another visible paradigm shift is the need for the leader to blend two different profiles in his persona viz. technical-mindedness and people-orientation in order to effectively bring about a digital transformation (Diamante & London, 2002). A challenge during such a process may be the resolution of generational conflicts between the tech-savvy Gen Y and the sceptical, change resistant, older generation (Coutu, 2000).

A bigger challenge is managing of virtual teams which have been defined as "interdependent groups of individuals that work across time, space, and organizational boundaries with communication links that are heavily dependent upon advanced information technologies" (Hambley et al., 2007, p. 1). These new age work groups depict a 'dispersed' organizational structure and the 'competency to network' finds a special application here. Virtual teamwork due to its very nature of heterogeneity brings together varied perspectives and enables easy accessibility of global talent (Jawadi et al., 2013; Gupta & Pathak, 2018). However, this geographical distance has a flip side to it in terms of the leader being devoid of a personal connect with the team members which results in difficulties in interpersonal relationships. In the absence of verbal and non verbal cues, the team's thoughts, feelings, moods and actions remain largely hidden from observation (Jawadi et al., 2013). Other than educational, functional, and geographical differences, cultural diversity between team members may undermine collaboration, thus restricting the leader from inculcating team spirit and trust (Gupta and Pathak, 2018). To manage a multicultural team with its share of similarities and differences, a virtual team leader needs to have good cross-cultural skills (Schwarzmüller et al., 2018). To avoid conflicts, clear communication norms in terms of regular feedback, unambiguity, recognition and monitoring of each member's performance and an early detection of communication problems, are more important than behavioural norms (Jawadi et al., 2013).

In the start up phase, it is imperative that the entire team is aware of the diverse skills possessed by each member (Malhotra et al., 2007) in order to clearly distribute the roles and tasks (Jawadi et al., 2013) and leverage its potential to arrive at innovative solutions. However, there are neutralizers and substitutes of virtual team leadership in the form of high performing, self -managing work teams (SMWTs) that can define their own collective leadership style (Gupta & Pathak, 2018). Pearce et al. (2009) refer to 'shared and empowered leadership' among virtual team members characterized by an equitable distribution of leadership responsibilities and participative decision making (Druskat & Wheeler, 2003) which lead to healthy power dynamics (Hoegl & Muethel, 2016).

From the aforementioned research it is quite evident that away from the traditional notions of leadership, the role of the c-suite executives has been recasted into that of a digital change agent or a digital enabler whose task is the development of a digital strategy by creating and sustaining a digital culture in the organization (Gerth & Peppard, 2016) with the aid of the Chief Information Officer (CIO). There is an increased ambidexterity in the role of CEOs and CIOs alike. A continual dialogue with the internal and external stakeholders by choosing the appropriate social media platform has transformed CEOs into "Chief Engagement Officers" who actively contribute to the engagement of followers and customers (Tsai & Men, 2017). Such a dialogue as suggested by Grafström & Falkman (2017) is a powerful tool to overcome organizational crisis and sustain the company image, build an employee value proposition, position the brand and propagate organizational values.

The competence model gives two dimensions that are crucial for e-leadership: (1) attitudes, competencies and behaviours required in the digital age e.g., digital literacy and (2) competencies that help drive digital transformation e.g., strong leadership skills (Capgemini Consulting, 2015; Westerman et al., 2012). In a study on upper level managers, Zeike et al. (2019) found a positive correlation between low digital skills and psychological well-being defined by WHO (2009) as "a state of well-being in which the individual realises his or her own abilities, can cope with the normal stresses of life, can work productively and fruitfully, and is able to make a contribution to his or her community". It is a blend of "feeling good and functioning effectively" (Huppert, 2009, p. 137). Digital leadership skills are seen as an internal job resource of leaders that help them cope with excessive job demands and hence, are associated with health outcomes. These are essentially personality characteristics such as self efficacy, optimism, resilience and social skills along with a sense of meaningfulness in life and a push towards realization of potential (Faltermaier et al., 2017).

From a macro perspective, an issue critical to e-leadership is that of ethics within the organization. Brown et al. (2005, p. 120) define ethical leadership as "the demonstration of normatively appropriate conduct through personal actions and interpersonal relationships, and the promotion of such conduct to followers through two-way communication, reinforcement, and decision making." The question addressed here is about the reciprocal influence between technology and organizational structure at the heart of which is the leader. The leader must display integrity in terms of:

a. Protecting workers' privacy by using sensitive personal data (such as that collected by way of electronic surveillance) discreetly (Kidwell & Sprague, 2009). Lack of face-to-face interactions in a virtual communication set-up may trigger aggressive and unethical behaviours. Hence, leaders must be role models in terms of implementation of national and international data security policies (Gheni et al., 2016).
b. Refraining from misuse of technology such as gaining access to confidential organizational information by breaching cyber security (Jones, 2017) and using it for the purpose for which it is intended. Transparent and authentic leadership is required because ethics affects power dynamics, safety perceptions of the employees, and human resource management.

DIGITAL WORKPLACE: EFFECTS ON EMPLOYEE BEHAVIOUR

The thoroughly complex information-intensive digital work environment is equally demanding for the employees. Corbin-Herbison (2019) has reported the effects of such a workplace on employee engagement, communication, talent acquisition and revenue generation. Increased employee engagement results from easy accessibility of documents through a quick search engine, from transparency in regard to business changes allowing informed decision-making, and a shared social network with instant messaging and also enabling stronger employee -customer relationships. In addition, those workers who might feel bored at work get variety and new challenges due to digital transformation. Some employees may find using new technologies a source of inspiration which may lead to techno-work engagement. Technology helps centralize organisational information and processes and facilitates in building a strong employee value proposition thus attracting talent. Customized software makes onboarding of new hires quicker and training easier. Digitalization has also led to positive changes in terms of making the work less physically or emotionally demanding by, for example, automating the repetitive, mundane, and physically challenging work processes. Resources are, thus, optimally utilized because of system efficiency resulting in increased revenue. Also, digital technologies such as advanced algorithms, robotics, and analytics amongst others are transforming the dynamics of the workforce and aiding in human resource management. The digital revolution has made companies think of re-designing and restructuring themselves.

However, technology-induced life has a downside to it. The loss of traditional face-to-face communication makes some employees isolated and unenthusiastic; heavy dependency on technology and system glitches lead to stress; and upgradation of software apart from being costly leads to employee resistance towards constant updation of their skills which further induces a fear of job loss. Also, a centralized information management system is a threat to data security and susceptible to cyber attacks.

Pirkkalainen and Salo (2016) after an extensive review of research concluded that there are four interrelated 'dark side' technology-related phenomena with negative consequences: technostress, IT 'addiction', IT anxiety, and information overload. These affect organizational outcomes and have a negative impact on attitudes, thoughts, and behaviours of the employees which further leads to ill-health and a decline in quality of life. Studies report that the increased use of information and communication technologies (ICTs) at work and the threat or fear of having to use them in the future have resulted in 'technostress'. It is caused by the constant need to adapt to fast evolving technologies, and the associated physical, social, and cognitive demands. The term 'technostress' was coined by Craig Brod in the early eighties. He defined it as "a modern disease of adaptation caused by an inability to cope with new computer technologies in a healthy manner". Cenfetelli and Schwarz (2011) define it as an individual state in which "too much information is provided beyond the user's needs resulting in perceptions of being overwhelmed". Technostress marked by feelings of anxiety, fatigue, and scepticism can also take the form of 'techno-addiction' – the compulsive and excessive use of technologies showing symptoms characteristic of substance addictions, a psychological state of maladaptive dependency on IT use that is manifested through IT-seeking obsessive-compulsive behaviours that take place at the expense of other important activities (Xu et al. 2012). The term 'IT or computer anxiety' was coined in the sixties to describe the trauma of employees undergoing computerisation in their company. In its extreme form it can become 'technophobia' marked by a high resistance to using technology. Deloitte research (Conner et al., 2018) suggests an increased 'cognitive overload' on the employee due to 'information overload'. Constant streams of information that remains unprocessed leads to 'cognitive scarcity' which results in poor decision making. Lack of perceptual selectivity results in heaps of unfiltered information, a lack of focus and a 'choice overload' hindering individuals from choosing the right alternative while decision making. The low priority e mails are received in a row and a lot of time is lost in reading them. There is a depletion of two of the scarcest resources viz. time and attention. Hence, the issue of employee technology-related well-being in the context of organizational digitalization remains of paramount importance to researchers and practitioners alike.

According to Marsh (2019), the above mentioned negative effects can be minimised in two ways:

a. Redesigning and Enriching a Digital Workplace
b. Training the employees

Deloitte research (Conner et al., 2018) in the context of designing work environments for digital health talks about 'positive technology'. For a positive transformative impact of digital and mobile technologies, it is important to design workplaces in a manner that healthy technology habits are imbibed by the employees. Flexitime, for instance, is devoid of rest pauses and ironically leads to overwork rather than giving autonomy. Among some of the other negative effects of digital gadgets is wakefulness because of exposure to blue screen light emitted by mobile devices which reduce melatonin required for good sleep. Also physical disconnection affects social well-being. The bulk of information to be processed in a limited time leads to FOMO i.e. fear of missing out. Comparisons with others' social profiles depicting an overly rosy picture prompt individuals to question the quality of their lives leading to anxiety and depression.

The challenge is to maintain a humane workplace through a blend of technology and physical connectedness. Digital addiction can be overcome by monitoring application usage patterns through smart meters. Artificial intelligence can be made use of to categorise mails making urgent mails easier to access. The Chatbot software containing a smart filter that blocks social media feed from refreshing and preventing distraction can be installed. CBT (Cognitive Behavioural Therapy) that sets into motion a positive thinking process through cognitive restructuring can be carried out by the AI-enabled Chatbot. The individual becomes aware of his automatic negative thoughts and is able to identify the reasons behind the same.

The 'nudge strategy' based on psychological principles encourages productive flows by helping users decide whether to continue a digital activity. This could be in the form of 'reminders' to break free from the flow of data usage; 'social proof' where employees are made aware of the work rules. Comparisons with other employees are made on IT usage as well as on number of working hours and a notification is sent likewise; or a 'commitment' to a digital detox. Employees can be alerted by employers to not attend emails while on vacation or in non-work hours. Nudging, thus, can be viewed as a human-centred design conducive to productive uses of technology. Committing to a 'digital detox' and striking a work-life balance is an interesting and effective technique which revolves around exercising self control in regard to technology usage. It is essentially a weekly schedule designed to make small changes each day such as unsubscribing from unnecessary emails; unfollowing unimportant people; cutting down on clutter by uninstalling mobile apps and; not attending to the phone while at home and, staying off social media on Sundays.

A digital skills gap was observed by Lloyds Bank UK Consumer Digital Index 2020. It says that 53% of the UK workforce does not have the digital skills for work and only 34% of employees report that their workplace gives them digital skills support which is critical today for productivity, engagement, wellbeing and other work-related outcomes. 47% of the workforce does not have the skills to communicate digitally at work, 33% don't know how to stay safe when working digitally, 44% are not competent enough to handle online information and content at work, and 41% are lacking in the ability to handle online transactions. The use of technology at home may not transfer to the workplace. Apart from investing in digital tools, it is imperative to train employees to use them optimally and to measure their digital readiness.

The content of a digital-training program, according to Marsh (2018) should include:

1. Raising the level of digital literacy of the employees:

"Digital literacy is the awareness, attitude and ability of individuals to appropriately use digital tools and facilities ...." (Martin & Grudziecki, 2006, p. 255). Becoming digitally literate is a process involving continuous learning and adaptation wherein the individual goes through three stages: digital competence (in which a range of skills are gained), digital usage (in which these skills are used in an applied setting), and finally digital transformation (in which the application of skills leads to innovation and creativity). Van Deursen, et al. (2012) have reported that employees are losing nearly 8 percent of productive time due to poor IT resources or inadequate digital skills. Soule et al. (2016) gave the concept of 'digital dexterity' to describe the ability of the organisation as a whole to move swiftly to exploit new digital opportunities. Digital dexterity is only possible if employees do not resist technology-related changes and are willing to retrain themselves.

Marsh (2018) has introduced the Digital Workplace Skills Framework which, apart from skills also includes approaches and mindsets that need to be fostered in employees. It is based on the conceptualisation of digital literacy as including technical, cognitive, and socio-emotional skills. The four overlapping skill areas of the framework include:

a. Using the digital workplace competently and safely
b. Finding, processing and applying information
c. Creating content and connecting with people
d. Reflecting on and adapting one's digital practices

The framework is all about training employees to establish (be aware of what is available and how to use it), safeguard (know about the potential risks in the digital environment and manage them), optimise (their personal digital working environment in order to maximise productivity) and, innovate (i.e. leverage digital workplace tools and resources to arrive at novel ideas, solutions, and ways of working).

2. Blending mindfulness principles with technology usage

Marsh (2017) talks about how technology enhances the mind's tendency to jump from one thought to the other, to remain distracted, reactive and in a 'quick mode'. This 'monkey mind', as mindfulness practitioners call it, needs to be quietened. For digital devices and apps to serve us we need to adopt the mindfulness approach which includes qualities of purposeful attention and broad awareness that help mitigate stress. "Using technology consciously" includes seven techniques (Marsh, 2017) viz. 'Zoning' which includes 'zoning out' from technology at specific times and places and intentionally 'zoning in' to technology at the appropriate time; 'focusing' by closing down distracting applications; 'filtering' out the 'noise' by connecting to people and content that is important; 'dialling down' by muting notifications from particular applications, for example; 'pausing' to restore presence and posture by logging off, 'de-cluttering' by deleting unimportant data, 'reflecting' on how one uses technology and continuously looking for ways to reduce its negative impact. Thus, mindfulness techniques of technology use pave the way for a digital detox.

CONCLUSION

Apart from its broader social implications and macroeconomic consequences, a profound re-alignment in the nature of doing business has surfaced due to Covid-19. A Bitkom study as reported by Roland Berger (2020, April 2), an international management consultancy headquarted in Munich, reveals that 43 percent of German companies surveyed predict that the number of employees working from home will increase in the next five to ten years. The same study shows that 30 percent of firms already rely on teleworking and 35 percent of the employees seek flexibility, prefer working from home and would quit their job if not allowed to do so. Home office does provide freedom, increased employee productivity, reduced turnover, and lower organizational costs but is, ironically, associated with a greater degree of personal responsibility and a blurring of the boundaries between professional and private lives. A study by Kaspersky, a cybersecurity company with headquarters in Moscow, reported by Financial Express Bureau (2020, May 27) also shows that the 'new normal' has resulted in work and family lives getting merged leading to a work-life imbalance. With an increase in social distancing and no travel, nearly a third (31%) of workers reported that they are spending more time working than before as opposed to 46% who said they spend more time on personal activities. Besides, half (51%) of employees have started watching more adult content and that too on the same devices that they use for work-related purposes. This risky behaviour can lead to malware infections if employees do not pay attention to the websites they visit. Companies somehow have to keep a check on such deviance by finding a balance between user convenience, business necessity and security.

Managers and affected employees must, therefore, jointly examine how the balance between private and professional needs can be maintained. Other than some concrete benefits like increased employee productivity, reduced turnover, and lower organizational costs, a major pitfall of flexible work arrangements is the loss of human connection aggravated due to 'social distancing'. A social disconnect takes a toll on idea generation, quick solution of problems, team cohesion, and the expression of human qualities of empathy and collaboration. Maintaining a meaningful interpersonal connect despite remote work arrangements is necessary for a positive company culture and employee experiences – a major challenge for leaders, managers, and organizations. Remote companies that have digital workplaces marked by a culture of close interaction, cooperation, and continuous socializing between organizational members will be successful in minimising business disruptions.

REFERENCES

Accenture. (2017). *Accenture Technology Vision 2017.* https://www.accenture.com/_acnmedia/PDF-45/Accenture-News-Release-Accenture-Technology-Vision-2017-Forecasts-A-Future-Of-Technology-For-People-By-People.pdf

Accenture. (2018). *Accenture Technology Vision 2018.* https://www.accenture.com/_acnmedia/Accenture/next-gen-7/tech-vision-2018/pdf/Accenture-TechVision-2018-Tech-Trends-Report.pdf

Avolio, B. J., Sosik, J. J., Kahai, S. S., & Baker, B. (2014). E-leadership: Re-examining transformations in leadership source and transmission. *The Leadership Quarterly, 25*(1), 105–131. doi:10.1016/j.leaqua.2013.11.003

Baraldi, E., & Nadin, G. (2006). The challenges in digitalising business relationships: The construction of an IT infrastructure for a textile-related business network. *Technovation, 26*(10), 1111–1126. doi:10.1016/j.technovation.2005.09.016

Barley, S. R. (2015). Why the internet makes buying a car less loathsome: How technologies change role relations. *Academy of Management Discoveries, 1*(1), 5–35. doi:10.5465/amd.2013.0016

Barney, J. (1991). Firm resources and sustained competitive advantage. *Journal of Management, 17*(1), 99–120. doi:10.1177/014920639101700108

Bloomberg. J. (2018, April 29). Digitization, digitalization, and digital transformation: Confuse them at your peril. *Forbes.* https://www.forbes.com/sites/jasonbloomberg/2018/04/29/digitization-digitalization-and-digital-transformation-confuse-them-at-your-peril/?sh=4b79bd632f2c

Brafman, O., & Beckstrom, R. A. (2007). *The starfish and the spider: The unstoppable power of leaderless organization.* Penguin Books.

Brod, C. (1984). *Technostress: The human cost of the computer revolution.* Addison-Wesley.

Brown, M. E., Trevino, L. K., & Harrison, D. A. (2005). Ethical leadership: A social learning perspective for construct development and testing. *Organizational Behavior and Human Decision Processes, 97*(2), 117–134. doi:10.1016/j.obhdp.2005.03.002

Buhse, W. (2014). Management by Internet: Neue Führungsmodelle für Unternehmen in Zeiten der digitalen Transformation. Kulmbach: Börsenmedien AG. doi:10.100740567-014-0039-y

Bureau, F. E. (2020, May 27). *Risky behaviour at work: How Covid-19 changed the way people work.* https://www.financialexpress.com/industry/technology/risky-behaviour-at-work-how-covid-19-changed-the-way-people-work/1971396/

Capgemini Consulting. (2015). *Digital Leadership—Führungskräfteentwicklung im Digitalen Zeitalter.* https://www.capgemini.com/consulting-de/wp content/uploads/sites/32/2017/08/14-10-16_digital_leadership_v11_web_17102016.pdf

Cenfetelli, R. T., & Schwarz, A. (2011). Identifying and testing the inhibitors of technology usage intentions. *Information Systems Research, 22*(4), 808–823. doi:10.1287/isre.1100.0295

Chakravarty, A., Grewal, R., & Sambamurthy, V. (2013). Information technology competencies, organizational agility, and firm performance: Enabling and facilitating roles. *Information Systems Research, 24*(4), 976–997. doi:10.1287/isre.2013.0500

Chen, H., Chiang, R. H., & Storey, V. C. (2012). Business intelligence and analytics: From big data to big impact. *Management Information Systems Quarterly, 36*(4), 1165–1188. doi:10.2307/41703503

Connor, J., Jen, F., Jim, G., & Hogan, S. K. (2018). Positive technology: Designing work environments for digital well-being. *Deloitte Insights.* https://www2.deloitte.com/us/en/insights/focus/behavioral-economics/negative-impact-technology-business.html/

Corbin-Herbison, C. (2019, September 13). Pros and cons of digital workplace – striking a human balance. *Interact.* https://www.interact-intranet.com/blog/pros-cons-digital-workplace/

Cortellazzo, L., Bruni, E., & Zampieri, R. (2019). The Role of Leadership in a Digitalized World: A Review. *Frontiers in Psychology, 10*, 1938. doi:10.3389/fpsyg.2019.01938 PMID:31507494

Coutu, D. L. (2000). Too old to learn? *Harvard Business Review, 78*(6), 37–42.

Diamante, T., & London, M. (2002). Expansive leadership in the age of digital technology. *Journal of Management Development, 21*(6), 404–416. doi:10.1108/02621710210430597

Druskat, V. U., & Wheeler, J. V. (2003). Managing from the boundary: The effective leadership of self-managing work teams. *Academy of Management Journal*, *46*(4), 435–457.

DuBrin, A. J. (2002). *Fundamentals of organizational behaviour: An applied perspective* (2nd ed.). Pergamon Press Inc.

Eggers, J. P., & Park, K. F. (2018). Incumbent adaptation to technological change: The past, present, and future of research on heterogeneous incumbent response. *The Academy of Management Annals*, *12*(1), 357–389. doi:10.5465/annals.2016.0051

Ernst & Young LLP. (2011). *The digitisation of everything: How organisations must adapt to changing consumer behaviour*. https://www.the-digital-insurer.com/wp-content/uploads/2014/04/200-EY_Digitisation_of_everything.pdf

Faltermaier, T., Ulich, D., Leplow, B., & von Salisch, M. (2017). *Grundriss der Psychologie* (2nd ed.). Kohlhammer Verlag.

Foerster-Metz, U., Marquardt, K., Golowko, N., Kompalla, A., & Hell, C. (2018). Digital transformation and its implications on organizational behaviour. *Journal of EU Research in Business*.

French, J. R. P., & Raven, B. H. (1959). The bases of social power. In D. Cartwright (Ed.), Studies in social power (pp. 150-167). Institute for Social Research.

Gerth, A. B., & Peppard, J. (2016). The dynamics of CIO derailment: How CIOs come undone and how to avoid it. *Business Horizons*, *59*(1), 61–70. doi:10.1016/j.bushor.2015.09.001

Gheni, A. Y., Jusoh, Y. Y., Jabar, M. A., Ali, N. M., Abdullah, R. H., Abdullah, S., & Khalefa, M. S. (2016). The virtual teams: E-leaders challenges. *Proceedings of the 2015 IEEE Conference on e-Learning, e-Management and e-Services (IC3e), Melaka, Malaysia, August 24-26, 2015*, 38–42. https://ieeexplore.ieee.org/document/7403483

Grafström, M., & Falkman, L. L. (2017). Everyday narratives: CEO rhetoric on Twitter. *Journal of Organizational Change Management*, *30*(3), 312–322. doi:10.1108/JOCM-10-2016-0197

Gupta, S., & Pathak, G. S. (2018). Virtual team experiences in an emerging economy: A qualitative study. *Journal of Organizational Change Management*, *31*(4), 778–794. doi:10.1108/JOCM-04-2017-0108

Hambley, L. A., O'Neill, T. A., & Kline, T. J. B. (2007 b). Virtual team leadership: The effects of leadership style and communication medium on team interaction styles and outcomes. *Organizational Behavior and Human Decision Processes*, *103*(1), 1–20. doi:10.1016/j.obhdp.2006.09.004

Harris, J. G., & Mehrotra, V. (2014). Getting value from your data scientists. *MIT Sloan Management Review*, *56*(1), 15–18.

Hoegl, M., & Muethel, M. (2016). Enabling shared leadership in virtual project teams: A practitioners' guide. *Project Management Journal*, *47*(1), 7–12. doi:10.1002/pmj.21564

Hojeghan, S. B., & Esfangareh, A. N. (2011). Digital economy and tourism impacts, influences and challenges. *Procedia: Social and Behavioral Sciences*, *19*, 308–316. doi:10.1016/j.sbspro.2011.05.136

Horner-Long, P., & Schoenberg, R. (2002). Does e-business require different leadership characteristics? An empirical investigation. *European Management Journal*, *20*(6), 611–619. doi:10.1016/S0263-2373(02)00112-3

Huppert, F. A. (2009). Psychological well-being: Evidence regarding its causes and consequences. *Applied Psychology. Health and Well-Being*, *1*(2), 137–164. doi:10.1111/j.1758-0854.2009.01008.x

Iansiti, M., & Lakhani, K. R. (2014). Digital ubiquity: How connections, sensors, and data are revolutionizing business. *Harvard Business Review*, *92*(11), 90–99.

Jawadi, N., Daassi, M., Favier, M., & Kalika, M. (2013). Relationship building in virtual teams: A leadership behavioral complexity perspective. *Human Systems Management*, *32*(3), 199–211. doi:10.3233/HSM-130791

Jones, M. (2017). E-leadership case study and the impact of (un)faithful appropriation of technology. *Proceedings of the 5th International Conference on Management Leadership and Governance (ICMLG 2017), Wits Business School, University of Witwatersrand, Johannesburg, South Africa, March 16-17, 2017*, 191–199. http://toc.proceedings.com/34017webtoc.pdf

Kane, G. C., Palmer, D., Philips, A. N., Kiron, D., & Buckley, N. (2015). Strategy, not technology, drives digital transformation. *MIT Sloan Management Review and Deloitte University Press*, *14*, 1–25.

Kannan, P. K., & Li, H. A. (2017). Digital marketing: A framework, review and research agenda. *International Journal of Research in Marketing*, *34*(1), 22–45. doi:10.1016/j.ijresmar.2016.11.006

Kidwell, R. E., & Sprague, R. (2009). Electronic surveillance in the global workplace: Laws, ethics, research, and practice. *New Technology, Work and Employment*, *24*(2), 194–208. doi:10.1111/j.1468-005X.2009.00228.x

Kübler, R. V., Wieringa, J. E., & Pauwels, K. H. (2017). Machine learning and big data. In P. Leeflang, J. Wieringa, T. Bijmolt, & K. Pauwels (Eds.), Advanced methods for modeling markets (pp. 631-670). Springer. doi:10.1007/978-3-319-53469-5_19

Lamberton, C., & Stephen, A. T. (2016). A thematic exploration of digital, social media, and mobile marketing: Research evolution from 2000 to 2015 and an agenda for future inquiry. *Journal of Marketing*, *80*(6), 146–172. doi:10.1509/jm.15.0415

Larjovuori, R. L., Bordi, L., Mäkiniemi, J. P., & Heikkilä-Tammi, K. (2016). The role of leadership and employee well-being in organisational digitalisation. *Proceedings of the 26th Annual European Association for Research on Services (RESER) Conference, University of Naples Federiico II, September 8-10, 2016,* 1141-1154. https://www.researchgate.net/profile/Milena_Jael_Silva-Morales/publication/308033532_Changes_in_the_intellectual_structure_of_service_innovation_and_service_system_research_in_the_digital_age_a_bibliometric_analysis_from_1986_to_2015/links/5b1844000f7e9b68b4245425/Changes-in-the-intellectual-structure-of-service-innovation-and-service-system-research-in-the-digital-age-a-bibliometric-analysis-from-1986-to-2015.pdf#page=1153

Lavie, D. (2006). Capability reconfiguration: An analysis of incumbent responses to technological change. *Academy of Management Review*, *31*(1), 153–174. doi:10.5465/amr.2006.19379629

Lee, O. K. D., Sambamurthy, V., Kim, K. H., & Wei, K. K. (2015). How does IT ambidexterity impact organizational agility? *Information Systems Research*, *26*(2), 398–417. doi:10.1287/isre.2015.0577

Leonhardt, D., Haffke, I., Kranz, J., & Benlian, A. (2017). Reinventing the IT function: the role of IT agility and IT ambidexterity in supporting digital business transformation. *Proceedings of the 25th European Conference on Information Systems (ECIS), Guimarães, Portugal, June 5-10, 2017, 1,* 968-984. https://www.researchgate.net/publication/317380735_Reinventing_the_IT_function_The_Role_of_IT_Agility_and_IT_Ambidexterity_in_Supporting_Digital_Business_Transformation

Leviäkangas, P. (2016). Digitalisation of Finland's transport sector. *Technology in Society*, *47*(1), 1–15. doi:10.1016/j.techsoc.2016.07.001

Li, F., Nucciarelli, A., Roden, S., & Graham, G. (2016). How smart cities transform operations models: A new research agenda for operations management in the digital economy. *Production Planning and Control*, *27*(6), 514–528. doi:10.1080/09537287.2016.1147096

Lloyds Bank UK Consumer Digital Index. (2020, May 21). UK Consumer Digital Index 2020. *Lloyds Bank*. https://www.lloydsbank.com/banking-with-us/whats-happening/consumer-digital-index.html

Lu, Y., & Ramamurthy, K. R. (2011). Understanding the link between information technology capability and organizational agility: An empirical examination. *Management Information Systems Quarterly*, *35*(4), 931–954. doi:10.2307/41409967

Lynn Pulley, M., & Sessa, V. I. (2001). E-leadership: Tackling complex challenges. *Industrial and Commercial Training*, *33*(6), 225–230. doi:10.1108/00197850110405379

Malhotra, A., Majchrzak, A., & Rosen, B. (2007). Leading virtual teams. *The Academy of Management Perspectives*, *21*(1), 60–70. doi:10.5465/amp.2007.24286164

Marsh, E. (2017, April 12). 7 approaches to mindful technology use. *LinkedIn*. https://www.linkedin.com/pulse/6-approaches-mindful-technology-use-elizabeth-marsh/

Marsh, E. (2018). The Digital Workplace Skills Framework: Ensuring the workforce is ready to work digitally. *Digital Work Research 2018*. https://digitalworkresearch.com/wp-content/uploads/2018/08/The-Digital-Workplace-Skills-Framework-final.pdf

Marsh, E. (2019, January 10). Is your organisation's digital workplace causing technostress? *LinkedIn*. https://www.linkedin.com/pulse/your-organisations-digital-workplace-causing-elizabeth-marsh/

Marsh, E. (2019, June 11). Half of the workforce isn't ready for the digital workplace. *LinkedIn*. https://www.linkedin.com/pulse/half-workforce-isnt-ready-digital-workplace-elizabeth-marsh/

Martin, A., & Grudziecki, J. (2006). DigEuLit: Concepts and tools for digital literacy development. *Innovation in Teaching and Learning in Information and Computer Sciences*, *5*(4), 1–9. doi:10.11120/ital.2006.05040249

McIntyre, D. P., & Srinivasan, A. (2017). Networks, platforms, and strategy: Emerging views and next steps. *Strategic Management Journal*, *38*(1), 141–160. doi:10.1002mj.2596

Newstrom, J. W., & Davis, K. (1997). *Organizational behavior: Human behavior at work*. McGraw-Hill.

Ng, I. C. L., & Wakenshaw, S. Y. L. (2017). The internet-of-things: Review and research directions. *International Journal of Research in Marketing*, *34*(1), 3–21. doi:10.1016/j.ijresmar.2016.11.003

Pagani, M., & Pardo, C. (2017). The impact of digital technology on relationships in a business network. *Industrial Marketing Management*, *67*, 185–192. doi:10.1016/j.indmarman.2017.08.009

Pearce, C. L., Manz, C. C., & Sims, H. P. Jr. (2009). Where do we go from here? Is shared leadership the key to team success? *Organizational Dynamics*, *38*(3), 234–238. doi:10.1016/j.orgdyn.2009.04.008

Pirkkalainen, H., & Salo, M. (2016). *Two decades of the dark side in the information systems basket: Suggesting five areas for future research*. https://aisel.aisnet.org/ecis2016_rp/101

Ramaswamy, V., & Ozcan, K. (2016). Brand value co-creation in a digitalized world: An integrative framework and research implications. *International Journal of Research in Marketing*, *33*(1), 93–106. doi:10.1016/j.ijresmar.2015.07.001

Richards, L. (2018, November 8). Factors affecting organizational behaviour. *bizfluent*. https://bizfluent.com/info-8131521-factors-affecting-organizational-behavior.html

Roland Berger. (2020, April 2). *Digital workplace in the era of Covid-19: How the current crisis will change the culture of our work*. https://www.rolandberger.com/ru/Insights/Publications/Digital-workplace-in-the-era-of-Covid-19.html

Roman, A., Van Wart, M., Wang, X., Liu, C., Kim, S., & McCarthy, A. (2018). Defining E- leadership as competence in ICT-mediated communications: An exploratory assessment. *Public Administration Review*, *79*(6), 853–866. doi:10.1111/puar.12980

Schwarzmüller, T., Brosi, P., Duman, D., & Welpe, I. M. (2018). How does the digital transformation affect organizations? Key themes of change in work design and leadership. *Management Review*, *29*(2), 114–138.

Sebastian, I. M., Ross, J. W., Beath, C., Mocker, M., Moloney, K. G., & Fonstad, N. O. (2017). How big old companies navigate digital transformation. *MIS Quarterly Executive*, *16*(3), 197–213.

SouleD. L.PuramA. D.WestermanG. F.BonnetD. (2016). *Becoming a digital organization: The journey to digital dexterity*. Working Paper. doi:10.2139srn.2697688

Tallon, P. P., & Pinsonneault, A. (2011). Competing perspectives on the link between strategic information technology alignment and organizational agility: Insights from a mediation model. *Management Information Systems Quarterly*, *35*(2), 463–486. doi:10.2307/23044052

Teece, D. J. (2010). Business models, business strategy and innovation. *Long Range Planning*, *43*(2–3), 172–194. doi:10.1016/j.lrp.2009.07.003

Thomas, L. D., Autio, E., & Gann, D. M. (2014). Architectural leverage: Putting platforms in context. *The Academy of Management Perspectives*, *28*(2), 198–219. doi:10.5465/amp.2011.0105

Tsai, W. H. S., & Men, L. R. (2017). Social CEOs: The effects of CEOs' communication styles and parasocial interaction on social networking sites. *New Media & Society*, *19*(11), 1848–1867. doi:10.1177/1461444816643922

Van Deursen, A. J. A. M., & Van Dijk, J. A. G. M. (2012). *Ctrl Alt Delete: Lost productivity due to IT problems and inadequate computer skills in the workplace.* Technical Report. Universiteit Twente. https://www.researchgate.net/publication/259703359_CTRL_ALT_DELETE_Lost_productivity_due_to_IT_problems_and_inadequate_computer_skills_in_the_workplace/citations

Van Doorn, J., Lemon, K. N., Mittal, V., Nass, S., Pick, D., Pirner, P., & Verhoef, P. C. (2010). Customer engagement behavior: Theoretical foundations and research directions. *Journal of Service Research*, *13*(3), 253–266. doi:10.1177/1094670510375599

Van Wart, M., Roman, A., Wang, X. H., & Liu, C. (2017). Integrating ICT adoption issues into (e) leadership theory. *Telematics and Informatics*, *34*(5), 527–537. doi:10.1016/j.tele.2016.11.003

Verhoef, P. C., Broekhuizen, T., Bart, Y., Bhattacharya, A., Dong, J. Q., Fabian, N., & Haenlein, M. (2019). Digital transformation: A multidisciplinary reflection and research agenda. *Journal of Business Research*, *122*, 889–901. doi:10.1016/j.jbusres.2019.09.022

Verhoef, P. C., Kooge, E., & Walk, N. (2016). *Creating value with big data analytics – Making smarter marketing decisions*. Routledge. doi:10.4324/9781315734750

Verhoef, P. C., Stephen, A. T., Kannan, P. K., Luo, X., Abhishek, V., Andrews, M., Bart, Y., Datta, H., Fong, N., Hoffman, D. L., Hu, M. M., Novak, T., Rand, W., & Zhang, Y. (2017). Consumer connectivity in a complex technology-enabled and mobile-oriented world with smart products. *Journal of Interactive Marketing*, *40*, 1–8. doi:10.1016/j.intmar.2017.06.001

Vidgen, R., Shaw, S., & Grant, D. B. (2017). Management challenges in creating value from business analytics. *European Journal of Operational Research, 261*(2), 626–639. doi:10.1016/j.ejor.2017.02.023

Westerman, G., Tannou, M., Bonnet, D., Ferraris, P., & McAfee, A. (2012) The digital advantage: How digital leaders outperform their peers in every industry. *MIT Sloan Management and Capgemini Consulting, 2,* 2–23. https://ide.mit.edu/sites/default/files/publications/TheDigitalAdvantage.pdf

World Health Organization. (2009). *Meeting of Regional Experts on Promotion of Mental Well-Being: Report of the Meeting*. http://www.searo.who.int/entity/mental_health/documents/seament-159.pdf

Xu, Z., Turel, O., & Yuan, Y. (2012). Online game addiction among adolescents: Motivation and prevention factors. *European Journal of Information Systems, 21*(3), 321–340. doi:10.1057/ejis.2011.56

Zeike, S., Bradbury, K., Lindert, L., & Pfa, H. (2019). Digital Leadership Skills and Associations with Psychological Well-Being. *International Journal of Environmental Research and Public Health, 16*(14), 2628. doi:10.3390/ijerph16142628 PMID:31340579

Zott, C., & Amit, R. (2008). The fit between product market strategy and business model: Implications for firm performance. *Strategic Management Journal, 29*(1), 1–26. doi:10.1002mj.642

Chapter 9
Online Advertising Strategies in Indian and Australian E-Commerce Companies:
A Comparative Study

Varinder Singh
Guru Kashi University, India

Sanjay Taneja
Guru Kashi University, India

Varinderjeet Singh
Guru Kashi University, India

Azad Singh
Guru Kashi University, India

Harmesh Lal Paul
Government College, Karamsar, India

ABSTRACT

Online advertising and marketing promote the different types of products through various kinds of advertising modes to customers. Online advertising is promotional messages that show up on the monitors of online laptops, desktops, tablets, televisions, and smart phones. The main objective of the study is to analyze the online advertising and impact comparison of online advertising strategy which is adopted by Indian and Australian e-commerce companies. To achieve the objectives of this study, the authors take the sample of 5 Indian and 5 Australian e-commerce companies. This study also found that the Indian and Australian e-commerce companies are inter-connected. Online advertising in India has been flowering and also increasing because

DOI: 10.4018/978-1-7998-7231-3.ch009

of 4G connections, which are good for the future of online marketing. This chapter explains comparisons of Indian and Australian e-commerce companies and also focuses on the top 10 platforms to increase sales and customer attraction through advertising. The future of online advertising is brilliant and unlimited.

INTRODUCTION

In present times, a large majority of the consumers view online advertisements that represent the modern dimension of traditional form of advertising. With the help of social media websites like Facebook and twitter etc. consumers are in the better position to connect with each other. Social media also enables consumers to create groups online that helps them to develop relationships and share valuable information within the network (Yang et al., 2006). Online advertisements have a large scope in future because users of internet and social media have been increasing rapidly across the entire world.

It is interesting to note that a large share of the worlds' population uses social media sites for different purposes. For instance, more than 70 percent of the US population use more than one type of social media (Shields 2007). Online advertisements have proved to be more economical for companies because firms can reach masses using online advertisements in contrast to traditional media. Rosenbush (2006) claimed that online advertisements are cheaper as companies are able to 70% rate of return from online advertisements. Findings of a study conducted by Goldsmith and Lafferty (2002) reported that 48.9% of the respondents, who were exposed to online advertising, liked the online advertisements. However, about 42% of the respondents reported that they like radio advertisements. Due to this reason, companies have been increasingly incurring more expenditure on online advertisements. Goldsmith and Lafferty (2002) reported that online advertising becomes more attractive when website of the company is attractive that also encourages consumers to have a positive feeling for brand among them. Moreover, consumers prefer to view advertisements that are more entertaining for them; such online advertisements can also be tailored as per needs and wants of the viewers.

The above discussion highlighted that online advertisements are important in determining consumer behaviour for purchasing products and services online. The previous literature on the influence of online advertising on consumer behaviour for India and Australia is nearly non-existent. Therefore, the present study aims to compare the influence of online advertising on intention to purchase online for India and Australia.

REVIEW OF LITERATURE

Hadija Z, Barnes S. B. and Hair N (2012) undertook a research study entitled "Why we ignore social networking advertising?" In this research, the authors attempted to investigate perceptions of online advertisements for college students. Authors used Zaltman Metaphor Elicitation Technique (ZMET) that helped them to interview 20 college students and the selected respondents were exposed to online advertisements that were able to reveal perceptions of online advertisements. Findings highlighted that respondents failed to dislike online advertisements that were shown to them by researchers.

Kumar, Mangla, Luthra, Rana and Dwivedi (2018) conducted a research study entitled "Predicting changing pattern: building model for consumer decision making in digital market". This research study attempted to investigate the changing consumer behaviour of Indian consumers in the light of digital era. This study included two phases; in the first phase, authors review previous literature for identifying important factors causing major changes in consumer behaviour in India. The second phase of this research consisted Analytic Hierarchy Process (AHP) that helped the authors to weigh the finalized factors. Findings indicated that consumers were found to be influenced by innovative and branded products.

RESEARCH METHODOLOGY

Research may be conceptualized as "a scientific enquiry into a pre-existing problem in any branch of science" (Naidoo, 2011). In other words, research may be defined as "the search for knowledge or search for pertinent information on a given topic" (Kothari 2004). According to Clifford Woody, "the process of research includes various steps like problem identification, reviewing the related literature, development of hypothesis, collecting and analyzing data, making interpretations and finding appropriate conclusions". The key characteristics of a research study are: "to gain familiarity with a phenomenon and to gain new insights into it"; "to portray accurately the characteristics of a particular individual, situation or a group"; and "to examine the causal relationships between variables".

Kothari (2004) defined research methodology as "a science that describes how research is done scientifically that includes various steps to be followed by a researcher during a research project". In this, researchers need to understand various techniques that may be useful in undertaking the research project and they also need to have an in-depth knowledge of the methods and criteria by which they can achieve research objectives in a scientific way. In sum, it is important for a researcher to design scientific steps for finding solution to a problem at hand.

Sample Size

There are many e-commerce companies in India and Australia that provide a plenty of products and services to consumers. Some agencies rate these e-commerce companies on the basis of traffic on the respective websites. In May, 2020; a company called SimilarWeb estimated monthly traffic on websites of e-commerce companies in India and Australia. The top 10 companies on the basis of traffic on their websites is given as under:

Table 1. Top 10 e-commerce companies in India and Australia

Rank	India		Australia	
	Name of the e-commerce company	Estimated monthly website traffic	Name of the e-commerce company	Estimated monthly website traffic
1	Amazon India	200 Million	eBay Australia	69.6 Million
2	Flipkart	157.5 Million	Amazon Australia	22.5 Million
3	IndiaMart	52.2 Million	Woolworths	20.4 Million
4	Myntra	14.2 Million	JB Hi-Fi	13.3 Million
5	Snapdeal	12.9 Million	Big W	11.9 Million
6	Firstcry	12.5 Million	Coles	10.7 Million
7	1mg	9.05 Million	Kogan.com	10.2 Million
8	BookMyShow	7.2 Million	Officeworks	9.45 Million
9	Nykaa	5.35 Million	Chemist Warehouse	9.1 Million
10	2GUD	4.65 Million	Catch	8.95 Million
Source: https://disfold.com/top-e-commerce-sites-india https://disfold.com/top-e-commerce-sites-australia/				

The present study selected top five e-commerce companies of both India and Australia. These companies float a plenty of online advertisements to consumers that attract them to buy products from the e-commerce companies. The present study selected respondents who have already purchase products from top five e-commerce companies. In the questionnaire, the first question asked respondents to provide information on how many times they have products/services from the selected e-commerce companies. The present study selected respondents who have purchased products at least twice from any of the selected e-commerce company. A respondent found to purchase products from the selected e-commerce company with less than the above mentioned frequency then that respondent was considered ineligible for providing information on the questionnaire. Such respondents were excluded from the final analysis. The present study prepared the online version of the questionnaire and floated on-line link to may social media groups. In total, first 150 complete responses from India and first 150 complete responses from Australia were considered for the final analysis. Therefore, the total sample size for the present study was 300 including 150 from India and 150 from Australia.

Developing Questionnaire

The present study developed a structured questionnaire to collect data from the selected respondents. In first section of the questionnaire, there were general questions that aimed to reveal demographic profile of the respondents. In second section of the questionnaire, statements measuring respondents' perceptions of on-line advertisements were included. The present study developed these statements with the help of existing literature relating to online advertising (Arora, Kumar and Agarwal 2020; Singh and Kathuria 2016; Santoso, Wright, Trinh and Avis 2020; Supriya and Aralelimath 2020; Souiden, Chtourou and Korai 2017; Wang and Sun 2010).

Statements Measuring Respondents' Perceptions of Online Advertising

Online advertising may be defined as "the advertising which uses the internet to deliver marketing messages to consumers." It has been observed that a majority of the consumers are exposed to a plenty of online advertisements every day; at the same time it has also been observed that some consumers perceive such online advertisements as disrupting and annoying. However, online advertisements have the ability to provide useful and timely information to consumers that provide value to the consumers. Therefore, it seems important to examine consumers' perceptions of online advertising and to study the differences between Indian and Australian consumers' perceptions of online advertising. For this, the present study collected previous literature that were used to develop statements for measuring different dimensions of consumers' perceptions of online advertising (Arora, Kumar and Agarwal 2020; Singh and Kathuria 2016; Santoso, Wright, Trinh and Avis 2020; Supriya and Aralelimath 2020; Souiden, Chtourou and Korai 2017; Wang and Sun 2010). For instance, Wang and Sun (2010) conducted a study aiming to study the relationship between perceptions and of online advertising and consumers'' attitude towards online advertising. The authors developed five dimensions of online advertisements and influence of these dimensions on attitude towards online advertising was also examines. The identified dimensions of online advertising were as under:

- Information
- Entertainment
- Credibility
- Economy
- Value

The above mentioned dimensions of online advertising were adopted in the present study as independent variables whereas intention to purchase products from the selected e-commerce companies was taken as dependent variable. The statements used for measuring the above mentioned variables are given as under:

Statements Measuring Information Provided by Online Advertising

The present study gathered many existing research studies relating to online advertising (Arora, Kumar and Agarwal 2020; Singh and Kathuria 2016; Santoso, Wright, Trinh and Avis 2020; Supriya and Aralelimath 2020; Souiden, Chtourou and Korai 2017); however we developed the statements relating to information provided by online advertising with the help of a study undertaken by Wang and Sun (2010):

- "Online advertising is a good source of product/service information"
- "Online advertising supplies relevant information"
- "Online advertising provides timely information"

Statements Measuring Entertainment Provided by Online Advertising

The present study gathered many existing research studies relating to online advertising (Arora, Kumar and Agarwal 2020; Singh and Kathuria 2016; Santoso, Wright, Trinh and Avis 2020; Supriya and Aralelimath 2020; Souiden, Chtourou and Korai 2017); however we developed the statements relating to entertainment provided by online advertising with the help of a study undertaken by Wang and Sun (2010):

- "Online advertising is entertaining"
- "Online advertising is enjoyable"
- "Online advertising is pleasing"
- "Online advertising is interesting"

Statements Measuring Credibility of Online Advertising

The present study gathered many existing research studies relating to online advertising (Arora, Kumar and Agarwal 2020; Singh and Kathuria 2016; Santoso, Wright, Trinh and Avis 2020; Supriya and Aralelimath 2020; Souiden, Chtourou and Korai 2017); however we developed the statements relating to credibility of online advertising with the help of a study undertaken by Wang and Sun (2010):

- "Online advertising is credible"
- "Online advertising is trustworthy"
- "Online advertising is believable"

Statements Measuring Economy of Online Advertising

The present study gathered many existing research studies relating to online advertising (Arora, Kumar and Agarwal 2020; Singh and Kathuria 2016; Santoso, Wright, Trinh and Avis 2020; Supriya and Aralelimath 2020; Souiden, Chtourou and Korai 2017); however we developed the statements relating to economy of online advertising with the help of a study undertaken by Wang and Sun (2010):

- "Online advertising has positive effects on the economy"
- "Online advertising raises our standard of living"
- "Online advertising results in better products for the public"

Statements Measuring Value of Online Advertising

The present study gathered many existing research studies relating to online advertising (Arora, Kumar and Agarwal 2020; Singh and Kathuria 2016; Santoso, Wright, Trinh and Avis 2020; Supriya and Aralelimath 2020; Souiden, Chtourou and Korai 2017); however we developed the statements relating to value of online advertising with the help of a study undertaken by Wang and Sun (2010):

- "Online advertising promotes undesirable values in our society"
- "Online advertising distorts the values of youth"

Statements Measuring Intention to Purchase Products Online

The present study gathered many existing research studies relating to online advertising (Arora, Kumar and Agarwal 2020; Singh and Kathuria 2016; Santoso, Wright, Trinh and Avis 2020; Supriya and Aralelimath 2020; Souiden, Chtourou and

Korai 2017); however we developed the statements relating to intention to purchase products online with the help of a study undertaken by Singh and Kathuria (2016):

- "I intend to purchase products online"
- "I wish to purchase products online"
- "I plan to purchase products online"

HYPOTHESES

The present study aimed to examine consumers' perceptions of online advertising and to compare Indian and Australian consumers' perceptions of online advertising. In order to achieve objectives of the study, the present study has formulated following hypotheses:

H1: The strength of relationship between "information provided by online advertising" and intention to purchase products online differs for Indian and Australian consumers.
H2: The strength of relationship between "entertainment provided by online advertising" and intention to purchase products online differs for Indian and Australian consumers.
H3: The strength of relationship between "credibility of online advertising" and intention to purchase products online differs for Indian and Australian consumers.
H4: The strength of relationship between "economy of online advertising" and intention to purchase products online differs for Indian and Australian consumers.
H5: The strength of relationship between "value of online advertising" and intention to purchase products online differs for Indian and Australian consumers.

STATISTICAL TOOLS USED

The present study used statistical tools like frequency, mean and regression analysis for testing hypotheses of the study. Regression analysis is an important statistical technique which is used for measuring the strength of relationship between independent variable(s) and a dependent variable (Zou, Tuncali and Silverman 2003). In a regression equation, which has only one dependent variable, we examine the linear relationship between independent and dependent variable. In the present study, we consider factors like "information provided by online advertising"; "entertainment provided by online advertising"; "credibility of online advertising"; "economy of online advertising"; and "value of online advertising" as independent variables; whereas intention to purchase products online was considered as a dependent variable. Using these variables, we develop a regression equation that may be expressed as follows:

$$ITP = a + b1\left(INF\right) + b2\left(ENT\right) + b3\left(CRD\right) + b4\left(ECO\right) + b5\left(VAL\right) + e$$

where, ITP = Intention to purchase online (Dependent variable)
INF = Information provided by online advertising
ENT = Entertainment provided by online advertising
CRD = Credibility of online advertising
ECO = Economy of online advertising
VAL = Value of online advertising
a = Intercept of regression line on y axis
b = Regression coefficient
e = Error term

In the above mentioned equation, the regression coefficient measures the intensity of the influence of an independent variable on dependent variable. In other words, it measures the change in the value of dependent variable when independent variable is changed by one unit. Moreover, higher the magnitude of regression coefficient, higher is the influence of independent variable on dependent variable.

DATA ANALYSIS AND INTERPRETATION

The present study developed a structured questionnaire and collected data from 300 respondents; including 150 from India and 150 from Australia. The demographic profile of the respondents is given in the table 2.

Table 2 revealed that out of the full sample, 53 percent respondents were male and 47 percent of the respondents were females. Out of the sample selected from India, 48 percent were males and 52 percent were females. However, out of the sample selected from Australia, 58 percent were males and 42 percent were females. Further, about 20 percent respondents from the full sample were between 15-25 years; out of the sample selected from India, 28 percent were between 15-25 years. Similarly, out of the sample selected from Australia, 13 percent were between 15-25 years. Further, about 32 percent respondents from the full sample were having bachelors' degree; out of the sample selected from India, 35 percent were having bachelor's degree. Similarly, out of the sample selected from Australia, 30 percent were having bachelor's degree.

Table 2. Demographic profile of respondents

		Full sample		India		Australia	
		Frequency	**Percent**	**Frequency**	**Percent**	**Frequency**	**Percent**
Gender	Male	159	53.00	72	48	87	58
	Female	141	47.00	78	52	63	42
	Total	**300**	**100.00**	**150**	**100**	**150**	**100**
Age	15-25 years	62	20.67	42	28	20	13.33
	26-35 years	73	24.33	31	20.67	42	28
	36-45 years	97	32.33	47	31.33	50	33.33
	Above 45 years	68	22.67	30	20	38	25.33
	Total	**300**	**100.00**	**150**	**100**	**150**	**100**
Level of education	Matriculation or below	45	15.00	23	15.33	22	14.67
	Intermediate	68	22.67	32	21.33	36	24
	Bachelors degree	98	32.67	53	35.33	45	30
	Masters Degree or above	89	29.67	42	28	47	31.33
	Total	**300**	**100.00**	**150**	**100**	**150**	**100**

PERCEPTIONS OF ONLINE ADVERTISING

The present study developed a structured questionnaire and collected data from 300 respondents; including 150 from India and 150 from Australia. Consumers' perceptions of five dimensions of online advertising were measured using five point Likert scale. The mean score of all statements were calculated and we used t-test to examine statistical difference between mean score of Indian and Australian consumers. The findings on consumers' perceptions of five dimensions of online advertising are given in the Table 3.

Table 3 revealed that consumers of India and Australia have different perceptions of information provided by online advertisements. Findings revealed that Australian consumers have stronger perceptions of "Online advertising is a good source of product/service information" then Indian consumers. Similarly, Australian consumers revealed that they have stronger perceptions of "Online advertising supplies relevant information" and "Online advertising provides timely information". Further, out of the four statements under the factor 'Entertaining'; Australian consumers have

Table 3. Perceptions of online advertising for India and Australia

	Mean (India)	Mean (Australia)	t-score	p-value
Information				
"Online advertising is a good source of product/service information"	3.14	3.78	-5.45	0.00*
"Online advertising supplies relevant information"	3.24	3.98	-4.15	0.00*
"Online advertising provides timely information"	3.41	4.12	-4.21	0.00*
Entertainment				
"Online advertising is entertaining"	3.11	3.76	-3.23	0.03*
"Online advertising is enjoyable"	3.23	3.31	-1.63	0.18**
"Online advertising is pleasing"	3.41	4.14	-4.52	0.00*
"Online advertising is interesting"	3.45	4.23	-3.45	0.01*
Credibility				
"Online advertising is credible"	3.14	3.19	-1.53	0.09**
"Online advertising is trustworthy"	3.31	3.98	-3.87	0.04*
"Online advertising is believable"	3.42	4.18	-2.76	0.03*
Economy				
"Online advertising has positive effects on the economy"	3.21	3.36	-1.67	0.13**
"Online advertising raises our standard of living"	3.12	3.78	-4.43	0.00*
"Online advertising results in better products for the public"	3.41	3.87	-3.76	0.04*
Value				
"Online advertising promotes undesirable values in our society"	2.76	2.62	1.57	0.12**
"Online advertising distorts the values of youth"	2.64	2.33	3.87	0.02*
Intention to purchase products online				
"I intend to purchase products online"	3.36	3.49	-1.77	0.09**
"I wish to purchase products online"	3.14	3.91	-4.32	0.00*
"I plan to purchase products online"	3.25	4.21	-5.21	0.00*
Notes: *significant at 5% ** insignificant				

higher perceptions of three statements. It means that consumers in Australia found online advertising for e-commerce sites is more entertaining. As far as credibility of online adverting in concerned, Australian consumers were found to have stronger perceptions of online advertising than their Indian counterparts. This finding suggested that e-commerce companies in India need to make their advertisements more trustworthy so that e-commerce companies can develop consumers' confidence in online advertising.

Findings revealed that Australian consumers perceived that they have higher perceptions of online advertising useful for the economy. For instance, Australian consumers revealed that online advertising helps to improve their standard of living and online advertisements also helps them to grab better products. However, it was interesting to note that both Indian and Australian consumers have positive perceptions of value of the online advertising. Findings in this regard revealed that mean score of statements under this factor like "Online advertising promotes undesirable values in our society" and "Online advertising distorts the values of youth" was found to be less than three. This indicates that both Indian and Australian consumers disagreed with the statement that online advertising encourages adverse values in the society. It was interesting to note that both Indian and Australian consumers revealed positive intention to purchase products online; however Australian consumers were found to have stronger perceptions of intention to purchase products online than for Indian consumers.

COMPARING INFLUENCE OF ONLINE ADVERTISING FOR INDIA AND AUSTRALIA

The present study considered factors like "information provided by online advertising"; "entertainment provided by online advertising"; "credibility of online advertising"; "economy of online advertising"; and "value of online advertising" as independent variables; whereas intention to purchase products online was considered as a

Table 4. Comparing influence of online advertising for India and Australia

Independent Variables	India			Australia		
	Standardized Beta	T	p	Standardized Beta	t	p
Information	0.154	2.73	0.007*	0.189	2.99	0.005*
Entertainment	0.217	5.42	0.000*	0.289	5.97	0.000*
Credibility	0.497	7.12	0.000*	0.564	8.45	0.000*
Economy	0.318	6.56	0.000*	0.091	1.81	0.07**
Value	0.028	1.32	0.12**	0.036	1.43	0.11**
Note: *significant at 5% level **insignificant						

dependent variable. Overall mean scores of the statements under above mentioned factors were calculated used in the regression model. Two separate regression models were in SPSS for Indian and Australian consumers. Findings in this regard have been presented in Table 4.

The above table indicated that the five factors of online advertising have significant influence on intention to purchase online for both Indian and Australian consumers. For Indian consumers, credibility of online advertising was found to be the strongest predictor of intention to purchase online (β= 0.497; $p<0.005$); followed by economy of the online advertisements (β= 0.318; $p<0.005$). Finding indicated that Indian consumers were influenced by four of the factors of online advertising except for value of the online advertising. Value of the online advertising failed to influence intention to purchase online for Indian consumers. However, Australian consumers were influenced by three factors of online advertising except for economy and value of the online advertising. Economy and value of the online advertising failed to influence intention to purchase online for Australian consumers. For Australian consumers, credibility of online advertising was found to be the strongest predictor of intention to purchase online (β= 0.564; $p<0.005$); followed by entertainment provided by online advertisements (β= 0.289; $p<0.005$). Findings suggested e-commerce companies to make their advertisements more credible for both Indian and Australian consumers so that consumer's intention to purchase online can be enhanced.

SUMMARY AND CONCLUSION

The present study selected top five e-commerce companies of both India and Australia. Total sample size for the present study was 300 including 150 from India and 150 from Australia. In the present study, we consider factors like "information provided by online advertising"; "entertainment provided by online advertising"; "credibility of online advertising"; "economy of online advertising"; and "value of online advertising" as independent variables; whereas intention to purchase products online was considered as a dependent variable. Findings revealed that Australian consumers perceived that they have higher perceptions of online advertising useful for the economy. For instance, Australian consumers revealed that online advertising helps to improve their standard of living and online advertisements also helps them to grab better products. For Indian consumers, credibility of online advertising was found to be the strongest predictor of intention to purchase online (β= 0.497; $p<0.005$); followed by economy of the online advertisements (β= 0.318; $p<0.005$). For Australian consumers, credibility of online advertising was found to be the strongest predictor of intention to purchase online (β= 0.564; $p<0.005$); followed by entertainment provided by online advertisements (β= 0.289; $p<0.005$).

REFERENCES

Arora, T., Kumar, A., & Agarwal, B. (2020). Impact of social media advertising on millennials buying behaviour. *International Journal of Intelligent Enterprise*, *7*(4), 481–500. doi:10.1504/IJIE.2020.110795

Goldsmith, R. E., & Lafferty, B. A. (2002). Consumer response to websites and their influence on advertising effectiveness. *Internet Research: Electronic Networking Applications and Policy*, *12*(4), 318–328. doi:10.1108/10662240210438407

Hadija, Z., Barnes, S. B., & Hair, N. (2012). Why we ignore social networking advertising? *Qualitative Market Research*, *15*(1), 19–32. doi:10.1108/13522751211191973

Kothari, C. R. (2004). *Research methodology: Methods and techniques*. New Age International.

Kumar, A., Mangla, S. K., Luthra, S., Rana, N. P., & Dwivedi, Y. K. (2018). Predicting changing pattern: Building model for consumer decision making in digital market. *Journal of Enterprise Information Management*, *31*(5), 674–703. doi:10.1108/JEIM-01-2018-0003

Naidoo, N. (2011). What is research? A conceptual understanding. *African Journal of Emergency Medicine*, *1*(1), 47–48. doi:10.1016/j.afjem.2011.05.011

Rosenbush, S. (2006). FaceBook's on the block. *Business Week*. Available at: www.businessweek.com/technology/content/mar2006/tc20060327_215976.htm

Santoso, I., Wright, M., Trinh, G., & Avis, M. (2020). Is digital advertising effective under conditions of low attention? *Journal of Marketing Management*, 1–24.

Shields, M. (2007). Study: Social networking ads take time to work. *Brandweek*, *23*(April), 6.

Singh, A., & Kathuria, L. M. (2016). Understanding drivers of branded food choice among low-income consumers. *Food Quality and Preference*, *52*, 52–61. doi:10.1016/j.foodqual.2016.03.013

Souiden, N., Chtourou, S., & Korai, B. (2017). Consumer attitudes toward online advertising: The moderating role of personality. *Journal of Promotion Management*, *23*(2), 207–227. doi:10.1080/10496491.2016.1267676

Supriya, C., & Aralelimath, S. S. (2020). Advertising messages impact on consumer buying behaviour of two-wheeler in Belgavi, Karanataka. Editorial Board, 9(7).

Wang, Y., & Sun, S. (2010). Assessing beliefs, attitudes, and behavioral responses toward online advertising in three countries. *International Business Review, 19*(4), 333–344. doi:10.1016/j.ibusrev.2010.01.004

Yang, W. S., Dia, J. B., Cheng, H. C., & Lin, H. T. (2006). Mining social networks for targeted advertising. *Proceedings of the 39th Hawaii International Conference on System Sciences.*

Zou, K. H., Tuncali, K., & Silverman, S. G. (2003). Correlation and simple linear regression. *Radiology, 227*(3), 617–628. doi:10.1148/radiol.2273011499 PMID:12773666

Chapter 10
An Empirical Study on Pharmaceutical and Personal Care Stocks Using Sharpe's Single-Index Model

Divya Bansal
Amity University, Noida, India

Srilakshmi Rao
ISBR, Bangalore, India

Karpagam T.
ISBR, Bangalore, India

ABSTRACT

As the various avenues for better returns in India are slowly dwindling due to various global scenarios as well as due to domestic government policies, more and more people are turning towards stock market for better returns. This poses a challenge to the fund managers when they have to construct a portfolio, which maximizes return and minimizes risk. This has become more and more challenging in the recent years as the investors are also becoming more knowledgeable. Timely and correct investment decision on the part of the investor requires an in-depth knowledge of the stock that he intends to procure and the theories behind portfolio management. This chapter mainly focuses on construction of an optimal portfolio comprising of top pharmaceutical companies and FMCG companies in India. Sharpe ratio return analysis is the tool that is used to construct the optimal portfolio. Monthly returns data of last 10 years of the said companies are regressed against monthly return data of Nifty for better comparison.

DOI: 10.4018/978-1-7998-7231-3.ch010

INTRODUCTION

We Indians have a very high propensity towards saving money rather than investing. There is a stark difference between Investing and Saving. When a part of income is put in a safe place, where it is considered to be risk-free, for example money deposited in a saving bank account, it is called saving. But the money does not grow in value over time. But when the money is put at work where it grows in value over time and generates higher return than normal, it is called investing. Investing involves committing ones money to a financial product involving risk proportion to expected returns. Portfolio management requires both emotional as well as analytical intelligence. It also involves matching goals to investment, allocating assets for institutions and individuals and having the right balance between and risk and return. Management of portfolio is the determination of opportunities and strengths, threats and weaknesses, involved in debt equity ratio, international or domestic, safety vs. growth and many such choices that are to be taken to achieve the maximum return for a risk level.

Individual securities and assets bundled and combined together form a portfolio. Normative approach is provided by the portfolio theory to investors who then take a decision to make their investment in assets or securities under risk. Investors are considered to be rational, and risk averse which means that the investors do not invest their all the wealth in few or single assets but they hold well diversified portfolios. If these risk-averse investors are offered additional risk premium, they are willing to include risky assets also. SIM was proposed by Sharpe. This model can help an investor to determine optimum portfolio within a class of assets. Markowitz has proposed MPT which takes into consideration many estimates. Single Index Model is an improvement over that Model. (Luskin, J. 2017) notes that historically when stocks are compared to bonds, the former contributes more return and volatility to portfolios. It is observed that optimum portfolio is chosen by a typical decision maker to maximise expected utility of his portfolio return (profit) (Thalheimer, R., & Ali, M. M., 1979).

Efficient diversification of investment portfolio has been done by Dr. Harry Markowitz by mainly using equity issues. If portfolio returns attain minimum variance along with expected rate of return desired by investor then it is known to be efficient diversification (Cheng, P. L., 1962). The author notes that there has been lot of focus exclusively on financial assets like corporate stocks in the recent research of investments (Bosch, J. C., 1986). Managing decisions are mostly made with in uncertain and risky environment. There are lot of reasons like existence of conflicting tendencies, lack of precise and complete information, unforeseen circumstances and so forth (Emelichev, V., Korotkov, V., & Nikulin, Y., 2014).

REVIEW OF LITERATURE

Five out of fifty stocks have been selected for optimum portfolio. Optimum portfolio has been constructed using Single Index Model in order find out the weightage of the selected stocks in nifty index. The author has studied the closing price of every day of the 50 securities (Giri, Laxmi, 2017). Professionals from the industry consider 20-30 assets in a portfolio in order to reduce the market risk. The author has tried to test this theory by simulating S&P500's various portfolios. The author found out that there were 25 stock positions in optimal stock (Adamiec, Cernauskas, 2019). The closing price of each month of 10 IT sector stocks and 10 stocks belonging to banking and NBFC sector companies which are listed in Bombay Stock Exchange (BSE) is considered for building an optimal portfolio. SIM model has been considered for calculating the same. The author concludes that this method of calculation is more adequate. Five years data has been taken to construct the portfolio. To get an optimal portfolio, two banking companies and one IT company have been taken for construction (Poornima, Remesh, 2015). An optimal portfolio has been constructed in Indian Market by the author by implementing SIM of Sharpe. . Optimum portfolio construction has been found a major challenge in recent years. The investors expect higher returns with least risk in their investments through their investments by having a right mix of assets in their portfolio (Patel, A. K. (2017). The authors has recognised that security information is not shared by the outside portfolio managers either with each other or with the decision makers. This generally leads to portfolios which are sub-optimal. Therefore an implementable set of rules have been derived which can be used by central decision maker to make optimal decisions (Elton, E. J., & Gruber, M. J., 2004). The author observes that there is a variation in the impact of crisis in terms of portfolio composition and risk which is posed by their proposed model (Mili, M., M'Hamdi, Y., Khalfallah, M., & Teulon, F., 2014). The author has studied the problem which has been neglected in the literature (Elton, E. J., & Gruber, M. J.,1987). Mean variance optimization techniques have been used to identify the right combination of all the assets. The autor has also identified the reason for how the utility of commodity changes, when the risk apetitie of the investor also changes. (Bansal, Y., Kumar, S., & Verma, P., 2014). Development of a case study on the Madrid Exchange is the objective of the author. The motivation behind this objective is that most of the mutual funds that are currently constructed on Madrid Market are index funds (Plà–Santamaría, D., & Ballestero, E., 2003) When expected values of two options are same, the one with the lower risk should be chosen.additionally it is known intuitively. High return expectations must be clubbed with high risk (Ben, B., 2006).

NEED FOR THE STUDY

The investors as well as fund managers both face a dilemma during the selection of securities that have to be included in their portfolio. Investors also face difficulty when they have to make a decision about deciding the proportion of investment to be made in each security. Sharpe's Single Index model can be used to get a solution to the problem. This model will prune the number of securities that are to be included in the portfolio based on the risk and return of the securities in comparison to the index.

RESEARCH METHODOLOGY

Source of Data

In the current study, 10 years monthly return of the top 20 stocks that is 10 from Pharmaceutical sector and 10 from FMCG sector are taken into consideration. Alongside, Nifty Index monthly return were calculated for which data was mined from National Stock Exchange (www.nseindia.com). The 10-year G-sec was taken as the risk free rate and it was converted into monthly yield.

Sample

In the current study, purposive sampling method has been used as this study intends to test the Sharpe's Single Index Model's efficiency. Hence a sample comprising 120 data points spreading over period of ten year from 1st February 2009 to 28th February 2019 is taken into consideration.

Technique

Sharpe's SIM model helps in pruning the number of securities to construct an optimal portfolio by calculating the excess return to the systematic risk ratio. In order to smoothen the data pertaining to returns, monthly log return is calculated for all the 20 securities. Then the systematic risk (Beta) is calculated for each of the stocks by dividing the covariance of excess return on a stock with that of the index excess return by the variance of index return. Ranking of the stocks is done on the basis of their excess return to beta. Then the cut off point (C*) is calculated with the help of the following formula.

$$\frac{\sigma^\wedge 2m \sum_{i=1}^{n} \frac{(Ri - Rf)\beta i}{\sigma^\wedge 2ei}}{1 + \sigma^\wedge 2m \Sigma_{i=1}^{n} \frac{\beta i^\wedge 2}{\sigma^\wedge 2ei}}$$

C* =Wherein

σ^2m ---

Nifty's Variance

σ^2ei ------

Stocks movement's variance which isn't associated with Nifty's movement; this is the unsystematic risk of the stock

Ri

stock i's return

Rf

Return which is risk free

βi

stock i's systematic risk

The group of securities that are having excess return to beta in comparison to the cut off point (C*) were selected as the securities that were to form the portfolio. The rest of securities which did not meet this criteria were discarded in the process. Then according to the fund availability, weightage were assigned to the selected securities of the portfolio indicating the amount of fund to be allocated to each and every security.

OBJECTIVES OF THE STUDY

1. Optimum portfolio to be constructed using Single Index Model.
2. Determination of each stocks' weightage in optimum portfolio

LIMITATIONS OF STUDY

1. The current study uses monthly return data rather than weekly or daily data.
2. The results of the study may not be applicable universally.

DATA ANALYSIS AND INTERPRETATION

Secondary data of the return of 20 stocks that are on NSE belonging to Pharmaceuticals and Personal care sector were chosen depending on the highest capital. The companies selected are listed below. The first 10 stocks belong to Personal Care Sector & the next 10 belongs to Pharmaceuticals sector.

Table 1. Mean Return and Beta value of the selected companies

Sl No	Securities	Mean Return	Beta Value
1	DABUR	0.0269	0.13166
2	COLGATE	0.0165	0.12873
3	P & G	0.0246	0.39500
4	JYOTHY LABS	0.02023	0.46910
5	MARICO	0.00225	0.40156
6	HLL	0.012	0.29273
7	PIRAMAL	0.0238	0.51657
8	GILLETTE	0.0209	0.47113
9	GODREJ	0.0236	1.67772
10	EMAMI	0.0204	0.94526
11	GODREJ IND	0.0236	1.67772
12	SUN PHARMA	0.015	0.41287
13	TORRENT	0.0305	0.53326
14	CIPLA	0.0113	0.34847
15	DIVIS LAB	0.0206	0.34883
16	CADILA	0.0218	0.39949
17	LUPIN	0.019	0.33879
18	BIOCON	0.0284	0.66125
19	DR REDDY	0.0179	0.45675
20	AUROBINDO	0.0405	1.56255

Source: Mean return and Beta through calculation

Table 1 indicates percentage mean return of companies and Systematic Risk or Beta values of the companies under study. The securities that have Beta value lesser than 1 implies that they are less volatile compared to the market. Godrej has the highest beta value of 1.67772 next is Aurobindo Pharma which has a Beta value of

Table 2. Securities ranked (Excess return to Beta)

SL NO	SECURITIES	BETA	EXCESS RETURN TO BETA	RANKING
1	DABUR	0.1316600	0.11621000	2
2	COLGATE	0.1287300	0.08467483	3
3	P & G	0.3950000	0.04784797	4
4	JYOTHY LABS	0.4691000	0.04519292	7
5	MARICO	0.4015600	0.04183662	9
6	HLL	0.2927300	0.04099000	10
7	PIRAMAL	0.5165700	0.03523253	13
8	GILLETTE	0.4711300	0.03226297	15
9	GODREJ	0.7073000	0.02827654	16
10	EMAMI	0.9452600	0.02158142	18
11	GODREJ IND	1.6777200	0.01066924	20
12	SUN	0.4128700	0.22525000	1
13	TORRENT	0.5332600	0.04650601	5
14	CIPLA	0.3484700	0.04648851	6
15	DIVIS LAB	0.3488300	0.04271396	8
16	CADILA	0.3994900	0.04055182	11
17	LUPIN	0.3387900	0.03925776	12
18	BIOCON	0.6612500	0.03432885	14
19	DR REDDY	0.4567500	0.02671063	17
20	AUROBINDO	1.5625500	0.02227131	19

Source: Computed by the author

1.56255. Majority of the companies under study have Beta values under 1 indicating that they are less volatile compared to the market.

Table 3, gives the the CUT-OFF value (C_i) of selected stocks. In the current study, the value of C_i is found to be in the range of 0.0175 to 0.0255. Therefore, 0.0255 is the "Cut-off point". The stocks, have lesser value than the C_i are not included in the portfolio. Only those securities, whose values are more than or equal to the C_i are considered during portfolio construction.

Table 3. Cut-off value of the selected Company stocks

SL NO	STOCK	(BETA/USR)2	CUM OF EX RET * BETA (USR)2	C*
1	SUN	28.89180286	6.507878595	0.01752456
2	DABUR	25.49169941	9.470268984	0.02386364
3	COLGATE	4.620180989	9.86148203	0.02456347
4	GODREJ IND	353.6263521	42.11954231	0.02552618
5	P & G	39.68247514	11.760208	0.02665796
6	TORRENT	55.29269037	14.33165039	0.02886858
7	EMAMI	118.7147122	38.34661733	0.02957871
8	CIPLA	25.5054238	15.51735959	0.02972959
9	AUROBINDO	201.3613736	35.78458582	0.03038485
10	JYOTHY LABS	23.25001158	16.56809556	0.03038902
11	DIVIS LAB	16.5175994	17.27362762	0.03075144
12	MARICO	49.93662207	19.3628073	0.03165646
13	HLL	23.86931836	20.34121066	0.03200701
14	DR REDDY	35.62389122	31.30000463	0.03205818
15	GODREJ	109.2794492	30.34846821	0.03226068
16	CADILA	28.11568513	21.48135276	0.03236902
17	LUPIN	18.84786917	22.22127795	0.03255926
18	PIRAMAL	37.15967956	23.5305074	0.03269730
19	GILLETTE	53.26938879	27.25842404	0.03278433
20	BIOCON	58.5305838	25.5397952	0.03282002

Source: Through calculation

FINDINGS

1. Aurobindo having the highest return ie. 40.5% and the Marico having the lowest return with 2.25%.
2. Colgate has the least beta value of 0.12873 and Godrej Industries with 1.6772 has the highest volatility .
3. The cut-off value is in the range of 0.01752 to 0.03282. Based on the C_i values twelve companies were selected.
4. Torrent having the weight of 16% with Z_i of 2.53.Colgate having a Z_i of 0.36 had the least allocation of 2%.

Table 4. Investment proportion for the optimal portfolio

Sl No	STOCK	C*	Z_i	WEIGHT	MEAN RETURNS
1	COLGATE	0.02456347	0.358393029	2%	0.0165
2	P & G	0.02665796	1.865905952	12%	0.0246
3	TORRENT	0.02886858	2.538622376	16%	0.0305
4	CIPLA	0.02972959	1.152889177	7%	0.02023
5	JYOTHY LABS	0.03038902	1.017915957	6%	0.00225
6	DIVIS LAB	0.03075144	0.672712048	4%	0.0206
7	MARICO	0.03165646	2.056359662	13%	0.00225
8	HLL	0.03200701	0.945583343	6%	0.012
9	CADILA	0.03236902	1.107322077	7%	0.0218
10	LUPIN	0.03255926	0.707105173	5%	0.019
11	PIRAMAL	0.03269730	1.276409433	8%	0.0238
12	BIOCON	0.03282002	1.976467788	13%	0.0284

Source: Computed by the author

CONCLUSION

Optimal Portfolio was constructed using SIM of Sharpe model by regressing the monthly returns for selected 20 stocks comprising of Pharmaceutical sector and Personal Care sector. Out of 20 stocks, only 12 stocks were chosen for portfolio construction. Out of which only 4 are from Personal Care sector and the rest 8 are from Pharmaceutical sector.

REFERENCES

Adamiec, L., & Cernauskas, D. (2019). *Optimal number of assets for reduction of market risk through diversification*. Academic Press.

Bădescu, A. V., Smeureanu, I., & Asimit, A. V. (2010). *Portfolio assets selection through Grey numbers implementation*. Academic Press.

Ballestero, E., & Plà–Santamaría, D. (2003). Portfolio selection on the Madrid exchange: A compromise programming model. *International Transactions in Operational Research*, *10*(1), 33–51. doi:10.1111/1475-3995.00391

Bansal, Y., Kumar, S., & Verma, P. (2014). Commodity futures in portfolio diversification: Impact on investor's utility. *Global Business and Management Research*, *6*(2), 112.

Ben, B. (2006). *Risk and Return: The Intuition Traps*. Wiley Periodicals, Inc..

Bosch, J. C. (1986). Portfolio Choices, Consumption, and Prices in a Market with Durable Assets. *Journal of Financial Research*, *9*(3), 239–250. doi:10.1111/j.1475-6803.1986.tb00454.x

Cheng, P. L. (1962). Optimum bond portfolio selections. *Management Science*, *8*(4), 490–499. doi:10.1287/mnsc.8.4.490

Elton, E. J., & Gruber, M. J. (1987). Portfolio analysis with partial information: The case of grouped data. *Management Science*, *33*(10), 1238–1246. doi:10.1287/mnsc.33.10.1238

Elton, E. J., & Gruber, M. J. (2004). Optimum centralized portfolio construction with decentralized portfolio management. *Journal of Financial and Quantitative Analysis*, *39*(3), 481–494. doi:10.1017/S0022109000003999

Emelichev, V., Korotkov, V., & Nikulin, Y. (2014). Post-optimal Analysis for Markowitz's Multicriteria Portfolio Optimization Problem. *Journal of Multi-Criteria Decision Analysis*, *21*(1-2), 95–100. doi:10.1002/mcda.1492

Giri, K. (2017). Optimum Portfolio Construction Using Single Index Model. *Intercontinental Journal of Finance Research Review, 5*(2).

Korteweg, P. (1972). Uncertainty and the behaviour of wealth-owner and policy-maker: The cases of the optimum portfolio-mix and the optimum policy-mix. *De Economist*, *120*(4), 367–377. doi:10.1007/BF02366911

Luskin, J. (2017). Examining Total Portfolio Performance: US Government Vs. Corporate Bonds. *Journal of Financial Planning*, *30*(12).

Mili, M., M'Hamdi, Y., Khalfallah, M., & Teulon, F. (2014). Fixed-income portfolio management in crisis period: Expected Tail Loss (ETL) approach. *Gestion 2000, 31*(1), 223-240.

PatelA. K. (2017). Construction of Optimal Portfolio Using Sharpe's Single Index Model and Markowitz Model: An Empirical Study on Nifty50 Stocks. Available at SSRN 3259328. doi:10.2139srn.3259328

Poornima, S., & Remesh, A. P. (2015). Construction of optimal portfolio using Sharpe's single index model–A study with reference to banking & IT sector. *International Journal of Applied Research*, *1*(13), 21–24.

Thalheimer, R., & Ali, M. M. (1979). Time series analysis and portfolio selection: An application to mutual savings banks. *Southern Economic Journal*, *45*(3), 821–837. doi:10.2307/1057480

Chapter 11
An Influence of Digitalization and Recent Innovations on the Hospitality and Tourism Sector

Varsha Singh
Chitkara College of Hospitality Management, Chitkara University, India

Deepika Puri
Chitkara College of Hospitality Management, Chitkara University, India

ABSTRACT

Our lifestyle cravings are voracious. The hospitality sector ensures guests are pleased with every new application and connected system that continues to become a business success. For guests, digital technology means a simple life where customer service is all about it. The transition of hospitality is at its tilt stage where everything is possible due to digital technology, where the ability to be improved by the correct technique from the movement of the reservation to check-out and from the ease of connecting to the hotel guest network to the temperature of the guest room when entering for the first time. Therefore, advancement in emerging technologies provides an opportunity for the hospitality business. Hotels strive for their growth to have more guest satisfaction with better experience, provisions, and management.

INTRODUCTION

Digitalization is the use of advanced innovation to modify an action plan to have fresh income and openness; it is a way to drive a technical Organisation forward. In the near and long term, digitalization has been described as one of the key elements

DOI: 10.4018/978-1-7998-7231-3.ch011

that will transform society and industry. Digitalization has been described as one of the key elements that will transform society and industry. The saving of "Time, Efforts, Energy and Fortune" is advantageous. It has stimulated and made human life effective and straightforward. In brief, technological innovation would be all the improvements that are aligned with the introduction of digital technology in any area of human society. This started with the launch of the first commercial websites in the 1990s, where the tendency to digital technology not only provided guests with ease, but also created hotel revenue. Developments in digital technology today present new possibilities for new products and services to be designed. The development of such digitalized goods and services, also poses new challenges for organizations pursuing innovation. In this article we examine the developments in the hospitality industry that are changing the landscape and address the needs of creative digital products and services in this industry. Just for recreation is the new century/generation becoming techno-savvy. In the 20th century, hotels have begun to head towards technology. In the very first 'HOTELTYPE' booking system built by Westin to the robots currently used in the hotels. For example, digital concierge, automated reservation systems, robot service for guests, etc., technology has helped hotels increase the comfort level of guests. Various websites such as trivago.in, irctc.com and many more have been built to ease the booking and reservation workload of customers. Hotels have also been aided by technology and digitalization in advertising and selling their services and facilities.

Various features such as Robots, Virtual Conferences, Wi-Fi, Infrared Sensors, Smart Room Keys, Cloud Services, Social Media Reviews, Near Field Communication (NFC) Technology, etc. have made it possible for hotels to give guests comfort and improve their facilities and services in the process of development. Any such automated software helps to determine the sales and development of an enterprise, which in turn tells where the organisation is lacking. The platform also allows the business to deliver services at reasonable prices.

DIGITAL TECHNOLOGY IN HOSPITALITY INDUSTRY

In human lives, technology has been the greatest edge and almost every industry has been penetrated by it. Hotels that harness the application of technology can have a direct effect on customer loyalty, from improving customer service to efficient energy use. The promotion of databases was a trend decades ago and is now a common method in everyday hotel operations. This is only proof that the future of technology is maybe predictable.

The hospitality industry focuses on the customer service field and its players have essentially provided their guests with enhanced experience of personalization.

Till date, conventional marketing tools have helped most hospitality companies to tap their target base, but modern day travelers and visitors are well versed and do a gazillion of research before preparing for their stay at hotels where they ultimately look for a customized and best-in-class experience to concentrate on the present day. Professionals in the industry agree that artificial intelligence has entered the hospitality market as a boon to hoteliers, allowing them to provide their guests with a range of facilities and services while saving valuable resources. Hotel employees can collect a whole range of information about their guests and customers through AI software and use that knowledge to provide their guests with informative experiences at all touch points such as travel, stay, and even up-selling other products and services. They can consider the needs of customers, travel options, their patterns of travel, and methods of payment.

In addition, while the hotel industry is adopting the latest technologies to provide experiences in tune with consumer experiences, the acceptance is not widespread. Although artificial intelligence (AI), mechanization, etc. may potentially revolutionize the processes and provide customer service, in the name of "personalization" there is some reluctance to implement them. There are some examples of industry-leading examples, however, such as 1) AI-based concierge, Connie, at Hilton hotels, 2) flotation pool in Taj Mahal palace, Mumbai, 3) Savvy Smart Mirror in Sinclair Hotel, a member of Marriott, Texas.

DIGITALISATION IN INDIA

Rising spending power and the emergence of entrepreneurs are increasingly embracing multiple mechanical resources, technology and digital channels to enhance customer service in the hospitality sector. "We are in a digital era and travel and hospitality is not an exception. According to the report, India was expected to account for 3.7 percent of global digital travel revenues, making it the third-largest value market in the Asia-Pacific (APAC) region. India is also experiencing a rise in technology-driven start-ups in the field of travel. With their niche offerings, these start-ups dominate the market, complementing the established players in certain respects and undermining them in others it added.

Guests in this country are now expecting state-of-the-art technology that is simple to use and accessible from multiple devices at such a rapid speed, says SharatDhall COO, Yatra.com. In order to draw more customers, it is therefore imperative for players in the Indian hospitality industry to make upgrades and be in line with international offerings.

Various developments have been noted in the Indian market—

- All is just a touch away for a guest at Marriott, Whitefield, Bengaluru. Via housekeeping, surprising anyone on a special occasion, ordering food, pulling the curtains, providing wake up call, mood lighting, even bathrooms, all are digitalized from placing requests in the room.
- In the Bengaluru Renaissance, this technology was adopted. Keyless check-in, in which the whole experience is simplified without the use of physical key and made seamless.
- Free bird" has been announced by Hyatt hotel, a friction-free web encryption allowing for a one-time central authentication to generate additional internet use a flawless event at any Hyatt property."
- Something can be ordered at ITC Kohenur through the I Pad given to the guest.

HOSPITALITY INDUSTRY DIGITAL TRENDS

In hospitality, modern technology is evolving at a rapid rate now, and many of the latest gadgets developed over the past years are anticipated to become popular shortly. We also presented some of the new technological trends in the hotel industry in this article.

Mobile phone- The truth is that we use them for more than communication, since mobile devices were invented to ease communication with each other through call, text, tweet, and so forth; they are a tool we use to perform tasks and make our lives seamless. In addition, in hotels, mobile applications have really reinterpreted the customer experience. In recent years, the value of mobile apps in hotels has been felt, and more hotels are switching to their adoption. "The Know" was developed by Virgin Hotels - a proprietary programme meant to generate delightful experience. The probability that repetitive company will take place is more likely by addressing visitors as entities rather than as a unified entity.

Virtual reality- The use of a VR headset usually requires virtual reality technology, which tends to familiarize a user in a digital world. The user is effectively put inside a virtual environment with the use of pictures, sounds and other physical sensations, which they can pass around and in some cases, communicate with in other ways. The use of technology for offering virtual tours of hotels and hotel rooms is one of the best examples of virtual reality in practice within the travel industry.

Blockchain Technology– The block chain technology pledge is- "A world with little or no intermediaries where there is no need to build trust between people and transactions are completed in seconds.

Internet of things- One of the most critical and influential new technology developments is the Internet of Things for those in the hospitality field. It has the opportunity to radically change the number of tourism firms, hotels, run, boost their sales management and boost the consumer experience. The term is more commonly used to refer to ordinary physical devices, appliances and other ‘things’ that have been equipped with internet connectivity, making them capable of sending and receiving data, although it theoretically encompasses absolutely anything that is connected to the internet.

Artificial Intelligence and Chatbots: As a business solution, artificial intelligence is evolving all the time, making it more efficient and appealing. AI applies to machines or computers carrying out activities that would usually require human intelligence to perform. This may be learning lessons, making choices, or hearing and reading speech, for instance. In hotels, one of AI’s most exciting trends is offering online customer service. In addition, the ability of Chatbots on social media sites as well as instant messaging applications has already been widely adopted. Robot utilizes artificial intelligence and recognition of speech to provide clients who talk to it with tourist information.

Robotic Butlers- Robotic Butlers was unveiled at Cupertino’s Aloft Hotel by Starwood, one of the largest hospitality firms in the world. The robots would perform duties in the front and back of the building, in addition to travelling around guests and using elevators. Robots are connected to the hotel and elevator apps to communicate using a WIFI / 4G hotel and can also get to and from the rooms without hurting anything or harming others. **Digital Concierge-** The Renaissance Midtown hotel in New York has built an innovative and interactive wall called ‘The Discovery Portal.’ By stepping through a circular hologram projected on the floor, such as entertainment, eating, adventure places and much more, it is a virtual concierge where guests can pick different categories.

Robotic Luggage Storage- Yotel in New York uses robotics and artificial intelligence to delight travelers. In order to make the check-in process simple for the consumer, Yotel has friendly robots to store luggage instead of touch-screen kiosks for front desk employees.

Near Field Communication Technology (NFC): The next-generation short-range high-frequency wireless communication technology is Near Field Communication (NFC) technology, which enables users to share data between devices.

FUTURISTIC HOTELS

In a quickly moving industry such as hospitality, futuristic hotels mean never standing still. The requirements of today’s visitors are the past of tomorrow, because smarter businesses are always peering over the horizon.

In a hotel room, bookable at the touch of a button on your mobile, any type, size, place, decor and functionality you could ever want. The way you would customize your salad or your food meal, in the same way there is a wide range of choices, but what if you could take one step further as a guest to take a freedom of choice and actually customize your room. The hyper-personalized rooms may be one of the major changes on the hospitality horizon in a study by intercontinental hotel groups and Amadeus and may even initiate the beginning of the end of "traditional" fixed interior hotel rooms and increase the new trend of attribute-based reservations.

Here, when it comes to music, fashion, entertainment and travel, customers may purchase precisely what they want or need. This new trend will allow the future travelers to get the option of bespoke option .it will be a breakthrough for the traditional standards and give the future customers, preferred price ranged commodities in terms of customized rooms

A Swiss based group has created a new concept of "Stay Kooook" which will debut soon in the coming next year with properties opening in Bern, Switzerland which is small hotel concept with advanced technology. The concept is going to be the basic 22sq m room which will be fully flexible, with fully customizable space. The walls move, the bed moves minimal furniture, plus the guests will be allowed to borrow fresh plants, frames of their choice, vases, some special cushions from one common pool area, in order to make tailor-make their rooms. This will be entirely their personalized space specially the long stay guest.

It is quite clear that in our lives, the role of travel is changing. Yet more individuals regard travel as a privilege and no longer as a luxury. A diverse collection of converging forces are driving the future of travel and tourism, obliging the industry to think about reshaping the overall experience. The hospitality sector is experiencing a time of unprecedented, irreversible changes and will look very different in the science, technology, entertainment, and energy sectors in 2020, which will change radically the hospitality experience for travelers. The globe is turning towards digital control. Young consumers born between 1981 and 2000 already account for one-third of visitors and upcoming projections state that this will grow to 50 percent by 2020. Thus, we will see millennials being the main buyers over the next few years. They will be compared to digital visitors, who in the future will expect the hotel to provide them with personalized service.

OLD PHENOMENA TRANSFORM

The modernization or automation of hotel technology started in the 1950s with the first In-Room Television, in the 1960s with hotel mini bars, in the 1970s with concierge services, in the 1980s with PCs, reservation systems, in-room phones, key cards, in the 1990s with online booking portals, in the 2000s with Wi-Fi. With the introduction of artificial intelligence (AI) to the hotel industry, this technological evolution has been accelerated. Increases in guest purchases and comfort have been achieved by responding to this.

DIGITIZATION BENEFITS

Both the hotel staff and visitors have been helped by digitization in the hotel industry. It has helped guests stay at the hotel with more ease and less tension. Digitization has allowed the hotel's HR department to evaluate employee results, pick the best applicants from different candidates, count staff holidays, bonuses and increases given to staff. Digitization will help workers provide visitors with the best and quickest services.

OBJECTIVE

1. This research paper aims to highlight the numerous developments and advancements related to digitalization in the hospitality industry.
2. To review the Indian hotels are inclined towards digital technology.
3. To understand the requirements of automation in the hospitality industry by raising the standards and level of satisfaction of both visitors and hoteliers.
4. To study the technical progress of the 21st century.

LITERATURE REVIEW

The quality of hotel service from different viewpoints has been studied by several scholars. Dimensions of service quality, its effect on satisfaction and loyalty, disparities in quality, and variables such as Gabbie and O'Neill (1997), Juwaheer T. D. (2004), respectively, Lau et al. Raspor S. with. (2010), Antoneta and Charles, respectively (2014). There are very few studies on the implementation of AI in the hotel industry, while AI is a recent development.

Olsen and Connolly (2000) stressed the value of data from hotel customers to fulfil their evolving needs and desires. Jurca and Fallings (2004) researched the AI-based Hotel Booking Reputation System and found it to be successful in preventing financial fraud. A cost benefit study of the implementation of robots, artificial intelligence and service automation was performed by Ivanov and Webster (2017).

The hospitality industry will be revolutionized by emerging digital innovations. As technological advances continue to change many industries, intelligent machine automation will be implemented, and by 2022, according to Forbes, five employees mostly engaged in non-routine functions will rely on AI to do many tasks relevant to their jobs.

According to Chip Rogers, president and CEO of the Asian American Hotel Owners Association "The accommodation industry has changed and helped hoteliers in several key areas in recent decades to intensify their products, attract more guests and create opportunities for expansion".

Many businesses struggle with digital transformation, according to Jane McConnell (December 30, 2015). Since digital allows expert skills to survive a challenging situation naturally when people ask and answer questions about networks in which each machine will serve the others as a server.

Enzi (2009) claims that technology adoption entails high Organisational costs, but at the same time provides the enterprise with several benefits.

V, Hitesh (2017) In the Food and Restaurant industry" there has been major digital transformation according to Hitesh. Kiosks, digital menus, desktop computers, digital tabletops and digital kitchens. In terms of customization, food distribution, and payment choices, the industry has achieved success. Zomato, Swiggy, and Food Panda have now made online table reservations, social media feedback, and mobile payment stuff of the past in India.

India Today web desk (2019); it will be of primary importance for hospitality brands to attract and retain clients, providing different experiences to meet visitors' different needs and desires, and this includes creativity. By 2020, Gen X will be overtaken by global millennial purchasing force, being greater than that of any other World Data Lab. Www.indiatoday.in/education-today-today.

Technological advances in the twenty-first century are one of the prime assets of hotel companies. But, when selecting overnight lodging, is it necessary for the hotel to answer questions such as which technology facilities their guests want? In addition, the standards of significance assigned by visitors to these different technology amenities? This study addressed the question of how, with regard to in-room technology facilities, leisure travelers could vary or be similar to business travelers.

Digital revolution in the travel space is on. Brands are embracing technology to transform themselves into experience platforms while automating operations. Corporate and consumer travel boundaries are already blurred. Incumbents are adapting swiftly to the emerging bouquet of travel start-ups. Creative digital business models will continue to reshape the future of travel. Among others, hospitality industry has gained a lot with the technological advancements.

The technology in the hospitality industry offers fair advantages for both visitors and the company, according to Nyheim and Connolly (2013). Guests find it easy to pick and interact with the aid of upgrading of digitalization and also consider technology as extremely relevant in the hospitality industry, as it allows room reservations, price comparisons, other guest interactions, accommodation facilities, infrastructure, etc. to be checked.

A 1995 article (Hansen & Owen) predicts that technical developments would be important for hotels to operate in the future. They spoke about "smart cards" that the consumer would use as a hotel key, as well as potential "kiosks" that will make it easier for hotel customers to register and save time.

KPMG India Partner and Head - Transport, Leisure and Sports, Jaideep Ghosh said "Digital revolution in the travel space is on. Brands are embracing technology to transform themselves into experience platforms while automating operations. Corporate and consumer travel boundaries are already blurred. Incumbents are adapting swiftly to the emerging bouquet of travel start-ups. Creative digital business models will continue to reshape the future of travel". Among others, hospitality industry has gained a lot with the technological advancements.

METHODOLOGY

The study adopted mainly a quantitative research design. A structured questionnaire was prepared to collect the research data. It consisted of 10 questions which enquired about the Digital transformation in Hospitality Sector. Qualitative approach was appropriate to get meaningful deep insight for analysis of data. Initially the study was collected by the secondary data primarily from books, journals and websites. Statistical analysis was also carried out. The surveys (48 in total) were taken from the hoteliers and executives of various hotels.

RESULTS AND DISCUSSIONS

Figure 1 represents that, during the study it was asked to find out from where the hoteliers came to know about various technologies, the following insights were found out:

There were four choices and multiple choices were permitted in which the responses from Verbal communication was15%which inclined three times for the case of Internet, where as the people who found out about robotics and automation through Newspapers and Magazines was 27% which almost declined twice folds for the case of Walk-in visit to13%. Internet co9mmunication accounts for about

Figure 1.

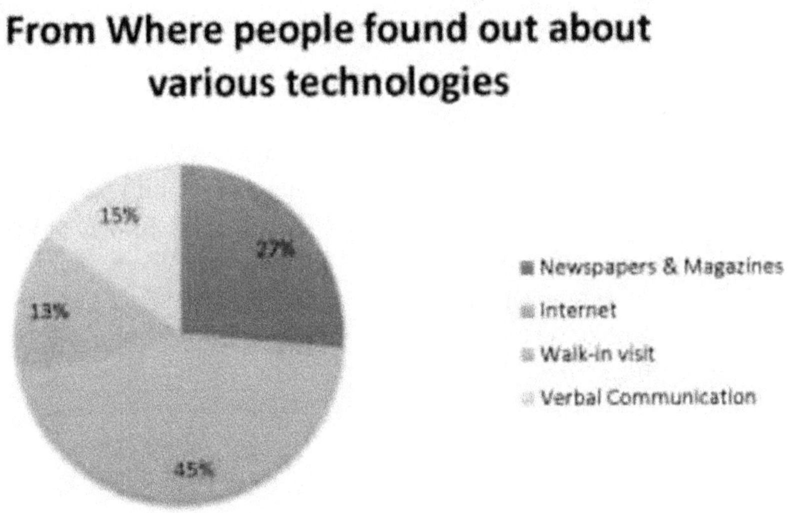

45%. The communication about these ICT technologies happened because of these four ways.

Figure 2 represents opinions about the factors from the hoteliers which prevents the usage of digital technology in the hotels. The categories taken in figure 2 are card keys, luggage scanners, express check in, WI fi, Automatic doors, sensory lightings. The results are given below:

Figure 2.

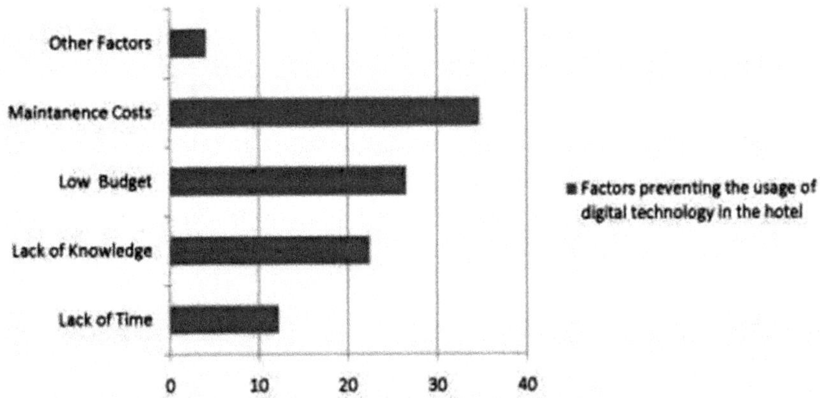

It gave the brief feedback that the maintenance costs were the major factor preventing the usage of digital technologies which were 34.09% whereas the least was of other factors which was 4.08%. The Lack of Time was 12.24% which inclined by 10% in the case of Lack of knowledge (22.45%). Low budget was considered second most preventing factor which was 26.53%.

Figure 2 represent the availability of the smart technologies available in the hotel people work or have visited and multiple options were allowed to be chosen:

The analysis of the data showed that the Card keys and Wi-Fi were present in the hotels and 20% people have opted for it. The Technologies like Express Check-in, Automatic Doors and Sensory lightning's present in the hotels were 13.91%, 12.17% and 15.65% respectively. Whereas, the Luggage Scanners present in the hotels were available approximately in 18% of hotels.

CONCLUSION

The whole research has been conducted to find out the increase in the Digital Technology in Hospitality Sector as well as the changing trends and innovations in the industry. The technology has evolved and has taken upliftment to a new level where study shows that the behavioural patterns of guest is ever evolving and one needs to be updated regarding the latest gadgets. This calls for hotels to keep a track of the changing trends. In the upcoming era, the innovation in hotels and their volution of technology will be leading force for creating guest experience to be simply a WOW Experience. The standards of the organisation can be inclined only when there is advancement in technology in Hotels. The analysis of paper shows us that advancement in technology is directly proportional to need of personalization and customization.

Technological activities in India are set to get a streamlined approach in travel and hospitality sector leading to innovation and seamless services. The efficient and effective technology being user-friendly is available in multiple regional languages for an array of guests as well as the hoteliers. Nowadays, Guest expects state-of-the-art-technology that is easy to use and accessible from multiple devices. Thus, it becomes imperative for the players of the Indian Hospitality Industry to make the upgrades and be in sync with universal technologies to attract more customers.

REFERENCES

Dave, C. (2020). *Global Social Media Summary August 2020.* Smart Insights.

Elisabeta, I., & Ivona, S. (2014). Social Media and its Impact on Consumers Behaviour. *International Journal of Economic Practices and Theories*, *4*(2), 295–302.

Fejzagic, E. (2017). *The Impact of Social Media on Consumer Behaviour.* Ligs University Blog Posts.

Gil, A., Grewal, L., Rhonda, H., & Stephen, A. T. (2019). Future of Social Media in Marketing. *Journal of the Academy of Marketing Science*, 79–95. PMID:32431463

Heinonen, K. (2011). Consumer activity in social media: Managerial approaches to consumers' social media behaviour. *Journal of Consumer Behaviour*, 356–364.

Kotler. (2017). *Marketing Management*. Prentice-Hall of India Private Limited.

Meenu, G., & Sahni, N. K. (2016). *Consumer Behaviour*. Kalyani Publishers.

Moustakas. (2015). Impact of Social Networking on Consumer Behaviour. Academic Press.

Parneet, R., & Gupta, S. K. (2016). *Business Research Methodology*. Kalyani publishers.

Singh, A., Jain, A., & Singla, B. (2019). Technological advancement-based paradigm shift: A focus shift from large screen to small screen. *International Journal of Innovative Technology and Exploring Engineering*, *8*(10), 48–53. Advance online publication. doi:10.35940/ijitee.I8613.0881019

Singh, A, Singh, A., Vij, T. S., & Pardesi, A. (2020). An empirical study of the factors affecting online shopping behavior of the Indian consumers. *International Journal of Advanced Science and Technology*.

Singh, A, Singla, B., & Sharma, S. (2020). An empirical study of factors affecting the selection of point of purchase location: A case of FMCG industry. *International Journal of Control and Automation*.

Sonnartakki, Neeti, & Anuj. (2015). Marketing management. Kalyani Publishers.

Chapter 12
Impact of Digital Marketing on the Buying Behavior of Youth With Special Reference to Uttarakhand State

Arun Kant Painoli
Quantum University, Roorkee, India

Rohit Bansal
https://orcid.org/0000-0001-7072-5005
Vaish College of Engineering, Rohtak, India

Ram Singh
https://orcid.org/0000-0002-6565-3091
Quantum University, Roorkee, India

Ankur Kukreti
Quantum University, Roorkee, India

ABSTRACT

The buying behaviors of the consumers are changing very rapidly in the today's consumer-oriented market. New technologies are evolving in the market to attract the customers. Smart phones have become necessities to cope with the changing dynamics of the market and society as a whole. Due to competitive price offer by the various cellular operators, it has become easy for all to reach the internet. Due to ease of use, the young generations are using the application of internet for various uses especially for purchasing goods and services. Today, every company is applying the digital marketing tool to attract customers, especially the young generation. As per a report published in Economics, the internet users in India are expected to reach 627 million by the end 2020. Due to the digital marketing, a new concept of shopping has evolved in the market, which the authors call off-the-shop retailing.
DOI: 10.4018/978-1-7998-7231-3.ch012

INTRODUCTION

Digital Marketing is the process of offering a products or services through the use of various digital search engines like Google, Yahoo, Bing etc. In this we use social media network like face book, Instagram, Twitter, LinkedIn, E-mail and with the use of mobile phone application tools to connect the prospective customers. Youth are the backbone of any nation and they are the major contributors in the economy. The youth are also called innovator because they adopt any innovation or change first. The buying behavior of the consumers is very complex and is influenced by the number of the factors which vary from individual to individual's as per report published by Hoot Suite in 2019 on average a person spent 6 hours 42 minutes per day online. This figure itself indicates the scope of digitalization. This is the reasons why every company today using digital marketing platform to promote their products and services. Every marketer want to connect directly to their customers and it is only possible through the use of online approach; where information is directly reach to individual users. The youth are very fascinated in using digital tolls and that is why if we talk about the figure of online shopping or use of digital marketing they figure is number one as compared to the other demographic segment. There are many communication sites evolved with the introduction of digital marketing and through which the companies promoting their products and services to the end users. Amazon is the world's largest on line shopping company with a turnover of 70 billion. Due to the ease of operation of internet and affordability of the service, the user of internet is increasing day by day.

Digital India: Transforming India

1. India is one of the largest growing digital markets with the 560 million internet subscriber in 2018
2. On an average 8.3 Gigabyte data is used by the Indian consumers
3. India has 1.2 billion phone subscribers
4. Approximately 1.2 billion apps download by the users in 2018
5. It was estimated that digital economy will create 60 to 65 million jobs by 2025.
6. It is estimated that India will increase the users of internet by about 40% and figure is estimated 750 million to 800 million.
7. The number of smart phone is estimated to increase between 650 million to 700 million by 2023

(Source: - McKinsey Global Institute report march 2019)

Youth Marketing

Youth marketing is an effort used by the marketers to attract young generation. This group is broken into small group depending upon their age. The age of this group is in between 23-34 years. Young people ay significant role in family decision making and influence the buying behavior of the family. It is also help in influencing the buying behavior of the friends. Almost all companies are using the digital marketing platform to influence the young generation, specially the companies who sell consumer goods. This approach is very particular in the case of the companies selling foods, cloths, entertainment and personal electronics. The youth are very brand conscious and fill delighted when the buy the particular brand.

Popular Social media network to use by the marketer to influence the buying behavior of the youth are:

1. Face book 10. Instagram
2. Whatsapp 11. You tube
3. LinkedIn 12. Messenger
4. Tumblr 13. E-mail
5. Reddit 14. Q-Zone
6. Twitter 15. Mobile phone app
7. Snap chat 16. Pinterest
8. Messenger
9. We chat

LITERATURE REVIEW

Wysocki (1997) suggested in his research that marketers must verify the tools and technique of online before applying to the teenagers. Taylor and Cosenza (2002) the authors concluded their research that the two important factors which play important role while selection of clothing among the teenagers are look and fit. Rebecca (2002) the author defines in his research that it is necessary to draw trend setter while understanding the behavior of the teenagers. During market research this component should be included in the research. Sadia Afzal et al., (2015) the researcher found that there is no direct relationship of online and conventional advertisement on buying behavior of the consumers when consumers decide to buy the branded garments. Davidson Alistair et al (2006) while buying through online factors like price features and technology etc influenced the decision of customers in selecting particular product/ brand through online. Marcel Gommans, et al. (2001) highlighted that e customers depends upon various factors like usage of the website and technology, value delivered, customer service branding and security. Weisman (2001) in his research found that customers like to search information about the product and compare it with the online alternative, but finally they purchased by using conventional store for purchase. Brimpong (2008) in his research found that financial institutions are making more user friendly approach to do business through e banking (Kotler, 2003). The key factors which make any website trustworthy for the customer is based on the usability and available online marketing mix displayed in the website which influences the buying decisions of the customers. Ming Wang (2005) identified in their research that the factors which bring satisfaction in the mind of the customers while online shopping are Technological factors which include privacy, relevance design of the site and usability. Vachani and Vallabhbhai (2014) found in their research that across the world there is a shift in the marketing trend from traditional offline store format to a mix format of both offline and online store.

OBJECTIVE OF THE RESEARCH

1. To identify the factors influencing the buying behavior of the youth while purchasing the product or service through digital channel by the youth

RESEARCH METHODOLOGY

To achieve the objective of the research secondary source of information was used. In this random sampling technique was used. The sample size for the research was 150. A structured questionnaire was used to achieve the objective of the research. Various statistical tools were used for the analysis of the data.

In this study author has taken responses from 800 respondents out of which 500 responses were considered fit for study. 800 self-developed questionnaires were sent to different respondents out of which 500 were found to be valid and reliable for further study with a success rate of 62.50%.

Out of the successful 500 questionnaires 275 were boys and 225 were girls with a demographic profile of 55% for boys and 45% for girls.

DATA ANALYSIS

Descriptive Statistics

Descriptive Statistics shows that there is no missing data.

Table 1.

Particulars	Mean	Standard Deviation	Number of Observations
Online products/services are high in quality	3.59	1.365	500
Digital Marketing provides several products to choose	3.62	1.311	500
Online products/services have good visual appearance	3.49	1.443	500
Online products/services portfolio up to customers' expectations	3.52	1.370	500
New product/service development is a continuous phenomenon in Digital Marketing	3.63	1.367	500
Pricing policy of Online products/services provides competitive edge	3.64	1.388	500
Digital Marketing provides price comparison	3.58	1.355	500
Pricing policy of Online products/services helps in maximizing profit	3.73	1.329	500
Digital Marketing is risky due to frauds, phishing pages	3.66	1.358	500
Digital Marketing provides value for money	3.63	1.336	500
Digital Marketing provides convenient	3.69	1.286	500
Digital Marketing is appealing	3.66	1.346	500
Digital Marketing serves customers well	3.59	1.429	500
Digital Marketing is easy & understandable	3.66	1.329	500
Digital Marketing provides location benefits	3.53	1.364	500
Digital Marketing shopping is able to inform its customer about new products/services well in time	3.60	1.324	500
Digital Marketing offer free home delivery	3.67	1.318	500
The promotional policies of Digital Marketing are good enough to persuade customers	3.56	1.435	500
The promotional policies of Digital Marketing helps out in attainment of objectives	3.56	1.389	500
Digital Marketing is popular for schemes	3.52	1.344	500
What was your level of satisfaction w.r.t online shopping	3.57	1.3787	500

Descriptive

Descriptive shows that the data collected is a normal data as skewness and kurtosis for all the variable is within the range.

Table 2.

			Statistic	Std. Error
Online products/ services are high in quality	Mean		3.59	.061
	95% Confidence Interval for Mean	Lower Bound	3.47	
		Upper Bound	3.71	
	5% Trimmed Mean		3.65	
	Median		4.00	
	Variance		1.862	
	Std. Deviation		1.365	
	Minimum		1	
	Maximum		5	
	Range		4	
	Interquartile Range		3	
	Skewness		-.623	.109
	Kurtosis		-.912	.218
Digital Marketing provides several products to choose	Mean		3.62	.059
	95% Confidence Interval for Mean	Lower Bound	3.50	
		Upper Bound	3.73	
	5% Trimmed Mean		3.69	
	Median		4.00	
	Variance		1.720	
	Std. Deviation		1.311	
	Minimum		1	
	Maximum		5	
	Range		4	
	Interquartile Range		2	
	Skewness		-.719	.109
	Kurtosis		-.660	.218
Online products/ services have good visual appearance	Mean		3.49	.065
	95% Confidence Interval for Mean	Lower Bound	3.36	
		Upper Bound	3.61	

continued on following page

Table 2. Continued

			Statistic	Std. Error
	5% Trimmed Mean		3.54	
	Median		4.00	
	Variance		2.082	
	Std. Deviation		1.443	
	Minimum		1	
	Maximum		5	
	Range		4	
	Interquartile Range		3	
	Skewness		-.601	.109
	Kurtosis		-1.026	.218
Online products/ services portfolio up to customers' expectations	Mean		3.52	.061
	95% Confidence Interval for Mean	Lower Bound	3.40	
		Upper Bound	3.64	
	5% Trimmed Mean		3.58	
	Median		4.00	
	Variance		1.877	
	Std. Deviation		1.370	
	Minimum		1	
	Maximum		5	
	Range		4	
	Interquartile Range		3	
	Skewness		-.605	.109
	Kurtosis		-.900	.218
New product/ service development is a continuous phenomenon in Digital Marketing	Mean		3.63	.061
	95% Confidence Interval for Mean	Lower Bound	3.51	
		Upper Bound	3.75	
	5% Trimmed Mean		3.70	
	Median		4.00	
	Variance		1.868	

continued on following page

Table 2. Continued

			Statistic	Std. Error
	Std. Deviation		1.367	
	Minimum		1	
	Maximum		5	
	Range		4	
	Interquartile Range		2	
	Skewness		-.742	.109
	Kurtosis		-.718	.218
Pricing policy of Online products/ services provides competitive edge	Mean		3.64	.062
	95% Confidence Interval for Mean	Lower Bound	3.52	
		Upper Bound	3.76	
	5% Trimmed Mean		3.71	
	Median		4.00	
	Variance		1.926	
	Std. Deviation		1.388	
	Minimum		1	
	Maximum		5	
	Range		4	
	Interquartile Range		2	
	Skewness		-.759	.109
	Kurtosis		-.715	.218
Digital Marketing provides price comparison	Mean		3.58	.061
	95% Confidence Interval for Mean	Lower Bound	3.46	
		Upper Bound	3.70	
	5% Trimmed Mean		3.64	
	Median		4.00	
	Variance		1.835	
	Std. Deviation		1.355	
	Minimum		1	
	Maximum		5	
	Range		4	

continued on following page

Table 2. Continued

			Statistic	Std. Error
	Interquartile Range		3	
	Skewness		-.653	.109
	Kurtosis		-.846	.218
Pricing policy of Online products/ services helps in maximizing profit	Mean		3.73	.059
	95% Confidence Interval for Mean	Lower Bound	3.61	
		Upper Bound	3.84	
	5% Trimmed Mean		3.81	
	Median		4.00	
	Variance		1.766	
	Std. Deviation		1.329	
	Minimum		1	
	Maximum		5	
	Range		4	
	Interquartile Range		2	
	Skewness		-.809	.109
	Kurtosis		-.549	.218
Digital Marketing is risky due to frauds, phishing pages	Mean		3.66	.061
	95% Confidence Interval for Mean	Lower Bound	3.54	
		Upper Bound	3.78	
	5% Trimmed Mean		3.73	
	Median		4.00	
	Variance		1.844	
	Std. Deviation		1.358	
	Minimum		1	
	Maximum		5	
	Range		4	
	Interquartile Range		2	
	Skewness		-.726	.109
	Kurtosis		-.747	.218

continued on following page

Table 2. Continued

			Statistic	Std. Error
Digital Marketing provides value for money	Mean		3.63	.060
	95% Confidence Interval for Mean	Lower Bound	3.52	
		Upper Bound	3.75	
	5% Trimmed Mean		3.70	
	Median		4.00	
	Variance		1.784	
	Std. Deviation		1.336	
	Minimum		1	
	Maximum		5	
	Range		4	
	Interquartile Range		2	
	Skewness		-.753	.109
	Kurtosis		-.634	.218
Digital Marketing provides convenient	Mean		3.69	.058
	95% Confidence Interval for Mean	Lower Bound	3.58	
		Upper Bound	3.80	
	5% Trimmed Mean		3.77	
	Median		4.00	
	Variance		1.653	
	Std. Deviation		1.286	
	Minimum		1	
	Maximum		5	
	Range		4	
	Interquartile Range		2	
	Skewness		-.792	.109
	Kurtosis		-.487	.218
Digital Marketing is appealing	Mean		3.66	.060
	95% Confidence Interval for Mean	Lower Bound	3.54	
		Upper Bound	3.78	
	5% Trimmed Mean		3.74	

continued on following page

Table 2. Continued

			Statistic	Std. Error
	Median		4.00	
	Variance		1.811	
	Std. Deviation		1.346	
	Minimum		1	
	Maximum		5	
	Range		4	
	Interquartile Range		2	
	Skewness		-.778	.109
	Kurtosis		-.625	.218
Digital Marketing serves customers well	Mean		3.59	.064
	95% Confidence Interval for Mean	Lower Bound	3.46	
		Upper Bound	3.72	
	5% Trimmed Mean		3.66	
	Median		4.00	
	Variance		2.042	
	Std. Deviation		1.429	
	Minimum		1	
	Maximum		5	
	Range		4	
	Interquartile Range		3	
	Skewness		-.697	.109
	Kurtosis		-.894	.218
Digital Marketing is easy & understandable	Mean		3.66	.059
	95% Confidence Interval for Mean	Lower Bound	3.55	
		Upper Bound	3.78	
	5% Trimmed Mean		3.74	
	Median		4.00	
	Variance		1.767	
	Std. Deviation		1.329	
	Minimum		1	
	Maximum		5	
	Range		4	

continued on following page

Table 2. Continued

			Statistic	Std. Error
	Interquartile Range		2	
	Skewness		-.745	.109
	Kurtosis		-.631	.218
Digital Marketing provides location benefits	Mean		3.53	.061
	95% Confidence Interval for Mean	Lower Bound	3.41	
		Upper Bound	3.65	
	5% Trimmed Mean		3.58	
	Median		4.00	
	Variance		1.861	
	Std. Deviation		1.364	
	Minimum		1	
	Maximum		5	
	Range		4	
	Interquartile Range		3	
	Skewness		-.583	.109
	Kurtosis		-.937	.218
Digital Marketing shopping is able to inform its customer about new products/ services well in time	Mean		3.60	.059
	95% Confidence Interval for Mean	Lower Bound	3.48	
		Upper Bound	3.71	
	5% Trimmed Mean		3.66	
	Median		4.00	
	Variance		1.752	
	Std. Deviation		1.324	
	Minimum		1	
	Maximum		5	
	Range		4	
	Interquartile Range		2	
	Skewness		-.679	.109
	Kurtosis		-.698	.218

continued on following page

Table 2. Continued

			Statistic	Std. Error
Digital Marketing offer free home delivery	Mean		3.67	.059
	95% Confidence Interval for Mean	Lower Bound	3.56	
		Upper Bound	3.79	
	5% Trimmed Mean		3.75	
	Median		4.00	
	Variance		1.736	
	Std. Deviation		1.318	
	Minimum		1	
	Maximum		5	
	Range		4	
	Interquartile Range		2	
	Skewness		-.778	.109
	Kurtosis		-.547	.218
The promotional policies of Digital Marketing are good enough to persuade customers	Mean		3.56	.064
	95% Confidence Interval for Mean	Lower Bound	3.43	
		Upper Bound	3.69	
	5% Trimmed Mean		3.62	
	Median		4.00	
	Variance		2.059	
	Std. Deviation		1.435	
	Minimum		1	
	Maximum		5	
	Range		4	
	Interquartile Range		3	
	Skewness		-.677	.109
	Kurtosis		-.922	.218
The promotional policies of Digital Marketing helps out in attainment of objectives	Mean		3.56	.062

continued on following page

Table 2. Continued

			Statistic	Std. Error
	95% Confidence Interval for Mean	Lower Bound	3.44	
		Upper Bound	3.68	
	5% Trimmed Mean		3.62	
	Median		4.00	
	Variance		1.930	
	Std. Deviation		1.389	
	Minimum		1	
	Maximum		5	
	Range		4	
	Interquartile Range		3	
	Skewness		-.642	.109
	Kurtosis		-.912	.218
Digital Marketing is popular for schemes	Mean		3.52	.060
	95% Confidence Interval for Mean	Lower Bound	3.40	
		Upper Bound	3.64	
	5% Trimmed Mean		3.58	
	Median		4.00	
	Variance		1.805	
	Std. Deviation		1.344	
	Minimum		1	
	Maximum		5	
	Range		4	
	Interquartile Range		3	
	Skewness		-.595	.109
	Kurtosis		-.872	.218
Satisfaction Level w.r.t Online shopping	Mean		3.57	.062
	95% Confidence Interval for Mean	Lower Bound	3.45	
		Upper Bound	3.69	
	5% Trimmed Mean		3.63	
	Median		4.00	
	Variance		1.901	

continued on following page

Table 2. Continued

			Statistic	Std. Error
	Std. Deviation		1.379	
	Minimum		1	
	Maximum		5	
	Range		4	
	Interquartile Range		2	
	Skewness		-.674	.109
	Kurtosis		-.830	.218

Reliability Analysis of Each Factor

The values shows of Reliability Analysis shows that if the same questionnaire is filled by same respondent then what is the probability that the respondent will fill the same response. The acceptable value of reliability analysis is from 0.50 to 0.99.

Table 3. Case Processing Summary

		N	%
Cases	Valid	500	100.0
	Excluded	0.00	0.00
	Total	500	100.0

Table 4. Reliability analysis of Product factor

Reliability Statistics of Product Factor	
Cronbach's Alpha	N of Items
0.687	5

Table 5. Reliability analysis of Price Factor

Reliability Statistics of Environmental Price Factor	
Cronbach's Alpha	N of Items
0.685	5

Table 6. Reliability analysis of Place Factor

Reliability Statistics of Place Factor	
Cronbach's Alpha	N of Items
0.695	5

Table 7. Reliability analysis of Promotion Factor

Reliability Statistics of Promotion Factor	
Cronbach's Alpha	N of Items
0.658	5

Table 8. Overall Reliability analysis

Overall Reliability Statistics	
Cronbach's Alpha	N of Items
0.898	21

Findings-: The value of Cronbach's alpha for all the factors such as product, Price, Place and Promotion is more than 0.50 which means that the self-designed is reliable.

Validity Analysis

The value of KMO and Bartlett's test is 0.945 which is more than 0.50 it means that research is 94.50% valid and is adequate to carry on a Factor Analysis.

Table 9. Validity analysis

Kaiser-Meyer-Olkin Measure of Sampling Adequacy.		0.945
Bartlett's Test of Sphericity	Approx. Chi-Square	2805.247
	Df	210
	Sig.	0.000

Source: Researchers data analysis, 2020

Communalities

Communalities represents that no value is below 0.50 hence no factor is going to distort result. Therefore, no variable should be deleted during Factor Analysis.

Table 10. Communalities

	Initial	Extraction
New product/service development is a continuous phenomenon in Digital Marketing	1.000	.539
Pricing policy of Online products/services provides competitive edge	1.000	.645
Digital Marketing provides price comparison	1.000	.510
Pricing policy of Online products/services helps in maximizing profit	1.000	.592
Digital Marketing is risky due to frauds, phishing pages	1.000	.620
Digital Marketing provides value for money	1.000	.755
Digital Marketing provides convenient	1.000	.533
Digital Marketing is appealing	1.000	.543
Digital Marketing serves customers well	1.000	.722
Digital Marketing is easy & understandable	1.000	.893
Digital Marketing provides location benefits	1.000	.749
Digital Marketing shopping is able to inform its customer about new products/services well in time	1.000	.526
Digital Marketing offer free home delivery	1.000	.780
The promotional policies of Digital Marketing are good enough to persuade customers	1.000	.502
The promotional policies of Digital Marketing helps out in attainment of objectives	1.000	.518
Digital Marketing is popular for schemes	1.000	.534
What was your level of satisfaction w.r.t online shopping	1.000	.534

Scree Plot

It is evident from the Scree plot that there are possible 4 factors out of the total 21 factors that affect adoption pattern of youths in Digital Marketing.

Component Plot in Rotated Space

The component plots show that out of 21 variables all 21 variables have high or low loading and all 21 variables are represented within the 3 components.

Figure 1.

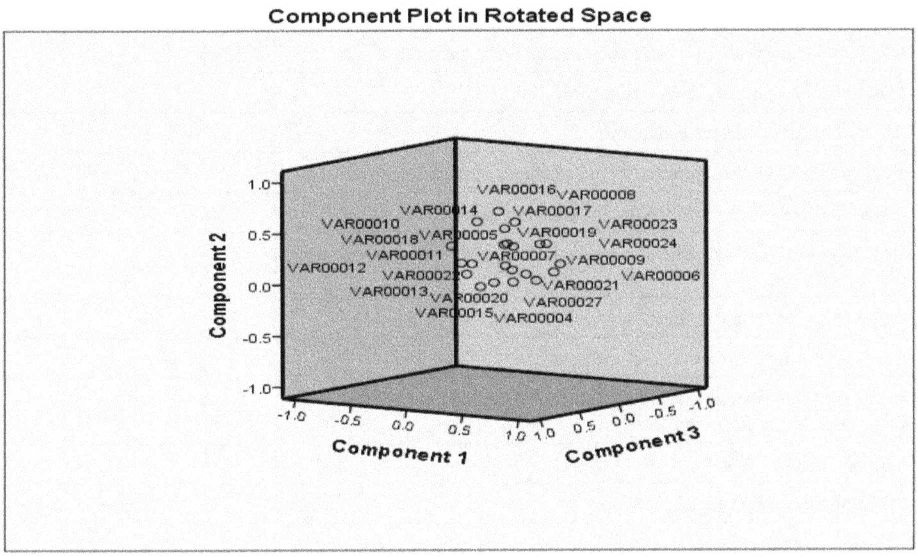

Factor Analysis

Factor Analysis shows that out of the possible 21 components 15 were found to be taken into consideration headed under 4 different factors that are most important.

These are the possible 4 factors are-:

Hence it is concluded that out of the 21 components taken for study 15 components are included under 4 factors i.e. accounting for (15/21) *100=71.43% acceptability of research. Hence result of the study is feasible.

These Factors are as follows:

1. Consumer Satisfaction
2. Policies of the Company
3. Information and Delivery Benefits
4. Additional benefits

Table 11.

Rotated Component Matrix				
	Component			
	1	2	3	4
Digital Marketing is appealing	0.703			
Digital Marketing provides value for money	0.607			
Digital Marketing serves customers well	0.579			
Online products/services portfolio up to customers' expectations	0.567			
Digital Marketing is easy & understandable				
Digital Marketing provides convenient		0.690		
Pricing policy of Online products/services helps in maximizing profit		0.619		
Digital Marketing is risky due to frauds, phishing pages		0.587		
The promotional policies of Digital Marketing are good enough to persuade customers		0.556		
Pricing policy of Online products/services provides competitive edge				
Digital Marketing provides price comparison				
Digital Marketing shopping is able to inform its customer about new products/services well in time			0.664	
Digital Marketing offer free home delivery			0.653	
Satisfaction Level w.r.t Online shopping			0.565	
New product/service development is a continuous phenomenon in Digital Marketing			0.542	
Online products/services are high in quality				
Online products/services have good visual appearance				
Digital Marketing provides several products to choose				0.741
The promotional policies of Digital Marketing helps out in attainment of objectives				0.647
Digital Marketing is popular for schemes				0.513
Digital Marketing provides location benefits				

Table 12. Factor naming

Factor 1 (Consumer Satisfaction)	Factor 2 (Policies of the company)	Factor 3 (Information and Delivery Benefits)	Factor 4 (Additional benefits)
Digital Marketing is appealing	Digital Marketing provides convenient	Digital Marketing shopping is able to inform its customer about new products/ services well in time	Digital Marketing provides several products to choose
Digital Marketing provides value for money	Pricing policy of Online products/services helps in maximizing profit	Digital Marketing offer free home delivery	The promotional policies of Digital Marketing helps out in attainment of objectives
Digital Marketing serves customers well	Digital Marketing is risky due to frauds, phishing pages	Satisfaction Level w.r.t Online shopping	Digital Marketing is popular for schemes
Online products/ services portfolio up to customers' expectations	The promotional policies of Digital Marketing are good enough to persuade customers	New product/service development is a continuous phenomenon in Digital Marketing	

FINDINGS & CONCLUSION

It is evident from factor Analysis that there is a significant relevance n Youths for digital marketing and is being highly affected by 4 factors:

1. Consumer Satisfaction
2. Policies of the company
3. Information and Delivery Benefits
4. Additional benefits

REFERENCES

Alistair, D., & Jonathan, C. (2006). anaging webmavens: Relationships with sophisticated customers via the internet can transform marketing and speed innovation. *Strategy and Leadership*, *34*(3), 14–22. doi:10.1108/10878570610660564

Brimpong, M. A. (2008). *A Project Submitted Entitled—The Effect of Customer Satisfaction on Loyalty A Case Study of First Allied Savings And Loans Ltd.* Academic Press.

Gommans, M., Krishnan, K. S., & Scheffold, K. B. (2001). From Brand Loyalty to E-Loyalty: A Conceptual Framework. *Journal of Economic and Social Research.*, *3*(1), 43–58.

Koester, A. W., & May, J. K. (1985). Profiles of adolescents' clothing practices: Purchase, daily selection and care. *Adolescense*, *20*(77), 97–113. PMID:3984818

Kotler, P. (2003). *Marketing Management* (11th ed.). Prentice-Hall International Editions.

Rebecca, A.F. (2002). *The effect of marketing on teens and how teens brain work. Inside the teenager brain.* PBS Frontline Report.

Taylor, S. L., & Cosenza, R. M. (2002). Profiling later aged female teens: Mall shopping behaviour and clothing choice. *Journal of Consumer Marketing*, *19*(4/5), 380–408. doi:10.1108/07363760210437623

Vachani, V. N. (2014). *A study to measure the impact of electronic (digital) marketing among the Gujarat based customers and firms*. Academic Press.

Wang. (2003). Assessment of E-service Quality via E-satisfaction in Ecommerce Globalization. The Electronic Journal on Information System in developing Countries, 11(10), 1-4.

Weisman, N.Y., Erokhina, I.D., & Zakharov, I.K. (2001). *Spectrum of visible mutations isolated out of wild populations of Drosophila melanogaster in 2000.* Academic Press.

Wysocki, B. J., & Wysocki, T. (1997). DS-CDMA Scheme with Reduced ISI and MAI. *Australian Telecommunications Research Institute, Design Note, RSL-DN, 002*, 1997.

Chapter 13
i-Branding as a Tool of Integrated Marketing:
An Empirical Study of Youngster Satisfaction

Sonu Dua
Lyallpur Khalsa College Technical Campus, India

Sakshi Dua
Lyallpur Khalsa College Technical Campus, India

Inderpal Singh
Lyallpur Khalsa College Technical Campus, India

ABSTRACT

i-Branding is one of the fastest-growing aspects of internet marketing. Internet marketing is still an experimental area that continues to grow, evolve, and adapt. The use of the internet as a branding tool is an important area of study since the literature on internet branding is currently in the formative stage. This study investigated the relationship of various factors with respect to customer satisfaction of youths towards purchasing through the internet. The sample size is comprised of 520 respondents from various regions of Punjab. For this purpose, CFA has been applied to analyze the customer satisfaction of internet marketing among youngsters. Finally, this chapter would help academicians as well as industry experts to analyze the potential of i-branding in the future.

DOI: 10.4018/978-1-7998-7231-3.ch013

INTRODUCTION

The concept of brand was not popular in earlier days i.e. 10-15 years ago. And it has been treated as a part of product, merely as an off-hand fashion of the product (Urde,1999). The concept of branding was again considered as an integral part of the product (Kotler,2000). Kapferer (1999) also discussed the few major concern related to the brand and it was only a sign to disclose the qualities of the product and it was also associated with tangible products and there was no significance of branding for service industry. Before 1980's, the corporate houses was having totally different approach towards the brand, the main focus was on product instead of creating distinctive place in the mind of the customer. Product was wholly solely a brand. For the service industry, service provider was considered as a brand.

In case of product, the branding efforts can be performed with the help of various others marketing activities such as packaging and labeling etc. and it was really difficult to perform branding activities for service industry, because service were less standardized, although services involved various attributes (Cobb-welgren, Rubble & Donthu,1995). Now here the importance of brand equity arises for the service industry. In case of service industry, the concept of brand equity helps the organization to get the higher profits and loyal customer, which would enable the organization to gain the competitive position in the market (Berry,2000). The concept of value services emerged as a dominant attribute, if a customer is satisfied with the services, it will directly lead to the customer loyalty.

The concept of internet branding in an initial stages of recognition in the corporate as well as academic world, so there is very less literature available pertaining to the internet branding. (Merisavo,2004 ; Ibah, 2005). During the last 8 months, due to COVID-2019, the demand of this concept has gained significant relevance. Most of the organizations, recognized the need of integrated marketing across offline and online channels. Branding on the platform of internet includes number of challenges and opportunities for the corporate world. Thus it is the need of the hour for every company to find out the impact of online platform for branding strategies

Online branding concept has so many advantages for companies, this is a platform where organization can avail the benefit of global world on the internet, even they can save the consumer time by reducing their extra search cost **(Ward and Lee, 2000).**

REVIEW OF LITERATURE

Churchill (1979) developed a paradigm for developing better measures of marketing constructs. The main objective was to suggest a procedure for developing better measures for marketing constructs. The procedure included various steps, which were as follow: 1) Specify domain of the construct, 2) Generate sample of items, 3) Collect data, 4) Purify measures, 5) Collect Data, 6) Assess reliability, 7) Develop norms. **Cobb-Walgren (1995)** studied brand equity, brand preferences and purchase intent. The main objective of the study was to measure the brand equity and to investigate the impact of brand equity on brand preferences and purchase intent. He explored four dimensions which were highly influenced from the study of Aaker four dimensions to measure the brand equity. The various dimensions which were studied such as Perceived quality, brand awareness, brand associations, advertising awareness. **Aaker (1996)** model selected as the foundation for the study. Background information were collected from surveys, reports and editorials in leading news papers on customer based brand equity and Antecedents of customer satisfaction. Several databases were then used to provide detailed information on specific research on customer based brand equity and Antecedents of customer satisfaction. These databases included EMRALD, DEEPDYVE and SSRN from which several peer reviewed academic journals were accessed. Books too formed a part of the literature review. **Aaker (1996)** explored four criteria to evaluating and tracking the brand equity over product and market. Firstly the measures should reflect the construct being measured named as brand equity. Secondly the measures should reflect constructs that truly drive the market. Thirdly selected measures should be sensitive. Lastly the measures should be applicable across brands, product categories, and markets. **Bergstrom (2000)** explored some conceptual fact about the cyber branding. The author presented some brand basics and model to build strong brand over the internet, because switching from offline to online is not straightforward task, it required significant attitudinal difference. **Ward (2000)** studied brand as a source of information over the internet. For this purpose, empirical study was conducted and result was very satisfactory, it was found that branding can facilitate consumer acceptance towards electronic commerce.

Krishnan (2001) explored Brand equity: is it more important in services?. The main objective of this study was to check whether the brand equity was important for the services as compare to goods. At the end, it was concluded that it is equally important for services industry. **Merisavo (2004)** examined the effect of e-mail marketing on brand loyalty. At the end results revealed that e-mail marketing is very important tool and it creates positive impact on brand loyalty. **Ibeh et al. (2005)** explored e-branding and communication strategies. The empirical analysis suggested that e-branding gained widespread appreciation. And the companies have applied various traditional as well as modern tools to communicate their brands to the customer. With the advancement and e-branding, companies are able to adopt localization strategies. **Simmons(2007)** explored "i-branding: developing the internet as a branding tool". The main purpose of this paper was to provide framework of branding via internet form by organizing and integrating current knowledge, assist market planners in the development of successful internet based branding strategies. **Simmons (2010)** explored Managing i-branding to create brand equity. The main aim of this study was to develop a conceptual framework to understand the concept of i-branding and implication for food industry in developing internet as branding tool and finally result was satisfactory in this regard. **Dua (2011)** studied "I-Branding as a Tool of internet marketing-an empirical study of youngsters". The main purpose of this study was to analyze the preference of internet marketing among youngsters. At the end it was concluded that that every factor was correlated with each other, and, for marketers every factor was equally important while identifying the customer on internet.

OBJECTIVE OF THE STUDY

To investigate the relationship of various factors with respect to customer satisfaction of youth behavior towards purchasing through internet.

Hypothesis of the Study

Following are the proposed hypothesis to test the primary objective of the study:

Figure 1. Conceptual Model on customer satisfaction of youth behavior towards purchasing through internet

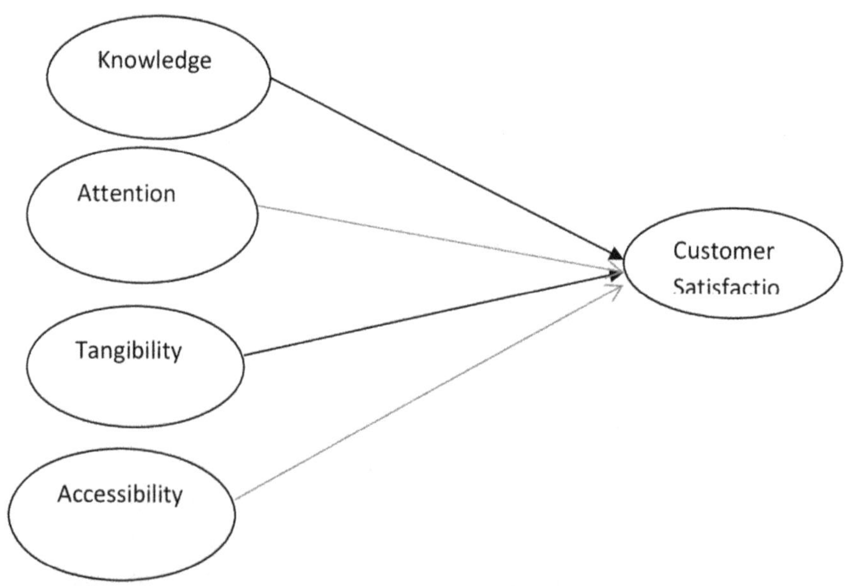

1) There is a positive relationship of Knowledge on Customer satisfaction.
2) There is positive relationship of Attention on Customer satisfaction.
3) There is positive relationship of Attitude on Customer satisfaction.
4) There is positive relationship of Accessibility on Customer satisfaction.

RESEARCH METHODOLOGY

The sample size is comprised of 520 respondents from various regions of Punjab. The sample belongs to different cities Malwa, Majha and Doaba region. Convenient Sampling has been used. The data was collected through structured questionnaire and further the data was coded to analyze the questionnaire. For this purpose, different tools have been applied to get the significant results. Various tools were CFA, SEM etc. For data analyzing, recent software's have been applied such as AMOS and SPSS

RESULTS AND DISCUSSIONS

Gender

This study consisted of 520 respondents (youth of Punjab region), out of which 300 are males and rest 220 respodents are females. Most of the male and females are working and rest are students. Table 1 indicates the contribution of both categories.

Table 1. Demographic Profile

Gender	Respondents	Percentage
Male	300	58
Female	220	42

Age

Four categories have been identified, which are described in Table 2 and the maximum respondents (male and female) lie in the category of 20-24 years which consist of almost 45 percent of the whole sample. (**Table 2**)

Table 2. Age Categories

Age	Frequency	Percentage
15-19	110	21
20-24	235	45
25-29	101	19
30 and above	84	15

Qualification

This is one of the important variable from our study point of view, because the nature of this study is dependent upon the educated respondents and the result shows that majority of the respondents are graduate i.e. 21 percent and 39 percent respondents are post graduate, which helps in gaining accurate picture of educated youth towards the various variables selected for this study. (Table 3)

Table 3. Qualification Categories

Qualification	Respondents	Percentage
10	110	21
12	100	19
Graduate	110	21
Post Graduate	200	39

Reliability of the Constructs

The reliability of the construct was assessed with the help of Cronbach's alpha. As per the reviews, the Cronbach's alpha of each construct must be higher than 0.70. (Nunnally,1978). Higher the Cronbach's alpha indicates reliable consistency among the items in the construct. The Cronbach's alpha of each construct in this study is higher than 0.70 as described in Table 4.

Table 4. Reliability of the Construct

Construct	Reliability (Cronbach's Alpha)
Knowledge (KN)	0.861
Attention (AT)	0.883
Tangibility (TN)	0.848
Accessibility (AC)	0.854
Customer Satisfaction (CUS)	0.811

Source: Result generated from SPSS

Exploratory Factor Analysis

Principal Component Analysis techniques were used to identify various constructs. five factors were extracted for this study. Only those factors were retained those Eigen value were high as compared to 1. The cumulative variance of all the factors were 63.63, which was up to the mark as per acceptable range (**Table 5**)

Table 5. Factor(s) & Eigen value Table

Factors	1 (KN)	2 (AT)	3 (TN)	4 (AC)	5 (CUS)
Eigen Value	5.050	3.289	2.880	2.684	1.520
% of variance	18.414	15.341	11.931	9.254	8.690
Cummulative Variance	18.414	33.755	45.686	54.94	63.63

Source: Result generated from SPSS

Validity Analysis: Discriminant Validity

While performing CFA and SEM, two issues have been strictly checked and verified: A) Average Variance Explained of each construct must be greater than Maximum Shared Variance. B) Average Variance Explained of each construct must be greater than Average Shared Variance. (**Table 6**)

Table 6. Comparison of Average Variance Explained, Maximum Shared Variance, Average Shared Variance and Alpha Value

Construct	Average Variance Explained	Maximum Shared Variance	Average Shared Variance	Alpha Value
Knowledge (KN)	0.614	0.033	0.012	0.861
Attention (AT)	0.602	0.023	0.008	0.883
Tangibility (TN)	0.528	0.105	0.035	0.848
Accessibility (AC)	0.540	0.105	0.041	0.854
Customer Satisfaction (CUS)	0.525	0.038	0.012	0.811

Source: Validity Master

Convergent Validity

The convergent validity could also be determined with the help of Average Variance Extracted (AVE) for each construct. The value of AVE must be 0.5 or higher for each construct. Thus, it is necessary to remove those items with low (below 0.5) factor l from the constructs otherwise that may lead to lower result during CFA.

At the time of measuring convergent validity, three issues were strictly checked and verified: (a) Alpha value of each construct should be greater than 0.7. (b) AVE of each construct must be greater than (0.50). (c) Alpha value of construct must be higher than Average variance explained (AVE) of each construct.

Table 7. Goodness of Fit Indices for Analysis

S. No	Name of Index	Results
1	Chi-square	610.71
2	Degree of freedom	352
3	Chi-square/ Degree of freedom	1.735
4	Comparative Fit Index (CFI)	0.96
5	Goodness of Fit Index (GFI)	0.93
6	Adjusted Goodness of Fit Index (AGFI)	0.91
7	Normed Fit Index (NFI)	0.92
8	Incremental Fit Index (IFI)	0.96
9	Root Mean Square Error of Approximation (RMEA)	0.03
10	Root Mean Square Residual (RMR)	0.02

Source: Output Generated from AMOS 20.0

The above table satisfied all the conditions of convergent and discriminant validity measures in all aspects. Thus it indicates that CFA can be proceed further analyzing the estimates.

After the reliability and validity measures that have satisfied all the pre-determined condition for applying the structural equation modeling's to get the desired results. **(Table 7)**

To investigate the relationship of various factors with respect to customer satisfaction of youth behaviour towards purchasing through internet

The above table showed the predicted model gave the desired. Now analysis was fit enough to perform further hypothesis testing.

HYPOTHESIS TESTING

H1: This hypothesis stated that the significant impact of knowledge of youth behavior was very important in customer satisfaction with respect to online purchasing. From the table no-8, the significant impact of knowledge was in right direction and statistically it was significant. (βeta = 0.123, $p < 0.05$). Finally it can be concluded that H1 hypothesis was significantly supported by this study.

Table 8. Brief Summary of all hypotheses

S. No	Hypothesis	Beta Value	Sig. T	Supported or Not Supported	Order of Importance
H1	**There is positive relationship of Knowledge on Customer satisfaction.**	0.423	0.001	**Supported**	**1**
H2	**There is positive relationship of Attention on Customer satisfaction.**	0.316	0.0001	**Supported**	**2**
H3	**There is positive relationship of Attitude on Customer satisfaction.**	0.223	0.001	**Supported**	**4**
H4	**There is positive relationship of Accessibility on Customer satisfaction**	0.274	0.001	**Supported**	**3**

Source: Output generated from SPSS 16.0 & Amos 20.0

H2: This hypothesis stated that the significant impact of Attention of youth behavior was very important in customer satisfaction with respect to online purchasing. From the table no-8, the significant impact of Attention was in right direction and statistically it was significant. (βeta = 0.116, $p < 0.05$) Finally it can be concluded that H2 hypothesis was significantly supported by this study.

H3: This hypothesis stated that the significant impact of Tangibility of youth behavior was very important in customer satisfaction with respect to online purchasing. From the table no-8, the significant impact of Tangibility was in right direction and statistically it was significant. (βeta = 0.116, $p < 0.05$). Finally it can be concluded that H3 hypothesis was significantly supported by this study.

H4: This hypothesis stated that the significant impact of Accessibility of youth behavior was very important in customer satisfaction with respect to online purchasing. From the above no-8, the effect of Accessibility was in right direction and statistically it was significant. (βeta = 0.223, $p < 0.05$) Finally it can be concluded that H4 hypothesis was significantly supported by this study. (**Table 8**)

CONCLUSION

This study was initiated to conclude the relationship of various factors with respect to customer satisfaction of youth behavior towards purchasing through internet. The interest in this study was to explore the new concept of i-branding. At the end, this study explained that that customer satisfaction, knowledge, accessibility and attention emerged as most significant factors which creates significant difference among gender (male and female) while purchasing or searching any product through i-branding. Several keys points have been emerged from the findings of the study. According to the conceptual model, there should be positive and direct effect of various variable on Customer satisfaction. And the results also revealed positive and direct effects of various i-branding variable on customer satisfaction. Knowledge factor emerged as one of the important as well as dominant factor in the conceptual model. And followed by the other factors such Attention, Accessibility and Attitude. And there was a significant correlation among the five factors of I-Branding. Finally it can be concluded that i-branding is creating an impact of every category of age and people and they are more satisfied with the way that the organizations are adopting to attract the customer.

SUGGESTIONS FOR FURTHER RESEARCH

At present the literature of "i-Branding" is at the initial stages. (Simmons, J) provided basic frame work for the exploration of the concept of i-branding. In this paper, we tried to analytically examine the relationship of various factors to the customer satisfaction in relation to the youth behavior towards online purchasing. Further, the researcher could enhance our study by taking different sectors. Even SERVQUAL model can also be applied in context of customer satisfaction.

Furthermore, researcher can enhance their study by using service extended marketing mix variable in i-branding.

REFERENCES

Aaker & Joachimsthaler. (2000). *Brand Leadership*. Free Press.

Aaker, D.A. (1991). *Managing brand equity*. The Free Press.

Berger, I. E., & Mitchell, A. A. (1989). The effect of advertising on attitude accessibility, attitude confidence, and attitude-behaviour relationship. *The Journal of Consumer Research*, *16*(3), 269–279. doi:10.1086/209213

Bergstrom, A. (2000). Cyberbranding: Leveraging your brand on the Internet. *Strategy and Leadership*, *28*(4), 10–15. doi:10.1108/10878570010378645

Buttle, F. (1996). *Relationship Marketing: Theory and Practice*. Chapman Hall.

Chen, A. C. (2001). Using free association to examine the relationship between the characteristics of brand associations and brand equity. *Journal of Product and Brand Management*, *10*(7), 439–451. doi:10.1108/10610420110410559

Churchill, G. Jr. (1979). A Paradigm for developing better measures of marketing constructs. *JMR, Journal of Marketing Research*, *16*(February), 64–73. doi:10.1177/002224377901600110

Cobb-Walgren, C. J., Ruble, C. A., & Donthu, N. (1995). Brand Equity, Brand Preferences, and Purchase Intent. *Journal of Advertising*, *24*(3), 25–40. doi:10.1080/00913367.1995.10673481

Court, D., McLaughlin, K., & Halsall, C. (2006). *Marketing spending effectiveness: how to winin a complex environment*. McKinsey White Paper. Available at: www.mckinsey.com

Doyle, P. (1998). *Marketing management and strategy* (2nd ed.). Prentice-Hall.

Dua, S., & Chahal, R. (2013). Interrelationship of Aaker's customer based brand equity dimensions: offering a model to banking sector. Asian Journal of Management Research, 4(2), 297-307.

Gobé, M. (2001). *Emotional branding: The new paradigm for connecting brands to people.* All Worth Press.

Ibeh, K. I. N., Luo, Y., & Dinnie, K. (2005). E-branding strategies of internet companies: Some preliminary insights from the UK. *Journal of Brand Management, 12*(5), 355–373. doi:10.1057/palgrave.bm.2540231

Keller, K. L. (1993). Conceptualizing, measuring, and managing customer-based brand equity. *Journal of Marketing, 57*(1), 1–22. doi:10.1177/002224299305700101

Kierzkowski, A., McQuade, S., Waltman, R., & Zelsser, M. (1996). Marketing to the digital consumer. *The McKinsey Quarterly, 79*(3), 5–21.

Kotler, P. (2000). M*arketing Management. The millennium edition.* Prentice Hall.

Krishnan, B. C., & Hartline, D. M. (2001). Brand equity: Is it more important in services? *Journal of Services Marketing, 15*(5), 328–342. doi:10.1108/EUM0000000005654

Lassar, W., Mittal, B., & Sharma, A. (1995). Measuring Customer-Based Brand Equity. *Journal of Consumer Marketing, 12*(4), 11–19. doi:10.1108/07363769510095270

McGovern, G. (2000). *The caring economy.* Available at: www.thecaringeconomy.com

Merisavo, M., & Raulas, M. (2004). The impact of e-mail marketing on brand loyalty. *Journal of Product and Brand Management, 13*(7), 498–505. doi:10.1108/10610420410568435

Newman, J. W., & Staelin, R. (1972). Prepurchase information seeking for new cars and major household appliances. *JMR, Journal of Marketing Research, 9*(3), 249–257. doi:10.1177/002224377200900302

Rowley, J. (2004). Just another channel? Marketing communities in e-business. *Marketing Intelligence & Planning, 22*(1), 24.

Simmon, G. J. (2007). i-Branding: Developing the internet as a branding tool. *Marketing Intelligence & Planning, 25*(6), 544–562. doi:10.1108/02634500710819932

Simmon, G. J., Traun, Y., & Thomas, B. (2007). Managing i-branding to create brand equity. *European Journal of Marketing, 44*(10), 1260–1582.

Ward, M., & Lee, M. (2000). Internet shopping, consumer search and product branding. *Journal of Product and Brand Management*, *9*(1), 6–20. doi:10.1108/10610420010316302

Chapter 14
OYO (The Journey): The Deeper Insights

Ruhi Bhardwaj
Chitkara Business School, Chitkara University, India

Namrata Sandhu
https://orcid.org/0000-0003-4428-5821
Chitkara Business School, Chitkara University, India

ABSTRACT

From a humble beginning in 2013, OYO is today the world's second-largest hospitality chain of franchised and leased hotels, living spaces, and homes. OYO has a global presence with large-scale operations in many countries. This case outlines OYO's complicated growth journey from a rapidly growing startup to an ethically maligned business venture. It also underscores OYO's business and revenue model, work culture, and growth strategies. It also provides a sneak peek about the major problems faced by OYO and how OYO should cope with these challenges.

INTRODUCTION

About OYO

OYO - "Own Your Own" is an Indian hotel chain. It is also known as OYO Rooms, Homes and Hotels. Initially known as "Oravel Stays Private Limited", OYO is today the world's second largest hospitality chain of franchised and leased hotels, living spaces and homes. OYO has a global presence with large-scale operations in India,

DOI: 10.4018/978-1-7998-7231-3.ch014

Malaysia, UK, Japan, Mexico, Sri Lanka, Indonesia, United States, UAE, Nepal, China, Philippines, Saudi Arabia, Vietnam and many more countries.

Ritesh Aggrawal founded OYO in 2013. OYO is headquartered at Gurugram, India. Aggarwal had an interesting philosophy behind starting this venture. It was his desire to *change the way people stayed away from home* that led him to start this venture.

To start with, Aggarwal first took charge of one small budget hotel in Gurugram and decided to clean it and redecorate it. He then decided to provide all the necessary amenities in the rooms such as towels, new beddings, Wi-Fi, Geysers, ACs etc. As time passed he was able to sell all the rooms. This small success encouraged him and he further leased numerous budget hotels and started selling rooms under the brand name.

PRODUCTS

OYO offers a range of interesting products listed below.

OYO Townhouse: It is a product customizable to the millennial traveler's need. Every townhouse is designed to complement its neighborhood. Each feature of the townhouse, right from the booking process to the breakfast, is engineered for convenience, comfort, affordability and efficiency.

OYO Home: OYO homes are unique, completely private beautiful homes stocked with high-quality amenities and located in serene local neighborhoods. OYO teams service OYO homes. Their USP is that they are a home away from home.

OYO Vacation Home: They are rental homes available for vacations. Their main aim is to create happiness and bright unforgettable memories for their guests, partners and homeowners.

SilverKey: It is the most suitable choice for business travelers. It has spacious rooms, professional staff and the accommodation is powered by technology. Silverkey units are located near corporate clusters. They are a home away from home, without the rules, formalities and rates of a hotel. These accommodations offer the following unique features: self-cooking counters, in-house laundry services, 24X7 caretakers, physical security, CCTV surveillance and in-house photocopying and printing.

Capital O: These are premium hotels located in the prime locations. They deliver quality experience at an affordable price.

Palette: These are OYO Resorts designed in French style. They have lush gardens and elegant social areas. They have designer rooms, private villas, beaches, spas and other recreational provisions. They deliver world-class hotel experience to the customers at competitive prices.

Collection O: These are premium hotels for stay, so that the guests enjoy a luxurious experience. These hotels are designed for guests travelling for business and leisure.

OYO LIFE: It is designed on the lines of a paying guest experience, where people can hire a room without restrictions. People can share the hired room with their friends too. OYO Life targets young professionals in search of fully managed homes with long-term rentals at affordable prices.

BUSINESS AND REVENUE MODEL

Since its inception in 2013, OYO aggressively pursued the target to attain the number one position in the global hospitality industry and became extremely successful within a short span of time (Sharma, 2020). There are five main reasons for it. One, OYO offers a very user-friendly experience. It is possible to book a room in under a minute with two or three clicks on the OYO app. Two, OYO's cheap pricing gains favor with the masses. Per day room tariffs offered by OYO are as less as INR500. Third, OYO adopted an aggressive business development policy. Its business development managers are charged with the responsibility of brining in more and more rooms, and more and more hotels under the OYO ambit to make OYO the world's number one hotel chain. Four, OYO offers flexibility. OYO does not apply strict checks to ensure that couples that hire OYO rooms are married. Most other players in this industry are extremely cautious on this front and prefer to rent rooms to only married couples. This is the reason for the popularity of OYO among youngsters. Further, OYO also offers flexibility in check-in and checkout timings. If a customer decides to use a room for 4 or 5 hours, they are more than happy with it, as it provides them the opportunity to rent out the same room to different customers with in the span of the same twenty-four hours. Five, OYO offers special discounts during festivals through the OYO app. Details of these offers are also available on various social media platforms, such as their Facebook page, Instagram page etc.

Furthermore, OYO gets most of its funding from Soft Bank Group. OYO's founder Ritesh Aggrawal has some shares, which are endorsed by his financial partners and global institutional banks.

WORK CULTURE

OYO is notorious for its work culture. Employees of OYO report that their job is very demanding. Employees are expected to be available to their customers 24X7. Consequently, employees have to answer calls on weekends, late in the evening as well as during the early hours of the day. Extended working hours interfere with the family/leisure time of the employees (Danna & Griffin, 1999; Sandhu & Prabhakar, 2012). Consequently, employees of OYO report difficulty in maintaining a good work-life balance. Further, since holidays are the busiest times for OYO employees, they do not get to enjoy festival breaks.

Employees of OYO are unhappy with their salary and incentive structure. It is their belief that their salary and incentive structure does not do justice to the amount of pressure they face at work. One of the employees of OYO, who preferred to remain anonymous, articulated her experience of working with OYO in the following words.

I have briefly worked with OYO. As an employee, my first responsibility was to seek good ratings from the customers. It was a challenging task. Further, I was responsible for handling customer shifts. This is a particularly difficult task because the customers find it very upsetting. Imagine what it is like to inform a customer who has planned to stay a particular hotel about a shift to another hotel because OYO dissolved its tie with the original hotel or entered into a payment disagreement with the hotel at the last minute. The shifting really irked the customers and our feedback and ratings suffered. It is very difficult to deal with such customers. Despite such day-to-day difficulties, I did make adequate money. It was not worth working with OYO.

AWARDS AND HONORS

OYO has received many awards, honors and accolades over the years. Some of these awards are listed in this section.

- In March 2020, Ivanka Trump (senior advisor to President Donald Trump) applauded the OYO Hotels' initiative to provide free stay to healthcare workers in the US to help the fight against the COVID19 pandemic. She described the gesture as "impactful acts of benevolence".
- In 2019, Ritesh Aggrawal (founder of OYO) featured in the
    - Bloomberg 50 list as 'The Amazingly Ambitious Hotelier'
    - Forbes's India's The Tycoons of Tomorrow' list
    - India Today's 50 Most Powerful People in India list
- Market Entrant of the Year Award, US-India Awards 2019
- Most Innovative Companies for 2019 Award, Fast Company's World's India edition
- Best Startup 2019 Award, SATTE Awards
- Topped LinkedIn's Top Startup in India maiden list in 2018
- LinkedIn recognized OYO as Top Employee Attractor in India for four consecutive years (2016-2019)

- Fast Company among the Top 10 Most Innovative Companies in India in 2018
- Startup of the Year, The Economic Times Startup Awards 2018
- TiE's QGlue Design-Led Entrepreneurship Awards 2018
- Best Travel Startup-Jury, Zee Business Travel Awards 2018
- India's Most Promising Hotel Network, Holiday IQ Better Holiday Awards 2017
- New Age Entrepreneur Award 2017, Asian Centre for Corporate Governance and Sustainability
- OneDirect Quest CX Award 2016 for Best Use of Social Media
- No.2 in BT Coolest Start-ups Survey 2016
- Startup of the Year, Express IT Award 2015

COMPETITORS

MakeMyTrip, Fab Hotels, Cleartrip, Trivago, Yatra and Treebo Hotels are the top competitors of OYO.

MakeMyTrip (MakeMyTrip Limited): It is an online travel company located in India. It was founded in 2000 and is headquartered at Gurugram, India. It provides facilities such as hotel reservations, rail tickets, bus tickets, flight tickets, domestic and international holiday packages etc.

Fab Hotels: It is a network of 3-star budget hotels in India. It was founded in 2014. Its headquarters are in Gurugram, India.

Cleartrip (Cleartrip Travel Services Private Limited): It is a global online travel company. It was founded in 2006. Its headquarters are in Dubai, UAE and Mumbai, India. It operates in the Middle East and India. It has an online travel aggregator website that books train tickets, flight tickets, hotel reservations and leisure activities packages.

Trivago: It specializes in internet-related services and products in hotels, lodging and metasearch space. It was founded in 2005. Its headquarters are in Germany.

Yatra (Yatra.com): It is an Indian online travel agency and travel search engine. It was founded in 2006. Its headquarters are in Gurugram, India.

Treebo (Treebo Hotels): It is an Indian budget hotel chain. It operates on a franchise model. It was founded in 2015. Its headquarters are in Bangalore, India.

MAJOR PROBLEMS

Carelessness in the facilities provided created major problems for OYO (Weinberg, 2020). During the initial years, OYO ensured that each and every facility, ranging from good food to Wi-Fi was provided to its customers. However, due to large-scale expansion, and that too in many countries, OYO was unable to closely monitor the quality of services provided. The consequent deterioration in service quality forced people to provide negative feedbacks and negative ratings for the services delivered by OYO. During this time, OYO also earned bad press. Many articles were published in newspapers and magazines that heavily criticized OYO. OYO lost favor with customers and its business suffered. The losses created a ripple effect – profits fell and many employees were fired. Further, OYO's relations with various hotels and their managers also suffered. Due to the continual bad feedback and delay in payments made to hotels by OYO, a lot of unpleasantness was created. In some cases it led to fights, in others it led to cancellation of contracts between the hotels and OYO.

Figure 1.

ET

TOP NEWS

APP

Oyo to sack 5,000 worldwide as business catches a cold

The Covid-19 outbreak, which has ravaged the world's second-largest economy, has hit the hotel room aggregator's operations in China, Oyo group CEO Ritesh Agarwal told Bloomberg in an interview on Wednesday.

By **ET Bureau** | Updated: Mar 05, 2020, 08.19 AM IST

BCCL - Non Copyright

Ritesh Agarwal told Bloomberg that Oyo's global headcount will be about 25,000 after the dismissals. It has a total of 20,000-22,000 employees in just India and China.

Figure 2.

ET | TOP NEWS | APP

Oyo likely to lay off 2,000 people by January end

By Anumeha Chaturvedi, **ET Bureau** | Updated: Dec 20, 2019, 09.14 AM IST

One of the people cited earlier said the company is looking to save on manpower costs by the end of January.

Figure 3.

ET tech.com

Oyo is laying off around 2,400 employees in India, may let go more in March

Layoffs are primarily in the mid-level management, business development, sales & operations roles

Biswarup Gooptu & Aditi Shrivastava | ETtech Updated: January 17, 2020, 17:20 IST

Figure 4.

ET | TOP NEWS | APP

Oyo plans to lay off sales staff

About 60 salespeople in Oyo's New Delhi and Gurgaon offices were the first to be fired and got their letters on Monday.

By Anumeha Chaturvedi, **ET Bureau** | Aug 22, 2019, 08.45 AM IST

The move to let go of some sales staff in India could be linked to business and operations getting affected because of disputes between Oyo and some hotel partners, said sources.

ETHICAL ISSUES

To highlight some of the ethical issues at OYO the authors have shared primary qualitative data collected from some ex-employees of OYO. (Use of qualitative data is recommended to capture sensitive issues (Sandhu, 2016)). These respondents though willing to share their views and experiences, preferred to stay anonymous. They shared their experiences with the authors in the following words.

I want to share one incident that involves a person who used an OYO room in Shimla. My team and I were mandated to collect 5 or 4 star ratings from customers of OYO. So, it was customary for us to make pre-check-in calls to the customers and provide the contact number of the hotel managers/owners. We also asked the customers to get in touch with us in case of any difficulty. One night I received a call at 12:05 AM. I was shocked, but despite the odd hour I decided to answer the call. On the other side was an irate customer whose driver could not locate the hotel. The customer though that I was the receptionist and he could talk to me in which ever manner he deemed fit.

Further, how is it possible to seek a 5 or 4 star rating from a dissatisfied customer? As difficult as the task is, it is equally unethical.

Figure 5.

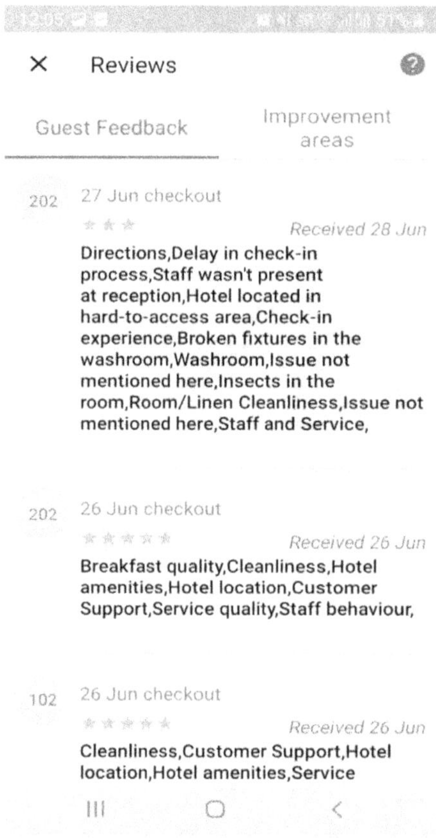

Figure 6.

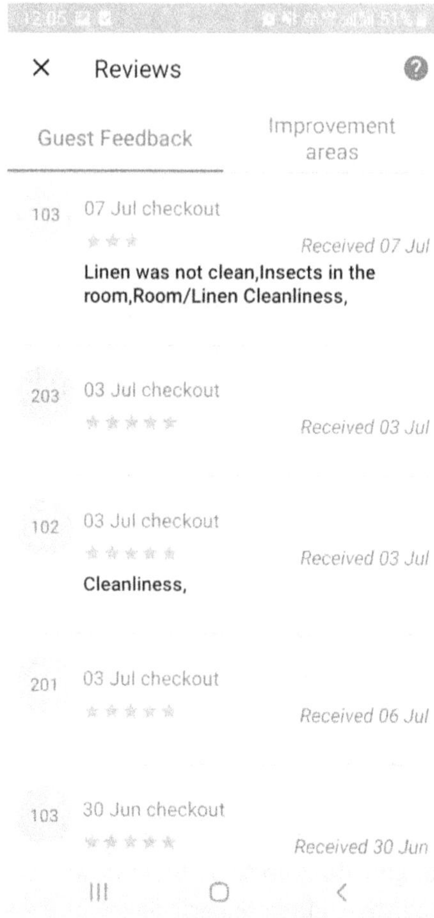

The behavior of the hotel owners towards the OYO staff is extremely rude. Such rudeness is unwarranted. The primary issue is delayed payments by OYO. Fights between hotel owners and OYO area managers have led to many police cases. The fights have also been the cause of many newspaper and magazine articles written against the services provided by OYO.

OYO employees are grossly overworked and underpaid. Weekends are as busy as weekdays. The culture is very disappointing.

I worked day and night for the company. All I earned was disappointment.

OYO was doing great business, but due to some mistakes OYO faced many problems (Alpeyev & Hyuga, 2020). All stakeholders, in particular the hotel owners, ex-employees and customers provided negative public and private feedback (Goel & Singh, 2020; Kaushik, 2020). Some hotel owners also terminated their contracts with OYO due to its growing bad reputation. Many controversial statements and stories were published in newspapers/magazines and aired on television. As a result, OYO lost business and had to resort to mass firing of employees (Chaturvedi, 2020; "Oyo to sack 5,000 worldwide as business catches a cold", 2020). Softbank also ended its tie-up with OYO.

REFERENCES

Alpeyev, P., & Hyuga, T. (2020, August 19). Softbank dispatches senior executives to turn around struggling Oyo. *The Economic Times*. https://economictimes.indiatimes.com/small-biz/startups/newsbuzz/softbank-dispatches-senior-executives-to-turn-around-struggling-oyo/articleshow/77626156.cms?from=mdr

Chaturvedi, A. (2020, January 21). Layoffs, rejig one-time exercise, will soon be over: Oyo CEO. *The Economic Times*. https://economictimes.indiatimes.com/small-biz/startups/newsbuzz/layoffs-rejig-one-time-exercise-will-be-over-soon-oyo-ceo/articleshow/73395167.cms

Danna, K., & Griffin, R. W. (1999). Health and well-being in the workplace: A review and synthesis of the literature. *Journal of Management*, *25*(3), 357–384. doi:10.1177/014920639902500305

Goel, V., & Singh, K. D. (2020, January 2). At SoftBank's jewel in India: 'Toxic' culture and troubling incidents. *The New York Times*. https://www.nytimes.com/2020/01/02/technology/oyo-softbank-india.html

Kaushik, M. (2020, March 8). Mystery of the Oyo rooms. *Business Today*. https://www.businesstoday.in/magazine/cover-story/mystery-of-the-oyo-rooms-ritesh-agarwal-investors-business-model/story/396392.html

Oyo to sack 5,000 worldwide as business catches a cold. (2020, March 5). *The Economic Times*. https://economictimes.indiatimes.com/small-biz/startups/newsbuzz/softbank-backed-oyo-to-cut-about-5000-jobs-in-overhaul/articleshow/74477429.cms?from=mdr

Purnell, N., & Dvorak, P. (2021, January 1). Oyo hotel chain suffered ailments beyond pandemic's travel slowdown. *The Wall Street Journal.* https://www.wsj.com/articles/oyo-hotel-chain-suffered-ailments-beyond-pandemics-travel-slowdown-11609525294

Sandhu, N. (2016). Behavioural red flags of fraud - A qualitative assessment. *Journal of Human Values, 22*(3), 221–237. doi:10.1177/0971685816650579

Sandhu, N., & Prabhakar, R. (2012). Factors influencing the quality of work life in the Indian banking industry – An empirical study. *International Proceedings of Economics Development and Research, 55*(23), 115–119.

Sharma, P. (2020, August 7). Oyo: A room with a 'troubled' view. *Forbes.* https://www.forbesindia.com/blog/business-strategy/oyo-a-room-with-a-troubled-view/

Weinberg, C. (2020, February 27). How SoftBank-backed chain Oyo lost its way in the U.S. *The Information.* https://www.theinformation.com/articles/how-softbank-backed-hotel-chain-oyo-lost-its-way-in-the-u-s?utm_source=google&utm_medium=cpc&utm_campaign=11543929116_112520154917&utm_content=477036477316&utm_term=dsa-304667822056&gclid=Cj0KCQjwp86EBhD7ARIsAFkgakhPU0VYBc-pURYtMVKeOCzwaZcz6vDztXx0ciQNUeIKt0GpssXnE8waAt2fEALw_wcB

ENDNOTE

It is time for OYO to constructively respond to its bad image. OYO must take concrete steps to rebuild its reputation in the market (Purnell & Dvorak, 2021). The feedback received from the hotel owners and customers should be critically reviewed with a view to take corrective action. Further, customer complaints related to food and service quality should be satisfactorily redressed. OYO should work on improving its reviews, which is the way to attract customers these days. OYO should also sincerely work on building and nurturing relationships with hotel owners. They are a key stakeholder in the overall business model of the company. Goodwill of the hotel owners will also help OYO acquire more properties.

Chapter 15
Social Media Marketing as New Marketing Tool

Sonal Trivedi
Chitkara Business School, Chitkara University, India

Reena Malik
Chitkara Business School, Chitkara University, India

ABSTRACT

Businesses are growing rapidly. They are using different strategies to connect customers. In this process, marketing is the most important thing. Most people use social media, and it has become one of the best platforms for marketing products. On social media, people can share their views and opinions and also get knowledge about the product and its updates. One of the fundamental reasons for utilizing social media in marketing is as a specialized apparatus that makes the organizations open to those interested in their products and makes them visible to the individuals who have no information of their products. These companies utilize social media to make a buzz and learn from and target customers. Therefore, companies need to look at various social media platforms where their customers exist. In this chapter, the concept of social media marketing is discussed with some practical examples of companies applying social media marketing tools.

INTRODUCTION

Economic development is the procedure by which a nation improves the prosperity of its natives through political or financial methods, is impacted by an assortment of components, including Marketing. The term is regularly mistaken for economic

DOI: 10.4018/978-1-7998-7231-3.ch015

growth, which alludes to an expansion in the capacity of an economy to create products or administrations after some time (Sheoran et al. 2018). Truth be told, economic development is just a single critical factor in the financial advancement of a region.

Marketing is viewed as the most critical action in a business enterprise while at the beginning period of advancement it was viewed as the last activity (Mago, 2017). For convenience, the significance of marketing might be clarified as follows:

i) Conveyance of Standard of Life to the General Public:

Present day marketing dependably goes for consumer satisfaction (Diaconescu, 2020). Along these lines, the fundamental obligation of marketing is to create goods and services for the society as per their necessities and tastes at a sensible cost.

ii) Reduction in Distribution Cost:

Through effective marketing, the organizations can diminish their distribution expenses to a great extent (Blazheska, Ristovska & Gramatnikovski, 2020). Reduction in the expense of distribution straightforwardly influences the costs of products in light of the fact that the expense of distribution is an important piece of the complete cost of the item.

iii) Enhancing Employment Opportunities:

Marketing contains advertising, sales, distribution, branding and a lot more exercises (Štrach, 2018). So, the advancement of marketing naturally offers to ascend to a requirement for individuals to work in a few zones of marketing. Along these lines, the business openings are conceived.

iv) National Income Growth:

The successful task of marketing activities creates, maintains and builds the demand for products and enterprises in the society (Subhashini & Kowsalya, 2020). To satisfy this expanded need the organizations need to build the dimension of production thus raising their income. This expansion, thusly, builds the national income.

Social Media Marketing can be communicated as the process toward making matter that marketers have customized to the setting of every social media platform so as to initiate client participation and belongingness (Duffett, 2017). But every social media platform is different and hence same content can be shared on all platforms, for few platforms video is apt and for few images can work better (Wang & Kim, 2017). Following graphic shows, the various available social media platforms.

One of the fundamental reasons for using social media in marketing field is that it provides direct information to the company related to customer preferences and awareness regarding their product (Keegan & Rowley, 2017). Additionally, companies use social medial to create buzz for their product in the market (Vinerean, 2017). Social media marketing is applicable at each stage of marketing from customer acquisition to customer retention.

LITERATURE REVIEW

Dwivedi et al. (2020) in their paper explained the opportunities and issues in social media marketing specially related to ethical issues, electronic word of mouth, B2B marketing, mobile marketing, digital content management and artificial intelligence. The findings of the study show that there are ample opportunities of technology like VR and AI in the field of social media marketing.

Jacobson, Gruzd & Hernández-García (2020) studied in their paper the requirement for professional norms in use of consumer data for social media marketing by marketers. The study recommends strategy for marketers to mitigate the concerns of consumers regarding use of their information on social media.

Iankova et al. (2019) explored in their paper the fundamental difference in usage and perceived importance of social media marketing. The study concludes that social media marketing is of less significance as communication channel in B2B.

Chen & Lin (2019) studied the impact of activities of social media marketing on purchase, participation and continuance intention of consumer. The findings of the study show that activities of social media marketing indirectly influence the perceived value and identification of goods.

Tafesse & Wien (2018) studied the impact of social media on company's marketing strategies. The study covers social media analytics, customer engagement initiatives, active presence, and social media strategy.

Bilgin (2018) studied the impact of social media marketing on brand loyalty, brand image and brand awareness. The findings of the study suggest that social media marketing has positive influence on brand image and is most effective in creating brand awareness. It was also found that social media marketing develops brand loyalty also.

Felix, Rauschnabel & Hinsch (2017) in their study explored social media marketing governance, networks and hierarchy, poles of modernism and conservations, social media marketing culture, and generic dimensions. The study also suggests a framework for social media marketing which fulfills the objective and mission of organization.

Alalwan et al. (2017) in their study reviewed and examined 144 articles on social media marketing. The areas which were covered in these articles were impact of social media marketing on firm's performance and brand, customer relationship management, e-WOM and advertisements. After review of these articles, the paper also suggests the scope of future studies in the field of social media marketing.

Godey et al. (2016) focused on the influence of social media marketing activities on creation of brand equity and behaviour of customer. The study was conducted over around 850 luxury brands and measured five parameters of social media marketing i.e. WOM, customization, trendiness, interaction and entertainment. The finding of the study suggested that there is positive influence of social media marketing on brand equity.

Stephen (2016) studied five themes of social media marketing i.e. eWOM, mobile environment, consumer behavior, digital advertising and digital culture. The study throws light on various aspects of consumer experience related to digital environment. The study concludes that majorly social media marketing revolves around eWOM and other aspects are not discovered. Thus, the study suggests that there is requirement of exploring wider scope of social media marketing.

Zhu & Chen (2015) studied the impact of social media advertising on buying decision of consumer of US. The study presents the typology of social media marketing on the basis of following categories – creative outlet, collaboration, self-media and relationship. The finding of the study shows how each element cater to need of consumer.

Dwivedi, Kapoor & Chen (2015) reviewed the literature of 71 articles based on social media marketing to understand SMM as new marketing channel. This study suggests the gap in the field of social media marketing and scope for future research.

Constantinides (2014) studied the present status, effects and nature of social media to understand its role as agent for customer empowerment. The findings of the paper recommend two strategies for social media marketing i.e. passive approach and active approach. Using social media marketing as customer voice is passive approach and using social media marketing as PR channel or direct marketing is active approach. The paper also suggests the future scope of research.

Dahnil et al. (2014) reviewed academic literature related to adoption of social media marketing by SMEs. The finding of the research suggests the level of adoption of social media marketing at global level.

Vinerean et al. (2013) studied the people interacting online and engage in communicating directly about brand. The study was conducted over around 250 social media users and different segments of social media users were identified. The findings of the study are useful for marketers to approach different social media users with different social media marketing strategy.

Paquette (2013) conducted a vast literature review to recognize the concept of social media marketing, virtual brand community, consumer motives, user generated content, and viral advertising. The study also suggests that there is scope of further study on social media marketing opportunities for small retailers.

Saravanakumar & SuganthaLakshmi (2012) explained in their paper the need for companies to realise the significance of social media marketing, use it as promotion mix, use it as communication channel and to build brand equity.

Erdoğmuş & Cicek (2012) focused on the influence of social media marketing on the brand loyalty of consumer. The study was conducted over 338 people who at least follow one brand on social media. The findings of the study suggest that brand loyalty of consumer is positively influenced when consumer directly offers applications on social media, appears on various platforms, offers popular content, offers relevant content and advantageous campaigns.

Neti (2011) explained in his paper the concept of social media marketing, its benefit, growth, strategies, relevance and role in marketing. The findings of the study suggests that social media marketing is gaining popularity day by day and other organizations should also adopt it as marketing strategy.

Akar & Topçu (2011) shows in their study the factors affecting the attitude of consumer towards social media marketing. The study was conducted over undergraduate students to understand their attitude over 32 items. The finding of the study shows that there are six factors which affects the attitudes of consumer.

Hoffman & Fodor (2010) in their study showed paths to effective social media strategy and relevant metrics for social media applications organized by key social media objectives.

Fogel (2010) in his paper studied the current issues in brand and product measurement conversation in social media. The finding of the study shows that companies should include eWOM in their advertising strategy.

Mangold & Faulds (2009) argued in their paper social media as a part of promotion mix. The paper present two views – one traditional and other non-traditional. The traditional view says that social media allows company to talk directly to consumer while non-traditional view says that social media allows consumer to converse with each other which is not control of manager.

Ray (2009) studied the impact of social media marketing investments and explained four perspective for marketers – risk management, brand management, digital and financial perspective.

Reuben (2008) in his paper studied 148 universities which are using social media as their marketing mix to reach their target customers. The popular social media platforms identified in this study are Twitter, Flickr, YouTube, MySpace, and Facebook.

The literature review shows that large companies, small businesses, universities and small retailers are using social media marketing in their promotion mix. But social media marketing is still seen as eWOM and its other application are still to be explored. Additionally, it shows that there is no framework for managers to control the WOM on social media. It also shows that there is a gap for research on scope of AI in social media marketing.

RESEARCH METHODOLOGY

Research Aim

The aim of the study is to identify social media marketing as a tool for companies to reach to the end consumer and create brand awareness. The research is done by thorough literature review using journals, book and other data in electronic form. The data from one company using social media in their promotion mix was collected and analyzed.

Research Strategy

The current study is conducted through case study method. Case study method is a method where a situation in analysed in depth (Harrison et al. 2017). Thus, case study method is a descriptive method where a situation is explained and analysed in depth. In the present study, the case of Coco-Cola company is taken to analyse the use of social media marketing by company.

Research Objective

1. To identify and analyse the way organizations are using social media marketing.
2. To identify the advantages and disadvantages of social media marketing to businesses.

Research Approach

The research approach used in the current study is deductive as the researcher has first identified the research problem and defined the research questions and then used case study method to identify the impact of social media marketing on businesses. Deductive approach was used in the present study as it helps in establishing relationship between two variables (Woiceshyn & Daellenbach, 2018) i.e. social media marketing in promotion mix of businesses.

Type of Research

The current research is descriptive research as the present study provides answers to research questions of 'how' companies are applying social media marketing and 'what' are its advantages and disadvantages. As descriptive research provides answers to questions like how, what, when and where (Kothari, 2004).

Collection of Data

In the present study, the data is collected from secondary sources such as official statistics, public documents, books, newspaper, magazines, articles, journals, and website of selected company. Secondary data is the data which exists either in published or electronic format (Noor, 2008). The data is collected in a way which ensures integrity (Marczyk and DeMatteo, 2005). Collection of secondary data is more convenient for researcher and further clears the research objective of the researcher.

CASE STUDY

Coca Cola and Facebook

As we all know that coca cola is one the biggest beverage brand in the market selling 3900 beverage choices and in 200 countries with over more than 500 brands. "We communicate exactly the same thing today as we did 125 years ago," M. Berquet (Director of Marketing, Coco-Cola) said, "and that is Coke's unique taste. We try to achieve brand love by communicating that message, and we have always been guided by the same principles: be unique, be simple, be honest and tell brand stories." According to him, brand image can be built through consistency. In one of the tests conducted in 2014, the blindfolded subjects were able to undoubtedly recognize only two shapes i.e. one of egg and another coke bottle. That is definitely an achievement.

One of the contributing factors for this success is the social media marketing on various social media platforms majorly Facebook (Rauschnabel, Praxmarer & Ivens, 2012). Coke uses many Facebook interfaces and products in its use that includes a news feed, posting ads, logout experience, etc. Coke worked with Starcom MediaVest to use the full range of Facebook products and the results that were analyzed with a study conducted by the Kantar Worldpanel study on the same in 2013.

The most noteworthy move of the Facebook marketing took place in 2013 when Coca- Cola launched a multichannel campaign and television and FB focusing a return of the polar bear family made by Ridley Scott (Refer figure 1). The 6-minute promotional video takes their journey across the Arctic and learns about leadership.

This Advertisement was broadcast on television into a 30-sec spot in prime time. Over a 3 days period, the company decided to use the FB target block using the logout experience i.e. the ad used to play when the users logged out of their Facebook accounts.

Figure 1. Coco-cola TV commercial used on FB
Source - digitaltveurope.com

As already mentioned the company is a popular brand in more than 20 countries and hence it has a different strategy of marketing to cover the diverse culture in these countries. Facebook has played a very important role in their social media strategy and we will consider success story for the most profitable cases where Facebook has played a significant role to help coke make huge ROI.

European Partners

The European partners of the company coke used the help of a local agency named PauwR Digital marketing to study the local market and audiences and device methods that increase the sale of the product in the local areas (Deighton & Kornfeld, 2011). For this reason, they made advertisements that were both local and personal. They devised the call to an action method, where people were invited to come and try the Fuze Tea which was absolutely free and claimed to return money back if they did not like the product on a refund page available to the customers.

Two types of advertisements were used to link ads and carousel method (Refer figure 2). The former was used if the vendor used to keep only one type of product/ flavor and the latter if the vendor has multiple products of flavor.

Facebook contributed very heavily in the entire campaign by helping got make advertisements by using Facebook APIs and the company was able to make over 10,000 + ad creatives as a part of 2,500 ad sets. With the help of this API, the company produced mathematical and statistical adjustments and increase campaign output.

Figure 2. Coke ad on Facebook
Source - www.cocacolaep.com/sustainability/this-is-forward

Coke Brazil

In the autumn of 2017, the coke campaigns with the help of eight Brazilian singers which were Simone and Simaria, Anitta, Luan Santana, Projota, Solange Almeida, PablloVittar, Thiaguinho, Valesca, and Ludmilla (Refer figure 3). The photos of these singers were made available on the coke cans and the final goal was a contract of a musical video by the top 3 singers that were picked by the audience at the end of the promotion (Kačániová & Bačíková, 2016). The winning trio of the promotional campaign was PablloVittar, Simone and Samaria and Luan Santana and hence came the record hit "Hasta la Viste".

Coke's and Facebook's partnership on this campaign involved a number of elements, let it be #FanFeat project, live broadcast of the trio' show and messenger live voting of their famous artist, etc. The company not only invested in FB but also

Figure 3. Coke Facebook partnership campaign
Source - oglobo.globo.com

much other social media feeds including Vertical Video, Live, Instant Experience ads, ads, Stories, and Insta feed. The result of this strategy was humongous and it was estimated that 3.6 million people were reached in 2 hours and around 600,000 views on Facebook live for a show in Sao Paulo.

Coke Taiwan

Targeting the audience in the age group of 11-20 and 20-30 who were interested in music and drinks, a multilevel campaign as launched consisting of the following objectives:

- To introduce a new bottle design
- The new bottles picturized 3 popular music artists who made promotional videos to make that the point the coke make summer fun and favorable (Refer figure 4).

The company also announced a launch of a new Messenger Bot along with a short video ad. The video was an adaptation of the tv commercial and it was converted in carousel format and uploaded in Instagram stories. It basically advertised the 3 artists featuring new Coca-Cola bottles. When people clicked on the advertisement it takes

Figure 4. Picture of 3 popular music artists on Coco-Cola bottles
Source – Perez, 2020

them to the bot which asked the people questions, increasing interest, and traffic. It encouraged a fun, personal, one-to-one interaction and also created awareness about the promotion in the target audience of young adults. It also created encouraged them to participate in Coca- Cola's lucky draw.

Coke and YouTube

Coco-Cola had created its own channel on YouTube with the objective to target young audience which spend their maximum time on iPhones, YouTube and Facebook (Refer figure 5).

Google as of late appealed that YouTube carries a ROI which 78% greater than television advertisements, with the research proposing that companies ought to spend anyplace between five to 25% of their advertisement spending plan on the channel.

The medium "CokeTV'' is a strategy adopted by Coke to catch the attention of social media generation. It is adjoined by Dodie Clark and vloggers Emmanuel "Manny" Brown. This idea was influenced from the success of marketing strategy of Red Bull (Brownbill, Miller & Braunack-Mayer, 2018). The marketing strategy adopted by Red Bull to connect to young generation was to present itself as an energy drink by sponsoring various thrilling sports. It widespread its marketing campaign from all possible digital channels to its own TV channel named RebBull TV.

Figure 5. CokeTV GB and Ireland
Source - Reporter, 2016

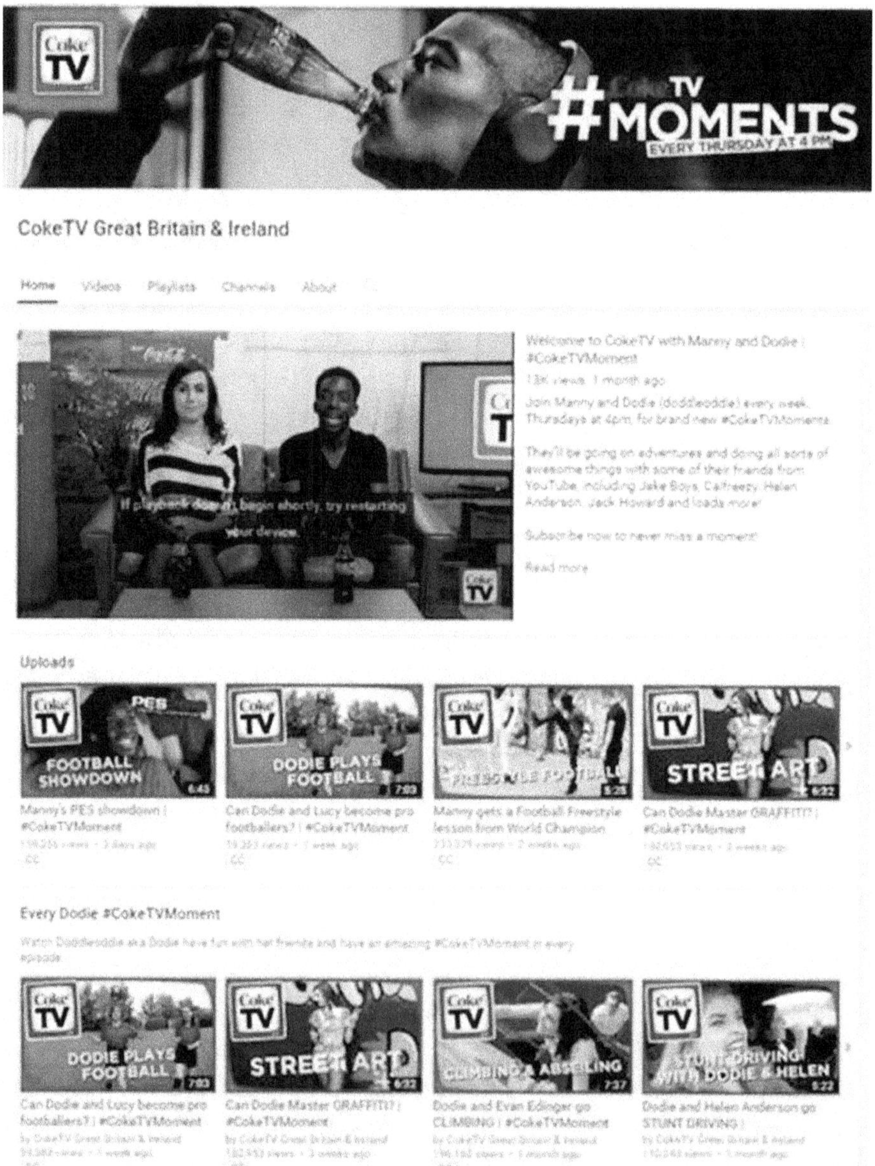

Coke entered into social media marketing but a bit late from its other competitors. Coke started its own YouTube channel in 2014. But as it is well said its never too late, So Coke at least made its presence on YouTube. It added to Coke's other marketing strategies. It also opted catchy tag lines to attract the attention of consumers. It also added varieties in its product line. It also product line with zero or low sugar content. The marketing Director 'Bobby Britain' says that CokeTV is different from others because it speaks the language of its customers.

"It will be the most engaging platform to reach young adults in GB and Ireland, entertaining them with relevant and authentic content, uniquely served in a way only Coca-Cola can," Britain added.

CASE ANALYSIS

Facebook

Case Analysis of the Coke Investment

The entire promotion was largely aimed at creating brand awareness. Using its campaign as a medium Coca-Cola wanted to encourage people to participate in various activities using FB adding as a compliment to the television resulting in a direct impact in sales. Delivering the message to a wider audience this strategy reaped incredible results. According to a study, Facebook leads in incremental sales with an ROI greater than all other media:

- Over 1.4 million unique shoppers reached
- Facebook was able to obtain 27% incremental sales with a mere 2% of gross media budget.
- 18% of the total potential buyers were exposed on the Facebook campaign.
- 3.6 times greater Return of Investment than television ROI.

Case Analysis of the Coke Investment in the European Market

According to Pieter Voogt, Managing Director, PauwR Digital Marketing "This campaign was a win-win-win for Coca-Cola European Partners, the vendors, and customers. For Coca-Cola European Partners Nederland, it provided the ideal solution to supporting thousands of outlets with local relevancy at scale. For vendors, that meant new customers and for the customers themselves, they got to try Fuze Tea for free." During the February–April 2018 campaign, Coca-Cola European Partners saw more than 32,000 people in the Netherlands try Fuze Tea for free.

- Over 1.4 million unique shoppers reached
- 32,170 offers redeemed

Case Analysis of the Coke Investment Brazil

Coca-Cola utilized the music as a base to reach out to the youth on Facebook in a new and way which was notably compelling, giving the target audience a chance to take part in the promotion and campaign. The entire success was only possible because of the combined result of Coca-Cola, FB, JWT, and KOLAB. This promotional method came out to be world's most intelligent way to form a community of fans and approach by giving them a cause and innovative formats like a celebration of the outcome and hand album

- 20-point ad recall in the second phase of the campaign
- 8-point increase in brand favourability
- 8-point increase in top-of-mind for association with music

Case Analysis of the Coke Investment Taiwan

Coca-Cola wanted to engage teens and young adults through its summer 2018 campaign to improve brand favourability as well as brand interest. The results were highly favorable for the company and the major credibility goes to the users of the Bot. The one to one interaction method boosted brand favourability and many customers were engaged with the brand via the bot to the Messenger to show their love for the videos, releasing quality results.

- 65% of the target audience reached
- 22% lift in sales in convenience store channel compared to before the campaign
- 15.6 interactions per person on Messenger

YouTube

In order to handle diminishing popularity of its image among the millennials, Coca-Cola chose to dispatch a channel on Youtube. Youtube is the most-well known video-sharing stage and is extremely mainstream among the youth. Coca-Cola began with youth-driven campaigns like "Share a-Coke" which was an enormous success. For connecting with much more prominent audience Coca-cola began working together with well-known youtubers. Coke has various videos on YouTube which are shot with Athletes, performing artists, and trending youtubers and these videos were trending in top 100.

In Croatia, a Youtube Talent show was launched. The point of the show was to discover new talent from among a huge number of Youtube users..

KPIs

The Key Performance Indicator of Coke marketing strategy is that it keep on submitting new videos on daily basis, kept those videos short and got various followers and likes on YouTube. The cost of this advertisement strategy was low and its reach and impact on people was high. The video of Coke which motivated viewers to share the bottle of coke got millions of likes and share. Thus, this strategy ensures that the video is effective, liked by people and reached to million of viewers. Additionally, it does not cost any additional money to company. It was all possible because of growing popularity of social media and smartphones and availability of internet everywhere.

CONCLUSION

Social media has been a very important source of marketing especially in recent times and many companies rely on the same. Let it be the newer companies who rely majorly on social media for marketing or let it be older companies who are shifting their traditional television advertisement-based approaches to social media marketing ones and earning huge profits. The case study of Coca-Cola confirms the statement as we have seen the shift from their traditional based approaches to social media ones. Facebook, Twitter, and YouTube play a very significant role in the same and location-based strategy is a cherry on a cake to customize the marketing pattern and model as per the geographical and cultural needs to ensure better results. Hence we conclude that social media marketing is a very significant method or part in any marketing strategy.

REFERENCES

Akar, E., & Topçu, B. (2011). An examination of the factors influencing consumers' attitudes toward social media marketing. *Journal of Internet Commerce*, *10*(1), 35–67. doi:10.1080/15332861.2011.558456

Alalwan, A. A., Rana, N. P., Dwivedi, Y. K., & Algharabat, R. (2017). Social media in marketing: A review and analysis of the existing literature. *Telematics and Informatics*, *34*(7), 1177–1190. doi:10.1016/j.tele.2017.05.008

Bell, E., & Bryman, A. (2007). The ethics of management research: An exploratory content analysis. *British Journal of Management*, *18*(1), 63–77. doi:10.1111/j.1467-8551.2006.00487.x

Beverage, F. (2020). *Coca-Cola TV Commercial, 'Snow Polar Bear' Song by Edvard Grieg*. Retrieved 9 November 2020, from https://www.ispot.tv/ad/ZIai/coca-cola-snow-polar-bear-song-by-edvard-grieg

Bilgin, Y. (2018). The effect of social media marketing activities on brand awareness, brand image and brand loyalty. *Business & Management Studies: An International Journal*, *6*(1), 128–148. doi:10.15295/bmij.v6i1.229

Blazheska, D., Ristovska, N., & Gramatnikovski, S. (2020). The impact of digital trends on marketing. *UTMS Journal of Economics (Skopje)*, *11*(1).

Boyatzis, R. E. (1998). *Transforming qualitative information: Thematic analysis and code development*. Sage.

Brownbill, A. L., Miller, C. L., & Braunack-Mayer, A. J. (2018). The marketing of sugar-sweetened beverages to young people on Facebook. *Australian and New Zealand Journal of Public Health*, *42*(4), 354–360. doi:10.1111/1753-6405.12801 PMID:29972262

Chen, S. C., & Lin, C. P. (2019). Understanding the effect of social media marketing activities: The mediation of social identification, perceived value, and satisfaction. *Technological Forecasting and Social Change*, *140*, 22–32. doi:10.1016/j.techfore.2018.11.025

Clarke, V., & Braun, V. (2013). Teaching thematic analysis: Overcoming challenges and developing strategies for effective learning. *The Psychologist*, *26*(2).

Constantinides, E. (2014). Foundations of social media marketing. *Procedia: Social and Behavioral Sciences*, *148*, 40–57. doi:10.1016/j.sbspro.2014.07.016

Dahnil, M. I., Marzuki, K. M., Langgat, J., & Fabeil, N. F. (2014). Factors influencing SMEs adoption of social media marketing. *Procedia: Social and Behavioral Sciences*, *148*, 119–126. doi:10.1016/j.sbspro.2014.07.025

Dahnil, M. I., Marzuki, K. M., Langgat, J., & Fabeil, N. F. (2014). Factors influencing SMEs adoption of social media marketing. *Procedia: Social and Behavioral Sciences*, *148*, 119–126. doi:10.1016/j.sbspro.2014.07.025

Deighton, J., & Kornfeld, L. (2011). *Coca-Cola on Facebook*. Harvard Business School Marketing Unit Case, (511-110).

Diaconescu, M. (2020). Some considerations regarding the new trends in marketing approaches. *Romanian Economic Journal, 23*(77), 2–10.

Duffett, R. G. (2017). Influence of social media marketing communications on young consumers' attitudes. *Young Consumers, 18*(1), 19–39. doi:10.1108/YC-07-2016-00622

Dwivedi, Y. K., Ismagilova, E., Hughes, D. L., Carlson, J., Filieri, R., Jacobson, J., ... Kumar, V. (2020). Setting the future of digital and social media marketing research: Perspectives and research propositions. *International Journal of Information Management*, 102168. doi:10.1016/j.ijinfomgt.2020.102168

Dwivedi, Y. K., Kapoor, K. K., & Chen, H. (2015). Social media marketing and advertising. *The Marketing Review, 15*(3), 289–309. doi:10.1362/14693471 5X14441363377999

Erdoğmuş, İ. E., & Cicek, M. (2012). The impact of social media marketing on brand loyalty. *Procedia: Social and Behavioral Sciences, 58*, 1353–1360. doi:10.1016/j.sbspro.2012.09.1119

Felix, R., Rauschnabel, P. A., & Hinsch, C. (2017). Elements of strategic social media marketing: A holistic framework. *Journal of Business Research, 70*, 118–126. doi:10.1016/j.jbusres.2016.05.001

Fogel, S. (2010). Issues in measurement of word of mouth in social media marketing. *International Journal of Integrated Marketing Communications, 2*(2).

Godey, B., Manthiou, A., Pederzoli, D., Rokka, J., Aiello, G., Donvito, R., & Singh, R. (2016). Social media marketing efforts of luxury brands: Influence on brand equity and consumer behavior. *Journal of Business Research, 69*(12), 5833–5841. doi:10.1016/j.jbusres.2016.04.181

Harrison, H., Birks, M., Franklin, R., & Mills, J. (2017, January). Case study research: Foundations and methodological orientations. In *Forum Qualitative Sozialforschung/ Forum: Qualitative. Social Research, 18*(1).

Hoffman, D. L., & Fodor, M. (2010). Can you measure the ROI of your social media marketing? *MIT Sloan Management Review, 52*(1), 41.

Iankova, S., Davies, I., Archer-Brown, C., Marder, B., & Yau, A. (2019). A comparison of social media marketing between B2B, B2C and mixed business models. *Industrial Marketing Management, 81*, 169–179. doi:10.1016/j.indmarman.2018.01.001

Jacobson, J., Gruzd, A., & Hernández-García, Á. (2020). Social media marketing: Who is watching the watchers? *Journal of Retailing and Consumer Services, 53*, 53. doi:10.1016/j.jretconser.2019.03.001

Kačániová, M., & Bačíková, Z. (2016). Emotional aspects of Facebook textual posts a framework for marketing research. *European Journal of Science and Theology, 12*(6), 187–197.

Keegan, B. J., & Rowley, J. (2017). Evaluation and decision making in social media marketing. *Management Decision, 55*(1), 15–31. doi:10.1108/MD-10-2015-0450

Kothari, C. R. (2004). *Research methodology: Methods and techniques*. New Age International.

Mago, Z. (2017). New trends of marketing communication based on digital games. *European Journal of Science and Theology, 13*(6), 171–182.

Mangold, W. G., & Faulds, D. J. (2009). Social media: The new hybrid element of the promotion mix. *Business Horizons, 52*(4), 357–365. doi:10.1016/j.bushor.2009.03.002

Marczyk, G., DeMatteo, D., & Festinger, D. (2005). *Essentials of research design and methodology*. John wiley & sons, Inc.

Neti, S. (2011). Social media and its role in marketing. *International Journal of Enterprise Computing and Business Systems, 1*(2), 1-15.

Noor, K. B. M. (2008). Case study: A strategic research methodology. *American Journal of Applied Sciences, 5*(11), 1602–1604. doi:10.3844/ajassp.2008.1602.1604

Paquette, H. (2013). *Social media as a marketing tool: A literature review*. Academic Press.

Perez, L. (2020). *Pin on Love Coca Cola*. Retrieved 9 November 2020, from https://www.pinterest.com/pin/597078863078710815/

Rauschnabel, P. A., Praxmarer, S., & Ivens, B. S. (2012). Social media marketing: How design features influence interactions with brand postings on Facebook. In *Advances in Advertising Research* (Vol. 3, pp. 153–161). Gabler Verlag. doi:10.1007/978-3-8349-4291-3_12

Ray, A. (2009). *The ROI Of Social Media Marketing*. Marketing.

Reporter, D. (2016). *Endemol Shine Beyond, Coca Cola Create Coketv*. Digital TV Europe. Available at: https://www.digitaltveurope.com/2016/07/19/endemol-shine-beyond-coca-cola-create-coketv/

Reuben, R. (2008). *The use of social media in higher education for marketing and communications: A guide for professionals in higher education*. Academic Press.

Santana & Juntos. (2020). Retrieved 9 November 2020, from https://oglobo.globo.com/cultura/musica/luan-santana-pabllo-vittar-simone-simaria-lancam-clipe-juntos-22647128

Saravanakumar, M., & SuganthaLakshmi, T. (2012). Social media marketing. *Life Science Journal*, *9*(4), 4444–4451.

Sheoran, M., Kumar, D., Kumar, V., & Verma, D. (2018). Understanding the trends of marketing research and its future directions: A citation analysis. *The Bottom Line (New York, N.Y.)*, *31*(3/4), 191–207. doi:10.1108/BL-04-2018-0022

Singh, Y. K. (2006). *Fundamental of research methodology and statistics*. New Age International.

Stephen, A. T. (2016). The role of digital and social media marketing in consumer behavior. *Current Opinion in Psychology*, *10*, 17–21. doi:10.1016/j.copsyc.2015.10.016

Štrach, P. (2018). Emerging Trends in Marketing Communications: Personalization and Eventization. *Marketing Identity*, *6*(1/1), 160-167.

Subhashini, M., & Kowsalya, M. (2020). Recent trends in marketing environment. *Studies in Indian Place Names*, *40*(40), 439–446.

Tafesse, W., & Wien, A. (2018). Implementing social media marketing strategically: An empirical assessment. *Journal of Marketing Management*, *34*(9-10), 732–749. doi:10.1080/0267257X.2018.1482365

This is Forward. (2020). Retrieved 9 November 2020, from https://www.cocacolaep.com/sustainability/this-is-forward/

Triangulation, D. S. (2014, September). The use of triangulation in qualitative research. *Oncology Nursing Forum*, *41*(5), 545–547. doi:10.1188/14.ONF.545-547 PMID:25158659

Vartanian, T. P. (2010). *Secondary data analysis*. Oxford University Press. doi:10.1093/acprof:oso/9780195388817.001.0001

Vinerean, S. (2017). Importance of strategic social media marketing. *Expert Journal of Marketing*, *5*(1).

Vinerean, S., Cetina, I., Dumitrescu, L., & Tichindelean, M. (2013). The effects of social media marketing on online consumer behavior. *International Journal of Business and Management*, *8*(14), 66. doi:10.5539/ijbm.v8n14p66

Wang, Z., & Kim, H. G. (2017). Can social media marketing improve customer relationship capabilities and firm performance? Dynamic capability perspective. *Journal of Interactive Marketing*, *39*, 15–26. doi:10.1016/j.intmar.2017.02.004

Weimer, W. B. (1979). *Notes on the methodology of scientific research* (No. 507.2 W45). Academic Press.

Woiceshyn, J., & Daellenbach, U. (2018). Evaluating inductive vs deductive research in management studies. *Qualitative Research in Organizations and Management*, *13*(2), 183–195. doi:10.1108/QROM-06-2017-1538

Zhu, Y. Q., & Chen, H. G. (2015). Social media and human need satisfaction: Implications for social media marketing. *Business Horizons*, *58*(3), 335–345. doi:10.1016/j.bushor.2015.01.006

Chapter 16
Developing a Framework to Study the Impact of Contingent Factors on Business Performance Using Strategic Cost Management:
A Meta-Analysis Study

Tanvi Verma
Chitkara Business School, Chitkara University, Punjab, India

Rashmi Aggarwal
Chitkara Business School, Chitkara University, Punjab, India

ABSTRACT

In the present scenario, cost and management accounting techniques have proved their effectiveness in decision making as they provide value creation. Therefore, the need for transforming traditional cost and management accounting to strategic cost management has been recognized. Manufacturing or service industries continuously seek to achieve business performance with the help of strategic cost management using contingency theory. This chapter provides a semi-systematic review of the articles and research papers examining major themes found in the literature focusing on the impact of various factors that are contingent in nature on the business performance through usage of strategic cost management. Systematic analysis of literature identified numerous relevant articles and research papers in eminent journals. The results indicated that there exists an interrelationship among variables, and the finding supports the central proposition of contingency theory where business performance increases with the usage of strategic cost management and contingent factors.

DOI: 10.4018/978-1-7998-7231-3.ch016

INTRODUCTION

Researchers have been exploring techniques of cost and management accounting along with their application, contingent factors and their effect on business performance over a couple of decades (Godil & Shabib-ul-hasan, 2018). It provides managers as well as internal staff shareholders with economic and financial information (Weygandt, Kimmel, and Kieso, 2010). This indicates that cost and management accounting play a vital role in the success and failure of the organization as it leads to effective decision- making of the company.

Some creative cost and management accounting methods have been presented in recent literature (Abdel-Kader & Luther, 2008; Zawawi & Hoque, 2010; Pavlatos, 2018). In the current business scenario, which is marked by constant competitive pressure, industries need to explore innovative strategies related to cost management and shall work on cost reduction which is a premise for value generation in order to achieve long term profitability and survival. Strategic cost management place greater reliance on strategic cost analysis which enables a firm to develop a framework for identification of superior strategies like cost leadership or differentiation with the help of strong information base so that a firm can achieve competitive advantage (Savić et al., 2014). It also leads to effective coordination between strategies, cost structure and organizational resources (Henri, Boiral, & Roy, 2016). This statement shows that one of the most important strategy is cost leadership in order to achieve an edge over competitors in the present challenging environment (Savić et al., 2014). So this aims at developing a sound and coherent framework by using contingency theory perspective. This paper aims to review studies focusing on impact of various factors that are contingent in nature on the business performance through usage of strategic cost management in manufacturing as well as services industries. This entails development of various themes depicting interrelationships among variables like contingent factors, strategic cost management and financial and non-financial business performance.

REVIEW OF LITERATURE

Numerous researchers examined the inaccuracy of traditional costing approaches because it focuses primarily on cost control and not on gaining competitive advantage and revenue growth, leading to the adoption of new cost accounting techniques in the manufacturing and service industries (Jinkens & Yallapragada, 2010; Messner, 2016; Pavlatos, 2015; Auzair, 2015). Strategic cost management is an ideology and a combination of methods that help define the company's future and compare it to conventional cost management (Kumar & Shafabi, 2011). The value provided by SCM and its array of accounting systems have been incorporated to provide a sustainable competitive advantage to the manufacturing and service industries (Savić et al., 2014). Liu (2015) also emphasized on the importance of SCM in modern businesses to strengthen the competitiveness of businesses.

In an attempt to gain competitive advantage, several researches about the use of contemporary strategic management techniques in companies were conducted and a perspective was taken from the respondents (Janjić et al., 2017). Another author (Sulanjaku & Shingjergji, 2015) aimed at evaluating the SCM framework and defining the most commonly used SCM accounting instruments. SCM strategies are used to prepare and execute short-term and long-term decisions, which in turn leads to cost savings as well as an enhancement in product value.

The SCM methods were initially introduced by Guilding et al. (2000) which also helped in identifying criteria for recognizing as to how a specific cost technique can be considered as strategic. SCM's key feature suggests a long- futuristic approach with highly centered context. Taking this point of view into consideration, SCM techniques shall incorporate two key elements: extrinsic business environment and long-term strategic approach. Guilding et al. (2000) found twelve Strategic cost management techniques from existing literature, then Cravens and Guilding, 2001

Figure 1. Strategic cost management techniques
Source: *"Cadez, S., & Guilding, C. (2008). An exploratory investigation of an integrated contingency model of strategic management accounting. Accounting, Organizations and Society, 33(7–8), 836–863. https://doi.org/10.1016/j.aos.2008.01.003"*

Costing	1. Attribute costing (Bromwich, 1990; Roslender and Hart, 2003) 2. Life-cycle costing (Czyzewski and Hull, 1991; Shields and Young, 1991; Dunk, 2004) 3. Quality costing (Heagy, 1991; Belohlav, 1993) 4. Target costing (Monden and Hamada, 1991; Cooper and Slagmulder, 1999) 5. Value-chain costing (Hergert and Morris, 1989; Shank and Govindarajan, 1992; Dekker, 2003)
Planning, control and performance measurement	1. Benchmarking (Elnathan et al; 1996, Brownlie, 1999) 2. Integrated performance measurement (Kaplan and Norton, 1992; 1996; Ittner et al, 2003; Libby et al, 2004; Chenhall, 2005)
Strategic decision-making	1. Strategic costing (strategic cost management) (Shank and Govindarajan, 1988; 1993; Shank, 1996) 2. Strategic pricing (Simmonds, 1982; Rickwood et al, 1990) 3. Brand valuation (Guilding, 1992; Cravens and Guilding, 1999)
Competitor accounting	1. Competitor cost assessment (Simmonds, 1981; Jones, 1988; Bromwich, 1990; Ward, 1992) 2. Competitive position monitoring (Simmonds, 1986; Rangone, 1997) 3. Competitor performance appraisal (Moon and Bates, 1993)
Customer accounting	1. Customer profitability analysis (Bellis-Jones, 1989; Ward, 1992; Zeithaml, 2000) 2. Lifetime customer profitability analysis (Foster and Gupta, 1994; Jacob, 1994) 3. Valuation of customers as assets (Slater and Narver, 1994; Foster and Gupta, 1996; Zeithaml, 2000)

introduced 3 additional approaches. Thus, Cadez and Guilding (2008) gathered 16 SCM techniques from previous literature and divided the techniques further into five major categories.

Most studies have used contingency theory approach as a method to analyze strategic cost control (Guilding, 1999; Chenhall & Langfield-Smith, 1998; Simons, 1987; Cinquini & Tenucci, 2010; Anderson & Lanen, 1999; Sayilar, 2016; Fisher, 1995). Otley (2016) indicated that wider view of contingency theory should be adopted so that individual firms are more concentrated. Following the same context, in a comprehensive contingent model, the impact contingent factors like strategic choices, company size and business orientation was analyzed by Cadez and Guilding (2008) on SCM and then mediating effect of SCM on business performance was also investigated. Several researchers have provided multiple contingent factors, depending upon the usage of strategic cost management. Such contingent factors include concentrating on major groups of contingencies: the external environment, technology and operational dimensions (Haldma & Lääts, 2002). There was also an attempt to examine the relationship between the contingent factors such as the policy, size, technology, national culture, structure, nature of the environment and control systems and usage (Chenhall, 2003; Cinquini & Tenucci, 2010). Other factors that can drive SCM use are: perceived environmental uncertainty, market orientation, Intensity of competition, quality of information system (IS) information in service and manufacturing industries (Pavlatos, 2015; Al-Mawali, 2015). An effect of coordination between strategies which competitive and strategic cost management was also examined for small manufacturing firms to obtain competitive advantages (Melo & Leone, 2015).

Several researches have been carried out in the context of strategic cost management (SCM) practices implemented by industries in India and how they influence business performance (Ganapaiah, 2017). There has been substantial empirical research into the relationship between management accounting usage and performance (Alamri, 2019). According to 'contingency-based' studies, "fit" is best defined as a cohesion between contingency factors and technique of strategic cost management (Chenhall, 2003). Studies investigating the same context claimed that when contingent factors like strategy and its choices, efficient cost and management accounting systems and improved organizational design will have an appropriate match among each other, organizational performance will automatically be improved (Jermias & Gani, 2004). The effect of contingent factors, including: organizational configurations, strategic choices, management accounting systems, and size of the company on the usage of SCM and in addition, its mediating effect on the performance of firms and the effectiveness of business units has been found in many studies (Alamri, 2019; Jeremias & Gani, 2004; Pavlatos, 2018). A collaboration has been defined between SCM including target costing and financial performance, along with non-financial performance including balance score card (Stanley, 2017; Yilmaz & Baral, 2010). The positive effect of advanced manufacturing technology, the implementation of Total Quality Management (TQM), Total Productivity Maintenance and the engagement of manufacturing managers in the strategic formulation on the competitiveness of the firm and the performance of manufacturing companies were also documented in the literature (Tracey et al., 1999; Fuentes et al., 2006; Al-Naser & Mohamed, 2017; Sahoo, 2018).

Semi -Systematic Literature Review

Figure 2. Flow of information through the different phases of a semi- systematic review

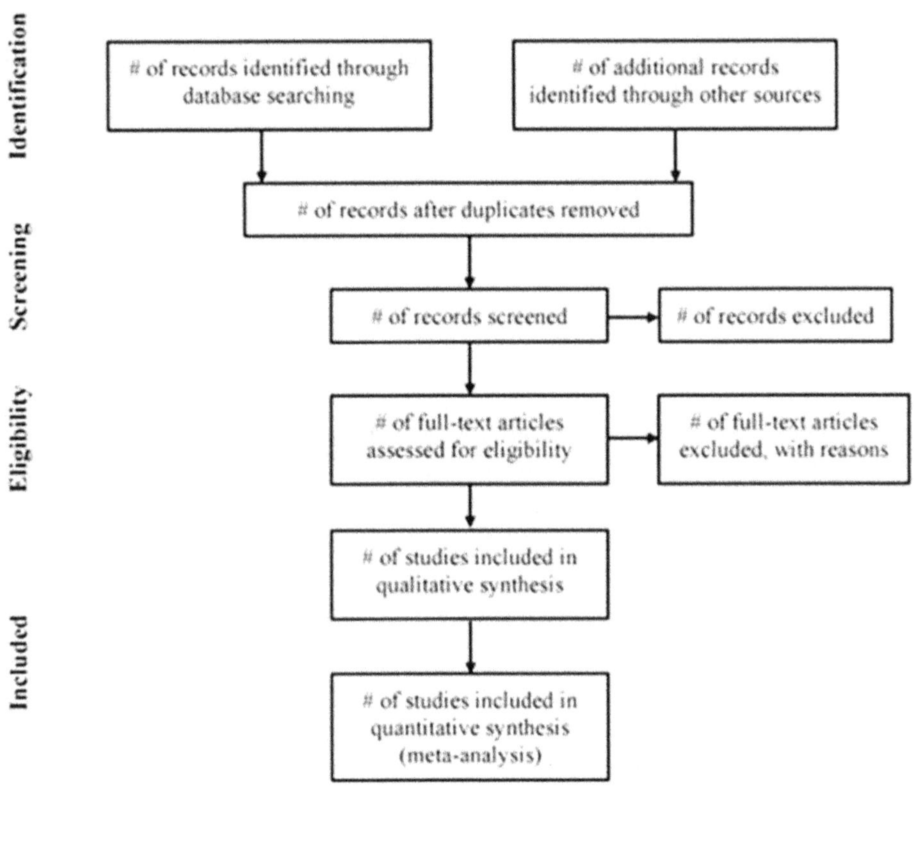

RESEARCH QUESTIONS

1. To what extent does contingent factors impact business performance?

2. To what extent does SCM adoption and usage mediates the relationship between contingent factors and business performance?

OBJECTIVES OF THE STUDY

1. To identify the important contingent factors that affect SCM adoption and usage and business performance.
2. To identify the dimensions of business performance.
3. To review studies exploring the interrelationship between contingent factors and business performance.
4. To review studies exploring the interrelationship between strategic cost management and business performance.
5. To review studies investigating the role of strategic cost management as a mediator on the relationship between contingent factors and business performance.

THEMES

1. The important contingent factors that affect SCM adoption and usage and business performance.

Among various theories of organizations, Structural contingency theory was the initial framework which was developed. It arose when organizational research studies were converged and developed since the 1950s with the help of open system theory. The basic concepts taken as base for the study were as organizational structure and environment and the interrelationship between them. The theory is established on organizational survival and success, thus considering and analyzing the relationships between organizations and their surrounding environment in context of their relevance to business performance. It mainly emphasized on inventing which factors in an organization lead to sustainability and growth. This also points out the compatibility between contingencies determined by characteristics of the organization. The theory indicates that contingencies identified by external environmental uncertainty, business strategy, technology and size of organization involve specific organizational structures (Sayilar, 2016).

The problem of fit between an organization and its contingent factors has been a focus for theory building and study in recent years. The changing economic climate has increased interest in improving the efficiency of organizational business processes and thereby leading to effective business performance (Trkman, 2010).

The theory of contingency claims that there is not a single optimal way to organize and an organizational approach that is successful in a particular scenario may not be effective in others (Fiedler, 1964). Organizations should adapt appropriate strategies and structure which is suitable to the environment to ensure smooth operations (Patrick et al., 1999). In other words: the optimum style of organization is dependent on different constraints, and there is no standardized of doing it. Burns and Stalker (1961), quoted by Fargnoli et al. (2012), were the originators of a research where there was usage of contingency approach. Interviews in British industries were taken in order to determine whether there was any association among these industries' administrative activities and its external environment. The findings showed a positive association. Therefore, the authors deduced that different organizational structure exists for different operational environment. Investigation was grounded on the perspective that environment arbitrates organization's structure and its functioning.

Fargnoli et al. (2012) investigated the interrelationship between organizational structure and technology. Findings indicated that there is impact of technology on the organizational structure and behavior, and this association results in improved organizational performance. According to Otley (1980), it is the assertion that the doctrine of theory of contingency is that all organizations within different locations do not have a commonly relevant accounting system. The selection of appropriate systems will therefore rely on the organizational circumstances. Chenhall (2003) found that the surge of contingency research is to explore the management accounting practices and how the selection of contingent variables is being practiced. Reported contingent factors which explain the effectiveness of cost management in organizations were size, organizational structure, technology, strategy, environment and organizational culture (Junqueira et al., 2016). Although usage of Contingency Theory and research on cost and management accounting is current, some time ago its interrelationship with organizational factors was also recognized. Many researchers like Haldma and Lääts (2002), Baines and Langfield-Smith (2003), Chenhall (2003), and Ahmad (2012) have acknowledged the interrelationship between contingent factors and management accounting and it resulted in the discovery of most common contingent factors like, intensity of competition, organizational performance, decentralization, technology, environment, organization size, organizational structure, strategy and culture. According to Chenhall (2003), the primary aim for implementing the paradigm for contingency theory is based on reasons like: the contingency framework would include probable causes for various applications of management accounting methods like performance measures (Otley, 1980). Next, analytical base is supplied by contingency framework (Jones, 1985). Ultimately, the contingency framework is an analytical system that enables this study to establish specific hypotheses and statistically evaluate them, based on the variables selected such as technology, TPM, organizational culture and strategy

(Xiao et al, 1996). Fisher (1995) highlighted the concept of Contingency Theory and it indicated various factors like external environment, mission and competitive strategy, technology, firm and industry variables and knowledge and observability factors. Langfield-smith (1997) analyzed the association between management control systems and business strategy using contingency approach. Major focus was on one of the most important contingent factor-Strategy. Strategic typologies focused on strategic variables like defenders, prospectors and analyzers (Miles &Snow, C1978), Strategic positioning involved cost leadership, differentiation and focus (Porter, 1980, 1985) and Strategic mission was build-hold-harvest-divest (Gupta & Govindarajan, 1984). Fuentes et al. (2006) explored the association between strategy and TQM and their effect on organizational performance. In strategy, the focus was on various strategic dimensions like Cost leadership (cost reduction efforts, price cutting ability of the firm), Marketing differentiation (brand image, marketing channels and service and advertising investment) and Innovation differentiation (Lee & Miller, 1996; Lee, 1989). Fakhri et al. (2009) also investigated the impact of contingent factors on the business performance of organizational performance of banking industry in developing countries. Contingent factors included organizational structure, organizational size, business strategy and level of competition. Pertusa-Ortega et al. (2010) analyzed how the structure of an organization impacts organizational performance by evaluating the same with competitive strategy on a sample of Spanish firms. The dimensions of organizational structure were Centralization, Complexity and Formalization (Cruz and Camps, 2003; Aiken et al., 1980; Miller and Dro¨ge, 1986; Miller 1992, 1987b; Pelham and Wilson, 1996). Strategic dimensions were Innovation differentiation, Marketing differentiation and Low cost (Miller, 1987b, 1988). Trkman (2010) proposed an underlying theoretical framework by utilizing contingency theory which majorly concentrated on the compatibility between business environment and process. Contingent factors were strategic alignment, investment level and level of employee's specialization. Sayilar (2016) examined the historical background, various theoretical developments along with a detailed description on structural contingency theory. The theory mainly emphasized on factors like strategy, size, technology, environment and structure. Strategy included product and price differentiation. Technology was based on three parameters- process of production, amount of variability and information technology. Environment factor focused on unpredictability, degree of competition, amount of change and resource munificence.

2. Dimensions of Business Performance

Research on performance measurement has grown immensely over the past decade, as reflected in the extensive literature. All non-financial & financial perspectives were included .The increased attention given by managers, consultants

Figure 3. Review of past studies on contingent factors
Source: *Author's own representation.*

Title	Year	Author	Journal	Focus	Contingent Factors
The Contingency Model and the Dynamics of the Leadership Process	1978	Fred E. Fiedler	Advances in experimental social psychology	Contingency Model	Organizational turbulence, leadership experience, training, and job rotation.
Contingency-based research on management control systems: Categorization by level of complexity	1995	Fisher, Joseph	Journal of Accounting Literature	Research on contingency theory and management control in complex organizations.	External environment, competitive strategy and mission, technology, unit, firm and industry variables and knowledge and observability factors.
Rainfall, commerce and politics	1997	Langfield-Smith, K I M	Science	Research on relationship between management control systems and business strategy	Strategy
Using information-processing theory to understand planning performance relationships in the context of strategy	1999	Patrick, Patrick. R Miller, Alex Judge, William. Q	Strategic Management Journal	Examining the importance viewing planning processes within the context of strategic orientation. (Patrick et al., 1999)	Strategy
Management control systems design within its organizational context: Findings from contingency-based research and directions for the future	2003	Chenhall, Robert H.	Accounting, Organizations and Society	Investigating the effectiveness of management control system with contingency theory.	Size, structure, environment, strategy, national culture and technology.
Total quality management, strategic orientation and organizational performance: The case of Spanish companies	2006	Fuentes, M. Mar Fuentes Montes, F. Javier Lloréns Fernandez, Luis M.	Total Quality Management and Business Excellence	Focus on relationship between strategy and total quality management (TQM) and their impact on business performance.	Strategic dimensions, TQM
The Impact of Contingent Factors on the Use of Performance Measurement System in the Banking Industry: The Case of Libya	2009	Fakhri, Gumma Menacere, Karim Pegum, Roger	A paper accepted for presentation at Salford Postgraduate Annual Research Conference	Focus on impact of contingent factors on organizational performance (financial and non-financial) of banking industry in developing countries	Organizational size, structure, level of competition and business strategy
The critical success factors of business process management	2010	Trkman, Peter	International Journal of Information Management	Creating a fit between business environment and business process by utilizing contingency theory	Strategic alignment, level of it investment, performance measurement, level of employee's specialization.
Competitive strategy, structure and firm performance: A comparison of the resource-based view and the contingency approach	2010	Pertusa-Ortega, Eva M. Molina-Azorin, José F. Claver-Cortés, Enrique	Management Decision	Focus on examining the impact of organizational structure and competitive strategy on organizational performance	Organizational structure and Strategy
The Past, Present and Future of Structural Contingency Theory	2016	Sayılar, Yücel	Industrial Relations and Human Resources Journal	Research on structural contingency theory	Strategy, size, technology, environment and structure
The effect of strategic choices and management control systems on organizational performance	2016	Junqueira, Emanuel Dutra, Eduardo Vieira Filho, Helio Zanquetto Gonzaga, Rosimeire Pimentel	Revista Contabilidade e Financas	Examination of effect of various strategic choices and management control system on business performance	Strategic choices
Contingent factors that influence the use of management accounting peactices in the Portuguese textile and clothing sector	2016	Akaisa Afonso Leite, Paula Odete Fernandes, Joaquim Mendes Leite	The International Journal of Management Science and Information Technology	Analyzing and verifying the relationship between management accounting practices and contingency factors	Competition, products diversity, organization size, importance of cost information for decision making and advanced production technology

and academicians to performance assessment reflects increased pressure on organizations to enhance efficiency and performance (Hoque, 2004). In addition to the contingency theory literature, practice of accounting methodologies and performance of business can get impacted from the environment of an entity (Otley, 1980; Ittner and Larcker, 2003a). In conjunction with that Otley (1999) examined that performance measurement frameworks used in one business may not be ideal for another facing specific circumstances. Earlier studies used different parameters to assess the efficiency of the company in terms of multidimensional construct, i.e. financial and non-financial indicators (Sarkindaji et al., 2014). Performance of an organization was evaluated by using instrument evolved by Govindarajan (1984) and then it was used by Chong and Chong (1997), Abernethy and Guthrie (1994), Chenhall and Langfield-Smith (1998), Abernethy and Stoelwinder (1991) and Govindarajan and Gupta (1985). Therefore, in order to evaluate the effect of contingent factors with adoption and usage of SCM, performance can be evaluated in terms of financial and non-financial measures.

Financial Performance- Financial performance is an instinctive indicator of how well an organization can leverage assets from its initial business mode to maximize revenue. Various financial measures have been used in the studies conducted by many researchers (Liao and Wu, 2009; Lopez et al., 2005; Ramanujan, 1986), which entails sales growth, competitive position, organizations' reputation, profitability, stock price, Return on Assets (ROA) Return on Investment (ROI) and Return on Sales (ROS).

Non-Financial Performance- In various studies, it has been reported by researchers that organizations have increased use of these measures for evaluating business performance in the past years (Govindarajan & Gupta, 1985; Ittner, Larcker, & Rajan, 1997; Nanni, Dixon, & Vollmann, 1992; Kaplan & Norton, 1992, 1996; Simons, 1987, 1990; Ittner & Larcker, 1998). Non-financial measures include customer satisfaction (quality), market share position, product quality, introduction of new product, operating efficiency and societal welfare as measuring variable. Researchers indicated that non-financial measures can assist managers in organizations to recognize variations in the existing environment of business and can also determine and evaluate progress of business activities towards objectives and performance goals (Kaplan & Norton, 1996).

3. To study the relationship between contingent factors and business performance.

The influence of contingent factors including organization size, structure, strategy, advanced manufacturing technology, environment uncertainty on business performance have been examined in the literature. Tracey et al. (1999) proposed that organizations that invest in advanced manufacturing technology and then focus

Figure 4. Review of past studies on dimensions of business performance
Source: *Author's own representation.*

Authors	Dimensions of Business Performance
(Govindarajan, 1984)	Sales growth rate, operating profits, market share, profit margins, return on investment, development of a new product, personnel development, research and development, market development, cash flows and cost reduction programs
(Venkatraman & Ramanujam 1986)	Financial measures (return on equity, return on investment) and operational measures (market share, sales growth, and, profit growth)
(Jaworski & Kohli, 1993)	Market share and overall performance
(Tracey et al., 1999)	Customer retention rate, sales growth, market share and overall competitive position
(Baker & Sinkula, 1999)	Overall performance, new product success, change in relative market share
(Ellinger et al., 2000)	Market share, sales growth, profitability, and customer satisfaction
(Thomas & Keithley, 2002) (Payne, 1986)	Aimed at improving the ability to attract, train, develop and retain an employee
(Sher & Lee, 2004)	Differentiated products, operating costs and shorten lead time
(Hoque, 2004)	Non-financial measures -material and labor efficiency, process improvements and reengineering, introduction of new product, employee training and development, customer satisfaction, on-time delivery, relation with suppliers, workplace relations, employee health and safety, customer response time and employee satisfaction
(Fuentes et al., 2006)	Financial performance (profitability growth), Operational performance (market share growth, sales growth, reduction in customer complaints, customer satisfaction, defects in products/services) and employee performance (level of employee satisfaction and absenteeism)
(Storey & Kahn, 2010)	Sustainable competitive advantage
(Vaccaro et al. 2010)	Profitability and cost
(López-Nicolás & Meroño-Cerdán, 2011)	Performance of processes (efficiency and quality); internal performance related to individual capabilities (creativity, employee's qualification), financial performance (customer satisfaction, growth and profitability)
(Abass et.al., 2011)	Financial performance, Overall organizational performance, employees' intimacy, operational excellence and organizational performance in terms of value discipline.
(Narver & Slater, 2012)	Return on assets, new product success and sales growth
(Deshpandé et al., 2012)	Relative growth rate, relative size, relative share of market and relative profitability
(X. Liu, 2013)	Innovative new products, improved coordination efforts, commercialization of new products, quick responsiveness to market change, improved ability to anticipate crises and reduced redundancy of information
(Tajali et al., 2014)	Employee and operational performance
(Rani, Rao and Kumar, 2014)	Financial performance in terms of deposits, investments, assets, expenditure, income and profitability
(Awan and Khalid, 2015)	Firm performance in terms of ratio of admissions to applications and increase in number of admissions to previous year
(Bourini, Khawaldeh and Al-Qudah, 2016)	Technical efficiency and innovation performance
(Jyoti and Rani, 2017)	Financial, employee and operational performance
(Bratianu, 2017)	Market performance
(García-Sánchez et al., 2017)	Organizational share in the market, return on assets, return on equity, return on sales, return on investments and sales growth
(Biswakarma, 2018)	Employee job performance
(Zaim, Muhammed and Tarim, 2018)	KM performance and quality performance
(Ahbabi et al., 2019)	Firm performance in terms of operational, quality and innovation performance

on developing mechanisms for strategy formulation leads to better organizational performance with improved capabilities. (Hoque, 2004) attempted to examine how performance measures are selected and also identified its relevance on the association between strategic choice, environment uncertainty and business performance on 52 manufacturing companies and the results concluded that association exists between the variables and major emphasis was on non-financial measures. Fuentes et al. (2006) also examined the relationship between strategy and implementation of total quality management (TQM) and also analyzed their effect on the organizational performance. It further concluded that organizations that have greater degree of alignment between strategy and TQM leads to higher level of performance. Many theories have proved the relationship between business strategy and TQM (Schonberger, 1992; Pruett & Thomas, 1996; Wilcox et al., 1996; Srinidhi, 1998). Garengo and Bititci (2007) also emphasized on the relevance of performance measurement system in order to support organizational development. It mainly focused on interrelationship between contingency factors and performance measurement practices in SMEs. The contingent factors included management information system, organization culture and management style, strategy, corporate governance structure, external environment and company size and all of these impacted positively on business performance. Studies investigating the relationship between strategy and performance measurement were conducted by Garengo et al. (2005) and it also quoted the relationship of strategy and various performance measurement systems. Fakhri et al. (2009) also aimed to investigate how contingent factors impact the usage of performance measures in banking industry. Considered contingent factors were level of competition, organizational size, organizational structure and business strategy. Pertusa-Ortega et al. (2010) examined how organizational structure impacts organizational performance by considering its association with competitive strategy. It concluded that structure of an organization has an indirect impact on performance through competitive strategy. Stock et al. (2013) has investigated the impact of innovation oriented corporate culture on product program effectiveness (PPI) leading to analysis of business performance. Innovation included -Innovation oriented cultural values, cultural norms and cultural artifacts moderated by market dynamism and technological turbulence in order to check its impact on product program effectiveness and then also examined the impact of PPI on organizational performance by measuring return on sales, profits and return on investments. Nzewi et al. (2016) aimed to determine the relationship between total productivity maintenance (TPM) and business performance of selected aluminum manufacturing companies in Anambra state, Nigeria. The findings concluded that TPM has a positive and significant influence on business performance. Ahuja (2008) claimed that TPM is widely recognized and acts as a strategy method for enhancing manufacturing performance through effective improvement of production facilities.

Al-Naser and Mohamed (2017) also examined the integration between total quality management (TQM) and business performance through balance scorecard (BSC) in Iraqi manufacturing industry. The findings showed that performance of Iraqi manufacturing industries can be increased by properly implementing TQM technique. Acar and Acar (2014) also cited in their study that organizational culture has a positive effect on organizational performance (in Turkish hospitals where business performance was measured in terms of employee performance, quality performance and financial performance). Scales used for measuring performance were taken from Venkatraman and Ramanujan (1986). Zahra, Neubaum, and El-Hagrassey (2003), Antoncic and Hisrich (2001), Rozenzweig, Roth, and Dean Jr. (2003), Chang et al. (2003), Baker and Sinkula (1999). Sahoo (2018) assessed the contribution of total quality management (TQM) and total productivity maintenance (TPM) on business performance in Indian manufacturing industry in Gandhinagar. The results showed that TQM and TPM collectively contributes effectively to organizational performance rather than implementing them individually. Ruiz et al. (2019) also attempted to analyze how high-performance work systems (HPWS) and total quality management (TQM) impact each other and its effect on business performance. The findings indicated that HPWS positively impacts the TQM which ultimately improves business performance. Performance measurement scales were taken from (Fuentes and Hurtado, 2002; Easton and Jarrell, 1998; Mohr-Jackson, 1998; Forker, Vickery and Droge, 1996, Anderson et al., 1999, Grandzol and Gershon, 1998; Adam, 1994).

4. To study the relationship between SCM and business performance

Managing the costs with a strategic perspective is very essential in response to today's challenging economic times. Strategic Cost Management (SCM) is an essential requirement for an organization to derive value in the competitive modern marketplace. It not only helps in driving business value but also assists in assigning right people at right place in order to achieve organizational goals along with tracking outcomes. Ganapaiah (2017) made an attempt to analyze Strategic Cost Management (SCM) practices in small and medium enterprises and investigated as it impacts business performance. It further concluded that adopting SCM practices positively impacts the organizational performance. Stanley (2017) examined the relationship between two components of SCM: Executional cost management which aims at performance improvement for a given strategy and Structural cost management which aims at changing the cost structure of a firm and financial performance in Canadian manufacturing firms. It also attempted to investigate the mediating impact of structural cost management between bot components of SCM. The specific context which was investigated was environmental costs. The results showed that both positively impacts financial performance. Pizzini (2006) also determined the impact of usage of strategic cost management on the financial performance of US hospitals .Findings indicated that if managers use SCM techniques efficiently, there would be increase in the financial performance of an organization. Alamri (2019) conceptualized facets of SCM and explored the impact of these facets on the business performance in Saudi Arabia. The two facets are the strategically adopted techniques of management accounting and accountant's involvement in strategic management process.

5. **To review studies investigating the role of strategic cost management as a mediator on the relationship between contingent factors and business performance.**

Literature of all other objectives also form part of this one as all are interrelated. Payne (1986) witnessed the interrelationship among business unit strategy and business performance with the usage of strategic cost management. Jermias and Gani (2004) realized that there is signification association between contingency factors, strategy, strategic cost management and business performance. Cadez and Guilding (2008) showed that if strategic cost management techniques are used, business performance will automatically increase. Wadongo and Abdel-Kader (2014) also claimed that the factors which are contingent in nature have affect business performance. Junqueira et al. (2016) and Diefenbach et al. (2018) also investigated that strategy effects business performance. Godil and Shabib-ul-hasan (2018) empirically validated utilization of contingent factors in Pakistan and also claimed that there is an interrelationship among factors, cost and management accounting and business performance. Pavlatos (2018) concluded that there is significant mediating impact of SCM on the interrelationship between factors and business performance.

ANALYSIS

As all the objectives in the form of themes have been explored and reviewed. It has been analyzed that common contingent factors which effect business performance are size, structure, technology, environment, strategy and its various choices and competition and total quality management from 1986 to 2019. Mostly followed dimensions by organizations to measure business performance include financial as well as non-financial measures. These are sales growth, market share, return on investment, return on sales, customer satisfaction, profitability and innovativeness in the process or product from 1984 to 2019. The analysis of theme 3,4 and 5 shows that majority of the studies reflect that there is an interrelationship among contingent factors, strategic cost management and business performance.

DISCUSSION AND CONCLUSION

The study focused on the reviewing the interrelationship among variables and the finding supports central proposition of contingency theory where the firm's business performance depends on the usage of strategic cost management and contingent factors. Strategic cost management has proved to be a significant mediator as it is evident from the review. However, as every study has some limitations, our main limitation was paucity of time and inability to access certain articles which could have made this more extensive.

This study has extended prior researches like theme classification can help in better understanding of the topic, additional insights have been provided in the domain of cost and management accounting, more extensive view can be developed on contingent factors influencing usage of SCM in service as well as manufacturing industries. Finally, this review will provide insight to industries, accounting practitioners, academicians, strategy, strategists who can design various strategies to enhance business performance accordingly. Further studies can be undertaken in order to extend domains of knowledge in context of cost and management accounting and more contingent factors like total productivity maintenance, culture, knowledge and specialization of the employee can be explored along with their interrelationship with business performance.

REFERENCES

Abdel-Kader, M., & Luther, R. (2008). The impact of firm characteristics on management accounting practices: A UK-based empirical analysis. *The British Accounting Review*, *40*(1), 2–27. doi:10.1016/j.bar.2007.11.003

Abernethy, M. A., & Guthrie, C. H. (1994). An empirical assessment of the "fit" between strategy and management information system design. *Accounting and Finance*, *34*(2), 49–66. doi:10.1111/j.1467-629X.1994.tb00269.x

Abernethy, M. A., & Stoelwinder, J. U. (1991). Budget use, task uncertainty, system goal orientation and subunit performance: A test of the 'fit' hypothesis in not-for-profit hospitals. *Accounting, Organizations and Society*, *16*(2), 105–120. doi:10.1016/0361-3682(91)90008-3

Acar, A. Z., & Acar, P. (2014). Organizational Culture Types and Their Effects on Organizational Performance in Turkish Hospitals. *EMAJ: Emerging Markets Journal*, *3*(3), 18–31. doi:10.5195/EMAJ.2014.47

Adam, E. E. Jr. (1994). Alternative quality improvement practices and organization performance. *Journal of Operations Management*, *12*(1), 27–44. doi:10.1016/0272-6963(94)90004-3

Ahmad, K. (2012). *The use of management accounting practices in Malaysian medium firms*. University of Exeter.

Ahuja, I. P. S., & Khamba, J. S. (2008). Justification of TPM initiatives in Indian Manufacturing Industry for achieving core competitiveness. *Journal of Manufacturing Technology*, *19*(5), 645–669. doi:10.1108/17410380810877302

Aiken, M., Bacharach, S. B., & French, J. L. (1980). Organizational structure, work process, and proposal making in administrative bureaucracies. *Academy of Management Journal*, *23*(4), 631–652.

Al Ahbabi, S. A., Singh, S. K., Balasubramanian, S., & Gaur, S. S. (2019). Employee perception of impact of knowledge management processes on public sector performance. *Journal of Knowledge Management*, *23*(2), 351–373. doi:10.1108/JKM-08-2017-0348

Al-Mawali, H. (2015). Contingent factors of Strategic Management Accounting. *Research Journal of Finance and Accounting Online*, *6*(11), 2222–2847.

Al-Naser, K., & Mohamed, R. (2017). The Integration between Strategic Cost Management Techniques to Improve the Performance of Iraqi Manufacturing Companies. *Asian Journal of Finance & Accounting*, *9*(1), 210. doi:10.5296/ajfa.v9i1.11003

Alamri, A. M. (2019). Association between strategic management accounting facets and organizational performance. *Baltic Journal of Management*, *14*(2), 212–234. doi:10.1108/BJM-12-2017-0411

Anderson, M., & Sohal, A. S. (1999). A study of the relationship between quality management practices and performance in small businesses. *International Journal of Quality & Reliability Management*, *16*(9), 859–877. doi:10.1108/02656719910289168

Anderson, S. W., & Lanen, W. N. (1999). Economic transition, strategy and the evolution of management accounting practices: The case of India. *Accounting, Organizations and Society*, *24*(5-6), 379–412. doi:10.1016/S0361-3682(97)00060-3

Antoncic, B., & Hisrich, R. D. (2001). Intrapreneurship: Construct refinement and cross-cultural validation. *Journal of Business Venturing*, *16*(5), 495–527. doi:10.1016/S0883-9026(99)00054-3

Auzair, S. (2015). A configuration approach to management control systems design in service organizations. *Journal of Accounting & Organizational Change*, *11*(1), 47–72. doi:10.1108/JAOC-08-2012-0064

Awan, A. G., & Khalid, M. I. (2015). Impact of Knowledge Management on Organizational Performance: A Case Study of Selected Universities in Southern Punjab-Pakistan. In Information and Knowledge Management (Vol. 5, No. 6, pp. 59-67). Academic Press.

Baines, A., & Langfield-Smith, K. (2003). Antecedents to management accounting change: A structural equation approach. *Accounting, Organizations and Society*, *28*(7-8), 675–698. doi:10.1016/S0361-3682(02)00102-2

Baker, W. E., & Sinkula, J. M. (1999). The synergistic effect of market orientation and learning orientation on organizational performance. *Journal of the Academy of Marketing Science*, *27*(4), 411–427. doi:10.1177/0092070399274002

Bourini, F., Khawaldeh, K., & Al-Qudah, S. (2013). The role of knowledge management in banks sector (analytical Study-Jordan). *Interdisciplinary Journal of Contemporary Research in Business*, *5*(3), 53–77.

Bratianu, C. (2017, November). Knowledge Management in the Sharing Economy. *Knowledge Management in the Sharing Economy.*, *6*, 290. doi:10.1007/978-3-319-66890-1

Cadez, S., & Guilding, C. (2008). An exploratory investigation of an integrated contingency model of strategic management accounting. *Accounting, Organizations and Society*, *33*(7–8), 836–863. doi:10.1016/j.aos.2008.01.003

Chang, S. C., Lin, N. P., Yang, C. L., & Sheu, C. (2003). Quality dimensions, capabilities and business strategy: An empirical study in high-tech industry. *Total Quality Management & Business Excellence*, *14*(4), 407–421. doi:10.1080/1478336032000047228

Chenhall, R. H. (2003). Management control systems design within its organizational context: Findings from contingency-based research and directions for the future. *Accounting, Organizations and Society*, *28*(2–3), 127–168. doi:10.1016/S0361-3682(01)00027-7

Chenhall, R. H., & Langfield-Smith, K. (1998). The relationship between strategic priorities, management techniques and management accounting: An empirical investigation using a systems approach. *Accounting, Organizations and Society*, *23*(3), 243–264. doi:10.1016/S0361-3682(97)00024-X

Chong, V. K., & Chong, K. M. (1997). Strategic choices, environmental uncertainty and SBU perform-ance: A note on the intervening role of management accounting systems. *Accounting and Business Research, 27*(4), 268–276. doi:10.1080/00014788.1997.9729553

Cinquini, L., &Tenucci, A. (2010). Strategic management accounting and business strategy: a loose coupling? *Journal of Accounting & Organizational Change, 6*(2), 228-259.

Cravens, K. S., & Guilding, C. (2001). An empirical study of the application of strategic management accounting techniques. *Advances in Management Accounting, 10*, 95–124.

Cruz, S., & Camps, J. (2003). Organic vs mechanistic structures. Construction and validation of a scale of measurement. *Management Research, 1*(1), 111–123. doi:10.1108/15365430380000521

Deshpandé, R., Farley, J. U., & Webster, F. E. (2012). Corporate Culture, Customer Orientation, and Innovativeness in Japanese Firms: A Quadrad Analysis. *Developing a Market Orientation, 57*, 79–102. doi:10.4135/9781452231426.n4

Diefenbach, U., Wald, A., & Gleich, R. (2018). Between cost and benefit: Investigating effects of cost management control systems on cost efficiency and organizational performance. *Journal of Management Control, 29*(1), 63–89. doi:10.100700187-018-0261-5

Easton, G. S., & Jarrell, S. L. (1998). The effects of total quality management on corporate performance: An empirical investigation. *The Journal of Business, 71*(2), 253–307. doi:10.1086/209744

Ellinger, A. E., Daugherty, P., & Keller, S. (2000). The relationship between marketing / logistics interdepartmental .... *Journal of Business Logistics, 21*(1), 1.

Fakhri, G., Menacere, K., & Pegum, R. (2009). The Impact of Contingent Factors on the Use of Performance Measurement System in the Banking Industry: The Case of Libya. *Salford Postgraduate Annual Research Conference, 44*(0), 1–5.

Fargnoli, E., Almeida, E., Palhares, G., Silvério, K., & Marques, R. (2012). Teoria da Contingência. *Administração e Negócio*, 61-80.

Fiedler, F. E. (1964). A contingency model of leadership effectiveness. In *Advances in experimental social psychology* (Vol. 1, pp. 149–190). Academic Press. doi:10.1016/S0065-2601(08)60051-9

Fisher, J. (1995). Contingency-based research on management control systems: Categorization by level of complexity. *Journal of Accounting Literature*, *14*, 24–53. http://search.proquest.com/docview/216311338?accountid=42455%5Cnhttp://sfx.library.tu.ac.th:3210/sfxlcl3?url_ver=Z39.882004&rft_val_fmt=info:ofi/fmt:kev:mtx:journal&genre=article&sid=ProQ:ProQ%3Aabiglobal&atitle=Contingency-based+research+on+management+c

Forker, L. B., Vickery, S. K., & Droge, C. L. (1996). The contribution of quality to business performance. *International Journal of Operations & Production Management*, *16*(8), 44–62. doi:10.1108/01443579610125778

Fuentes, M., & Hurtado, N. (2002). Variables críticasen la medición del desempeñoenempresas con implantación de la gestión de la calidad total. *Investigaciones Europeas de Dirección y Economía de la Empresa*, *8*(2), 87–102.

Fuentes, M. M. F., Montes, F. J. L., & Fernández, L. M. (2006). Total quality management, strategic orientation and organizational performance: The case of Spanish companies. *Total Quality Management & Business Excellence*, *17*(3), 303–323. doi:10.1080/14783360500451358

Ganapaiah, C. (2017). Strategic Cost Management and Business Performance: A Study of SME's in India-An Analysis. *BIMS International Journal of Social Science Research*, *2*(1), 17–29.

García-Sánchez, E., García-Morales, V. J., & Bolívar-Ramos, M. T. (2017). The influence of top management support for ICTs on organizational performance through knowledge acquisition, transfer, and utilisation. *Review of Managerial Science*, *11*(1), 19–51. doi:10.100711846-015-0179-3

Garengo, P., Biazzo, S., & Bititci, U. S. (2005). Performance measurement systems in SMEs: A review for a research agenda. *International Journal of Management Reviews*, *7*(1), 25–47. doi:10.1111/j.1468-2370.2005.00105.x

Garengo, P., & Bititci, U. (2007). Towards a contingency approach to performance measurement: An empirical study in Scottish SMEs. *International Journal of Operations & Production Management*, *27*(8), 802–825. doi:10.1108/01443570710763787

Godil, D. I., & Shabib-ul-hasan, S. (2018). An Investigation of a Contingency Framework of Management Accounting Practices in Manufacturing Companies of Pakistan. *Gmjacs*, *8*(1), 53–65.

Govindarajan, V. (1984). Appropriateness of accounting data in performance evaluation: An empirical examination of environmental uncertainty as an intervening variable. *Accounting, Organizations and Society*, *9*(2), 125–135. doi:10.1016/0361-3682(84)90002-3

Govindarajan, V., & Gupta, A. K. (1985). Linking control systems to business unit strategy: Impact on performance. *Accounting, Organizations and Society*, *10*(1), 51–66. doi:10.1016/0361-3682(85)90031-5

Grandzol, J. R., & Gershon, M. (1998). A survey instrument for standardizing TQM modeling research. *International Journal of Quality Science*, *3*(1), 80–105. doi:10.1108/13598539810203887

Guilding, C. (1999). Competitor-focused accounting: An exploratory note. *Accounting, Organizations and Society*, *24*(7), 583–595. doi:10.1016/S0361-3682(99)00007-0

Guilding, C., Cravens, K. S., & Tayles, M. (2000). An international comparison of strategic management accounting practices. *Management Accounting Research*, *11*(1), 113–135. doi:10.1006/mare.1999.0120

Gupta, A. K., & Govindarajan, V. (1984). Business unit strategy, managerial characteristics, and business unit effectiveness at strategy implementation. *Academy of Management Journal*, *27*(1), 25–41.

Haldma, T., & Lääts, K. (2002). Contingencies influencing the management accounting practices of Estonian manufacturing companies. *Management Accounting Research*, *13*(4), 379–400. doi:10.1006/mare.2002.0197

Henri, J. F., Boiral, O., & Roy, M. J. (2016). Strategic cost management and performance: The case of environmental costs. *The British Accounting Review*, *48*(2), 269–282. doi:10.1016/j.bar.2015.01.001

Hoque, Z. (2004). A contingency model of the association between strategy, environmental uncertainty and performance measurement: Impact on organizational performance. *International Business Review*, *13*(4), 485–502. doi:10.1016/j.ibusrev.2004.04.003

Ittner, C. D., & Larcker, D. F. (1998). Innovations in performance measurement: Trends and research implications. *Journal of Management Accounting Research*, *10*, 205–238.

Ittner, C. D., & Larcker, D. F. (2003a). Coming up short on non-financial performance measurement. *Harvard Business Review*, *81*(11), 88–95. PMID:14619154

Ittner, C. D., Larcker, D. F., & Rajan, M. V. (1997, April). The choice of performance measures in annual bonus contract. *The Accounting Review*, *2*(2), 231–256.

Janjić, V., Karapavlović, N., & Damjanović, J. (2017). Технике Стратегијског Управљања Трошковима – Случај Републике Србије. *Teme*, *441*, 441. Advance online publication. doi:10.22190/TEME1702441J

Jaworski, B. J., & Kohli, A. K. (1993). Market Orientation: Antrcendent and Consequances. *Journal of Marketing*, *57*(1), 53–70. doi:10.1177/002224299305700304

Jermias, J., & Gani, L. (2004). Integrating business strategy, organizational configurations and management accounting systems with business unit effectiveness: A fitness landscape approach. *Management Accounting Research*, *15*(2), 179–200. doi:10.1016/j.mar.2004.03.002

Jinkens, R., & Yallapragada, R. R. (2010). Cost Accounting In Auto Manufacturing Companies In Germany And The United States. *International Business & Economics Research Journal*, *9*(3), 121–126. doi:10.19030/iber.v9i3.542

Jones, C. S. (1985). An empirical study of the evidence for contingency theories of management accounting systems in conditions of rapid change. *Accounting, Organizations and Society*, *10*(3), 303–328. doi:10.1016/0361-3682(85)90022-4

Junqueira, E., Dutra, E. V., Filho, H. Z., & Gonzaga, R. P. (2016). The effect of strategic choices and management control systems on organizational performance. *Revista Contabilidade & Finanças*, *27*(72), 334–348. doi:10.1590/1808-057x201601890

Jyoti, J., & Rani, A. (2017). High performance work system and organizational performance: Role of knowledge management. *Personnel Review*, *46*(8), 1770–1795. doi:10.1108/PR-10-2015-0262

Kaplan, R. S., & Norton, D. P. (1996). Using the balanced scorecard as a strategic management system. *Harvard Business Review*, *74*(1), 75–85.

Kimmel, P. D., Weygandt, J. J., & Kieso, D. E. (2010). *Financial accounting: Tools for business decision making*. John Wiley & Sons.

Kumar, A., & Shafabi. (2011). Strategic Cost Management – Suggested Framework for 21st Century. *Journal of Business and Management Research*, *5*(2), 118–131.

Langfield-smith, K. I. M. (1997). Rainfall, commerce and politics. *Science*, *15*(368), 110–111. doi:10.1016/S0361-3682(95)00040-2

Lee, J. (1989). Environmental change, strategy type and performance: Comparative-static analysis. *Korean Management Review*, *18*, 245–273.

Lee, J., & Miller, D. (1996). Strategy, environment and performance in two technological contexts: Contingency theory in Korea. *Organization Studies, 17*(5), 729–750. doi:10.1177/017084069601700502

Liao, S. H., & Wu, C. C. (2009). The relationship among knowledge management, organizational learning, and organizational performance. *International Journal of Business and Management, 4*(4), 64–76. doi:10.5539/ijbm.v4n4p64

Liberati, A., Altman, D. G., Tetzlaff, J., Mulrow, C., Gøtzsche, P. C., Ioannidis, J. P., Clarke, M., Devereaux, P. J., Kleijnen, J., & Moher, D. (2009). The PRISMA statement for reporting systematic reviews and meta-analyses of studies that evaluate health care interventions: Explanation and elaboration. *Journal of Clinical Epidemiology, 62*(10), e1–e34. doi:10.1016/j.jclinepi.2009.06.006 PMID:19631507

Liu, Q. (2015). Research on Strategic Cost Management in Modern Enterprises. *Management & Engineering, 21*. doi:10.5503/J.ME.2015.21.005

Liu, X., Zhang, J., & Guo, C. (2013). Full-Text Citation Analysis: A New Method to Enhance. *Journal of the American Society for Information Science and Technology, 64*(July), 1852–1863. doi:10.1002/asi.22883

Lopez, S. P., Peón, J. M. M., & Ordás, C. J. V. (2005). Organizational learning as a determining factor in business performance. *The Learning Organization.*

López-Nicolás, C., & Meroño-Cerdán, Á. L. (2011). Strategic knowledge management, innovation and performance. *International Journal of Information Management, 31*(6), 502–509. doi:10.1016/j.ijinfomgt.2011.02.003

Melo, M., & Leone, R. (2015). Alignment between Competitive Strategies and Cost Management: A Study of Small Manufacturing Companies. *Brazilian Business Review, 12*(5), 78–96. doi:10.15728/bbr.2015.12.5.5

Messner, M. (2016). Does industry matter? How industry context shapes management accounting practice. *Management Accounting Research, 31*, 103–111. doi:10.1016/j.mar.2015.09.001

Miles, R. E., & Snow, C. G. (1978). Organizational Strategy, Structure, and Process, McGraw-Hill, New York, NY. model of strategic management accounting. Accounting, Organizations and Society.

Miller, D. (1987b). Strategy making and structure: Analysis and implications for performance. *Academy of Management Journal, 30*(1), 7–32.

Miller, D. (1988). Relating Porter's business strategies to environment and structure: Analysis and performance implications. *Academy of Management Journal, 31*(2), 280–308.

Miller, D. (1992). Environmental fit versus internal fit. *Organization Science, 3*(2), 159–178. doi:10.1287/orsc.3.2.159

Miller, D., & Droge, C. (1986). Psychological and traditional determinants of structure. *Administrative Science Quarterly, 31*(4), 539–560. doi:10.2307/2392963

Mohr-Jackson, I. (1998). Conceptualizing total quality orientation. *European Journal of Marketing, 32*(1/2), 13–22. doi:10.1108/03090569810197390

Narver, J. C., & Slater, S. F. (2012). The Effect of Market Orientation on Business Profitability. *Developing a Market Orientation*, (October), 45–78. doi:10.4135/9781452231426.n3

Nzewi. (2016). Total Productivity Maintenance and Performance of Selected Aluminium Manufacturing Companies in Anambra State. *IOSR Journal of Business and Management, 18*(1). doi:10.9790/487X-18116773

Otley, D. (1980). The contingency theory of management accounting: Achievement and prognosis. *Accounting, Organizations and Society, 5*(4), 13–28. doi:10.1016/0361-3682(80)90040-9

Otley, D. (1999). Performance management: A framework for management control systems research. *Management Accounting Research, 10*(4), 363–382. doi:10.1006/mare.1999.0115

Otley, D. (2016). The contingency theory of management accounting and control: 1980–2014. *Management Accounting Research, 31*, 45–62. doi:10.1016/j.mar.2016.02.001

Patrick, P. R., Miller, A., & Judge, W. Q. (1999). Using information-processing theory to understand. *Strategic Management Journal, 20*(6), 567–577. doi:10.1002/(SICI)1097-0266(199906)20:6<567::AID-SMJ36>3.0.CO;2-K

Pavlatos, O. (2015). An empirical investigation of strategic management accounting in hotels. *International Journal of Contemporary Hospitality Management, 27*(5), 756–767. doi:10.1108/IJCHM-12-2013-0582

Pavlatos, O. (2018). Strategic cost management, contingent factors and performance in services. *Journal of Accounting and Management Information Systems, 12*(2), 215–233. doi:10.24818/jamis.2018.02002

Payne, J. L. (1986). Rejoinder Reproduced with permission of the copyright owner. Further reproduction prohibited without permission. *Preventing School Failure, 51*(3), 49–51.

Pelham, A. M., & Wilson, D. T. (1996). A longitudinal study of the impact of market structure, firm structure, strategy, and market orientation culture on dimensions of small-firm performance. *Journal of the Academy of Marketing Science, 24*(1), 27–43. doi:10.1007/BF02893935

Pertusa-Ortega, E. M., Molina-Azorín, J. F., & Claver-Cortés, E. (2010). Competitive strategy, structure and firm performance: A comparison of the resource-based view and the contingency approach. *Management Decision, 48*(8), 1282–1303. doi:10.1108/00251741011076799

Pizzini, M. J. (2006). The relation between cost-system design, managers' evaluations of the relevance and usefulness of cost data, and financial performance: An empirical study of US hospitals. *Accounting, Organizations and Society, 31*(2), 179–210. doi:10.1016/j.aos.2004.11.001

Porter, M. (1980). *Competitive strategy: Techniques for analyzing industries and competitors*. Free.

Porter, M. (1985). *Competitive Advantage*. The Free Press.

Pruett, M., & Thomas, H. (1996). Thinking about quality and its links with strategic management. *European Management Journal, 14*(1), 37–46. doi:10.1016/0263-2373(95)00045-3

Ramanujan, V. (1986). Onmeasurementofb1135Venk. *The Journal of Management and Governance, 1*, 1–30.

Rogers, P. R., Miller, A., & Judge, W. Q. (1999). Using information-processing theory to understand planning/performance relationships in the context of strategy. *Strategic Management Journal, 20*(6), 567–577. doi:10.1002/(SICI)1097-0266(199906)20:6<567::AID-SMJ36>3.0.CO;2-K

Rosenzweig, E. D., Roth, A. V., & Dean, J. W. Jr. (2003). The influence of an integration strategy on competitive capabilities and business performance: An exploratory study of consumer products manufacturers. *Journal of Operations Management, 21*(4), 437–456. doi:10.1016/S0272-6963(03)00037-8

Ruiz, E., De Pablo, J. D. S., Muñoz, R. M., & Peña, I. (2019). Do high performance work systems enhance business performance? Examining the mediating influence of total quality management. *Zbornik Radova Ekonomskog Fakultet Au Rijeci*, *37*(1), 235–258. doi:10.18045/zbefri.2019.1.235

Sahoo, S. (2018). An empirical exploration of TQM, TPM and their integration from Indian manufacturing industry. *Journal of Manufacturing Technology Management*, *29*(7), 1188–1210. doi:10.1108/JMTM-03-2018-0075

Sarkindaji, B. D., Hashim, N. A. B., & Abdullateef, A. O. (2014). Knowledge Management and Organizational Performance of Mobile Service Firms in Nigeria: A Proposed Framework. *Information and Knowledge Management, 4*(11), 88–95. https://iiste.org/Journals/index.php/IKM/article/view/17216

Savić, B., Vasiljević, Z., & Đorđević, D. (2014). Strategic Cost Management As Instrument for. *Economics of Agriculture*, *4*(6), 1005–1020.

Sayilar, Y. (2016). The Past, Present and Future Of Structural Contingency Theory. *Industrial Relations and Human Resources Journal*, *18*(4), 95–124. doi:10.4026/2148-9874.2016.0333.X

Schonberger, R. J. (1992). Is strategy strategic? Impact of total quality management on strategy. *The Academy of Management Executive*, *6*(3), 80–87.

Sher, P. J., & Lee, V. C. (2004). Information technology as a facilitator for enhancing dynamic capabilities through knowledge management. *Information & Management*, *41*(8), 933–945. doi:10.1016/j.im.2003.06.004

Simons, R. (1987). Accounting control systems and business strategy. *Accounting, Organizations and Society*, *12*(4), 357–374. doi:10.1016/0361-3682(87)90024-9

Simons, R. (1990). The role of management control systems in creating competitive advantage: New per-spectives. *Accounting, Organizations and Society*, *15*(1–2), 127–143. doi:10.1016/0361-3682(90)90018-P

Skinner, W. (1971). The anachronistic factory. *Harvard Business Review*, (January–February), 61–70.

Snyder, H. (2019). Literature review as a research methodology: An overview and guidelines. *Journal of Business Research*, *104*(March), 333–339. doi:10.1016/j.jbusres.2019.07.039

Srinidhi, B. (1998). Strategic quality management. *International Journal of Quality Science*, *3*(1), 38–70. doi:10.1108/13598539810196877

Stanley, C. (2017). Strategic Cost Management and Performance: The Case of Environmental Costs. *Social and Environmental Accountability Journal, 37*(2), 150–151. doi:10.1080/0969160X.2017.1345812

Stock, R. M., Six, B., & Zacharias, N. A. (2013). Linking multiple layers of innovation-oriented corporate culture, product program innovativeness, and business performance: A contingency approach. *Journal of the Academy of Marketing Science, 41*(3), 283–299. doi:10.100711747-012-0306-5

Storey, C., & Kahn, K. B. (2010). The role of knowledge management strategies and task knowledge in stimulating service innovation. *Journal of Service Research, 13*(4), 397–410. doi:10.1177/1094670510370988

Sudha Rani, D., Mohana, R. K. R., & Vijay Kumar, P. (2014). Knowledge Management and Decennial Growth of a Private Sector Bank–A Case Study of ICICI Bank. *IOSR Journal of Business and Management, 16*(1), 25–37. doi:10.9790/487X-16142537

Sulanjaku, M., & Shingjergji, A. (2015). Strategic Cost Management Accounting Instrument and their Usage in Albanians Companies. European Journal of Business. *Economics and Accountancy, 3*(5), 44–50.

Thomas, D., & Keithley, T. (2002). Knowledge management improves performance. *AACE International Transactions*, PM171.

Tracey, M., Vonderembse, M. A., & Lim, J. S. (1999). Manufacturing technology and strategy formulation: Keys to enhancing competitiveness and improving performance. *Journal of Operations Management, 17*(4), 411–428. doi:10.1016/S0272-6963(98)00045-X

Trkman, P. (2010). The critical success factors of business process management. *International Journal of Information Management, 30*(2), 125–134. doi:10.1016/j.ijinfomgt.2009.07.003

Vaccaro, A., Parente, R., & Veloso, F. M. (2010). Knowledge management tools, interorganizational relationships, innovation and firm performance. *Technological Forecasting and Social Change, 77*(7), 1076–1089. doi:10.1016/j.techfore.2010.02.006

Venkatraman, N., & Ramanujam, V. (1986). Measurement of business performance in strategy research: A comparison of approaches. *Academy of Management Review, 11*(4), 801–814. doi:10.5465/amr.1986.4283976

Wadongo, B., & Abdel-Kader, M. (2014). Contingency theory, performance management and organizational effectiveness in the third sector: A theoretical framework. *International Journal of Productivity and Performance Management, 63*(6), 680–703. doi:10.1108/IJPPM-09-2013-0161

Wilcox, M., & … . (1996). Managing for quality: The strategic issues. *International Journal of Technology Management, 12*(1), 59–74.

Xiao, Z., Dyson, J. R., & Powell, P. L. (1996). The impact of information Technology on corporate financial Reporting: A contingency perspective. *The British Accounting Review, 28*(3), 203–227. doi:10.1006/bare.1996.0015

Yilmaz, R., & Baral, G. (2010). Target costing as a strategic cost management tool for success of balanced scorecard system. *China-USA Business Review, 9*(3), 39–53.

Zahra, S. A., Neubaum, D. O., & El–Hagrassey, G. M. (2002). Competitive analysis and new venture performance: Understanding the impact of strategic uncertainty and venture origin. *Entrepreneurship Theory and Practice, 27*(1), 1–28. doi:10.1111/1540-8520.t01-2-00001

Zaim, H., Muhammed, S., & Tarim, M. (2019). Relationship between knowledge management processes and performance: Critical role of knowledge utilization in organizations. *Knowledge Management Research and Practice, 17*(1), 24–38. doi:10.1080/14778238.2018.1538669

Zawawi, N. H. M., & Hoque, Z. (2010). Research in management accounting innovations: An overview of its recent development. *Qualitative Research in Accounting & Management, 7*(4), 505–568. doi:10.1108/11766091011094554

Compilation of References

Ranjan, J., & Foropon, C. (2021). Big data analytics in building the competitive intelligence of organizations. *International Journal of Information Management*, *56*, 102231. doi:10.1016/j.ijinfomgt.2020.102231

Sun, Z., & Stranieri, A. (2021). The Nature of Intelligent Analytics. In *Intelligent Analytics With Advanced Multi-Industry Applications* (pp. 1–21). IGI Global. doi:10.4018/978-1-7998-4963-6.ch001

Essakimuthu, A., Ganesh, R. K., Krishnan, R. S., & Robinson, Y. H. (2021). Enhanced Hadoop Distribution File System for Providing Solution to Big Data Challenges. *Further Advances in Internet of Things in Biomedical and Cyber Physical Systems*, *193*, 71–83. doi:10.1007/978-3-030-57835-0_7

Hajjaji, Y., Boulila, W., Farah, I. R., Romdhani, I., & Hussain, A. (2021). Big data and IoT-based applications in smart environments: A systematic review. *Computer Science Review*, *39*, 100318. doi:10.1016/j.cosrev.2020.100318

Rehman, A., Naz, S., & Razzak, I. (2021). Leveraging big data analytics in healthcare enhancement: Trends, challenges and opportunities. *Multimedia Systems*, 1–33.

Kaffash, S., Nguyen, A. T., & Zhu, J. (2021). Big data algorithms and applications in intelligent transportation system: A review and bibliometric analysis. *International Journal of Production Economics*, *231*, 107868. doi:10.1016/j.ijpe.2020.107868

Yu, W., Zhao, G., Liu, Q., & Song, Y. (2021). Role of big data analytics capability in developing integrated hospital supply chains and operational flexibility: An organizational information processing theory perspective. *Technological Forecasting and Social Change*, *163*, 120417. doi:10.1016/j.techfore.2020.120417

Roul, R. K. (2021). Topic modeling combined with classification technique for extractive multi-document text summarization. *Soft Computing*, *25*(2), 1113–1127. doi:10.100700500-020-05207-w

Chen, F., Han, K., & Chen, G. (2002). An Approach to sentence selection based text summarization. *Proceedings of the IEEE, TENCON02*, 489–493.

Kiani, & Akbarzadeh. (2006). AutomaticText Summarization Using: Hybrid Fuzzy GA-GP. *IEEE International Conference on Fuzzy Systems*, 977-983.

Jaruskulchai, C., & Kruengkrai, C. (2003). Text Summarization Using Local and Global Properties. *Proceedings of the IEEE/WIC International Conference on web Intelligence*, 201-206.

Radev, D. R., Jing, H., & Budzikowska, M. (2000). *Centroid-based summarization of multiple documents: Sentence extraction, utility based evaluation, and user studies.* In ANLP/NAACL Workshop on Summarization, Seattle, WA.

Osborne, M. (2002). Using Maximum Entropy for Sentence Extraction. *ACL Workshop on Text Summarization.* 10.3115/1118162.1118163

Neto, Freitas, & Kaestner. (2002). Automatic Text Summarization using a Machine Learning Approach. In *Advances in Artificial Intelligence: Lecture Notes in Computer Science*. Springer.

Edmundson, H. P. (2008, April). New methods in automatic extracting. *Journal of the Association for Computing Machinery*, *16*(2), 264–285. doi:10.1145/321510.321519

Prudhvi, K., Chowdary, A. B., Reddy, P. S. R., & Prasanna, P. L. (2021). Text Summarization Using Natural Language Processing. In *Intelligent System Design* (pp. 535–547). Springer. doi:10.1007/978-981-15-5400-1_54

Zhang, X., & Liu, S. (2021, January). Automatic Text Summarization for Marine Natural Products Literature. *Journal of Physics: Conference Series*, *1732*(1), 012047. doi:10.1088/1742-6596/1732/1/012047

Aaker & Joachimsthaler. (2000). *Brand Leadership*. Free Press.

Aaker, D.A. (1991). *Managing brand equity*. The Free Press.

Abdel-Kader, M., & Luther, R. (2008). The impact of firm characteristics on management accounting practices: A UK-based empirical analysis. *The British Accounting Review*, *40*(1), 2–27. doi:10.1016/j.bar.2007.11.003

Abernethy, M. A., & Guthrie, C. H. (1994). An empirical assessment of the "fit" between strategy and management information system design. *Accounting and Finance*, *34*(2), 49–66. doi:10.1111/j.1467-629X.1994.tb00269.x

Abernethy, M. A., & Stoelwinder, J. U. (1991). Budget use, task uncertainty, system goal orientation and subunit performance: A test of the 'fit'hypothesis in not-for-profit hospitals. *Accounting, Organizations and Society*, *16*(2), 105–120. doi:10.1016/0361-3682(91)90008-3

Acar, A. Z., & Acar, P. (2014). Organizational Culture Types and Their Effects on Organizational Performance in Turkish Hospitals. *EMAJ: Emerging Markets Journal*, *3*(3), 18–31. doi:10.5195/EMAJ.2014.47

Acar, O. A. (2019). Why Crowdsourcing Often Leads to Bad Ideas. *Harvard Business Review*.

Accenture. (2017). *Accenture Technology Vision 2017.* https://www.accenture.com/_acnmedia/PDF-45/Accenture-News-Release-Accenture-Technology-Vision-2017-Forecasts-A-Future-Of-Technology-For-People-By-People.pdf

Accenture. (2018). *Accenture Technology Vision 2018.* https://www.accenture.com/_acnmedia/Accenture/next-gen-7/tech-vision-2018/pdf/Accenture-TechVision-2018-Tech-Trends-Report.pdf

Adam, E. E. Jr. (1994). Alternative quality improvement practices and organization performance. *Journal of Operations Management*, *12*(1), 27–44. doi:10.1016/0272-6963(94)90004-3

Adamiec, L., & Cernauskas, D. (2019). *Optimal number of assets for reduction of market risk through diversification.* Academic Press.

Advance, H. E. (2020). *Coronavirus (COVID-19) updates.* https://www.advance-he.ac.uk/coronavirus-COVID-19-updates

Aggarwal, P., Vaidyanathan, R., & Venkatesh, A. (2009). Using lexical semantic analysis to derive online brand positions: An application to retail marketing research. *Journal of Retailing*, *85*(2), 145–158. doi:10.1016/j.jretai.2009.03.001

Ahmad, K. (2012). *The use of management accounting practices in Malaysian medium firms.* University of Exeter.

Ahuja, I. P. S., & Khamba, J. S. (2008). Justification of TPM initiatives in Indian Manufacturing Industry for achieving core competitiveness. *Journal of Manufacturing Technology*, *19*(5), 645–669. doi:10.1108/17410380810877302

Aiken, M., Bacharach, S. B., & French, J. L. (1980). Organizational structure, work process, and proposal making in administrative bureaucracies. *Academy of Management Journal*, *23*(4), 631–652.

Akar, E., & Topçu, B. (2011). An examination of the factors influencing consumers' attitudes toward social media marketing. *Journal of Internet Commerce*, *10*(1), 35–67. doi:10.1080/15332861.2011.558456

Al Ahbabi, S. A., Singh, S. K., Balasubramanian, S., & Gaur, S. S. (2019). Employee perception of impact of knowledge management processes on public sector performance. *Journal of Knowledge Management*, *23*(2), 351–373. doi:10.1108/JKM-08-2017-0348

Alalwan, A. A., Rana, N. P., Dwivedi, Y. K., & Algharabat, R. (2017). Social media in marketing: A review and analysis of the existing literature. *Telematics and Informatics*, *34*(7), 1177–1190. doi:10.1016/j.tele.2017.05.008

Alamri, A. M. (2019). Association between strategic management accounting facets and organizational performance. *Baltic Journal of Management*, *14*(2), 212–234. doi:10.1108/BJM-12-2017-0411

Alcaraz, R. (2014). The business case for better analytics: A retrospective and the future of theory and practice of marketing science. *Journal of Brand Strategy*, *3*(3), 295–303.

Alistair, D., & Jonathan, C. (2006). anaging webmavens: Relationships with sophisticated customers via the internet can transform marketing and speed innovation. *Strategy and Leadership*, *34*(3), 14–22. doi:10.1108/10878570610660564

Al-Mawali, H. (2015). Contingent factors of Strategic Management Accounting. *Research Journal of Finance and Accounting Online*, *6*(11), 2222–2847.

Al-Naser, K., & Mohamed, R. (2017). The Integration between Strategic Cost Management Techniques to Improve the Performance of Iraqi Manufacturing Companies. *Asian Journal of Finance & Accounting*, *9*(1), 210. doi:10.5296/ajfa.v9i1.11003

Alpeyev, P., & Hyuga, T. (2020, August 19). Softbank dispatches senior executives to turn around struggling Oyo. *The Economic Times.* https://economictimes.indiatimes.com/small-biz/startups/newsbuzz/softbank-dispatches-senior-executives-to-turn-around-struggling-oyo/articleshow/77626156.cms?from=mdr

Alves, Fernandes, & Raposo. (2016). Value co-creation: Concept and contexts of application and study. *Journal of Business Research, 69*(5), 1626–1633. es.2015.10.029 doi:10.1016/j.jbusr

AMA. (2017). *2017 AMA gold global top 25 market research companies*. Retrieved from https://www.ama.org/publications/MarketingNews/Pages/2017-ama-gold-global-report.aspx

Ambler, T., & Roberts, J. H. (2008). Assessing marketing performance: Don't settle for a silver metric. *Journal of Marketing Management*, *24*(7-8), 733–750. doi:10.1362/026725708X345498

Anderson, M., & Sohal, A. S. (1999). A study of the relationship between quality management practices and performance in small businesses. *International Journal of Quality & Reliability Management*, *16*(9), 859–877. doi:10.1108/02656719910289168

Anderson, S. W., & Lanen, W. N. (1999). Economic transition, strategy and the evolution of management accounting practices: The case of India. *Accounting, Organizations and Society*, *24*(5-6), 379–412. doi:10.1016/S0361-3682(97)00060-3

Andolo, D. (2013). From time to talk about workplace stress. In Personal Resilience for Healthcare Staff. When the Going Gets Tough. Radcliffe Publishing.

Antoncic, B., & Hisrich, R. D. (2001). Intrapreneurship: Construct refinement and cross-cultural validation. *Journal of Business Venturing*, *16*(5), 495–527. doi:10.1016/S0883-9026(99)00054-3

Arnold, S. J., Ma, S., & Tigert, D. J. (1978). A comparative analysis of determinant attributes in retail store selection. *Advances in Consumer Research. Association for Consumer Research (U. S.)*, *5*(1), 663–667.

Arnold, S. J., Oum, T. H., & Tigert, D. J. (1983). Determinant attributes in retail patronage: Seasonal, temporal, regional, and international comparisons. *JMR, Journal of Marketing Research*, *20*(2), 149–157. doi:10.1177/002224378302000205

Arora, T., Kumar, A., & Agarwal, B. (2020). Impact of social media advertising on millennials buying behaviour. *International Journal of Intelligent Enterprise*, *7*(4), 481–500. doi:10.1504/IJIE.2020.110795

Artola, C., Pinto, F., & García, D. P. (2015). Can internet searches forecast tourism inflows? *International Journal of Manpower*, *36*(1), 103–116. doi:10.1108/IJM-12-2014-0259

Atwong, C. T. (2015). A social media practicum: An action-learning approach to social media marketing and analytics. *Marketing Education Review*, *25*(1), 27–31. doi:10.1080/10528008.2015.999578

Auzair, S. (2015). A configuration approach to management control systems design in service organizations. *Journal of Accounting & Organizational Change*, *11*(1), 47–72. doi:10.1108/JAOC-08-2012-0064

Avolio, B. J., Sosik, J. J., Kahai, S. S., & Baker, B. (2014). E-leadership: Re-examining transformations in leadership source and transmission. *The Leadership Quarterly*, *25*(1), 105–131. doi:10.1016/j.leaqua.2013.11.003

Awan, A. G., & Khalid, M. I. (2015). Impact of Knowledge Management on Organizational Performance: A Case Study of Selected Universities in Southern Punjab-Pakistan. In Information and Knowledge Management (Vol. 5, No. 6, pp. 59-67). Academic Press.

Ayanso, A., & Lertwachara, K. (2014). *Harnessing the power of social media and web analytics*. IGI Global. doi:10.4018/978-1-4666-5194-4

Bădescu, A. V., Smeureanu, I., & Asimit, A. V. (2010). *Portfolio assets selection through Grey numbers implementation*. Academic Press.

Baesens, B., Bapna, R., Marsden, J. R., Vanthienen, J., & Zhao, J. L. (2016). Transformational issues of big data and analytics in net- worked business. *Management Information Systems Quarterly*, *40*(4), 807–818. doi:10.25300/MISQ/2016/40:4.03

Baines, A., & Langfield-Smith, K. (2003). Antecedents to management accounting change: A structural equation approach. *Accounting, Organizations and Society*, *28*(7-8), 675–698. doi:10.1016/S0361-3682(02)00102-2

Baker, J., Grewal, D., & Levy, M. (1992). An experimental approach to making retail store environmental decisions. *Journal of Retailing*, *68*(4), 445–460.

Baker, J., Parasuraman, A., Grewal, D., & Voss, G. B. (2002). The influence of multiple store environment cues on perceived merchandise value and patronage intentions. *Journal of Marketing*, *65*(1), 120–141. doi:10.1509/jmkg.66.2.120.18470

Baker, W. E., & Sinkula, J. M. (1999). The synergistic effect of market orientation and learning orientation on organizational performance. *Journal of the Academy of Marketing Science*, *27*(4), 411–427. doi:10.1177/0092070399274002

Ballestero, E., & Plà–Santamaría, D. (2003). Portfolio selection on the Madrid exchange: A compromise programming model. *International Transactions in Operational Research, 10*(1), 33–51. doi:10.1111/1475-3995.00391

Bansal, Y., Kumar, S., & Verma, P. (2014). Commodity futures in portfolio diversification: Impact on investor's utility. *Global Business and Management Research, 6*(2), 112.

Bao, W. (2020). COVID -19 and online teaching in higher education: A case study of Peking University. *Human Behavior and Emerging Technologies, 2*(2), 113–115. doi:10.1002/hbe2.191 PMID:32510042

Baraldi, E., & Nadin, G. (2006). The challenges in digitalising business relationships: The construction of an IT infrastructure for a textile-related business network. *Technovation, 26*(10), 1111–1126. doi:10.1016/j.technovation.2005.09.016

Barczak, G. (2017). Writing a review article. *Journal of Product Innovation Management, 34*(2), 120–121. doi:10.1111/jpim.12365

Barley, S. R. (2015). Why the internet makes buying a car less loathsome: How technologies change role relations. *Academy of Management Discoveries, 1*(1), 5–35. doi:10.5465/amd.2013.0016

Barman, A., & Das, K. (2020). *E-Learning and E-education during COVID-19 Pandemic -A study on the e-learning initiatives with special reference to North-East India.* Academic Press.

Barney, J. (1991). Firm resources and sustained competitive advantage. *Journal of Management, 17*(1), 99–120. doi:10.1177/014920639101700108

Bassett, R. M. (2020, May). *Sustaining the Values of Tertiary Education during the COVID-19 Crisis.* Retrieved from https://www.internationalhighereducation.net/api-v1/article/!/action/getPdfOfArticle/articleID/2922/productID/29/filename/article-id-2922.pdf

Bawab, N. (2020, March 19). *Here's what Texas universities and colleges are doing in response to COVID-19.* WFAA8 ABC. https://www.wfaa.com/article/news/health/coronavirus/ list-texas-universities-that-have-suspended-study-abroad-or-travel-programs/287-4242e7fe-f39b-4322-a8d1-3de59cff46f3

BBC News. *(2014, August 27). Ebola Outbreak: Nigeria Closes All Schools until October.* BBC News.

BBC News. (2020a, February 1). *Health: Coronavirus: UK patient is University of York student.* BBC. https://www.bbc. com/news/health-51337400

BBC News. (2020c, March 15). *Coronavirus: Scottish universities and colleges announce new measures.* BBC. https://www.bbc.com/news/uk-scotland-51880666

BBC News. (2020g, March 23). *Universities must stop unconditional offers in virus confusion.* BBC. https://www.bbc.com/news/education-52010858

BBC News. (2020h, March 18). *Coronavirus: Oxford University students set up help group.* BBC. https://www.bbc.com/news/uk-england-oxfordshire-51946854

BBC News. (2020i, March 18). *Coronavirus: Oxford University students set up help group.* BBC. https://www.bbc.com/news/uk-england-oxfordshire-51946854

Bell, D. R., Ho, T., & Tang, C. S. (2001). Store choice and shopping behavior: How price format works. *California Management Review, 43*(2), 352–369.

Bell, D. R., & Lattin, J. M. (1998). Shopping behavior and consumer preference for retail price format: Why 'large basket' shoppers prefer EDLP. *Marketing Science, 17*(1), 66–88. doi:10.1287/mksc.17.1.66

Bell, E., & Bryman, A. (2007). The ethics of management research: An exploratory content analysis. *British Journal of Management, 18*(1), 63–77. doi:10.1111/j.1467-8551.2006.00487.x

Bellenger, D. N., Robertson, D. H., & Greenberg, B. A. (1977). Shopping centre patronage motives. *Journal of Retailing, 53*(2), 29–38.

Belsky, S. (2010). *Crowdsourcing is broken: How to fix it.* Bloomberg Businessweek.

Ben, B. (2006). *Risk and Return: The Intuition Traps.* Wiley Periodicals, Inc..

Bendle, N. T., Farris, P. W., Pfeifer, P. E., & Reibstein, D. J. (2015). *Marketing metrics: The manager's guide to measuring marketing performance* (3rd ed.). Pearson Education.

Berezina, K., Bilgihan, A., Cobanoglu, C., & Okumus, F. (2016). Understanding satisfied and dissatisfied hotel customers: Text mining of online hotel reviews. *Journal of Hospitality Marketing & Management, 25*(1), 1–24. doi:10.1080/19368623.2015.983631

Berger, I. E., & Mitchell, A. A. (1989). The effect of advertising on attitude accessibility, attitude confidence, and attitude-behaviour relationship. *The Journal of Consumer Research, 16*(3), 269–279. doi:10.1086/209213

Bergstrom, A. (2000). Cyberbranding: Leveraging your brand on the Internet. *Strategy and Leadership, 28*(4), 10–15. doi:10.1108/10878570010378645

Berman, B., & Evans, J. R. (2007). *Retailing management: A strategic approach* (8th ed.). Pearson Education.

Beverage, F. (2020). *Coca-Cola TV Commercial, 'Snow Polar Bear' Song by Edvard Grieg.* Retrieved 9 November 2020, from https://www.ispot.tv/ad/ZIai/coca-cola-snow-polar-bear-song-by-edvard-grieg

Bijmolt, T. H. A., Leeflang, P. S. H., Block, F., Eisenbeiss, M., Hardie, B. G. S., Lemmens, A., & Saffert, P. (2010). Analytics for customer engagement. *Journal of Service Research, 13*(3), 341–356. doi:10.1177/1094670510375603

Bilgin, Y. (2018). The effect of social media marketing activities on brand awareness, brand image and brand loyalty. *Business & Management Studies: An International Journal*, *6*(1), 128–148. doi:10.15295/bmij.v6i1.229

Blazheska, D., Ristovska, N., & Gramatnikovski, S. (2020). The impact of digital trends on marketing. *UTMS Journal of Economics (Skopje)*, *11*(1).

Bloch, P. H., Dawson, S., & Ridgway, N. M. (1994). The shopping mall as consumer habitat. *Journal of Retailing*, *70*(1), 132–145. doi:10.1016/0022-4359(94)90026-4

Bloomberg. J. (2018, April 29). Digitization, digitalization, and digital transformation: Confuse them at your peril. *Forbes*. https://www.forbes.com/sites/jasonbloomberg/2018/04/29/digitization-digitalization-and-digital-transformation-confuse-them-at-your-peril/?sh=4b79bd632f2c

Bosch, J. C. (1986). Portfolio Choices, Consumption, and Prices in a Market with Durable Assets. *Journal of Financial Research*, *9*(3), 239–250. doi:10.1111/j.1475-6803.1986.tb00454.x

Bothwell, E. (2020, March 18). Flexible admissions could mitigate COVID-19 impact. *Times Higher Education*. https:// www.timeshighereducation.com/news/flexible-admissions-could-mitigate-COVID-19-impact

Bourini, F., Khawaldeh, K., & Al-Qudah, S. (2013). The role of knowledge management in banks sector (analytical Study-Jordan). *Interdisciplinary Journal of Contemporary Research in Business*, *5*(3), 53–77.

Boyatzis, R. E. (1998). *Transforming qualitative information: Thematic analysis and code development*. Sage.

Bozkurt, A., & Sharma, R. C. (2020). Emergency remote teaching in a time of global crisis due to CoronaVirus pandemic. *Asian Journal of Distance Education*, *15*(1).

Brabham, D. C. (2008). Crowdsourcing as a model for problem solving: An introduction and cases. *Convergence*, *14*(1), 75–90. doi:10.1177/1354856507084420

Bradlow, E. T., Gangwar, M., Kopalle, P., & Voleti, S. (2017). The role of big data and predictive analytics in retailing. *Journal of Retailing*, *93*(1), 79–95. doi:10.1016/j.jretai.2016.12.004

Brafman, O., & Beckstrom, R. A. (2007). *The starfish and the spider: The unstoppable power of leaderless organization*. Penguin Books.

Brar, T. P. S., & Basra, R. (2018). Business Intelligence Technology: A Study Of Bi Implementation And Challenges. Advances in Wireless Communication and Mathematics.

Bratianu, C. (2017, November). Knowledge Management in the Sharing Economy. *Knowledge Management in the Sharing Economy.*, *6*, 290. doi:10.1007/978-3-319-66890-1

Brimpong, M. A. (2008). *A Project Submitted Entitled—The Effect of Customer Satisfaction on Loyalty A Case Study of First Allied Savings And Loans Ltd*. Academic Press.

Brod, C. (1984). *Technostress: The human cost of the computer revolution*. Addison-Wesley.

Brownbill, A. L., Miller, C. L., & Braunack-Mayer, A. J. (2018). The marketing of sugar-sweetened beverages to young people on Facebook. *Australian and New Zealand Journal of Public Health*, *42*(4), 354–360. doi:10.1111/1753-6405.12801 PMID:29972262

Brown, M. E., Trevino, L. K., & Harrison, D. A. (2005). Ethical leadership: A social learning perspective for construct development and testing. *Organizational Behavior and Human Decision Processes*, *97*(2), 117–134. doi:10.1016/j.obhdp.2005.03.002

Brown, S. (1989). Retail location theory: The legacy of Harold hoteling. *Journal of Retailing*, *65*(4), 450–470.

Bucklin, L. P. (1966). *A theory of distribution channel structure*. Institute of Business and Economic Research.

Bucklin, L. P., Ramaswamy, V., & Majumdar, S. K. (1996). Analyzing channel structures of business markets via the structure-output paradigm. *International Journal of Research in Marketing*, *13*(1), 73–87. doi:10.1016/0167-8116(95)00035-6

Buhse, W. (2014). Management by Internet: Neue Führungsmodelle für Unternehmen in Zeiten der digitalen Transformation. Kulmbach: Börsenmedien AG. doi:10.100740567-014-0039-y

Bureau, F. E. (2020, May 27*). Risky behaviour at work: How Covid-19 changed the way people work.* https://www.financialexpress.com/industry/technology/risky-behaviour-at-work-how-covid-19-changed-the-way-people-work/1971396/

Business Standard. (2012). *Madras HC orders shutdown of Subhiksha*. Available at: https://www.business-standard.com/article/companies/madras-hc-orders-shutdown-of-subhiksha-112030100064_1.html

Business Today. (2012). *The devil is in retail*. Available at: https://www.businesstoday.in/magazine/cover-story/organised-retail-india-problems/story/184980.html

Buttle, F. (1996). *Relationship Marketing: Theory and Practice*. Chapman Hall.

Cadez, S., & Guilding, C. (2008). An exploratory investigation of an integrated contingency model of strategic management accounting. *Accounting, Organizations and Society*, *33*(7–8), 836–863. doi:10.1016/j.aos.2008.01.003

Campbell-Sills, L., Cohan, S. L., & Stein, M. B. (2006). Relationship of resilience to personality, coping, and psychiatric symptoms in young adults. *Behaviour Research and Therapy*, *44*(4), 585–599. doi:10.1016/j.brat.2005.05.001 PMID:15998508

Capgemini Consulting. (2015). *Digital Leadership—Führungskräfteentwicklung im Digitalen Zeitalter.* https://www.capgemini.com/consulting-de/wp content/uploads/sites/32/2017/08/14-10-16_digital_leadership_v11_web_17102016.pdf

Cenfetelli, R. T., & Schwarz, A. (2011). Identifying and testing the inhibitors of technology usage intentions. *Information Systems Research*, *22*(4), 808–823. doi:10.1287/isre.1100.0295

Chaffey, D., & Patron, M. (2012). From web analytics to digital marketing optimization: Increasing the commercial value of digital analytics. *Journal of Direct, Data and Digital Marketing Practice*, *14*(1), 30–45. doi:10.1057/dddmp.2012.20

Chaffey, D., & Smith, P. R. (2013). *Emarketing excellence: Planning and optimizing your digital marketing* (4th ed.). Taylor & Francis. doi:10.4324/9780203082812

Chakravarty, A., Grewal, R., & Sambamurthy, V. (2013). Information technology competencies, organizational agility, and firm performance: Enabling and facilitating roles. *Information Systems Research*, *24*(4), 976–997. doi:10.1287/isre.2013.0500

Chandrasekaran, D., Srinivasan, R., & Sihi, D. (2017). Effects of offline ad content on online brand search: Insights from super bowl advertising. *Journal of the Academy of Marketing Science*, *46*(3), 403–430. doi:10.100711747-017-0551-8

Chang, S. C., Lin, N. P., Yang, C. L., & Sheu, C. (2003). Quality dimensions, capabilities and business strategy: An empirical study in high-tech industry. *Total Quality Management & Business Excellence*, *14*(4), 407–421. doi:10.1080/1478336032000047228

Chaturvedi, A. (2020, January 21). Layoffs, rejig one-time exercise, will soon be over: Oyo CEO. *The Economic Times*. https://economictimes.indiatimes.com/small-biz/startups/newsbuzz/layoffs-rejig-one-time-exercise-will-be-over-soon-oyo-ceo/articleshow/73395167.cms

Chen, A. C. (2001). Using free association to examine the relationship between the characteristics of brand associations and brand equity. *Journal of Product and Brand Management*, *10*(7), 439–451. doi:10.1108/10610420110410559

Cheng, P. L. (1962). Optimum bond portfolio selections. *Management Science*, *8*(4), 490–499. doi:10.1287/mnsc.8.4.490

Chen, H., Chiang, R. H., & Storey, V. C. (2012). Business intelligence and analytics: From big data to big impact. *Management Information Systems Quarterly*, *36*(4), 1165–1188. doi:10.2307/41703503

Chenhall, R. H. (2003). Management control systems design within its organizational context: Findings from contingency-based research and directions for the future. *Accounting, Organizations and Society*, *28*(2–3), 127–168. doi:10.1016/S0361-3682(01)00027-7

Chenhall, R. H., & Langfield-Smith, K. (1998). The relationship between strategic priorities, management techniques and management accounting: An empirical investigation using a systems approach. *Accounting, Organizations and Society*, *23*(3), 243–264. doi:10.1016/S0361-3682(97)00024-X

Chen, S. C., & Lin, C. P. (2019). Understanding the effect of social media marketing activities: The mediation of social identification, perceived value, and satisfaction. *Technological Forecasting and Social Change*, *140*, 22–32. doi:10.1016/j.techfore.2018.11.025

Chong, V. K., & Chong, K. M. (1997). Strategic choices, environmental uncertainty and SBU perform-ance: A note on the intervening role of management accounting systems. *Accounting and Business Research*, *27*(4), 268–276. doi:10.1080/00014788.1997.9729553

Chung, T. S., Wedel, M., & Rust, R. T. (2016). Adaptive personalization using social networks. *Journal of the Academy of Marketing Science*, *44*(1), 66–87. doi:10.100711747-015-0441-x

Churchill, G. Jr. (1979). A Paradigm for developing better measures of marketing constructs. *JMR, Journal of Marketing Research*, *16*(February), 64–73. doi:10.1177/002224377901600110

Cinquini, L., &Tenucci, A. (2010). Strategic management accounting and business strategy: a loose coupling? *Journal of Accounting & Organizational Change*, *6*(2), 228-259.

Clark, E. (2020, March 13). Hundreds of universities closing across the US in response to coronavirus threat. *Chemistry World*. https://www.chemistryworld.com/news/hundredsof-universities-closing-across-the-us-in-response-to coronavirus- threat/4011337.article

Clark, B. H., Abela, A. V., & Ambler, T. (2006). Behind the wheel: Align marketing goals and corporate strategies through dashboards. *Marketing Management*, *15*(3), 19–23.

Clarke, V., & Braun, V. (2013). Teaching thematic analysis: Overcoming challenges and developing strategies for effective learning. *The Psychologist*, *26*(2).

Cobb-Walgren, C. J., Ruble, C. A., & Donthu, N. (1995). Brand Equity, Brand Preferences, and Purchase Intent. *Journal of Advertising*, *24*(3), 25–40. doi:10.1080/00913367.1995.10673481

Connor, J., Jen, F., Jim, G., & Hogan, S. K. (2018). Positive technology: Designing work environments for digital well-being. *Deloitte Insights*. https://www2.deloitte.com/us/en/insights/focus/behavioral-economics/negative-impact-technology-business.html/

Constantinides, E. (2014). Foundations of social media marketing. *Procedia: Social and Behavioral Sciences*, *148*, 40–57. doi:10.1016/j.sbspro.2014.07.016

Corbin-Herbison, C. (2019, September 13). Pros and cons of digital workplace – striking a human balance. *Interact*. https://www.interact-intranet.com/blog/pros-cons-digital-workplace/

Coronavirus disease 2019 (COVID-19) in the U.S. (2020, May 21). Retrieved from https://www.cdc.gov/coronavirus/2019-ncov/cases-updates/cases-in-us.html

Corrigan, H. B., Craciun, G., & Powell, A. M. (2014). How does Target know so much about its customers? Utilizing customer analytics to make marketing decisions. *Marketing Education Review*, *24*(2), 159–165. doi:10.2753/MER1052-8008240206

Cortellazzo, L., Bruni, E., & Zampieri, R. (2019). The Role of Leadership in a Digitalized World: A Review. *Frontiers in Psychology*, *10*, 1938. doi:10.3389/fpsyg.2019.01938 PMID:31507494

Côrte-Real, N., Oliveira, T., & Ruivo, P. (2017). Assessing business value of Big Data Analytics in European firms. *Journal of Business Research*, *70*, 379–390. doi:10.1016/j.jbusres.2016.08.011

Coursaris, C. K., van Osch, W., & Balogh, B. A. (2016). Informing brand messaging strategies via social media analytics. *Online Information Review*, *40*(1), 6–24. doi:10.1108/OIR-02-2015-0062

Court, D., McLaughlin, K., & Halsall, C. (2006). *Marketing spending effectiveness: how to winin a complex environment.* McKinsey White Paper. Available at: www.mckinsey.com

Coutu, D. L. (2000). Too old to learn? *Harvard Business Review, 78*(6), 37–42.

Craig, S. C., Ghosh, A., & McLafferty, S. (1984). Department store cross-shoppers. *JMR, Journal of Marketing Research, 14*(2), 187–192.

Cravens, K. S., & Guilding, C. (2001). An empirical study of the application of strategic management accounting techniques. *Advances in Management Accounting, 10*, 95–124.

Crawford, J., Butler-Henderson, K., Rudolph, J., & Glowatz, M. (2020). COVID-19: 20 Countries' Higher Education Intra-Period Digital Pedagogy Responses. *Journal of Applied Teaching and Learning, 3*(1).

Cruz, S., & Camps, J. (2003). Organic vs mechanistic structures. Construction and validation of a scale of measurement. *Management Research, 1*(1), 111–123. doi:10.1108/15365430380000521

Culotta, A., & Cutler, J. (2016). Mining brand perceptions from Twitter social networks. *Marketing Science, 35*(3), 343–362. doi:10.1287/mksc.2015.0968

Dahnil, M. I., Marzuki, K. M., Langgat, J., & Fabeil, N. F. (2014). Factors influencing SMEs adoption of social media marketing. *Procedia: Social and Behavioral Sciences, 148*, 119–126. doi:10.1016/j.sbspro.2014.07.025

Danna, K., & Griffin, R. W. (1999). Health and well-being in the workplace: A review and synthesis of the literature. *Journal of Management, 25*(3), 357–384. doi:10.1177/014920639902500305

Dann, S. (2010). Redefining social marketing with contemporary commercial marketing definitions. *Journal of Business Research, 63*(2), 147–153. doi:10.1016/j.jbusres.2009.02.013

Dave, C. (2020). *Global Social Media Summary August 2020.* Smart Insights.

Davenport, T. H. (2006). Competing on analytics. *Harvard Business Review, 84*(1), 99–107. PMID:16447373

Davenport, T. H., & Harris, J. G. (2007). *Competing on analytics: The new science of winning.* Harvard Business School Press.

Definition of regional groupings. (n.d.). Retrieved from https://www.who.int/healthinfo/global_burden_disease/definition_regions/en/

Deighton, J., & Kornfeld, L. (2011). *Coca-Cola on Facebook.* Harvard Business School Marketing Unit Case, (511-110).

Deng & Li. (2018). Feeling a destination through the 'right' photos: A machine learning model for DMOs' photo selection. *Tourism Management*, 267-278.

Deshpandé, R., Farley, J. U., & Webster, F. E. (2012). Corporate Culture, Customer Orientation, and Innovativeness in Japanese Firms: A Quadrad Analysis. *Developing a Market Orientation, 57*, 79–102. doi:10.4135/9781452231426.n4

Diaconescu, M. (2020). Some considerations regarding the new trends in marketing approaches. *Romanian Economic Journal*, *23*(77), 2–10.

Diamante, T., & London, M. (2002). Expansive leadership in the age of digital technology. *Journal of Management Development*, *21*(6), 404–416. doi:10.1108/02621710210430597

Diefenbach, U., Wald, A., & Gleich, R. (2018). Between cost and benefit: Investigating effects of cost management control systems on cost efficiency and organizational performance. *Journal of Management Control*, *29*(1), 63–89. doi:10.100700187-018-0261-5

Dodge, R. H., & Summer, H. (1969). Choosing between retail stores. *Journal of Retailing*, *45*(3), 11–21.

Doyle, P. (1998). *Marketing management and strategy* (2nd ed.). Prentice-Hall.

Druskat, V. U., & Wheeler, J. V. (2003). Managing from the boundary: The effective leadership of self-managing work teams. *Academy of Management Journal*, *46*(4), 435–457.

Dua, S., & Chahal, R. (2013). Interrelationship of Aaker's customer based brand equity dimensions: offering a model to banking sector. Asian Journal of Management Research, 4(2), 297-307.

DuBrin, A. J. (2002). *Fundamentals of organizational behaviour: An applied perspective* (2nd ed.). Pergamon Press Inc.

Duffett, R. G. (2017). Influence of social media marketing communications on young consumers' attitudes. *Young Consumers*, *18*(1), 19–39. doi:10.1108/YC-07-2016-00622

Duong, V., Pham, P., Yang, T., Wang, Y., & Luo, J. (2020). *The ivory tower lost: How college students respond differently than the general public to the covid-19 pandemic*. arXiv preprint arXiv:2004.09968.

Dutta, A., & Goswami, A. L. (2020, May 4). *Corona Pandemic and Higher Education*. Academic Press.

Dwivedi, Y. K., Ismagilova, E., Hughes, D. L., Carlson, J., Filieri, R., Jacobson, J., ... Kumar, V. (2020). Setting the future of digital and social media marketing research: Perspectives and research propositions. *International Journal of Information Management*, 102168. doi:10.1016/j.ijinfomgt.2020.102168

Dwivedi, Y. K., Kapoor, K. K., & Chen, H. (2015). Social media marketing and advertising. *The Marketing Review*, *15*(3), 289–309. doi:10.1362/146934715X14441363377999

Easton, G. S., & Jarrell, S. L. (1998). The effects of total quality management on corporate performance: An empirical investigation. *The Journal of Business*, *71*(2), 253–307. doi:10.1086/209744

Ebner, W., Leimeister, J. M., & Krcmar, H. (2009). Community engineering for innovations: The ideas competition as a method to nurture a virtual community for innovations. *R & D Management*, *39*(4), 342–356. doi:10.1111/j.1467-9310.2009.00564.x

Egeland, B., Carlson, E., & Sroufe, L. A. (1993). Resilience as process. *Development and Psychopathology*, *5*(4), 517–528. doi:10.1017/S0954579400006131

Eggers, J. P., & Park, K. F. (2018). Incumbent adaptation to technological change: The past, present, and future of research on heterogeneous incumbent response. *The Academy of Management Annals*, *12*(1), 357–389. doi:10.5465/annals.2016.0051

Elisabeta, I., & Ivona, S. (2014). Social Media and its Impact on Consumers Behaviour. *International Journal of Economic Practices and Theories*, *4*(2), 295–302.

Ellinger, A. E., Daugherty, P., & Keller, S. (2000). The relationship between marketing / logistics interdepartmental .... *Journal of Business Logistics*, *21*(1), 1.

Elton, E. J., & Gruber, M. J. (1987). Portfolio analysis with partial information: The case of grouped data. *Management Science*, *33*(10), 1238–1246. doi:10.1287/mnsc.33.10.1238

Elton, E. J., & Gruber, M. J. (2004). Optimum centralized portfolio construction with decentralized portfolio management. *Journal of Financial and Quantitative Analysis*, *39*(3), 481–494. doi:10.1017/S0022109000003999

Emelichev, V., Korotkov, V., & Nikulin, Y. (2014). Post-optimal Analysis for Markowitz's Multicriteria Portfolio Optimization Problem. *Journal of Multi-Criteria Decision Analysis*, *21*(1-2), 95–100. doi:10.1002/mcda.1492

Engel, J. F., Blackwell, R. D., & Miniard, P. W. (1995). *Consumer behaviour*. Dryden Press.

Erdoğmuş, İ. E., & Cicek, M. (2012). The impact of social media marketing on brand loyalty. *Procedia: Social and Behavioral Sciences*, *58*, 1353–1360. doi:10.1016/j.sbspro.2012.09.1119

Erevelles, S., Fukawa, N., & Swayne, L. (2016). Big Data consumer analytics and the transformation of marketing. *Journal of Business Research*, *69*(2), 897–904. doi:10.1016/j.jbusres.2015.07.001

Ernst & Young LLP. (2011). *The digitisation of everything: How organisations must adapt to changing consumer behaviour*. https://www.the-digital-insurer.com/wp-content/uploads/2014/04/200-EY_Digitisation_of_everything.pdf

eYeka. (2015). *The state of crowdsourcing in 2015*. Analyst report #CSReport 2015.

Fakhri, G., Menacere, K., & Pegum, R. (2009). The Impact of Contingent Factors on the Use of Performance Measurement System in the Banking Industry: The Case of Libya. *Salford Postgraduate Annual Research Conference*, *44*(0), 1–5.

Faltermaier, T., Ulich, D., Leplow, B., & von Salisch, M. (2017). *Grundriss der Psychologie* (2nd ed.). Kohlhammer Verlag.

Fang, Kucukusta, & Law. (2016). Analysis of the perceived value of online tourism reviews: Influence of readability and reviewer characteristics. *Tourism Management*, •••, 498–506.

Fargnoli, E., Almeida, E., Palhares, G., Silvério, K., & Marques, R. (2012). Teoria da Contingência. *Administração e Negócio*, 61-80.

Fejzagic, E. (2017). *The Impact of Social Media on Consumer Behaviour*. Ligs University Blog Posts.

Felix, R., Rauschnabel, P. A., & Hinsch, C. (2017). Elements of strategic social media marketing: A holistic framework. *Journal of Business Research*, *70*, 118–126. doi:10.1016/j.jbusres.2016.05.001

Fiedler, F. E. (1964). A contingency model of leadership effectiveness. In *Advances in experimental social psychology* (Vol. 1, pp. 149–190). Academic Press. doi:10.1016/S0065-2601(08)60051-9

Fisher, J. (1995). Contingency-based research on management control systems: Categorization by level of complexity. *Journal of Accounting Literature*, *14*, 24–53. http://search.proquest.com/docview/216311338?accountid=42455%5Cnhttp://sfx.library.tu.ac.th:3210/sfxlcl3?url_ver=Z39.882004&rft_val_fmt=info:ofi/fmt:kev:mtx:journal&genre=article&sid=ProQ:ProQ%3Aabiglobal&atitle=Contingency-based+research+on+management+c

Fluss, D. (2010). Why marketing needs speech analytics. *Journal of Direct, Data and Digital Marketing Practice*, *11*(4), 324–331. doi:10.1057/dddmp.2010.12

Foerster-Metz, U., Marquardt, K., Golowko, N., Kompalla, A., & Hell, C. (2018). Digital transformation and its implications on organizational behaviour. *Journal of EU Research in Business*.

Fogel, S. (2010). Issues in measurement of word of mouth in social media marketing. *International Journal of Integrated Marketing Communications*, *2*(2).

Ford, R. C., Richard, B., & Ciuchta, M. P. (2015). Crowdsourcing: A new way of employing non-employees? *Business Horizons*, *58*(4), 377–388.

Forker, L. B., Vickery, S. K., & Droge, C. L. (1996). The contribution of quality to business performance. *International Journal of Operations & Production Management*, *16*(8), 44–62. doi:10.1108/01443579610125778

Fredrickson, B. L., Tugade, M. M., Waugh, C. E., & Larkin, G. R. (2003). What good are positive emotions in crises? A prospective study of resilience and emotions following the terrorist attacks on the United States on September 11th, 2001. *Journal of Personality and Social Psychology*, *84*(2), 365–376. doi:10.1037/0022-3514.84.2.365 PMID:12585810

French, J. R. P., & Raven, B. H. (1959). The bases of social power. In D. Cartwright (Ed.), Studies in social power (pp. 150-167). Institute for Social Research.

Freymann, J. V. (2002). Grocery store pricing and its effect on initial and ongoing store choice. *Marketing Management Journal*, *12*(1), 107–119.

Fuentes, M. M. F., Montes, F. J. L., & Fernández, L. M. (2006). Total quality management, strategic orientation and organizational performance: The case of Spanish companies. *Total Quality Management & Business Excellence*, *17*(3), 303–323. doi:10.1080/14783360500451358

Fuentes, M., & Hurtado, N. (2002). Variables críticasen la medición del desempeñoenempresas con implantación de la gestión de la calidad total. *Investigaciones Europeas de Dirección y Economía de la Empresa*, *8*(2), 87–102.

Furness, P. (2011). Applications of Monte Carlo Simulation in marketing analytics. *Journal of Direct, Data and Digital Marketing Practice*, *13*(2), 132–147. doi:10.1057/dddmp.2011.25

Gale, B. T., & Klavans, R. (1985). Formulating a quality improvement strategy. *The Journal of Business Strategy*, *5*(3), 21–31. doi:10.1108/eb039072

Ganapaiah, C. (2017). Strategic Cost Management and Business Performance: A Study of SME's in India-An Analysis. *BIMS International Journal of Social Science Research*, *2*(1), 17–29.

Gandomi & Haider. (2017). Beyond the hype: Big data concepts, methods, and analytics. *International Journal of Information Management*, •••, 137–144.

Ganesha, H. R., Aithal, P. S., & Kirubadevi, P. (2020). Changes in Consumer Perspective towards Discount at Brick-and-Mortar Stores owing to Emergence of Online Store Format in India. I*nternational Journal of Management. Technology, and Social Sciences*, *5*(1), 43–83.

García-Sánchez, E., García-Morales, V. J., & Bolívar-Ramos, M. T. (2017). The influence of top management support for ICTs on organizational performance through knowledge acquisition, transfer, and utilisation. *Review of Managerial Science*, *11*(1), 19–51. doi:10.100711846-015-0179-3

Garengo, P., Biazzo, S., & Bititci, U. S. (2005). Performance measurement systems in SMEs: A review for a research agenda. *International Journal of Management Reviews*, *7*(1), 25–47. doi:10.1111/j.1468-2370.2005.00105.x

Garengo, P., & Bititci, U. (2007). Towards a contingency approach to performance measurement: An empirical study in Scottish SMEs. *International Journal of Operations & Production Management*, *27*(8), 802–825. doi:10.1108/01443570710763787

Gartner. (2014, November). *Gartner Survey Reveals Digital Marketing Budgets Will Increase by 8 Percent in 2015.* Available at: https://www.gartner.com/newsroom/id/2895817

Germann, F., Lilien, G. L., Fiedler, L., & Kraus, M. (2014). Do retailers benefit from deploying customer analytics? *Journal of Retailing*, *90*(4), 587–593. doi:10.1016/j.jretai.2014.08.002

Germann, F., Lilien, G. L., & Rangaswamy, A. (2013). Performance implications of deploying marketing analytics. *International Journal of Research in Marketing*, *30*(2), 114–128. doi:10.1016/j.ijresmar.2012.10.001

Gerth, A. B., & Peppard, J. (2016). The dynamics of CIO derailment: How CIOs come undone and how to avoid it. *Business Horizons*, *59*(1), 61–70. doi:10.1016/j.bushor.2015.09.001

Gheni, A. Y., Jusoh, Y. Y., Jabar, M. A., Ali, N. M., Abdullah, R. H., Abdullah, S., & Khalefa, M. S. (2016). The virtual teams: E-leaders challenges. *Proceedings of the 2015 IEEE Conference on e-Learning, e-Management and e-Services (IC3e), Melaka, Malaysia, August 24-26, 2015*, 38–42. https://ieeexplore.ieee.org/document/7403483

Ghosh, P., Tripathi, V., & Kumar, A. (2010). Customer expectations of store attributes: A Study of organized retail outlets in India. *Journal of Retail & Leisure Property*, *9*(1), 75–87. doi:10.1057/rlp.2009.27

Gil, A., Grewal, L., Rhonda, H., & Stephen, A. T. (2019). Future of Social Media in Marketing. *Journal of the Academy of Marketing Science*, 79–95. PMID:32431463

Giri, K. (2017). Optimum Portfolio Construction Using Single Index Model. *Intercontinental Journal of Finance Research Review, 5*(2).

Gobé, M. (2001). *Emotional branding: The new paradigm for connecting brands to people.* All Worth Press.

Godey, B., Manthiou, A., Pederzoli, D., Rokka, J., Aiello, G., Donvito, R., & Singh, R. (2016). Social media marketing efforts of luxury brands: Influence on brand equity and consumer behavior. *Journal of Business Research*, *69*(12), 5833–5841. doi:10.1016/j.jbusres.2016.04.181

Godil, D. I., & Shabib-ul-hasan, S. (2018). An Investigation of a Contingency Framework of Management Accounting Practices in Manufacturing Companies of Pakistan. *Gmjacs*, *8*(1), 53–65.

Goel, V., & Singh, K. D. (2020, January 2). At SoftBank's jewel in India: 'Toxic' culture and troubling incidents. *The New York Times.* https://www.nytimes.com/2020/01/02/technology/oyo-softbank-india.html

Goh, K. T., Cutter, J., Heng, B. H., Ma, S., Koh, B. K., Kwok, C., ... Chew, S. K. (2006). Epidemiology and control of SARS in Singapore. *Annals of the Academy of Medicine, Singapore*, *35*(5), 301. PMID:16829997

Goh, T. T., & Sun, P.-C. (2015). Teaching social media analytics: An assessment based on natural disaster postings. *Journal of Information Systems Education*, *26*(1), 27–38.

Goldsmith, R. E., & Lafferty, B. A. (2002). Consumer response to websites and their influence on advertising effectiveness. *Internet Research: Electronic Networking Applications and Policy*, *12*(4), 318–328. doi:10.1108/10662240210438407

Gommans, M., Krishnan, K. S., & Scheffold, K. B. (2001). From Brand Loyalty to E-Loyalty: A Conceptual Framework. *Journal of Economic and Social Research.*, *3*(1), 43–58.

Goodwin, D., & McElwee, R. (1999). Grocery shopping and an ageing population: Research note. *International Journal of Retail, Distribution and Consumer Research, 9*(4), 403-409.

Gov.UK. (2020). *Travel advice: Coronavirus (COVID-19).* https://www.gov.uk/guidance/travel-advice-novel-coronavirus

Government of South Africa. (2020). *Minister Angie Motshekga on Basic Education Sector Plans to support learners during Coronavirus COVID-19 lockdown.* Accessed 08/04/2020, available from https://www.gov.za/speeches/minister-angie-motshekga-basic-educationsector-plans-support-learners-during-covid-19

Govindarajan, V. (1984). Appropriateness of accounting data in performance evaluation: An empirical examination of environmental uncertainty as an intervening variable. *Accounting, Organizations and Society*, *9*(2), 125–135. doi:10.1016/0361-3682(84)90002-3

Govindarajan, V., & Gupta, A. K. (1985). Linking control systems to business unit strategy: Impact on performance. *Accounting, Organizations and Society*, *10*(1), 51–66. doi:10.1016/0361-3682(85)90031-5

Grafström, M., & Falkman, L. L. (2017). Everyday narratives: CEO rhetoric on Twitter. *Journal of Organizational Change Management*, *30*(3), 312–322. doi:10.1108/JOCM-10-2016-0197

Grandzol, J. R., & Gershon, M. (1998). A survey instrument for standardizing TQM modeling research. *International Journal of Quality Science*, *3*(1), 80–105. doi:10.1108/13598539810203887

Guilding, C. (1999). Competitor-focused accounting: An exploratory note. *Accounting, Organizations and Society*, *24*(7), 583–595. doi:10.1016/S0361-3682(99)00007-0

Guilding, C., Cravens, K. S., & Tayles, M. (2000). An international comparison of strategic management accounting practices. *Management Accounting Research*, *11*(1), 113–135. doi:10.1006/mare.1999.0120

Gujarati, D. N. (2008). *Basic econometrics*. McGraw Hill.

Gunasekaran, A., Papadopoulos, T., Dubey, R., Wamba, S. F., Childe, S. J., Hazen, B., & Akter, S. (2017). Big data and predictive analytics for supply chain and organizational performance. *Journal of Business Research*, *70*, 308–317. doi:10.1016/j.jbusres.2016.08.004

Gupta, A. K., & Govindarajan, V. (1984). Business unit strategy, managerial characteristics, and business unit effectiveness at strategy implementation. *Academy of Management Journal*, *27*(1), 25–41.

Gupta, S., & Pathak, G. S. (2018). Virtual team experiences in an emerging economy: A qualitative study. *Journal of Organizational Change Management*, *31*(4), 778–794. doi:10.1108/JOCM-04-2017-0108

Hadija, Z., Barnes, S. B., & Hair, N. (2012). Why we ignore social networking advertising? *Qualitative Market Research*, *15*(1), 19–32. doi:10.1108/13522751211191973

Hair, J. F. Jr. (2007). Knowledge creation in marketing: The role of predictive analytics. *European Business Review*, *19*(4), 303–315. doi:10.1108/09555340710760134

Haldma, T., & Lääts, K. (2002). Contingencies influencing the management accounting practices of Estonian manufacturing companies. *Management Accounting Research*, *13*(4), 379–400. doi:10.1006/mare.2002.0197

Hambley, L. A., O'Neill, T. A., & Kline, T. J. B. (2007 b). Virtual team leadership: The effects of leadership style and communication medium on team interaction styles and outcomes. *Organizational Behavior and Human Decision Processes*, *103*(1), 1–20. doi:10.1016/j.obhdp.2006.09.004

Hansen, T., Cumberland, F., & Sologaard, H. S. (2004). *How the measurement of store choice behavior moderates the relationship between distance and store choice behavior*. Available at: www.marketing-trends-congress.com/archives/2013/pages/PDF/665.pdf

Hanssens, D. M., & Pauwels, K. H. (2016). Demonstrating the value of marketing. *Journal of Marketing*, *80*(6), 173–190. doi:10.1509/jm.15.0417

Hanssens, D. M., Pauwels, K. H., Srinivasan, S., Vanhuele, M., & Yildirim, G. (2014). Consumer attitude metrics for guiding marketing mix decisions. *Marketing Science*, *33*(4), 534–550. doi:10.1287/mksc.2013.0841

Harris, J. G., & Mehrotra, V. (2014). Getting value from your data scientists. *MIT Sloan Management Review*, *56*(1), 15–18.

Harrison, H., Birks, M., Franklin, R., & Mills, J. (2017, January). Case study research: Foundations and methodological orientations. In *Forum Qualitative Sozialforschung/Forum: Qualitative. Social Research*, *18*(1).

Hauser, W.J. 2007. Marketing analytics: The evolution of marketing research in the twenty-first century. *Direct Marketing: An Inter- national Journal, 1*(1), 38–54.

HBS Digital Initiative. (2017). *The biggest challenge to the future of crowdsourcing in business*. Retrieved from: https://digital.hbs.edu/platforms-crowds/biggest-challenge-future-crowdsourcing-business/

Heinonen, K. (2011). Consumer activity in social media: Managerial approaches to consumers' social media behaviour. *Journal of Consumer Behaviour*, **•••**, 356–364.

Hempel, J. (2006). Crowdsourcing: Milk the masses for inspiration. *Business Week*, *25*, 38–39.

Henri, J. F., Boiral, O., & Roy, M. J. (2016). Strategic cost management and performance: The case of environmental costs. *The British Accounting Review*, *48*(2), 269–282. doi:10.1016/j.bar.2015.01.001

Herpich, N. (2020, March 10). Q&A on Harvard's move to online learning. *Harvard Gazette*. https://news.harvard.edu/ gazette/story/2020/03/officials-detail-university's-move-to online-learning-to-combat-coronavirus/

Herrington, J. D., & Capella, L. M. (1994). Practical applications of music in retail and service settings. *Journal of Services Marketing*, *8*(4), 50–65. doi:10.1108/08876049410065615

Hildebrandt, L. (1988). Store image and the prediction of performance in retailing. *Journal of Business Research*, *17*(1), 91–100. doi:10.1016/0148-2963(88)90026-4

Hoegl, M., & Muethel, M. (2016). Enabling shared leadership in virtual project teams: A practitioners' guide. *Project Management Journal*, *47*(1), 7–12. doi:10.1002/pmj.21564

Hofacker, C. F., Malthouse, E. C., & Sultan, F. (2016). Big Data and consumer behaviour: Imminent opportunities. *Journal of Consumer Marketing*, *33*(2), 89–97. doi:10.1108/JCM-04-2015-1399

Hoffman, D. L., & Fodor, M. (2010). Can you measure the ROI of your social media marketing? *MIT Sloan Management Review*, *52*(1), 41.

Hojeghan, S. B., & Esfangareh, A. N. (2011). Digital economy and tourism impacts, influences and challenges. *Procedia: Social and Behavioral Sciences*, *19*, 308–316. doi:10.1016/j.sbspro.2011.05.136

Hoppner, J. J., & Griffith, D. A. (2015). Looking back to move forward: A review of the evolution of research in international marketing channels. *Journal of Retailing*, *91*(4), 610–626. doi:10.1016/j.jretai.2015.04.005

Hoque, Z. (2004). A contingency model of the association between strategy, environmental uncertainty and performance measurement: Impact on organizational performance. *International Business Review*, *13*(4), 485–502. doi:10.1016/j.ibusrev.2004.04.003

Horner-Long, P., & Schoenberg, R. (2002). Does e-business require different leadership characteristics? An empirical investigation. *European Management Journal*, *20*(6), 611–619. doi:10.1016/S0263-2373(02)00112-3

Ho, S. Y., & Bodoff, D. (2014). The effects of Web personalization on user attitude and behavior: An integration of the Elaboration Likelihood Model and consumer search theory. *Management Information Systems Quarterly*, *38*(2), 497–520. doi:10.25300/MISQ/2014/38.2.08

Houlden, S., & Veletsianos, G. (2020). Coronavirus pushes universities to switch to online classes – but are they ready? *The Conversation*. https://theconversation.com/coronaviruspushes-universities-to-switch-to-online-classes-but-arethey-ready-132728

Howe, J. (2008). *Crowdsourcing: How the power of the crowd is driving the future of business*. Random House.

Ho, Y., Chung, Y., & Lau, K. (2010). Unfolding large-scale marketing data. *International Journal of Research in Marketing*, *27*(2), 119–132. doi:10.1016/j.ijresmar.2009.12.009

Huang, M.-H., & Rust, R. T. (2017). Technology-driven service strategy. *Journal of the Academy of Marketing Science*, *45*(6), 906–924. doi:10.100711747-017-0545-6

Hudgins, T. A. (2016). Resilience, job satisfaction and anticipated turnover in nurse leaders. *Journal of Nursing Management*, *24*(1), E62–E69. doi:10.1111/jonm.12289 PMID:25782613

Huff, D. (1964). Declining and estimating a trading area. *Journal of Marketing*, *28*(3), 34–38. doi:10.1177/002224296402800307

Huppert, F. A. (2009). Psychological well-being: Evidence regarding its causes and consequences. *Applied Psychology. Health and Well-Being*, *1*(2), 137–164. doi:10.1111/j.1758-0854.2009.01008.x

Iankova, S., Davies, I., Archer-Brown, C., Marder, B., & Yau, A. (2019). A comparison of social media marketing between B2B, B2C and mixed business models. *Industrial Marketing Management*, *81*, 169–179. doi:10.1016/j.indmarman.2018.01.001

Iansiti, M., & Lakhani, K. R. (2014). Digital ubiquity: How connections, sensors, and data are revolutionizing business. *Harvard Business Review*, *92*(11), 90–99.

IBEF. (2018). *Retail industry in India*. Available at: https://www.ibef.org/industry/retail-india.aspx

Ibeh, K. I. N., Luo, Y., & Dinnie, K. (2005). E-branding strategies of internet companies: Some preliminary insights from the UK. *Journal of Brand Management*, *12*(5), 355–373. doi:10.1057/palgrave.bm.2540231

ICEF. (2020). Coronavirus triggers travel restrictions and other countermeasures. *ICEF Monitor*. https://monitor.icef.com/2020/01/coronavirus-triggers-travel-restrictions-andother-countermeasures/

Ikediego, H. O., Ilkan, M., Abubakar, A. M., & Victor Bekun, F. (2018). Crowd-sourcing (who, why and what). *International Journal of Crowd Science*, *2*(1), 27–41. doi:10.1108/ijcs-07-2017-0005

Ittner, C. D., & Larcker, D. F. (1998). Innovations in performance measurement: Trends and research implications. *Journal of Management Accounting Research*, *10*, 205–238.

Ittner, C. D., & Larcker, D. F. (2003a). Coming up short on non-financial performance measurement. *Harvard Business Review*, *81*(11), 88–95. PMID:14619154

Ittner, C. D., Larcker, D. F., & Rajan, M. V. (1997, April). The choice of performance measures in annual bonus contract. *The Accounting Review*, *2*(2), 231–256.

Itweb. (2020). *Government makes provision for virtual learning during lockdown*. Accessed 08/04/2020, available from https://www.itweb.co.za/content/Gb3BwMW8LQKq2k6V

Jacobson, J., Gruzd, A., & Hernández-García, Á. (2020). Social media marketing: Who is watching the watchers? *Journal of Retailing and Consumer Services*, *53*, 53. doi:10.1016/j.jretconser.2019.03.001

Janjić, V., Karapavlović, N., & Damjanović, J. (2017). Технике Стратегијског Управљања Трошковима – Случај Републике Србије. *Teme*, *441*, 441. Advance online publication. doi:10.22190/TEME1702441J

Järvinen, J., & Karjaluoto, H. (2015). The use of Web analytics for digital marketing performance measurement. *Industrial Marketing Management*, *50*, 117–127. doi:10.1016/j.indmarman.2015.04.009

Jawadi, N., Daassi, M., Favier, M., & Kalika, M. (2013). Relationship building in virtual teams: A leadership behavioral complexity perspective. *Human Systems Management*, *32*(3), 199–211. doi:10.3233/HSM-130791

Jaworski, B. J., & Kohli, A. K. (1993). Market Orientation: Antrcendent and Consequances. *Journal of Marketing*, *57*(1), 53–70. doi:10.1177/002224299305700304

Jermias, J., & Gani, L. (2004). Integrating business strategy, organizational configurations and management accounting systems with business unit effectiveness: A fitness landscape approach. *Management Accounting Research*, *15*(2), 179–200. doi:10.1016/j.mar.2004.03.002

Jinkens, R., & Yallapragada, R. R. (2010). Cost Accounting In Auto Manufacturing Companies In Germany And The United States. *International Business & Economics Research Journal*, *9*(3), 121–126. doi:10.19030/iber.v9i3.542

Jobs, C. G., Aukers, S. M., & Gilfoil, D. M. (2015). The impact of big data on your firms marketing communications: A framework for understanding the emerging marketing analytics industry. *Inter- national. Academy of Marketing Studies Journal*, *19*(2), 81–94.

Jobs, C. G., Gilfoil, D. M., & Aukers, S. M. (2016). How marketing organizations can benefit from big data advertising analytics. *Academy of Marketing Studies Journal*, *20*(1), 18–36.

Jones, M. (2017). E-leadership case study and the impact of (un)faithful appropriation of technology. *Proceedings of the 5th International Conference on Management Leadership and Governance (ICMLG 2017), Wits Business School, University of Witwatersrand, Johannesburg, South Africa, March 16-17, 2017*, 191–199. http://toc.proceedings.com/34017webtoc.pdf

Jones, C. S. (1985). An empirical study of the evidence for contingency theories of management accounting systems in conditions of rapid change. *Accounting, Organizations and Society*, *10*(3), 303–328. doi:10.1016/0361-3682(85)90022-4

Junqueira, E., Dutra, E. V., Filho, H. Z., & Gonzaga, R. P. (2016). The effect of strategic choices and management control systems on organizational performance. *Revista Contabilidade & Finanças*, *27*(72), 334–348. doi:10.1590/1808-057x201601890

Jyoti, J., & Rani, A. (2017). High performance work system and organizational performance: Role of knowledge management. *Personnel Review*, *46*(8), 1770–1795. doi:10.1108/PR-10-2015-0262

Kačániová, M., & Bačíková, Z. (2016). Emotional aspects of Facebook textual posts a framework for marketing research. *European Journal of Science and Theology*, *12*(6), 187–197.

Kane, G. C., Palmer, D., Philips, A. N., Kiron, D., & Buckley, N. (2015). Strategy, not technology, drives digital transformation. *MIT Sloan Management Review and Deloitte University Press*, *14*, 1–25.

Kannan, P. K., & Li, H. A. (2017). Digital marketing: A framework, review and research agenda. *International Journal of Research in Marketing*, *34*(1), 22–45. doi:10.1016/j.ijresmar.2016.11.006

Kantrowitz, A. (2014). The CMO's guide to marketing automation. *Advertising Age*, *85*(17), 24.

Kantur, D., & İşeri-Say, A. (2012). Organizational resilience: A conceptual integrative framework. *Journal of Management & Organization*, *18*(6), 762–773. doi:10.5172/jmo.2012.18.6.762

Kaplan, A. M., & Haenlein, M. (2010). Users of the world, unite! The challenges and opportunities of Social Media. *Business Horizons*, *53*(1), 59–68.

Kaplan, R. S., & Norton, D. P. (1996). Using the balanced scorecard as a strategic management system. *Harvard Business Review*, *74*(1), 75–85.

Kaushik, M. (2020, March 8). Mystery of the Oyo rooms. *Business Today*. https://www.businesstoday.in/magazine/cover-story/mystery-of-the-oyo-rooms-ritesh-agarwal-investors-business-model/story/396392.html

Keegan, B. J., & Rowley, J. (2017). Evaluation and decision making in social media marketing. *Management Decision*, *55*(1), 15–31. doi:10.1108/MD-10-2015-0450

Keller, K. L. (1993). Conceptualizing, measuring, and managing customer-based brand equity. *Journal of Marketing*, *57*(1), 1–22. doi:10.1177/002224299305700101

Kerr, G., & Kelly, L. (2017). IMC education and digital disruption. *European Journal of Marketing*, *51*(3), 406–420. doi:10.1108/EJM-08-2015-0603

Ketter, W., Peters, M., Collins, J., & Gupta, A. (2016). Competitive benchmarking: An IS research approach to address wicked problems with big data and analytics. *Management Information Systems Quarterly*, *40*(4), 1057–1080. doi:10.25300/MISQ/2016/40.4.12

Khare, A., Khare, A., & Singh, S. (2012). Attracting Shoppers to Shop Online—Challenges and Opportunities for the Indian Retail Sector. *Journal of Internet Commerce*, *11*(2), 161–185. doi:10.1080/15332861.2012.689570

Kidwell, R. E., & Sprague, R. (2009). Electronic surveillance in the global workplace: Laws, ethics, research, and practice. *New Technology, Work and Employment*, *24*(2), 194–208. doi:10.1111/j.1468-005X.2009.00228.x

Kierzkowski, A., McQuade, S., Waltman, R., & Zelsser, M. (1996). Marketing to the digital consumer. *The McKinsey Quarterly*, *79*(3), 5–21.

Kietzmann, J. H., Hermkens, K., McCarthy, I. P., & Silvestre, B. S. (2011). Social media? Get serious! Understanding the functional building blocks of social media. *Business Horizons*, *54*(3), 241–251.

Kim, B., & Park, K. (1997). Studying patterns of grocery shopping trips. *Journal of Retailing*, *73*(4), 501–517. doi:10.1016/S0022-4359(97)90032-4

Kimmel, P. D., Weygandt, J. J., & Kieso, D. E. (2010). *Financial accounting: Tools for business decision making*. John Wiley & Sons.

Kirk, N. (2018). Compliance and Personal Data Protection: The EU is getting serious about data protection via the GDPR. *Journal of Property Management*, *83*(3), 40–41.

Koester, A. W., & May, J. K. (1985). Profiles of adolescents' clothing practices: Purchase, daily selection and care. *Adolescense*, *20*(77), 97–113. PMID:3984818

Korteweg, P. (1972). Uncertainty and the behaviour of wealth-owner and policy-maker: The cases of the optimum portfolio-mix and the optimum policy-mix. *De Economist, 120*(4), 367–377. doi:10.1007/BF02366911

Kothari, C. R. (2004). *Research methodology: Methods and techniques*. New Age International.

Kotler, P. (2000). M*arketing Management. The millennium edition*. Prentice Hall.

Kotler, P. (2003). *Marketing Management* (11th ed.). Prentice-Hall International Editions.

Kotler. (2017). *Marketing Management*. Prentice-Hall of India Private Limited.

Kotler, P. (1973). Atmospherics as a marketing tool. *Journal of Retailing, 49*(4), 48–64.

Kozinets, R. V., de Valck, K., Wojnicki, A. C., & Wilner, S. J. S. (2010). Networked narratives: Understanding word-of-mouth marketing in online communities. *Journal of Marketing, 74*(March), 71–89. doi:10.1509/jm.74.2.71

Krishen, A. S., & Petrescu, M. (2017). The world of analytics: Interdisciplinary, inclusive, insightful, and influential. *Journal of Marketing Analytics, 5*(1), 1–4. doi:10.105741270-017-0016-4

Krishnamurthy, S. (2006). Introducing e-markplan: A practical methodology to plan e-marketing activities. *Business Horizons, 49*(1), 51–60. doi:10.1016/j.bushor.2005.05.008

Krishnan, B. C., & Hartline, D. M. (2001). Brand equity: Is it more important in services? *Journal of Services Marketing, 15*(5), 328–342. doi:10.1108/EUM0000000005654

Krush, M. T., Agnihotri, R., & Trainor, K. J. (2016). A contingency model of marketing dashboards and their influence on marketing strategy implementation speed and market information management capability. *European Journal of Marketing, 50*(12), 2077–2102. doi:10.1108/EJM-06-2015-0317

Kshetri, N., & Voas, J. (2019). Online Advertising Fraud. *Computer, 52*(1), 58–61. doi:10.1109/MC.2018.2887322

Kübler, R. V., Wieringa, J. E., & Pauwels, K. H. (2017). Machine learning and big data. In P. Leeflang, J. Wieringa, T. Bijmolt, & K. Pauwels (Eds.), Advanced methods for modeling markets (pp. 631-670). Springer. doi:10.1007/978-3-319-53469-5_19

Kumar, A., & Shafabi. (2011). Strategic Cost Management – Suggested Framework for 21st Century. *Journal of Business and Management Research, 5*(2), 118–131.

Kumar, A., Bezawada, R., Rishika, R., Janakiraman, R., & Kannan, P. K. (2016b). From social to sale: The effects of firm-generated content in social media on customer behavior. *Journal of Marketing, 80*(1), 7–25. doi:10.1509/jm.14.0249

Kumar, A., Mangla, S. K., Luthra, S., Rana, N. P., & Dwivedi, Y. K. (2018). Predicting changing pattern: Building model for consumer decision making in digital market. *Journal of Enterprise Information Management, 31*(5), 674–703. doi:10.1108/JEIM-01-2018-0003

Kumar, V., Dixit, A., Javalgi, R. G., & Dass, M. (2016a). Research frame- work, strategies, and applications of intelligent agent technologies (IATs) in marketing. *Journal of the Academy of Marketing Science, 44*(1), 24–45. doi:10.100711747-015-0426-9

Kumar, V., Sharma, A., & Gupta, S. (2017). Accessing the influence of strategic marketing research on generating impact: Moderating roles of models, journals, and estimation approaches. *Journal of the Academy of Marketing Science, 45*(2), 164–185. doi:10.100711747-017-0518-9

Kyama, R., Kokutse, F., & Dell, S. (2020, February 21). COVID-19 – Kenya, Ghana, and South Africa students stay put. *University World News*. https://www.universityworldnews.com/post.php?story=20200221140301259

Lai, C., Shih, T., Ko, W., Tang, H., & Hsueh, P. (2020). Severe acute respiratory syndrome coronavirus 2 (SARS-Cov-2) and coronavirus disease-2019 (COVID-19): The epidemic and the challenges. *International Journal of Antimicrobial Agents, 55*(3), 105924. doi:10.1016/j.ijantimicag.2020.105924 PMID:32081636

Lall, S., & Singh, N. (2020). CoVid-19: Unmasking the new face of Education. *International Journal of Research in Pharmaceutical Sciences, 11*(SPL1), 48-53.

Lamberton, C., & Stephen, A. T. (2016). A thematic exploration of digital, social media, and mobile marketing: Research evolution from 2000 to 2015 and an agenda for future inquiry. *Journal of Marketing, 80*(6), 146–172. doi:10.1509/jm.15.0415

Langfield-smith, K. I. M. (1997). Rainfall, commerce and politics. *Science, 15*(368), 110–111. doi:10.1016/S0361-3682(95)00040-2

LaPointe, P. (2012). The dog ate my analysis: The hitchhiker's guide to marketing analytics. *Journal of Advertising Research, 52*(4), 395–396. doi:10.2501/JAR-52-4-395-396

Larjovuori, R. L., Bordi, L., Mäkiniemi, J. P., & Heikkilä-Tammi, K. (2016). The role of leadership and employee well-being in organisational digitalisation. *Proceedings of the 26th Annual European Association for Research on Services (RESER) Conference, University of Naples Federiico II, September 8-10, 2016,* 1141-1154. https://www.researchgate.net/profile/Milena_Jael_Silva-Morales/publication/308033532_Changes_in_the_intellectual_structure_of_service_innovation_and_service_system_research_in_the_digital_age_a_bibliometric_analysis_from_1986_to_2015/links/5b1844000f7e9b68b4245425/Changes-in-the-intellectual-structure-of-service-innovation-and-service-system-research-in-the-digital-age-a-bibliometric-analysis-from-1986-to-2015.pdf#page=1153

Lassar, W., Mittal, B., & Sharma, A. (1995). Measuring Customer-Based Brand Equity. *Journal of Consumer Marketing, 12*(4), 11–19. doi:10.1108/07363769510095270

Lau, R. Y. K., Li, C., & Liao, S. S. Y. (2014). Social analytics: Learning fuzzy product ontologies for aspect-oriented sentiment analysis. *Decision Support Systems, 65*, 80–94. doi:10.1016/j.dss.2014.05.005

Lavie, D. (2006). Capability reconfiguration: An analysis of incumbent responses to technological change. *Academy of Management Review, 31*(1), 153–174. doi:10.5465/amr.2006.19379629

Leeflang, P. S. H., Verhoef, P. C., Dahlström, P., & Freundt, T. (2014). Challenges and solutions for marketing in a digital era. *European Management Journal, 32*(1), 1–12. doi:10.1016/j.emj.2013.12.001

Lee, J. (1989). Environmental change, strategy type and performance: Comparative-static analysis. *Korean Management Review, 18*, 245–273.

Lee, J., & Miller, D. (1996). Strategy, environment and performance in two technological contexts: Contingency theory in Korea. *Organization Studies, 17*(5), 729–750. doi:10.1177/017084069601700502

Lee, O. K. D., Sambamurthy, V., Kim, K. H., & Wei, K. K. (2015). How does IT ambidexterity impact organizational agility? *Information Systems Research, 26*(2), 398–417. doi:10.1287/isre.2015.0577

Leonhardt, D., Haffke, I., Kranz, J., & Benlian, A. (2017). Reinventing the IT function: the role of IT agility and IT ambidexterity in supporting digital business transformation. *Proceedings of the 25th European Conference on Information Systems (ECIS), Guimarães, Portugal, June 5-10, 2017, 1*, 968-984. https://www.researchgate.net/publication/317380735_Reinventing_the_IT_function_The_Role_of_IT_Agility_and_IT_Ambidexterity_in_Supporting_Digital_Business_Transformation

Leszczyc, P. T. L. P., Sinha, A., & Timmermans, H. J. P. (2000). Consumer store choice dynamics: An analysis of the competitive market structure for grocery stores. *Journal of Retailing, 76*(3), 323–345. doi:10.1016/S0022-4359(00)00033-6

Leung, M., & Sharma, Y. (2020, February 21). *Online classes try to fill education gap during epidemic.* University World News. https://www.universityworldnews.com/post.php?story=20200221083603325

Leventhal, B. (2010). An introduction to data mining and other techniques for advanced analytics. *Journal of Direct, Data and Digital Marketing Practice, 12*(2), 137–153. doi:10.1057/dddmp.2010.35

Leviäkangas, P. (2016). Digitalisation of Finland's transport sector. *Technology in Society, 47*(1), 1–15. doi:10.1016/j.techsoc.2016.07.001

Levy, M., & Weitz, B. (1998). *Retailing management* (3rd ed.). McGraw Hill.

Liao, S. H., & Wu, C. C. (2009). The relationship among knowledge management, organizational learning, and organizational performance. *International Journal of Business and Management, 4*(4), 64–76. doi:10.5539/ijbm.v4n4p64

Liberati, A., Altman, D. G., Tetzlaff, J., Mulrow, C., Gøtzsche, P. C., Ioannidis, J. P., Clarke, M., Devereaux, P. J., Kleijnen, J., & Moher, D. (2009). The PRISMA statement for reporting systematic reviews and meta-analyses of studies that evaluate health care interventions: Explanation and elaboration. *Journal of Clinical Epidemiology*, *62*(10), e1–e34. doi:10.1016/j.jclinepi.2009.06.006 PMID:19631507

Li, F., Nucciarelli, A., Roden, S., & Graham, G. (2016). How smart cities transform operations models: A new research agenda for operations management in the digital economy. *Production Planning and Control*, *27*(6), 514–528. doi:10.1080/09537287.2016.1147096

Li, L. (2011). Marketing metrics' usage: Its predictors and implications for customer relationship management. *Industrial Marketing Management*, *40*(1), 139–148. doi:10.1016/j.indmarman.2010.09.002

Lilien, G. L. (2011). Bridging the academic–practitioner divide in marketing decision models. *Journal of Marketing*, *75*(4), 196–210. doi:10.1509/jmkg.75.4.196

Lilien, G. L. (2016). The B2B knowledge gap. *International Journal of Research in Marketing*, *33*(3), 543–556. doi:10.1016/j.ijresmar.2016.01.003

Littell, J., Corcoran, J., & Pillai, V. (2008). *Systematic reviews and meta-analysis*. Oxford University Press. doi:10.1093/acprof:oso/9780195326543.001.0001

Liu, Q. (2015). Research on Strategic Cost Management in Modern Enterprises. *Management & Engineering, 21*. doi:10.5503/J.ME.2015.21.005

Liu, X., Singh, P. V., & Srinivasan, K. (2016). A structured analysis of unstructured big data by leveraging cloud computing. *Marketing Science*, *35*(3), 363–388. doi:10.1287/mksc.2015.0972

Liu, X., Zhang, J., & Guo, C. (2013). Full-Text Citation Analysis: A New Method to Enhance. *Journal of the American Society for Information Science and Technology*, *64*(July), 1852–1863. doi:10.1002/asi.22883

Li, X., & Petrick, J. F. (2008). Examining the antecedents of brand loyalty from an investment model perspective. *Journal of Travel Research*, *47*(1), 25–34.

Li, Y.-M., Hsieh, C.-Y., Lin, L.-F., & Wei, C.-H. (2020). A social mechanism for task-oriented crowdsourcing recommendations. *Decision Support Systems*, 113449.

Lloyds Bank UK Consumer Digital Index. (2020, May 21). UK Consumer Digital Index 2020. *Lloyds Bank*. https://www.lloydsbank.com/banking-with-us/whats-happening/consumer-digital-index.html

López-Nicolás, C., & Meroño-Cerdán, Á. L. (2011). Strategic knowledge management, innovation and performance. *International Journal of Information Management*, *31*(6), 502–509. doi:10.1016/j.ijinfomgt.2011.02.003

Lopez, S. P., Peón, J. M. M., & Ordás, C. J. V. (2005). Organizational learning as a determining factor in business performance. *The Learning Organization*.

Loudon, D. L., & Bitta, A. J. (1993). *Consumer behavior: Concepts and applications*. McGraw-Hill.

Lumpkin, J. R., Greenberg, B. A., & Goldstucker, J. L. (1985). Marketplace needs of the elderly: Determinant attributes and store choice. *Journal of Retailing*, *61*(2), 75–105.

Lupia, T., Scabini, S., Mornese Pinna, S., Di Perri, G., De Rosa, F. G., & Corcione, S. (2020). 2019 novel coronavirus (2019-nCoV) outbreak: A new challenge. *Journal of Global Antimicrobial Resistance*, *21*, 22–27. doi:10.1016/j.jgar.2020.02.021 PMID:32156648

Luskin, J. (2017). Examining Total Portfolio Performance: US Government Vs. Corporate Bonds. *Journal of Financial Planning*, *30*(12).

Luthar, S. (2006). Resilience in development: a synthesis of research across five decades. In D. Cicchetti & D. Cohen (Eds.), *Risk, Disorder, and Adaptation* (pp. 740–795). Wiley.

Lu, Y., & Ramamurthy, K. R. (2011). Understanding the link between information technology capability and organizational agility: An empirical examination. *Management Information Systems Quarterly*, *35*(4), 931–954. doi:10.2307/41409967

Lynn Pulley, M., & Sessa, V. I. (2001). E-leadership: Tackling complex challenges. *Industrial and Commercial Training*, *33*(6), 225–230. doi:10.1108/00197850110405379

Mago, Z. (2017). New trends of marketing communication based on digital games. *European Journal of Science and Theology*, *13*(6), 171–182.

Mahalakshmi & Radha. (2020). COVID 19: A massive exposure towards web based learning. *Journal of Xidian University*, *14*(4). . doi:10.37896/jxu14.4/266

Majchrzak, A., & Malhotra, A. (2013). Towards an information systems perspective and research agenda on crowdsourcing for innovation. *The Journal of Strategic Information Systems*, *22*(4), 257–268.

Maklan, S., Peppard, J., & Klaus, P. (2015). Show me the money: Improving our understanding of how organizations generate return from technology-led marketing change. *European Journal of Marketing*, *49*(3/4), 561–595. doi:10.1108/EJM-08-2013-0411

Malhotra, A., Majchrzak, A., & Rosen, B. (2007). Leading virtual teams. *The Academy of Management Perspectives*, *21*(1), 60–70. doi:10.5465/amp.2007.24286164

Malhotra, N. K. (2008). *Marketing research: An applied orientation*. Prentice-Hall. doi:10.1108/S1548-6435(2008)4

Malthouse, E. C., Haenlein, M., Skiera, B., Wege, E., & Zhang, M. (2013). Managing customer relationships in the social media era: Introducing the social CRM house. *Journal of Interactive Marketing*, *27*(4), 270–280. doi:10.1016/j.intmar.2013.09.008

Malthouse, E., & Hofacker, C. (2010). Looking back and looking forward with interactive marketing. *Journal of Interactive Marketing*, *24*(3), 181–184. doi:10.1016/j.intmar.2010.04.005

Mangold, W. G., & Faulds, D. J. (2009). Social media: The new hybrid element of the promotion mix. *Business Horizons*, *52*(4), 357–365. doi:10.1016/j.bushor.2009.03.002

Mansoor, S. (2020, March 12). India is the world's second most populous country. Can it handle the coronavirus outbreak? *Time*. https://time.com/5801507/coronavirusindia/

Marczyk, G., DeMatteo, D., & Festinger, D. (2005). *Essentials of research design and methodology*. John wiley & sons, Inc.

Marr, B. (2018). A Very Brief History Of Blockchain Technology Everyone Should Read. *Forbes*. Available via: https://www.forbes.com/sites/bernardmarr/2018/02/16/a-very-brief-history-of-blockchain-technology-everyone-should-read/#68257227bc47

Marsh, E. (2017, April 12). 7 approaches to mindful technology use. *LinkedIn*. https://www.linkedin.com/pulse/6-approaches-mindful-technology-use-elizabeth-marsh/

Marsh, E. (2018). The Digital Workplace Skills Framework: Ensuring the workforce is ready to work digitally. *Digital Work Research 2018*. https://digitalworkresearch.com/wp-content/uploads/2018/08/The-Digital-Workplace-Skills-Framework-final.pdf

Marsh, E. (2019, January 10). Is your organisation's digital workplace causing technostress? *LinkedIn*. https://www.linkedin.com/pulse/your-organisations-digital-workplace-causing-elizabeth-marsh/

Marsh, E. (2019, June 11). Half of the workforce isn't ready for the digital workplace. *LinkedIn*. https://www.linkedin.com/pulse/half-workforce-isnt-ready-digital-workplace-elizabeth-marsh/

Martens, D., Provost, F., Clark, J., & de Fortuny, E. J. (2016). Mining massive fine-grained behavior data to improve predictive analytics. *Management Information Systems Quarterly*, *40*(4), 869–888. doi:10.25300/MISQ/2016/40.4.04

Martin, A., & Grudziecki, J. (2006). DigEuLit: Concepts and tools for digital literacy development. *Innovation in Teaching and Learning in Information and Computer Sciences*, *5*(4), 1–9. doi:10.11120/ital.2006.05040249

Martineau, P. (1958). The personality of the retail store. *Harvard Business Review*, *36*(1), 47–56.

Martin, K. D., & Murphy, P. E. (2017). The role of data privacy in marketing. *Journal of the Academy of Marketing Science*, *45*(2), 135–155. doi:10.100711747-016-0495-4

McGovern, G. (2000). *The caring economy*. Available at: www.thecaringeconomy.com

McIntyre, D. P., & Srinivasan, A. (2017). Networks, platforms, and strategy: Emerging views and next steps. *Strategic Management Journal*, *38*(1), 141–160. doi:10.1002mj.2596

McKenzie, L. (2020, February 25). Coronavirus forces universities online. *Inside Higher Education*. https://www.insidehighered.com/news/2020/02/25/coronavirus-forcesus-universities-online-china

McManus, S., Seville, E., Vargo, J., & Brunsdon, D. (2008). Facilitated process for improving organizational resilience. *Natural Hazards Review*, *9*(2), 81–90. doi:10.1061/(ASCE)1527-6988(2008)9:2(81)

Medina, S., & Ward, R. W. (1999). A model of retail outlet selection for beef. *The International Food and Agribusiness Management Review*, *2*(2), 195–219. doi:10.1016/S1096-7508(00)00021-5

Meenu, G., & Sahni, N. K. (2016). *Consumer Behaviour*. Kalyani Publishers.

Melo, M., & Leone, R. (2015). Alignment between Competitive Strategies and Cost Management: A Study of Small Manufacturing Companies. *Brazilian Business Review*, *12*(5), 78–96. doi:10.15728/bbr.2015.12.5.5

Merisavo, M., & Raulas, M. (2004). The impact of e-mail marketing on brand loyalty. *Journal of Product and Brand Management*, *13*(7), 498–505. doi:10.1108/10610420410568435

Messner, M. (2016). Does industry matter? How industry context shapes management accounting practice. *Management Accounting Research*, *31*, 103–111. doi:10.1016/j.mar.2015.09.001

Miles, R. E., & Snow, C. G. (1978). Organizational Strategy, Structure, and Process, McGraw-Hill, New York, NY. model of strategic management accounting. Accounting, Organizations and Society.

Miles, D. A. (2014). Measuring customer behavior and profitability: Using marketing analytics to examine customer and marketing behavioral patterns in business ventures. *Academy of Marketing Studies Journal*, *18*(1), 141–170.

Mili, M., M'Hamdi, Y., Khalfallah, M., & Teulon, F. (2014). Fixed-income portfolio management in crisis period: Expected Tail Loss (ETL) approach. *Gestion 2000*, *31*(1), 223-240.

Miller, A., & Cioffi, J. (2004). Measuring marketing effectiveness and value: The Unisys marketing dashboard. *Journal of Advertising Research*, *44*(3), 237–243. doi:10.1017/S0021849904040334

Miller, D. (1987b). Strategy making and structure: Analysis and implications for performance. *Academy of Management Journal*, *30*(1), 7–32.

Miller, D. (1988). Relating Porter's business strategies to environment and structure: Analysis and performance implications. *Academy of Management Journal*, *31*(2), 280–308.

Miller, D. (1992). Environmental fit versus internal fit. *Organization Science*, *3*(2), 159–178. doi:10.1287/orsc.3.2.159

Miller, D., & Droge, C. (1986). Psychological and traditional determinants of structure. *Administrative Science Quarterly*, *31*(4), 539–560. doi:10.2307/2392963

Miner, T. (2005). The wisdom of crowds: Why the many are smarter than the few, and how collective wisdom shapes business, economies, societies, and nations. *Journal of Experiential Education*, *27*(3), 351.

Ministry of Education of the People's Republic of China. (2020e). *Relevant Person in Charge of the Ministry of Education Answered Reporters' Questions on the Postponement of the "Suspending Classes without Stopping Learning" in Primary and Secondary Schools*. Available online: http://www.moe.gov.cn/jyb_xwfb/s271/202002/t20200211_420109.html

Moe, W. W., & Schweidel, D. A. (2017). Opportunities for innovation in social media analytics. *Journal of Product Innovation Management, 34*(5), 697–702. doi:10.1111/jpim.12405

Mohr-Jackson, I. (1998). Conceptualizing total quality orientation. *European Journal of Marketing, 32*(1/2), 13–22. doi:10.1108/03090569810197390

Montgomery, A. L., & Smith, M. D. (2009). Prospects for personalization on the Internet. *Journal of Interactive Marketing, 23*(2), 130–137. doi:10.1016/j.intmar.2009.02.001

Monto, A. (2009). The risk of seasonal and pandemic influenza: Prospects for control. *Clinical Infectious Diseases, 48*(S1), S20–S25. doi:10.1086/591853 PMID:19067611

Moorman, C. (2016). Celebrating marketing's dirty word. *Journal of the Academy of Marketing Science, 44*(5), 562–564. doi:10.100711747-016-0483-8

Morgan, J. (2020, March 19). Schools shutdown creates UK university admissions uncertainty. *Times Higher Education*. https://www.timeshighereducation.com/news/schoolsshutdown-creates-uk-university-admissions-uncertainty

Morgan, R. M., & Hunt, S. D. (1994). The commitment-trust theory of relationship marketing. *Journal of Marketing, 58*(3), 20–38.

Motamarri, S., Akter, S., & Yanamandram, V. (2017). Does big data analytics influence frontline employees in services marketing? *Business Process Management Journal, 23*(3), 623–644. doi:10.1108/BPMJ-12-2015-0182

Moustakas. (2015). Impact of Social Networking on Consumer Behaviour. Academic Press.

Mraznica, E. (2017). GDPR: A new challenge for personal data protection. *Bankarstvo, 46*(4), 166–177. doi:10.5937/bankarstvo1704166M

Mulhern, F. (2009). Integrated marketing communications: From media channels to digital connectivity. *Journal of Marketing Communications, 15*(2-3), 85–101. doi:10.1080/13527260902757506

Naidoo, N. (2011). What is research? A conceptual understanding. *African Journal of Emergency Medicine, 1*(1), 47–48. doi:10.1016/j.afjem.2011.05.011

Nair, H. S., Misra, S., Hornbuckle, W. J. IV, Mishra, R., & Acharya, A. (2017). Big data and marketing analytics in gaming: Combining empirical models and field experimentation. *Marketing Science, 36*(5), 699–725. doi:10.1287/mksc.2017.1039

Narver, J. C., & Slater, S. F. (2012). The Effect of Market Orientation on Business Profitability. *Developing a Market Orientation*, (October), 45–78. doi:10.4135/9781452231426.n3

Neti, S. (2011). Social media and its role in marketing. *International Journal of Enterprise Computing and Business Systems, 1*(2), 1-15.

Netzer, O., Feldman, R., Goldenberg, J., & Moshe, F. (2012). Mine your own business: Market structure surveillance through text mining. *Marketing Science, 31*(3), 521–543. doi:10.1287/mksc.1120.0713

Newman, J. W., & Staelin, R. (1972). Prepurchase information seeking for new cars and major household appliances. *JMR, Journal of Marketing Research, 9*(3), 249–257. doi:10.1177/002224377200900302

Newstrom, J. W., & Davis, K. (1997). *Organizational behavior: Human behavior at work.* McGraw-Hill.

Ng, I. C. L., & Wakenshaw, S. Y. L. (2017). The internet-of-things: Review and research directions. *International Journal of Research in Marketing, 34*(1), 3–21. doi:10.1016/j.ijresmar.2016.11.003

Niranjan, P. S. (2020). Corona virus Pandemic impact on Global Education: A Blessing in disguise. *Sustainable Humanosphere, 16*(2), 68–72.

Noor, K. B. M. (2008). Case study: A strategic research methodology. *American Journal of Applied Sciences, 5*(11), 1602–1604. doi:10.3844/ajassp.2008.1602.1604

Nzewi. (2016). Total Productivity Maintenance and Performance of Selected Aluminium Manufacturing Companies in Anambra State. *IOSR Journal of Business and Management, 18*(1). doi:10.9790/487X-18116773

Obaid, R. (2020). *Saudi students, educators take on virtual education challenge amid coronavirus suspension.* Retrieved from https://www.arabnews.pk/node/1640211/saudi-arabia

Oliver, R. L. (1980). A cognitive model of the antecedents and consequences of satisfaction decisions. *JMR, Journal of Marketing Research, 17*(4), 46–49. doi:10.1177/002224378001700405

Otley, D. (1980). The contingency theory of management accounting: Achievement and prognosis. *Accounting, Organizations and Society, 5*(4), 13–28. doi:10.1016/0361-3682(80)90040-9

Otley, D. (1999). Performance management: A framework for management control systems research. *Management Accounting Research, 10*(4), 363–382. doi:10.1006/mare.1999.0115

Otley, D. (2016). The contingency theory of management accounting and control: 1980–2014. *Management Accounting Research, 31*, 45–62. doi:10.1016/j.mar.2016.02.001

Oyo to sack 5,000 worldwide as business catches a cold. (2020, March 5). *The Economic Times.* https://economictimes.indiatimes.com/small-biz/startups/newsbuzz/softbank-backed-oyo-to-cut-about-5000-jobs-in-overhaul/articleshow/74477429.cms?from=mdr

Ozimek, J. F. (2010). Issues with statistical forecasting: The problems with climate science—And lessons to be drawn for marketing analytics. *Journal of Database Marketing & Customer Strategy Management, 17*(2), 138–150.

Pacauskas, D., Rajala, R., Westerlund, M., & Mäntymäki, M. (2018). Harnessing user innovation for social media marketing: Case study of a crowdsourced hamburger. *International Journal of Information Management*, *43*, 319–327.

Pagani, M., & Pardo, C. (2017). The impact of digital technology on relationships in a business network. *Industrial Marketing Management*, *67*, 185–192. doi:10.1016/j.indmarman.2017.08.009

Palacios, M., Martinez-Corral, A., Nisar, A., & Grijalvo, M. (2016). Crowdsourcing and organizational forms: Emerging trends and research implications. *Journal of Business Research*, *69*(5), 1834–1839.

Palacios-Marqués, D., Gallego-Nicholls, J. F., & Guijarro-García, M. (2021). A recipe for success: Crowdsourcing, online social networks, and their impact on organizational performance. *Technological Forecasting and Social Change*, *165*, 120566.

Paniagua, J., & Sapena, J. (2014). Business performance and social media: Love or hate? *Business Horizons*, *57*(6), 719–728.

Paquette, H. (2013). *Social media as a marketing tool: A literature review*. Academic Press.

Parmigiani, A. (2007). Why do firms both make and buy? An investigation of concurrent sourcing. *Strategic Management Journal*, *28*(3), 285–311.

Parneet, R., & Gupta, S. K. (2016). *Business Research Methodology*. Kalyani publishers.

PatelA. K. (2017). Construction of Optimal Portfolio Using Sharpe's Single Index Model and Markowitz Model: An Empirical Study on Nifty50 Stocks. Available at SSRN 3259328. doi:10.2139srn.3259328

Patrick, P. R., Miller, A., & Judge, W. Q. (1999). Using information-processing theory to understand. *Strategic Management Journal*, *20*(6), 567–577. doi:10.1002/(SICI)1097-0266(199906)20:6<567::AID-SMJ36>3.0.CO;2-K

Paul, W. (2009). Crowdsourcing and its application in marketing activities. *Contemporary Management Research*, *5*(1).

Pauwels, Aksehirli, & Lackman. (2016). Like the ad or the brand? Marketing stimulates different electronic word-of-mouth content to drive online and offline performance. *International Journal of Research in Marketing*, *33*(3), 639–655.

Pauwels, K. (2015). Truly accountable marketing: The right metrics for the right results. *GfK Marketing Intelligence Review*, *7*(1), 8–15.

Pavlatos, O. (2015). An empirical investigation of strategic management accounting in hotels. *International Journal of Contemporary Hospitality Management*, *27*(5), 756–767. doi:10.1108/IJCHM-12-2013-0582

Pavlatos, O. (2018). Strategic cost management, contingent factors and performance in services. *Journal of Accounting and Management Information Systems, 12*(2), 215–233. doi:10.24818/jamis.2018.02002

Paye-Layleh, J. (2015, February 17). Liberia Schools Reopen after 6-month Ebola Closure. *The Boston Globe.*

Payne, J. L. (1986). Rejoinder Reproduced with permission of the copyright owner. Further reproduction prohibited without permission. *Preventing School Failure, 51*(3), 49–51.

Peacock, S. E. (2014). How web tracking changes user agency in the age of Big Data: The used user. *Big Data & Society, 1*(2), 1–11. doi:10.1177/2053951714564228

Pearce, C. L., Manz, C. C., & Sims, H. P. Jr. (2009). Where do we go from here? Is shared leadership the key to team success? *Organizational Dynamics, 38*(3), 234–238. doi:10.1016/j.orgdyn.2009.04.008

Pelham, A. M., & Wilson, D. T. (1996). A longitudinal study of the impact of market structure, firm structure, strategy, and market orientation culture on dimensions of small-firm performance. *Journal of the Academy of Marketing Science, 24*(1), 27–43. doi:10.1007/BF02893935

Perez, L. (2020). *Pin on Love Coca Cola.* Retrieved 9 November 2020, from https://www.pinterest.com/pin/597078863078710815/

Persson & Ryals. (2014). Making customer relationship decisions: Analytics v rules of thumb. *Journal of Business Research, 67*(8), 1725–1732.

Pertusa-Ortega, E. M., Molina-Azorín, J. F., & Claver-Cortés, E. (2010). Competitive strategy, structure and firm performance: A comparison of the resource-based view and the contingency approach. *Management Decision, 48*(8), 1282–1303. doi:10.1108/00251741011076799

Petersen, McAlister, Reibstein, Winer, Kumar, & Atkinson. (2009). Choosing the right metrics to maximize profit-ability and shareholder value. *Journal of Retailing, 85*(1), 95–111.

Petrescu & Krishen. (2017). Marketing analytics: From prac-tice to academia. *Journal of Marketing Analytics, 5*(2), 45–46.

Piller, F., Vossen, A., & Ihl, C. (2012). From social media to social product development: The impact of social media on co-creation of innovation. *Die Unternehmung, 66*, 7–27.

Pirkkalainen, H., & Salo, M. (2016). *Two decades of the dark side in the information systems basket: Suggesting five areas for future research.* https://aisel.aisnet.org/ecis2016_rp/101

Pizzini, M. J. (2006). The relation between cost-system design, managers' evaluations of the relevance and usefulness of cost data, and financial performance: An empirical study of US hospitals. *Accounting, Organizations and Society, 31*(2), 179–210. doi:10.1016/j.aos.2004.11.001

Poornima, S., & Remesh, A. P. (2015). Construction of optimal portfolio using Sharpe's single index model–A study with reference to banking & IT sector. *International Journal of Applied Research, 1*(13), 21–24.

Porter, M. (1980). *Competitive strategy: Techniques for analyzing industries and competitors*. Free.

Porter, M. (1985). *Competitive Advantage*. The Free Press.

Press Trust of India. (2020, March 13). Several states in shutdown mode, total number of coronavirus cases 81. *Press Trust of India*. https://www.indiatoday.in/india/story/states-shutdown-coronavirus-case-1655258-2020-03-13

Pries & Dunnigan. (2015). *Big Data Analytics: A practical guide for managers*. CRC Press.

Pruett, M., & Thomas, H. (1996). Thinking about quality and its links with strategic management. *European Management Journal, 14*(1), 37–46. doi:10.1016/0263-2373(95)00045-3

Purnell, N., & Dvorak, P. (2021, January 1). Oyo hotel chain suffered ailments beyond pandemic's travel slowdown. *The Wall Street Journal*. https://www.wsj.com/articles/oyo-hotel-chain-suffered-ailments-beyond-pandemics-travel-slowdown-11609525294

Quinn, Dibb, & Simkin, Canhoto, & Analogbei. (2016). Troubled waters: The transformation of marketing in a digital world. *European Journal of Marketing, 50*(12), 2103–2133.

Raich, Müller, & Abfalter. (2014). Hybrid analysis of textual data: Grounding managerial decisions on intertwined qualitative and quantitative analysis. *Management Decision, 52*(4), 737–754.

Ramanujan, V. (1986). Onmeasurementofb1135Venk. *The Journal of Management and Governance, 1*, 1–30.

Ramaswamy, V., & Ozcan, K. (2016). Brand value co-creation in a digitalized world: An integrative framework and research implications. *International Journal of Research in Marketing, 33*(1), 93–106. doi:10.1016/j.ijresmar.2015.07.001

Rauschnabel, P. A., Praxmarer, S., & Ivens, B. S. (2012). Social media marketing: How design features influence interactions with brand postings on Facebook. In *Advances in Advertising Research* (Vol. 3, pp. 153–161). Gabler Verlag. doi:10.1007/978-3-8349-4291-3_12

Ray, A. (2009). *The ROI Of Social Media Marketing*. Marketing.

Rebecca, A.F. (2002). *The effect of marketing on teens and how teens brain work. Inside the teenager brain*. PBS Frontline Report.

Ren, J., Han, Y., Genc, Y., Yeoh, W., & Popovič, A. (2021). The boundary of crowdsourcing in the domain of creativity. *Technological Forecasting and Social Change, 165*, 120530.

Reporter, D. (2016). *Endemol Shine Beyond, Coca Cola Create Coketv*. Digital TV Europe. Available at: https://www.digitaltveurope.com/2016/07/19/endemol-shine-beyond-coca-cola-create-coketv/

Reuben, R. (2008). *The use of social media in higher education for marketing and communications: A guide for professionals in higher education*. Academic Press.

Reynolds, K. E., & Arnold, M. J. (2000). Customer loyalty to the salesperson and the store: Examining relationship customers in an upscale retail context. *Journal of Personal Selling & Sales Management, 20*(2), 89–98.

Richards, L. (2018, November 8). Factors affecting organizational behaviour. *bizfluent*. https://bizfluent.com/info-8131521-factors-affecting-organizational-behavior.html

Ringel & Skiera. (2016). *Visualizing asymmetric competition among more than 1,000 products using big search data*. Marketing.

Roland Berger. (2020, April 2). *Digital workplace in the era of Covid-19: How the current crisis will change the culture of our work*. https://www.rolandberger.com/ru/Insights/Publications/Digital-workplace-in-the-era-of-Covid-19.html

Roman, A., Van Wart, M., Wang, X., Liu, C., Kim, S., & McCarthy, A. (2018). Defining E-leadership as competence in ICT-mediated communications: An exploratory assessment. *Public Administration Review, 79*(6), 853–866. doi:10.1111/puar.12980

Rosenbush, S. (2006). FaceBook's on the block. *Business Week*. Available at: www.businessweek.com/technology/content/mar2006/tc20060327_215976.htm

Rosenzweig, E. D., Roth, A. V., & Dean, J. W. Jr. (2003). The influence of an integration strategy on competitive capabilities and business performance: An exploratory study of consumer products manufacturers. *Journal of Operations Management, 21*(4), 437–456. doi:10.1016/S0272-6963(03)00037-8

Rowley, J. (2004). Just another channel? Marketing communities in e-business. *Marketing Intelligence & Planning, 22*(1), 24.

Ruiz, E., De Pablo, J. D. S., Muñoz, R. M., & Peña, I. (2019). Do high performance work systems enhance business performance? Examining the mediating influence of total quality management. *Zbornik Radova Ekonomskog Fakultet Au Rijeci, 37*(1), 235–258. doi:10.18045/zbefri.2019.1.235

Rust & Huang. (2014). The service revolution and the transformation of marketing science. *Marketing Science, 33*(2), 206–221.

Rutter, M. (2008). Developing concepts in developmental psychopathology. *Developmental psychopathology and wellness: Genetic and environmental influences*, 3-22.

Saboo, Kumar, & Park. (2016). Using big data to model time-varying effects for marketing resource (re)allocation. *Management Information Systems Quarterly, 40*(4), 911–939.

Sahoo, S. (2018). An empirical exploration of TQM, TPM and their integration from Indian manufacturing industry. *Journal of Manufacturing Technology Management, 29*(7), 1188–1210. doi:10.1108/JMTM-03-2018-0075

Salehan & Kim. (2016). Predicting the performance of online consumer reviews: A sentiment mining approach to big data analytics. *Decision Support Systems*, *81*, 30–40.

Sandhu, N., Singh, D., & Dhall, R. (2012, March). *Determinants of retail store choice: An empirical analysis.* Paper presented at 2nd National Conference on Retailing in India: Opportunities and Challenges, BFCMT, Bathinda, India.

Sandhu, N. (2016). Behavioural red flags of fraud - A qualitative assessment. *Journal of Human Values*, *22*(3), 221–237. doi:10.1177/0971685816650579

Sandhu, N., & Prabhakar, R. (2012). Factors influencing the quality of work life in the Indian banking industry – An empirical study. *International Proceedings of Economics Development and Research*, *55*(23), 115–119.

Santana & Juntos. (2020). Retrieved 9 November 2020, from https://oglobo.globo.com/cultura/musica/luan-santana-pabllo-vittar-simone-simaria-lancam-clipe-juntos-22647128

Santoso, I., Wright, M., Trinh, G., & Avis, M. (2020). Is digital advertising effective under conditions of low attention? *Journal of Marketing Management*, 1–24.

Saravanakumar, M., & SuganthaLakshmi, T. (2012). Social media marketing. *Life Science Journal*, *9*(4), 4444–4451.

Sarkindaji, B. D., Hashim, N. A. B., & Abdullateef, A. O. (2014). Knowledge Management and Organizational Performance of Mobile Service Firms in Nigeria: A Proposed Framework. *Information and Knowledge Management, 4*(11), 88–95. https://iiste.org/Journals/index.php/IKM/article/view/17216

Savić, B., Vasiljević, Z., & Đorđević, D. (2014). Strategic Cost Management As Instrument for. *Economics of Agriculture*, *4*(6), 1005–1020.

Saxton, G. D., Oh, O., & Kishore, R. (2013). Rules of crowdsourcing: Models, issues, and systems of control. *Information Systems Management*, *30*(1), 2–20.

Sayilar, Y. (2016). The Past, Present and Future Of Structural Contingency Theory. *Industrial Relations and Human Resources Journal*, *18*(4), 95–124. doi:10.4026/2148-9874.2016.0333.X

Schonberger, R. J. (1992). Is strategy strategic? Impact of total quality management on strategy. *The Academy of Management Executive*, *6*(3), 80–87.

Schuckert, Liu, & Law. (2015). Hospitality and tourism online reviews: Recent trends and future directions. *Journal of Travel & Tourism Marketing*, 608-621.

Schwarzmüller, T., Brosi, P., Duman, D., & Welpe, I. M. (2018). How does the digital transformation affect organizations? Key themes of change in work design and leadership. *Management Review*, *29*(2), 114–138.

Scott, D. M. (2015). *The new rules of marketing and PR: how to use social media, blogs, news releases, online video, and viral marketing to reach buyers directly*. John Wiley & Sons.

Sebastian, I. M., Ross, J. W., Beath, C., Mocker, M., Moloney, K. G., & Fonstad, N. O. (2017). How big old companies navigate digital transformation. *MIS Quarterly Executive*, *16*(3), 197–213.

Sharma, P. (2020, August 7). Oyo: A room with a 'troubled' view. *Forbes*. https://www.forbesindia.com/blog/business-strategy/oyo-a-room-with-a-troubled-view/

Sharma, R., Brar, T. P. S., & Gandhi, P. (2020). Defense and Isolation in the Internet of Things. *Internet of Things in Business Transformation: Developing an Engineering and Business Strategy for Industry*, *5*(0), 141–168.

Sheoran, M., Kumar, D., Kumar, V., & Verma, D. (2018). Understanding the trends of marketing research and its future directions: A citation analysis. *The Bottom Line (New York, N.Y.)*, *31*(3/4), 191–207. doi:10.1108/BL-04-2018-0022

Sher, P. J., & Lee, V. C. (2004). Information technology as a facilitator for enhancing dynamic capabilities through knowledge management. *Information & Management*, *41*(8), 933–945. doi:10.1016/j.im.2003.06.004

Shields, M. (2007). Study: Social networking ads take time to work. *Brandweek*, *23*(April), 6.

Shmueli & Koppius. (2011). Predictive analytics in information systems research. *Management Information Systems Quarterly*, *35*(3), 553–572.

Sifferlin, A. (2014, Dec. 17). Million Kids Aren't in School Because of Ebola. *Time*.

Silva & Schegg. (2015). The interactive effects of online reviews on the determinants of Swiss hotel performance: A neural network analysis. *Tourism Management*, •••, 130–141.

Simmon, G. J. (2007). i-Branding: Developing the internet as a branding tool. *Marketing Intelligence & Planning*, *25*(6), 544–562. doi:10.1108/02634500710819932

Simmon, G. J., Traun, Y., & Thomas, B. (2007). Managing i-branding to create brand equity. *European Journal of Marketing*, *44*(10), 1260–1582.

Simons, R. (1987). Accounting control systems and business strategy. *Accounting, Organizations and Society*, *12*(4), 357–374. doi:10.1016/0361-3682(87)90024-9

Simons, R. (1990). The role of management control systems in creating competitive advantage: New per-spectives. *Accounting, Organizations and Society*, *15*(1–2), 127–143. doi:10.1016/0361-3682(90)90018-P

Singh, A, Singh, A., Vij, T. S., & Pardesi, A. (2020). An empirical study of the factors affecting online shopping behavior of the Indian consumers. *International Journal of Advanced Science and Technology*.

Singh, A, Singla, B., & Sharma, S. (2020). An empirical study of factors affecting the selection of point of purchase location: A case of FMCG industry. *International Journal of Control and Automation*.

Singh, A., Jain, A., & Singla, B. (2019). Technological advancement-based paradigm shift: A focus shift from large screen to small screen. *International Journal of Innovative Technology and Exploring Engineering*, *8*(10), 48–53. Advance online publication. doi:10.35940/ijitee.I8613.0881019

Singh, A., & Kathuria, L. M. (2016). Understanding drivers of branded food choice among low-income consumers. *Food Quality and Preference*, *52*, 52–61. doi:10.1016/j.foodqual.2016.03.013

Singh, Y. K. (2006). *Fundamental of research methodology and statistics*. New Age International.

Sinha, P. K., & Banerjee, A. (2004). Store choice behavior in an evolving market. *International Journal of Retail & Distribution Management*, *32*(10), 482–494. doi:10.1108/09590550410558626

Sinha, P. K., Banerjee, A., & Uniyal, D. P. (2002). Deciding where to buy: Store choice behaviour of Indian shoppers. *Vikalpa*, *27*(2), 13–28. doi:10.1177/0256090920020203

Siry, L. (2019). Cloudy days ahead: Cross-border evidence collection and its impact on the rights of EU citizens. *New Journal of European Criminal Law*, *10*(3), 227–250. doi:10.1177/2032284419865608

Skiera, B. (2016). Data, data and even more data: Harvesting insights from the data jungle. *GfK Marketing Intelligence Review*, *8*(2), 10–17.

Skinner, W. (1971). The anachronistic factory. *Harvard Business Review*, (January–February), 61–70.

Sloan Consortium. (2008). *About academic continuity*. Retrieved from http://www.academiccontinuity.org/node/272

Smith & Humphreys. (2006). Evaluation of unsupervised semantic mapping of natural language with Leximancer concept mapping. *Behavior Research Methods*, *38*(2), 262–279.

Snyder, H. (2019). Literature review as a research methodology: An overview and guidelines. *Journal of Business Research*, *104*(March), 333–339. doi:10.1016/j.jbusres.2019.07.039

Sobuwa, Y. (2020). Universities cancelling in-person classes due to coronavirus. *Sowetan Live*. https://www.sowetanlive. co.za/news/south-africa/2020-03-16-universitiescancelling-in-person-classes-due-to-coronavirus/

Sohrabi, C., Alsafi, Z., O'Neill, N., Khan, M., Kerwan, A., Al-Jabir, A., Iosifidis, C., & Agha, R. (2020). World Health Organization declares global emergency: A review of the 2019 novel coronavirus (COVID-19). *International Journal of Surgery*, *76*, 71–76. doi:10.1016/j.ijsu.2020.02.034 PMID:32112977

Sonnartakki, Neeti, & Anuj. (2015). Marketing management. Kalyani Publishers.

Souiden, N., Chtourou, S., & Korai, B. (2017). Consumer attitudes toward online advertising: The moderating role of personality. *Journal of Promotion Management*, *23*(2), 207–227. doi:10.1080/10496491.2016.1267676

SouleD. L.PuramA. D.WestermanG. F.BonnetD. (2016). *Becoming a digital organization: The journey to digital dexterity.* Working Paper. doi:10.2139srn.2697688

South African Government. (2020). *Minister Blade Nzimande: Measures to deal with the Coronavirus COVID-19 in the post-school education and training sector.* https://www. gov.za/speeches/minister-higher-education-science-andinnovation-statement-measures-deal-COVID-19-threat

South African News Agency. (2020). *Coronavirus 101.* https:// www.sanews.gov.za/south-africa/coronavirus-101

Spiegel, E. (2014). *Six challenges of Big Data.* https://blogs.wsj.com/experts/2014/03/26/six-challenges-of-big-data/

Sridhar, Naik, & Kelkar. (2017). Metrics unreliability and marketing overspending. *International Journal of Research in Marketing*, *34*(4), 761–779.

Srinidhi, B. (1998). Strategic quality management. *International Journal of Quality Science*, *3*(1), 38–70. doi:10.1108/13598539810196877

Stanley, C. (2017). Strategic Cost Management and Performance: The Case of Environmental Costs. *Social and Environmental Accountability Journal*, *37*(2), 150–151. doi:10.1080/0969160X.2017.1345812

Stephen, A. T. (2016). The role of digital and social media marketing in consumer behavior. *Current Opinion in Psychology*, *10*, 17–21. doi:10.1016/j.copsyc.2015.10.016

Stern, L. W., & El-Ansary, A. I. (1988). *Marketing channels.* Prentice-Hall Inc.

Stibbe, M. (2006). All contributions welcome. *Director*, *60*(4), 76–81.

Stock, R. M., Six, B., & Zacharias, N. A. (2013). Linking multiple layers of innovation-oriented corporate culture, product program innovativeness, and business performance: A contingency approach. *Journal of the Academy of Marketing Science*, *41*(3), 283–299. doi:10.100711747-012-0306-5

Storey, C., & Kahn, K. B. (2010). The role of knowledge management strategies and task knowledge in stimulating service innovation. *Journal of Service Research*, *13*(4), 397–410. doi:10.1177/1094670510370988

Štrach, P. (2018). Emerging Trends in Marketing Communications: Personalization and Eventization. *Marketing Identity, 6*(1/1), 160-167.

Streiner, D., & Norman, G. (1995). *Health measurement scales: A practical guide to their development and use.* Oxford University Press.

Subhashini, M., & Kowsalya, M. (2020). Recent trends in marketing environment. *Studies in Indian Place Names*, *40*(40), 439–446.

Sudha Rani, D., Mohana, R. K. R., & Vijay Kumar, P. (2014). Knowledge Management and Decennial Growth of a Private Sector Bank–A Case Study of ICICI Bank. *IOSR Journal of Business and Management, 16*(1), 25–37. doi:10.9790/487X-16142537

Sulanjaku, M., & Shingjergji, A. (2015). Strategic Cost Management Accounting Instrument and their Usage in Albanians Companies. European Journal of Business. *Economics and Accountancy, 3*(5), 44–50.

Supriya, C., & Aralelimath, S. S. (2020). Advertising messages impact on consumer buying behaviour of two-wheeler in Belgavi, Karanataka. Editorial Board, 9(7).

Surwiecki, J. (2005). *The Wisdom of Crowds: Why the Many Are Smarter than the Few and How Collective Wisdom Shapes Business, Economies, Societies, and Nations*. Doubleday.

Tafesse, W., & Wien, A. (2018). Implementing social media marketing strategically: An empirical assessment. *Journal of Marketing Management, 34*(9-10), 732–749. doi:10.1080/0267257X.2018.1482365

Takala, T. (2016). *The Use of Digital Analytics for Measuring and Optimizing Digital Marketing Performance. Jyväskylä University Printing House.*

Tallon, P. P., & Pinsonneault, A. (2011). Competing perspectives on the link between strategic information technology alignment and organizational agility: Insights from a mediation model. *Management Information Systems Quarterly, 35*(2), 463–486. doi:10.2307/23044052

Tanveer, M., Bhaumik, A., & Hassan, S. (2020). Covid-19 Pandemic, Outbreak Educational Sector and Students Online Learning in Saudi Arabia. *Journal of Entrepreneurship Education, 23*(3).

Taylor, S. L., & Cosenza, R. M. (2002). Profiling later aged female teens: Mall shopping behaviour and clothing choice. *Journal of Consumer Marketing, 19*(4/5), 380–408. doi:10.1108/07363760210437623

Teece, D. J. (2010). Business models, business strategy and innovation. *Long Range Planning, 43*(2–3), 172–194. doi:10.1016/j.lrp.2009.07.003

Thalheimer, R., & Ali, M. M. (1979). Time series analysis and portfolio selection: An application to mutual savings banks. *Southern Economic Journal, 45*(3), 821–837. doi:10.2307/1057480

The Economic Times. (2020, March 19). *UGC tells universities to postpone exams, suspend evaluation work due to COVID-19*. https://economictimes.indiatimes.com/industry/ services/ education/ugc-tells-universities-to-postpone exams- suspend-evaluation-work-due-to-COVID-19-spread/articleshow/74707411.cms?from=mdr

The Economist. (2020, March 21). The billion-person question if covid-19 takes hold in India the toll will be grim. *The Economist*. https://www.economist.com/asia/2020/03/21/if-covid-19-takes-hold-in-india-the-toll-will-be-grim

The total population. (2020, January 1). Retrieved from https://www.stats.gov.sa/en/indicators/1

This is Forward. (2020). Retrieved 9 November 2020, from https://www.cocacolaep.com/sustainability/this-is-forward/

Thomas, D., & Keithley, T. (2002). Knowledge management improves performance. *AACE International Transactions*, PM171.

Thomas, L. D., Autio, E., & Gann, D. M. (2014). Architectural leverage: Putting platforms in context. *The Academy of Management Perspectives*, *28*(2), 198–219. doi:10.5465/amp.2011.0105

Times Malta. (2021). *Two out of the three believe social media 'very important' for their business*. Retrieved from: https://timesofmalta.com/articles/view/two-out-of-three-believe-social-media-very-important.850025

Tracey, M., Vonderembse, M. A., & Lim, J. S. (1999). Manufacturing technology and strategy formulation: Keys to enhancing competitiveness and improving performance. *Journal of Operations Management*, *17*(4), 411–428. doi:10.1016/S0272-6963(98)00045-X

Triangulation, D. S. (2014, September). The use of triangulation in qualitative research. *Oncology Nursing Forum*, *41*(5), 545–547. doi:10.1188/14.ONF.545-547 PMID:25158659

Tripathi, S., & Sinha, P. K. (2008). *Choice of a retail store and retail store format: A hierarchical logit model*. Available at: www.iimahd.ernet.in/publications/data/2008-04-03Tripathi.pdf

Trkman, P. (2010). The critical success factors of business process management. *International Journal of Information Management*, *30*(2), 125–134. doi:10.1016/j.ijinfomgt.2009.07.003

Trusov, Ma, & Jamal. (2016). Crumbs of the cookie: User profiling in customer-base analysis and behavioral targeting. *Marketing Science*, *35*(3), 405–426.

Tsai, W. H. S., & Men, L. R. (2017). Social CEOs: The effects of CEOs' communication styles and parasocial interaction on social networking sites. *New Media & Society*, *19*(11), 1848–1867. doi:10.1177/1461444816643922

U.S. News. (2018). *Best global universities for economics and business*. Accessed January 15, 2018, from https://www.usnews.com/educaion/best-global-universities/economics-business?page=3

Underwood, S. (2016). Blockchain Beyond Bitcoin: Blockchain technology has the potential to revolutionize applications and redefine the digital economy. *Communications of the ACM*, *59*(11), 15–17. doi:10.1145/2994581

UNESCO. (2020, March 13). *COVID-19 educational disruption and response*. Retrieved from https://en.unesco.org/covid19/educationresponse

UNESCO. (2020a). *COVID-19 education response*. Retrieved from https://en.unesco.org/covid19/educationresponse/globalcoalition

UNESCO. (2020b). *COVID-19 Educational disruption and response*. Retrieved from https://en.unesco.org/covid19/educationresponse

UNESCO. (2020c). *Global education coalition*. Retrieved from https://en.unesco.org/covid19/educationresponse/globalcoalition

UNESCO. (2020d). *National learning platforms and tools*. Retrieved from https://en.unesco.org/covid19/educationresponse/nationalresponses#WESTERN%20EUROPE%20&%20NORTH%20AMERICA

UNESCO. (2020e). *Distance learning solutions*. Retrieved from https://en.unesco.org/covid19/educationresponse/solutions

UNICEF. (2020). *UNICEF and Microsoft launch global learning platform to help address COVID-19 education crisis*. Retrieved from https://www.unicef.org/press-releases/unicef-and-microsoft-launch-global-learning-platform-help-address-covid-19-education

Vaccaro, A., Parente, R., & Veloso, F. M. (2010). Knowledge management tools, interorganizational relationships, innovation and firm performance. *Technological Forecasting and Social Change*, *77*(7), 1076–1089. doi:10.1016/j.techfore.2010.02.006

Vachani, V. N. (2014). *A study to measure the impact of electronic (digital) marketing among the Gujarat based customers and firms*. Academic Press.

Van Deursen, A. J. A. M., & Van Dijk, J. A. G. M. (2012). *Ctrl Alt Delete: Lost productivity due to IT problems and inadequate computer skills in the workplace*. Technical Report. Universiteit Twente. https://www.researchgate.net/publication/259703359_CTRL_ALT_DELETE_Lost_productivity_due_to_IT_problems_and_inadequate_computer_skills_in_the_workplace/citations

Van Doorn, J., Lemon, K. N., Mittal, V., Nass, S., Pick, D., Pirner, P., & Verhoef, P. C. (2010). Customer engagement behavior: Theoretical foundations and research directions. *Journal of Service Research*, *13*(3), 253–266. doi:10.1177/1094670510375599

Van Wart, M., Roman, A., Wang, X. H., & Liu, C. (2017). Integrating ICT adoption issues into (e) leadership theory. *Telematics and Informatics*, *34*(5), 527–537. doi:10.1016/j.tele.2016.11.003

Vartanian, T. P. (2010). *Secondary data analysis*. Oxford University Press. doi:10.1093/acprof:oso/9780195388817.001.0001

Vashishtha, S., & Sharma, S. (2016). Store choice behaviour in a developing economy: An empirical evidence on household consumer durables. *IOSR Journal of Business and Management*, *18*(8), 30–35. doi:10.9790/487X-1808013035

Venkatesan, R. (2017). Executing on a customer engagement strategy. *Journal of the Academy of Marketing Science*, *45*(3), 289–293.

Venkatraman, N., & Ramanujam, V. (1986). Measurement of business performance in strategy research: A comparison of approaches. *Academy of Management Review*, *11*(4), 801–814. doi:10.5465/amr.1986.4283976

Verhoef, Kooge, & Walk. (2016). *Creating Value with Big Data Analytics: Making Smarter Marketing Decisions*. London: Routledge.

Verhoef, P. C., Broekhuizen, T., Bart, Y., Bhattacharya, A., Dong, J. Q., Fabian, N., & Haenlein, M. (2019). Digital transformation: A multidisciplinary reflection and research agenda. *Journal of Business Research, 122*, 889–901. doi:10.1016/j.jbusres.2019.09.022

Verhoef, P. C., Kooge, E., & Walk, N. (2016). *Creating value with big data analytics – Making smarter marketing decisions*. Routledge. doi:10.4324/9781315734750

Verhoef, P. C., Stephen, A. T., Kannan, P. K., Luo, X., Abhishek, V., Andrews, M., Bart, Y., Datta, H., Fong, N., Hoffman, D. L., Hu, M. M., Novak, T., Rand, W., & Zhang, Y. (2017). Consumer connectivity in a complex technology-enabled and mobile-oriented world with smart products. *Journal of Interactive Marketing*, *40*, 1–8. doi:10.1016/j.intmar.2017.06.001

Vidgen, R., Shaw, S., & Grant, D. B. (2017). Management challenges in creating value from business analytics. *European Journal of Operational Research*, *261*(2), 626–639. doi:10.1016/j.ejor.2017.02.023

Vinerean, S. (2017). Importance of strategic social media marketing. *Expert Journal of Marketing*, *5*(1).

Vinerean, S., Cetina, I., Dumitrescu, L., & Tichindelean, M. (2013). The effects of social media marketing on online consumer behavior. *International Journal of Business and Management*, *8*(14), 66. doi:10.5539/ijbm.v8n14p66

Vorvoreanu, Boisvenue, Wojtalewicz, & Dietz. (2013). Social media marketing analytics: A case study of the public's perception of Indianapolis as Super Bowl XLVI host city. *Journal of Direct. Data and Digital Marketing Practice*, *14*(4), 321–328.

Wadongo, B., & Abdel-Kader, M. (2014). Contingency theory, performance management and organizational effectiveness in the third sector: A theoretical framework. *International Journal of Productivity and Performance Management*, *63*(6), 680–703. doi:10.1108/IJPPM-09-2013-0161

Walters, R. G., & Heikki, J. R. (1986). An empirical investigation into the imapct of price promotions on reatil store performance. *Journal of Retailing*, *62*(3), 237–266.

Wang. (2003). Assessment of E-service Quality via E-satisfaction in Ecommerce Globalization. The Electronic Journal on Information System in developing Countries, 11(10), 1-4.

Wang, Y., & Sun, S. (2010). Assessing beliefs, attitudes, and behavioral responses toward online advertising in three countries. *International Business Review*, *19*(4), 333–344. doi:10.1016/j.ibusrev.2010.01.004

Wang, Z., & Kim, H. G. (2017). Can social media marketing improve customer relationship capabilities and firm performance? Dynamic capability perspective. *Journal of Interactive Marketing*, *39*, 15–26. doi:10.1016/j.intmar.2017.02.004

Ward, M., & Lee, M. (2000). Internet shopping, consumer search and product branding. *Journal of Product and Brand Management*, *9*(1), 6–20. doi:10.1108/10610420010316302

Webster, F. E., Malter, A. J., & Ganesan, S. (2005). The decline and dispersion of marketing competence. *MIT Sloan Management Review*, *46*(4), 35–43.

Wedel & Kannan. (2016). Marketing analytics for data-rich environments. *Journal of Marketing*, *80*(6), 97–121.

Weimer, W. B. (1979). *Notes on the methodology of scientific research* (No. 507.2 W45). Academic Press.

Weinberg, C. (2020, February 27). How SoftBank-backed chain Oyo lost its way in the U.S. *The Information.* https://www.theinformation.com/articles/how-softbank-backed-hotel-chain-oyo-lost-its-way-in-the-u-s?utm_source=google&utm_medium=cpc&utm_campaign=11543929116_112520154917&utm_content=477036477316&utm_term=dsa-304667822056&gclid=Cj0KCQjwp86EBhD7ARIsAFkgakhPU0VYBc-pURYtMVKeOCzwaZcz6vDztXx0ciQNUeIKt0GpssXnE8waAt2fEALw_wcB

Weisman, N.Y., Erokhina, I.D., & Zakharov, I.K. (2001). *Spectrum of visible mutations isolated out of wild populations of Drosophila melanogaster in 2000.* Academic Press.

Westerman, G., Tannou, M., Bonnet, D., Ferraris, P., & McAfee, A. (2012) The digital advantage: How digital leaders outperform their peers in every industry. *MIT Sloan Management and Capgemini Consulting, 2,* 2–23. https://ide.mit.edu/sites/default/files/publications/TheDigitalAdvantage.pdf

Whitla, P. (2009). Crowdsourcing and its application in marketing activities. *Contemporary Management Research*, *5*(1).

Wilcox, M., & … . (1996). Managing for quality: The strategic issues. *International Journal of Technology Management*, *12*(1), 59–74.

Wilson, R. (2010). Using clickstream data to enhance business-to-business web site performance. *Journal of Business and Industrial Marketing*, *25*(3), 177–187. doi:10.1108/08858621011027768

Wilson, R. D. (2010). Using clickstream data to enhance business-to- business web site performance. *Journal of Business and Industrial Marketing*, *25*(3), 177–187.

Woiceshyn, J., & Daellenbach, U. (2018). Evaluating inductive vs deductive research in management studies. *Qualitative Research in Organizations and Management*, *13*(2), 183–195. doi:10.1108/QROM-06-2017-1538

Woodside, A. G., & Trappey, R. J. (1992). Finding out why customers shop your store and buy your brand. *Journal of Advertising Research*, *32*(6), 59–78.

World Health Organization. (2009). *Meeting of Regional Experts on Promotion of Mental Well-Being: Report of the Meeting*. http://www.searo.who.int/entity/mental_health/documents/seament-159.pdf

World Health Organization. (2020a). *Coronavirus disease (COVID-2019) situation reports.* Situation report – 64 (29 March 2020). https://www.who.int/emergencies/diseases/ novel-coronavirus-2019/situation-reports

Wu, Z. (2020). *How a top Chinese university is responding to coronavirus*. https://www.weforum.org/agenda/2020/03/coronavirus-china-the-challenges-of-online-learning-foruniversities/

Wymbs, C. (2011). Digital marketing: The time for a new "academic major" has arrived. *Journal of Marketing Education*, *33*(1), 93–106. doi:10.1177/0273475310392544

Wysocki, B. J., & Wysocki, T. (1997). DS-CDMA Scheme with Reduced ISI and MAI. *Australian Telecommunications Research Institute, Design Note, RSL-DN*, *002*, 1997.

Xiao, Z., Dyson, J. R., & Powell, P. L. (1996). The impact of information Technology on corporate financial Reporting: A contingency perspective. *The British Accounting Review*, *28*(3), 203–227. doi:10.1006/bare.1996.0015

Xu, Frankwick, & Ramirez. (2016). Effects of big data analytics and traditional marketing analytics on new product success: A knowledge fusion perspective. *Journal of Business Research*, *69*(5), 1562–1566.

Xu, Z., Turel, O., & Yuan, Y. (2012). Online game addiction among adolescents: Motivation and prevention factors. *European Journal of Information Systems*, *21*(3), 321–340. doi:10.1057/ejis.2011.56

Yang, W. S., Dia, J. B., Cheng, H. C., & Lin, H. T. (2006). Mining social networks for targeted advertising. *Proceedings of the 39th Hawaii International Conference on System Sciences.*

Yilmaz, R., & Baral, G. (2010). Target costing as a strategic cost management tool for success of balanced scorecard system. *China-USA Business Review*, *9*(3), 39–53.

Zahay, D. (2014). Beyond interactive marketing. *Journal of Research in Interactive Marketing*, *8*(4). Advance online publication. doi:10.1108/JRIM-08-2014-0047

Zahra, S. A., Neubaum, D. O., & El–Hagrassey, G. M. (2002). Competitive analysis and new venture performance: Understanding the impact of strategic uncertainty and venture origin. *Entrepreneurship Theory and Practice*, *27*(1), 1–28. doi:10.1111/1540-8520.t01-2-00001

Zaim, H., Muhammed, S., & Tarim, M. (2019). Relationship between knowledge management processes and performance: Critical role of knowledge utilization in organizations. *Knowledge Management Research and Practice*, *17*(1), 24–38. doi:10.1080/14778238.2018.1538669

Zautra, A., Hall, J., & Murray, K. (2010). Resilience: a new definition of health for people and communities. In J. Reich, A. Zautra, & J. Hall (Eds.), Handbook of Adult Resilience (pp. 3–34). Academic Press.

Zawawi, N. H. M., & Hoque, Z. (2010). Research in management accounting innovations: An overview of its recent development. *Qualitative Research in Accounting & Management*, *7*(4), 505–568. doi:10.1108/11766091011094554

Zeike, S., Bradbury, K., Lindert, L., & Pfa, H. (2019). Digital Leadership Skills and Associations with Psychological Well-Being. *International Journal of Environmental Research and Public Health*, *16*(14), 2628. doi:10.3390/ijerph16142628 PMID:31340579

Zhang, W., Wang, Y., Yang, L., & Wang, C. (2020). Suspending classes without stopping learning: China's education emergency management policy in the COVID-19 outbreak. *Journal of Risk and Financial Management, 13*(3), 55. doi:10.3390/jrfm13030055

Zhang, Y., Liu, X., Fan, F., Zhou, P., & Bai, Q. (2015). Factors Influencing on Teachers' ICT Application Level of Primary and Secondary Schools: An Empirical Analysis Based on the 14 cities of X Province. *Modern Educational Technology, 25*, 44–50.

Zhong, R. (2020, March 17). The coronavirus exposes education's digital divide. *The New York Times*. https://www.nytimes.com/2020/03/17/technology/china-schoolscoronavirus.html

Zhu, Y. Q., & Chen, H. G. (2015). Social media and human need satisfaction: Implications for social media marketing. *Business Horizons, 58*(3), 335–345. doi:10.1016/j.bushor.2015.01.006

Zott, C., & Amit, R. (2008). The fit between product market strategy and business model: Implications for firm performance. *Strategic Management Journal, 29*(1), 1–26. doi:10.1002mj.642

Zou, K. H., Tuncali, K., & Silverman, S. G. (2003). Correlation and simple linear regression. *Radiology, 227*(3), 617–628. doi:10.1148/radiol.2273011499 PMID:12773666

Županič, I. (2013). Social media as enabler of crowdsourcing. In *Social Media in Human Resources Management*. Emerald Group Publishing Limited.

About the Contributors

Amandeep Singh has done BIT, MBA, PhD, and he is also UGC-NET qualified. Currently, he is working as Professor Chitkara Business School, Chitkara University, Punjab, India. He is having more than 14 years of teaching experience. He has served as Dean / Principal in various reputed Universities and colleges. He has published 28 research papers in various journals and conferences. He has also chaired many National and International Conferences. He is on the editorial board for 3 International Journals. He was awarded as the Best Teacher in 2008.

* * *

Karpagam A. is a seasoned academician and a specialist in the area of Supply Chain Management and Analytics. Her research area spans from supply chain management to marketing with special emphasis on sustainable supply chain, humanitarian supply chain, O2O supply chain, green supply chain, FSCM, the sandwich strategy for brand equity. Expert in teaching operations and Supply chain Management. Her areas of interest include Sales & Distribution, Last Mile Delivery, Manufacturing Technologies, Operations Strategy, Production Planning & Control, Sourcing & Supply Chain Management. Published papers in various international journals. She runs various YouTube channel for Excel, MS-Project, Tableau and Power BI. She is also a trainer in the areas of Supply Chain Analytics and Data Visualization.

Rashmi Aggarwal is working as Professor and Assistant Dean at Chitkara Business School, Chitkara University, Punjab, India.

Martin Aruldoss is an Assistant Professor in the Department of Computer Science, School of Mathematics and Computer Science, Central University of Tamil Nadu. He has more than 16 years of work experience which includes academic, research, and teaching. His research interest includes evolutionary computing, data analytics, business intelligence, multi-criteria decision making, and machine learning techniques. He has published research papers in world highly recognized

Journals such as IEEE transactions on evolutionary computation, Elsevier - International Journal of Information Management, Emerald, Inderscience, and other top journals. He has received 800 citation indices for his publications. His h-index is 14 and his i-10 index is 16. His research work on “Qualitative Bankruptcy Data Set” has been recognized by the Center for Machine Learning and Intelligent Systems, Bren School of Information and Computer Science, University of California, USA. Since its launching (Feb’, 2014) more than 80,000 researchers have visited the qualitative bankruptcy data set. He has received a project grant from “Tamilnadu state council for science and technology” under “Student Project Scheme – 2020”. Recently he completed the “Big Data Analytics for Smart Grid” course certificate from SWAYAM. He is an EMC2 certified “Data Science and Big Data Analytics” programmer and Oracle Java 2 Certified Programmer. He has received many awards and recognition for his research work, teaching and training. He has received Faculty Mentor Certification for ‘The Great Mind Challenge 2007, 2008 & 2010’ from IBM. He played a key role in IBM ‘The Great Mind Challenge’ as a Coordinator to bring the Best Performing College award consecutively for 6 years since 2007. PROJECTS Agency: Tamil Nadu State Council for Science and Technology (TNSCST) - Student Project Scheme 2019-2020 Project Title: A Study and Development of Mobile App for Fisherwomen in Nagapattinam District to Reduce Complexities for Selling of Fishes

Shradhha Awasthi is currently working as Associate Professor at Chitkara Business School. Possess 15+ years of work experience in the field of HR and OB besides a Doctorate in Managment from Amity University.

Divya Bansal is a lecturer and researcher with 10+ years of experience teaching courses in both undergraduate and postgraduate levels, Passion for learning new things and sharing knowledge has led Dr. Divya Bansal to a conscious decision of opting teaching as a profession. She comes from a business family, which has helped her in hands on training in entrepreneurial skills. She has done her MBA from APJ University. She has come a long way, both in terms of academics and research. She was awarded the doctoral for her research in Universal Banking. She has published around more than twenty research articles in various journals and presented lot of papers in National and International conferences. Her research interests are in the diverse areas of marketing, Universal Banking, customer satisfaction, and entrepreneurship. She has keen interest in learning new packages and analytical tools in Statistics. Currently she is working as an Assistant Professor at Amity University, Noida.

Rohit Bansal is working as Assistant Professor in Department of Management Studies in Vaish College of Engineering, Rohtak. He obtained Ph.D. in Management from Maharshi Dayanand University, Rohtak. With a rich experience of 13 years, he has achieved growth through robust and proactive academic initiatives. He has authored & edited 8 books as well as published 95 research papers in national and international journals of repute including chapters in edited books. He has also presented papers in 30 conferences and seminars. His area of interest includes marketing management, human resource management, organizational behaviour, services marketing and organizational development. He has proficiency in handling graduate and post graduate students by using interactive discussions and "hands-on" approaches to help them undergo experiential learning He is on Editorial Advisory Board as a member in 110 national and international peer reviewed journals. He is Managing Editor of International Journal of 360° Management Review & International Journal of Techno – Management Research.

Devesh Bathla is an industry practitioner and a Business Analytics' Trainer to Working professionals and Management students who demand innovation & continuous improvement. Experienced in marketing analytics, consistently achieved business objectives, reduced marketing / operating costs and improved productivity.

Ruhi Bhardwaj is an MBA Marketing Student from Chitkara University.

Surbhi Chauhan is M.Tech, B.Tech in computer science and engineering. She has more than 7 year of teaching experience.

Rishu Chhabra received her PhD from Banasthali Vidyapith, India, and also an Associate Professor at Chitkara University Institute of Engineering and Technology, Chitkara University, Punjab, India. Her research interests include wireless networks, ad hoc networks, vehicular ad hoc networks, and programming.

Sakshi Dua is presently working as an Assistant Professor, in the esteemed Institution, Lyallpur Khalsa College for women, Jalandhar. She has completed her Doctoral degree in the field of IT. Till the date, she has 10 years of experience in Academics. She owes the credit of 10 national & International Publications.

Sonu Dua is presently working as an Associate Professor, in the esteemed Institution, Khalsa College Lyallpur Institute of Management & Technology, Jalandhar. He has completed his Doctoral degree in the field of management. Till the date, He has 11 years of experience (Both Academics and Industry). He owes the credit of

10 national & International Publications, 02 Book and 11 chapters and completed 30 online courses including NPTEL, COURSERA and SAYLOR.

Ankur Kukreti is working as an Assistant Professor in Department of Management Studies Quantum School of Business, Quantum University, Roorkee, Uttarakhand having a teaching experience of Six Years. He enjoys a privilege of publishing 18 research articles in leading international journals such as Sustainable Humanosphere, International Journal of Business Excellence, Advances in Engineering Technology and Management etc. The research publications had good citation and indexing such as Scopus and ABDC. Currently he is pursuing PhD. in Management from Motherhood University on Total Quality Management. Ankur is also a reviewer for various journals (e.g. Asian journal of Management, International Journal of Creative Research Thoughts and International Journal of Business Excellence). Area of specializations includes Research Methodology, Marketing management and Total Quality Management.

Reena Malik has around 8 years of teaching experience. She has published 2 books and various research papers in varied reputed journals.

Arun Kant Painoli is currently working as a Associate Professor and Head of Department Management Program in the Quantum University. His area of research is Consumer Behavior, Retail Management, Digital Marketing. He has been into teaching profession from last 15 years.

Harmesh Lal Paul is Vice Principal, Government College Karamsar, Rara Sahib, Ludhiana (Punjab).

Jaya Krishna Raguru received his M.Tech degree in Computer Science and Engineering from Manipal Institute of Technology in 2009. He has been working as an Assistant Professor in the Department of Computer Science and Engineering at Manipal University Jaipur since 2013. His research interests include Social Network Analysis. Massive graph processing, parallel computing, and Machine Learning.

Srilakshmi Rao, with an excellent understanding of the underlying principles of business management and their interaction with and relevance to other domains, has relevant teaching as well as industrial experience on various Finance and HR domain. She is a NET qualified doctoral student from Mysore University with outstanding and consistent academic record. She is highly motivated and with an aptitude for learning and combined with strong communication skills, she has published various research articles in reputed journals and presented papers in National and International conferences. Her research interest lies in the area of Finance especially in risk management and investment.

Namrata Sandhu has sixteen years of experience in research, consulting and teaching graduate management courses. She has authored/edited three books and published over 60 research articles in journals of academic repute such as Development Policy Review, Development, Journal of Financial Crime, Global Business Review, Journal of Human Values, International Journal of Business and Globalization, Paradigm, Business Perspectives and Research, Indian Journal of Women and Social Change, FIIB Business Review etc. In the capacity of a consultant she has worked with United Nations Development Program and Metamorph Consultants, Mumbai. Her areas of interest include Ethics, Finance and Gender Studies.

Nitin Sharma is pursuing his PHD from Manipal University Jaipur.

Vijay Kumar Sharma has an Assistant professor in the School of Computing and Information Technology, Manipal University Jaipur. His area of Research is an Information security and image processing.

Arjun Singh is working as Associate Professor in Computer and Communication Engineering department, Manipal University Jaipur, India.

Azad Singh is Dean, Assistant Professor at University College of Commerce and Management.

Dilpreet Singh, Ph.D. (Strategy), MBA (Marketing), has over fifteen years of academic and industry experience. He is an accomplished teacher, researcher, consultant and trainer with expertise in Strategy and Sales. He has presented research articles in various conferences, besides publishing them in journals of repute. He is the author of the books titled 'Bank Marketing Strategies – An Indian Perspective' and 'Contemporary Issues in Business' published by renowned international publishers. He received the Best Research Paper Award at IMRA-IIMB International Conference, 2015, Indian Institute of Management, Bangalore. He is also an avid trainer and consultant and has imparted training/consultancy to various organisations including Reliance Communications, Hero Cycles, Subhiksha Trading Services, Punjab State Cooperative Development Bank, Punjab Agriculture Department etc. He is currently working as Assistant Dean, BBA Programmes with Chitkara Business School, Chitkara University, Punjab, India.

Inderpal Singh is presently working as an Associate Professor & HOD Management, in the esteemed Institution, Khalsa College Lyallpur Institute of Management & Technology, Jalandhar, since July, 15th 2010. Ph.D completed in the year 2010 . Owes the credit of more than 20 Books published in the field of Commerce and Management, Bio-Technology & Research. More than 60 research papers presented in National & International Conferences and 40 papers published in National & International Journals including Scopus Indexed Journals. Six Papers Published in Scopus Indexed Journals. Gold Medalist in M.Phil & Awarded "Exemplary Educationist Award" by Indo Global Chamber of Commerce, Industry Trade & Agriculture & "Best Faculty Award" by Indian Society of Technical Education (ISTE) for academic excellence and Outstanding Educator Award from I2OR Australia.

Kuber Singh has a Bachelor of Applied Science - BASc Field Of Study Mechatronics Engineering and Minors in Management Sciences at University of Waterloo, Canada. Possess 6+ years of global work experience and currently working as Manager of Information Systems at triOS College.

Ram Singh is Sr. Assistant Professor & Coordinator Department of Commerce, Quantum School of Business, Quantum University Roorkee India. Dr. Singh has completed his Ph.D. degree in Commerce from HNB Garhwal Central University Srinagar Uttarakhand India. Currently, Dr. Singh is a member and secretary of Research Council of Quantum University, member of BOF/BOS (Commerce), a member of Editorial Board of numeral Journals, and Reviewer in various peer reviewed National and International Journals of Accounting, Finance & General Management. He has published 2 books and several research papers & articles in different SCOPUS/UGC listed/Peer-Reviewed journals. Besides this, he has also attended various FDPs, workshops, national & international webinars conducted by renowned institutions & organizations. He also presented papers in various national & International Seminars & Conferences and published more than a dozen articles/ Chapters in proceedings of seminars & Conferences.

Varinderjeet Singh is an Assistant Professor at University college of commerce and management, Guru Kashi University, Talwandi Sabo, Bathinda (Punjab).

Sanjay Taneja is an Assistant Professor at University college of commerce and management, Guru Kashi University, Talwandi Sabo, Bathinda (Punjab).

Miranda Lakshmi Travis is an Assistant Professor with the PG and Research Department of Computer Science, St. Joseph's College (Autonomous), Cuddalore and completed Ph.D. degree in computer science with Bharathiar University, Coimbatore,

India. She has received 611 citations indices for her publications. Her h-index is 11 and i-10 index is 10. Her research interests include multicriteria decision making, business intelligence and software engineering.

Sonal Trivedi has 10 years of experience in teaching. She has completed her PhD from University of Kota.

Tanvi Verma is pursuing her Ph.D. from Panjab University Chandigarh. She is working as assistant professor at Chitkara Business School, Chitkara University, Punjab, India.

Index

G

H

I

K

M

N

O

P

R

S

T

V

W

Y

www.ingramcontent.com/pod-product-compliance
Lightning Source LLC
LaVergne TN
LVHW061546290926
849162LV00004B/926
* 9 7 8 1 7 9 9 8 7 2 3 1 3 *